NATIONAL AND REGIONAL PARLIAMENTS IN THE EU-LEGISLATIVE PROCEDURE POST-LISBON

Much has changed in European constitutional law after the Lisbon Treaty, not least the efforts to increase democratic legitimacy by engaging national legislatures and introducing a stricter subsidiary review process (namely the Early Warning Mechanism (EWM)). This collection looks at the how national parliaments have adapted to their new roles and at how the new system has impacted on relations between the EU legislative bodies and these national parliaments. A team of experts from across Europe explores the effect of the EWM on the national constitutional orders, analyses the regional impact of EWM and evaluates the new system of scrutiny.

National and Regional Parliaments in the EU-Legislative Procedure Post-Lisbon

The Impact of the Early Warning Mechanism

Edited by
Anna Jonsson Cornell and Marco Goldoni

•HART•
OXFORD • LONDON • NEW YORK • NEW DELHI • SYDNEY

HART PUBLISHING
Bloomsbury Publishing Plc
Kemp House, Chawley Park, Cumnor Hill, Oxford, OX2 9PH, UK

HART PUBLISHING, the Hart/Stag logo, BLOOMSBURY and the Diana logo are trademarks of Bloomsbury Publishing Plc
First published in Great Britain 2017

First published in hardback, 2017
Paperback edition, 2019

A catalogue record for this book is available from the British Library.

Library of Congress Cataloging-in-Publication Data

Names: Jonsson Cornell, Anna, 1973– editor. | Goldoni, Marco, editor.

Title: National and regional parliaments in the EU-legislative procedure post-Lisbon : the impact of the early warning mechanism / edited by Anna Jonsson Cornell and Marco Goldoni.

Description: Oxford [UK] ; Portland, Oregon : Hart Publishing, 2017. | Includes bibliographical references and index.

Identifiers: LCCN 2016037924 (print) | LCCN 2016038129 (ebook) | ISBN 9781782259176 (hardback) | ISBN 9781782259183 (Epub)

Subjects: LCSH : Legislative bodies—European Union countries. | Parliamentary practice—European Union countries. | Constitutional law—European Union countries. | International and municipal law—European Union countries. | Subsidiarity—European Union countries. | Central-local government relations—European Union countries. | Treaty on European Union (1992 February 7). Protocols, etc. (2007 December 13)

Classification: LCC KJE5390 .N35 2017 (print) | LCC KJE5390 (ebook) | DDC 328.4—dc23

LC record available at https://lccn.loc.gov/2016037924

ISBN: HB: 978-1-78225-917-6
PB: 978-1-50992-969-6
ePDF: 978-1-78225-919-0
ePub: 978-1-78225-918-3

Typeset by Compuscript Ltd, Shannon

ACKNOWLEDGEMENTS

This book is the result of two workshops organised in Uppsala and Stockholm between 2014 and 2015, and a conference arranged jointly by the Uppsala Forum for Democracy, Peace and Justice, SIEPS and the Swedish Riksdag in 2015. These workshops and the conference were generously funded by the Swedish Research Council and the Swedish Foundation for Humanities and Social Sciences. The project was initiated by Anna Jonsson Cornell and Marco Goldoni under the umbrella of the Uppsala Forum for Democracy, Peace and Justice at Uppsala University, for which Anna Jonsson Cornell was Research Director between 2010 and 2015. We would like to express our sincere gratitude to Per Olov Hammargren, at that time Research Assistant at the Uppsala Forum for Democracy, Peace and Justice. Without his devotion, efficiency and hard work these workshops and the book would not have seen the light of day. We would also like to express our gratitude to the editors at Hart Publishing for their support throughout the publication process. The authors contributing to this book have been generous and patient. Our most heartfelt thanks goes out to all of you; your contributions have made it an absolute pleasure to work on this book.

Anna Jonsson Cornell and Marco Goldoni
Uppsala, May 2016

CONTENTS

Part III: The Early Warning Mechanism in National Constitutional Orders

LIST OF CONTRIBUTORS

Katrin Auel is Associate Professor in Political Science at the Institute for Advanced Studies in Vienna. After completing her studies at the University of Konstanz, she held positions at the University of Halle-Wittenberg, the University of Hagen, the University of Oxford and the European University Viadrina. Her research focuses on Europeanisation, multilevel governance and, in particular, legislative studies with a specific interest in the role of national parliaments in the EU. Recent publications include special issues of the *Journal of Legislative Studies* (2014, co-edited with T Raunio) and *West European Politics* (2015, co-edited with T Christiansen) as well as articles in *Comparative European Politics* (2014, 2016) and the *Journal of Common Market Studies* (2014).

Karolina Borońska-Hryniewiecka is an Assistant Professor at the Political Science Institute of the University of Wrocław and a Senior Fellow in the EU Programme of the Polish Institute of International Affairs (PISM). In the past, she was a Jean Monnet Fellow at the European University Institute in Florence and a Postdoctoral Research and Teaching Fellow at the University of Masaryk in Brno. Her research interests concern the European Union's institutional reform, EU democratic legitimacy and the role of parliamentary actors in EU policy-making.

Ian Cooper is a Research Associate, Department of Politics and International Studies, University of Cambridge. His research interest is in the fields of constitutionalism, legitimacy and democracy in the European Union, international relations theory, and Catholic social philosophy.

Anna Jonsson Cornell is Associate Professor in constitutional law and senior lecturer in comparative constitutional law at the Faculty of Law at Uppsala University. She is the former Research Director of the Uppsala Forum for Democracy, Peace and Justice. Her research interests are in the fields of comparative constitutional law, EU constitutional law, international socialisation processes, international police cooperation and human trafficking.

Adam Cygan is a Professor at the School of Law, University of Leicester, and visiting Professor at the Faculty of Law at the University of Brescia. His research interests lie in the field of EU public law and governance with a focus on the relationship between national parliaments and the EU Institutions within the context of the decision-making process.

1

Introduction

ANNA JONSSON CORNELL AND MARCO GOLDONI

Having been stifled for a long time, the attention of scholars to the role of national parliaments in EU constitutional law seems to be, by now, at its peak. The historical context has possibly played an instrumental role in changing the tide. It has to be borne in mind that parliamentary politics has long been subject to discredit as a 'talking shop' and Europeanisation considered a factor in the further deterioration of parliamentary relevance.[1] In particular, two events occurring over the final years of the past decade have contributed to the resurgence of interest around national parliaments. The first is the Euro crisis, which has weakened dramatically the foundations of EU law-making because it has triggered the adoption of a mix of measures of different legal natures. Moreover, the adoption of them without proper and robust deliberation by national parliaments has made things even worse.[2] The measures adopted to cope with the Euro crisis might have been effective in the short term, but they conveyed the message that it was a matter of *necessity* to ratify them. National parliamentary politics was directly threatened by this arrangement, even though this was clearly the case more for certain Member States than others. If parliamentary politics is above all representative politics and representative law-making,[3] then the necessity of ratifying new legislation in a condition of emergency is a denial of this point. In other words, the political deficit intrinsic to the process of EU law-making (actually, not only EU law-making, but the so-called Union Method too) was exposed beyond any reasonable doubt. Such a deficit does not only shake the legitimacy of EU ordinary law-making, but would also put further pressure on the domestic role of national parliaments by hollowing out their effective capacity of political representation. The second factor is the ratification and the entry into force of the Lisbon Treaty, which included

[1] This criticism is actually quite dated (for a classic statement see C Schmitt, *The Crisis of Parliamentary Democracy*, E Kennedy (trans) (Cambridge MA, MIT Press, 1985 [1923]).

[2] For a quantitative analysis and an assessment of parliaments' performance during the Euro crisis see K Auel and O Höing, 'Parliaments in the Euro Crisis: Can the Losers of Integration Still Fight Back?' (2014) 52 *Journal of Common Market Studies* 1184.

[3] Among many, see J Waldron, 'Representative Lawmaking' in (2009) 89 *Boston University Law Review* 335.

workshops held in Uppsala in September 2014 and in Stockholm in January 2015, organised out of the necessity of analysing and possibly assessing the recently introduced EWM for subsidiarity review. The original problem was that the available numbers did not seem to settle the question of its value in an unequivocal way. In 2012 and 2013 two yellow cards were finally issued after a period of diffuse scepticism; yet, the numbers of reasoned opinions issued by national parliaments, after having grown steadily between 2010 and 2013, fell drastically in 2014. Once again it is not easy to assess properly this latter bit of information: the diminution might be due to the European Parliament elections in May 2014 or, on the contrary, it could have been determined by a diminished interest in the principle of subsidiarity due to frustration at the ineffective two yellow cards or the more general sense of parliamentary impotency.

The aim of the workshops and then of the volume is to review, compare and when possible assess the performance of the EWM, reflecting upon its impact not only on EU law-making but also within the domestic constitutional and political context. Contributors were invited to analyse the use of the EWM under a theoretical and normative point of view or from the vantage point of the experience of a particular Member State or a group of them. Therefore, the aim of the contributions was not to produce a judgment on the success or failure of the EWM. As has been noted, it is not easy to assess the impact of the EWM just through a quantitative study.[16] Rather, contributors were asked to analyse:

1) how the EWM had been implemented into national constitutional orders and how reasoned opinions were shaped,
2) its effect on the national constitutional dynamic,
3) its impact on the relation between national parliaments and the Commission, and
4) in specific case studies of national and regional parliaments, what was peculiar in their experiences.

Two points need to be highlighted before describing the content of the volume. In light of the ambiguous nature of the EWM and the unsettled definition of the content of subsidiarity, it was necessary to involve both legal scholars and political scientists to take part in the two workshops. In fact, the point of the review of subsidiarity is still disputed, in particular whether it is possible to combine a political with a legal scrutiny of the principle. This issue requires a plurality of perspectives on the analysis of the EWM. Such an interdisciplinary approach is captured in the following chapters by the diversity of the contributors' backgrounds and their approaches. Moreover, in light of the research questions submitted to the participants, it is clear that this collection of essays is grounded upon a solid comparative

[16] K Auel et al, 'Fighting Back? And if so How? Measuring Parliamentary Strength and Activity in EU Affairs' in Hefftler et al (eds), *The Palgrave Handbook of National Parliaments and the European Union* (Basingstoke/New York, Palgrave Macmillan, 2015), 74.

position, one that makes room both for comparative political studies and comparative constitutional law. The privileged point of view of the analysis is usually (but not exclusively) at the national level. The comparative approach yields important dividends for constitutional analysis and policy-reform likewise. Constitutionally, contrasting the practices of subsidiarity review of different national parliaments makes it possible to draw lines of continuity and discontinuity between different experiences. Such an analysis paves the way for a reconstruction of different understandings of subsidiarity review sensitive to national constitutional features, which constitute factors in explaining the practice of the EWM. Some of these factors include: the distribution of the competences of subsidiarity review, which can vary between more or less centralised forms of review and between a light or heavy involvement of the plenary; the institutional and administrative capacities of each parliamentary chamber; the specific sensitivity of each parliamentary chamber toward different subjects of policy-making, so that certain issues trigger a heightened level of scrutiny and others a lessened level (motivational factor).[17] This is functional to an accurate assessment of potential policy-making reforms and the possibility of a uniform and unique European solution to issues affecting the EWM like the possibility of a common understanding of subsidiarity, the drafting of reasoned opinions, and the involvement of subnational legislatures. Hence, the volume reflects the necessity both of inquiring into the actual practices of application of the EWM and, at the same time, looking at possible reforms of this instrument. A key question, which needs to be properly mentioned at this stage, concerns the relation between subsidiarity review and the so-called Political Dialogue.[18] The latter is an informal practice launched by the Barroso Commission in 2006[19] in order to enhance the dialogue between the Commission and national parliaments. It gives the opportunity to each parliamentary chamber to address its concerns over or make suggestions on a draft legislative act or a consultation paper.[20] The considerations sent through the Political Dialogue might overlap with those contained in national parliaments' reasoned opinions. An analysis of the practice of the EWM cannot ignore the use of the Political Dialogue and any proposal for the reform of subsidiarity review has to consider also the role of the Barroso Initiative.

This volume is organised in three parts, each one contributing to separate but related aspects of the use of the EWM. The first part of the volume is devoted to a theoretical reconstruction of how the EWM *ought* to be understood and what *ought*

[17] For a recent survey of the factors explaining whether national parliaments decide to scrutinise EU legislative proposals see K Auel, O Rozenberg and A Tacea, 'To Scrutinise or not to Scrutinise? Explaining Variation in EU-Related Activities in National Parliaments' (2015) 38 *West European Politics* 282.

[18] For a recent impressive reflection on this point see D Jančić, 'The Game of Cards: National Parliaments in the EU and the Future of the Early Warning Mechanism and the Political Dialogue' (2005) 52 *Common Market Law Review* 939.

[19] COM(2006) 211 final.

[20] For an evaluation of the impact of the Political Dialogue see D Jančić, 'The Barroso Initiative: Political Boost or Window Dressing?' (2012) 8 *Utrecht Law Review* 78.

the function and role that are (and could be) played by regional parliaments. Her analysis offers a general reconstruction of the current impact by regional parliaments upon the EWM, and her normative view is organised around the binary distinction between regional parliaments with legislative powers and those without. The former have a higher stake (and more power) in being involved in subsidiarity review because their legislative competences might be directly affected by a Commission proposal. In light of these considerations and of practical constraints (ie, the limited amount of time available to parliaments in order to perform their review, and the different relations, in each Member State, between the national legislature and the regional parliaments), she suggests involving regional parliaments in the process of subsidiarity review in a consistent but limited way. She concludes that

> there is a need for reflection as to the effectiveness and, in the end, the sense it makes for regional parliaments to participate systematically in the EWM as it currently stands in the light of all the existing difficulties highlighted here …
>
> Regional parliaments with legislative competences should hence only participate in the EWM in limited cases of particular political importance whereas all regional assemblies should be given the possibility to express their opinion, through their national parliament, in the framework of the Political Dialogue.[24]

The importance of cooperation and communication for an effective use of subsidiarity review at the regional level is further explored by Karolina Borońska-Hryniewiecka. Her chapter includes a theoretical contribution expanding the notion of the multilevel parliamentary field[25] to the subnational level. There are at least two solid reasons for this operation: the inclusion of subnational institutions captures the new dynamics generated by the EWM in a more accurate way[26] and, as a matter of fact, it is stated that over 70 per cent of EU legislation and programmes have to be implemented by, and are of concern to, regional parliaments. Empirically, the comparative analysis of the chapter is based on document review and interviews conducted among regional parliaments in five Member States (Spain, Belgium, the United Kingdom, Italy, and Germany). The reconstruction of horizontal (within the subnational entities of the same Member State or of different Member States) and vertical (with other legislative entities) cooperation is conducted under a strict definition of cooperation, understood as 'an active engagement and exchange of resources (ie information, expertise, support) between the actors'. The findings are of a dual nature: there has been clear mobilisation from certain subnational institutional actors because networking and exchange

[24] See Chapter 6, Section IV of this volume at 136.

[25] The classic reference here is B Crum and J Fossum, 'The Multilevel Parliamentary Field: a Framework for Theorizing Representative Democracy in the EU' (2009) *European Political Science Review* 249.

[26] For a comparative assessment of the new mobilization see K Borońska-Hryniewiecka, 'Differential Europeanization? Explaining the Impact of the Early Warning System on Subnational Parliaments in Europe' in (2016) 8 *European Political Science Review* (forthcoming).

position, one that makes room both for comparative political studies and comparative constitutional law. The privileged point of view of the analysis is usually (but not exclusively) at the national level. The comparative approach yields important dividends for constitutional analysis and policy-reform likewise. Constitutionally, contrasting the practices of subsidiarity review of different national parliaments makes it possible to draw lines of continuity and discontinuity between different experiences. Such an analysis paves the way for a reconstruction of different understandings of subsidiarity review sensitive to national constitutional features, which constitute factors in explaining the practice of the EWM. Some of these factors include: the distribution of the competences of subsidiarity review, which can vary between more or less centralised forms of review and between a light or heavy involvement of the plenary; the institutional and administrative capacities of each parliamentary chamber; the specific sensitivity of each parliamentary chamber toward different subjects of policy-making, so that certain issues trigger a heightened level of scrutiny and others a lessened level (motivational factor).[17] This is functional to an accurate assessment of potential policy-making reforms and the possibility of a uniform and unique European solution to issues affecting the EWM like the possibility of a common understanding of subsidiarity, the drafting of reasoned opinions, and the involvement of subnational legislatures. Hence, the volume reflects the necessity both of inquiring into the actual practices of application of the EWM and, at the same time, looking at possible reforms of this instrument. A key question, which needs to be properly mentioned at this stage, concerns the relation between subsidiarity review and the so-called Political Dialogue.[18] The latter is an informal practice launched by the Barroso Commission in 2006[19] in order to enhance the dialogue between the Commission and national parliaments. It gives the opportunity to each parliamentary chamber to address its concerns over or make suggestions on a draft legislative act or a consultation paper.[20] The considerations sent through the Political Dialogue might overlap with those contained in national parliaments' reasoned opinions. An analysis of the practice of the EWM cannot ignore the use of the Political Dialogue and any proposal for the reform of subsidiarity review has to consider also the role of the Barroso Initiative.

This volume is organised in three parts, each one contributing to separate but related aspects of the use of the EWM. The first part of the volume is devoted to a theoretical reconstruction of how the EWM *ought* to be understood and what *ought*

[17] For a recent survey of the factors explaining whether national parliaments decide to scrutinise EU legislative proposals see K Auel, O Rozenberg and A Tacea, 'To Scrutinise or not to Scrutinise? Explaining Variation in EU-Related Activities in National Parliaments' (2015) 38 *West European Politics* 282.

[18] For a recent impressive reflection on this point see D Jančić, 'The Game of Cards: National Parliaments in the EU and the Future of the Early Warning Mechanism and the Political Dialogue' (2005) 52 *Common Market Law Review* 939.

[19] COM(2006) 211 final.

[20] For an evaluation of the impact of the Political Dialogue see D Jančić, 'The Barroso Initiative: Political Boost or Window Dressing?' (2012) 8 *Utrecht Law Review* 78.

to be the role of national and regional parliaments. A common theme behind all chapters of this part is the link between the idea of subsidiarity and the use of the EWM. It is open to different interpretations whether subsidiarity ought to be conceived according to political or legal rationality (or both, if possible).[21] The opening chapter, by one of the major experts of subsidiarity review, Ian Cooper identifies three approaches to the understanding of the EWM: 1) subsidiarity review seen as a rule-following practice (exemplified by the practice of the Finnish *Eduskunta*); 2) subsidiarity review as political bargaining (exemplified by the Danish *Folketing*); and 3) subsidiarity review as policy arguing (exemplified by the Swedish *Riksdag*). Each approach entails a different conception of subsidiarity[22] and normative consequences in the relation with the Commission. The chapter shows how the content of subsidiarity review is shaped by the interaction between the Commission and the relevant national constitutional culture, but Cooper also puts forward an argument in favour of the model of argumentation. The latter vindicates the political role of national parliaments in checking subsidiarity but at the same time does not unleash centrifugal or anti-integration forces because the engagement with the Commission would be driven by the dialogue on how to legislate on the basis of the best argument and not of self-interest. However, while some parliamentary chambers have adopted this approach, he recognises that the Commission has not been willing to cooperate in this way with national parliaments because it has favoured an understanding of the EWM based on a strictly formal and legal conception of subsidiarity.

Jörgen Hettne provides an overview of the functioning of the EWM and its link with both political and legal conceptions of subsidiarity. His aim is to find a solution to the potential conflict between the political and legal understandings of subsidiarity and to articulate an encompassing proposal of rationalisation of the subsidiarity review, compatible with the current constitutional balance in the EU. His proposal, termed a constitutional dialogue, comprises several aspects: the facilitating of constitutional issues through reasoned opinions which would serve as a mechanism for signalling potential dangers in a Commission proposal; the ex ante involvement of the Court of Justice of the European Union to settle constitutional issues; the modification of the threshold for the yellow card according to the rules of decision-making in the Treaties; the inclusion of proportionality reasoning in reasoned opinions together with issues relating to the principle of conferred powers and issues of national/constitutional identity. Overall, Hettne's chapter offers a challenging blueprint for a reform of the EWM which would hold

[21] See, for an example of a legal interpretation of the EWM, F Fabbrini and K Granat, 'Yellow Card, but no Foul: The Role of National Parliaments under the Subsidiarity Protocol and the Commission Proposal for an EU Regulation on the Right to Strike' (2013) 50 *Common Market Law Review* 116.

[22] Cf C Fasone, 'Competing Concepts of Subsidiarity and the Early Warning Mechanism' in N Lupo, M Cartabia and A Simoncini (eds), *Democracy and Subsidiarity in the EU* (Bologna, Il Mulino, 2013) 157–96.

together two potentially contrasting objectives: maintaining the current balance of powers in the EU and resolving the conflict over subsidiarity review.

Anne Wetter adds a further dimension to this debate on how to improve the application of the EWM by introducing an argument in favour of procedural indicators in performing subsidiarity review. While aware that procedures are not absolute guarantees of involvement, Wetter's reasoning is that they constitute the very starting point of national parliaments' participation in EU law-making. Following the *Isoglucose* case and Maduro's opinion in *Vodafone*, she elaborates what the role of the Court of Justice could be in enforcing the respect of procedural requirements in order to protect the rights of national parliaments within the EWM. She argues that a contextual and purpose-oriented method of interpretation in the future would allow for the ECJ to annul legislation adopted in violation of procedural requirements, aiming for the implementation of the principle of subsidiarity.

The trajectory of inter-parliamentary cooperation among national parliaments is the core issue treated by Bruno Dias Pinheiro in his chapter. It is uncontested that the EWM cannot fly without some form of cooperation among national parliaments. The question, therefore, is not *if* but *how* cooperation should take place in order to make the EWM effective.[23] Hence, subsidiarity review might be a catalyst practice for strengthening the exchange of information and networking among national parliamentarians even beyond the EWM. By adopting an institutionalist approach, and on the basis of his professional experience, Dias Pinheiro reconstructs in a systematic way all the possible forms of inter-parliamentary cooperation (vertical and horizontal) and then assesses the influence of national parliaments in each of them. He also underlines the material and institutional factors which make national parliaments' participation in those forums more or less influential. With the recognition that there are two practical drivers of cooperation—that is, a possibility to generate some electoral reward or the chance of having a policy impact—Dias Pinheiro proposes to use forms of inter-parliamentary cooperation for gearing subsidiarity review toward a more proactive and affirmative role of the national parliaments. Inter-parliamentary cooperation can play a positive role in re-interpreting subsidiarity scrutiny from a veto mechanism to an input-based practice (for example, the green card) which would transform the national parliaments into active shapers of EU law-making.

Part II of the book is devoted to regional parliaments and the impact that the EWM has had on them. Given that the protocol on subsidiarity gives the national parliaments the right to consult the regional parliaments and include their comments in reasoned opinions, the inclusion of regional parliaments is necessary for a more accurate account of the dynamics of the EWM. Diane Fromage addresses

[23] Ian Cooper has famously suggested that the EWM ought to nudge the national parliaments to operate as if they were a collective institution, a 'third chamber' of the European Union: I Cooper, 'A "Virtual Third Chamber" for the European Union? National Parliaments after the Lisbon Treaty' (2013) 35 *West European Politics* 441.

the function and role that are (and could be) played by regional parliaments. Her analysis offers a general reconstruction of the current impact by regional parliaments upon the EWM, and her normative view is organised around the binary distinction between regional parliaments with legislative powers and those without. The former have a higher stake (and more power) in being involved in subsidiarity review because their legislative competences might be directly affected by a Commission proposal. In light of these considerations and of practical constraints (ie, the limited amount of time available to parliaments in order to perform their review, and the different relations, in each Member State, between the national legislature and the regional parliaments), she suggests involving regional parliaments in the process of subsidiarity review in a consistent but limited way. She concludes that

> there is a need for reflection as to the effectiveness and, in the end, the sense it makes for regional parliaments to participate systematically in the EWM as it currently stands in the light of all the existing difficulties highlighted here …
>
> Regional parliaments with legislative competences should hence only participate in the EWM in limited cases of particular political importance whereas all regional assemblies should be given the possibility to express their opinion, through their national parliament, in the framework of the Political Dialogue.[24]

The importance of cooperation and communication for an effective use of subsidiarity review at the regional level is further explored by Karolina Borońska-Hryniewiecka. Her chapter includes a theoretical contribution expanding the notion of the multilevel parliamentary field[25] to the subnational level. There are at least two solid reasons for this operation: the inclusion of subnational institutions captures the new dynamics generated by the EWM in a more accurate way[26] and, as a matter of fact, it is stated that over 70 per cent of EU legislation and programmes have to be implemented by, and are of concern to, regional parliaments. Empirically, the comparative analysis of the chapter is based on document review and interviews conducted among regional parliaments in five Member States (Spain, Belgium, the United Kingdom, Italy, and Germany). The reconstruction of horizontal (within the subnational entities of the same Member State or of different Member States) and vertical (with other legislative entities) cooperation is conducted under a strict definition of cooperation, understood as 'an active engagement and exchange of resources (ie information, expertise, support) between the actors'. The findings are of a dual nature: there has been clear mobilisation from certain subnational institutional actors because networking and exchange

[24] See Chapter 6, Section IV of this volume at 136.

[25] The classic reference here is B Crum and J Fossum, 'The Multilevel Parliamentary Field: a Framework for Theorizing Representative Democracy in the EU' (2009) *European Political Science Review* 249.

[26] For a comparative assessment of the new mobilization see K Borońska-Hryniewiecka, 'Differential Europeanization? Explaining the Impact of the Early Warning System on Subnational Parliaments in Europe' in (2016) 8 *European Political Science Review* (forthcoming).

of knowledge are considered strategic assets for what are on average relatively under-empowered institutions; and yet inter-parliamentary cooperation still takes place in a fragmented and incoherent way. Borónska-Hryniewiecka concludes that inter-parliamentary cooperation in all the analysed cases leaves much scope for improvement. Regional parliaments are mostly guardians and controllers of their executives, while remaining weak networkers and policy entrepreneurs. One of the main explanations for this is a weakness in the necessary EU expertise, as well as insufficient political engagement on the side of members of regional parliaments. Thus, there is still a large amount of leeway regarding the tools for making their engagement more efficient, faster and meaningful under the constraints of the European decision-making process.

Another case concerning regions with legislative powers is represented by Italy, here tackled by Cristina Fasone.[27] Her chapter is particularly illuminating because it contrasts the Italian experience with the Spanish. The Spanish territorial organisation is deemed to have inspired the reform of Italian regionalism. Yet, compared to the Spanish context, Italian regions come across as weaker, both in political and legislative terms. Nonetheless, Fasone shows that the implementation of EWM in Italy has benefitted Italian regions more than Spanish ones by generating three unexpected positive externalities. The first one is that it has strengthened the previously tenuous relation between the Italian Parliament and the regional councils. This has been possible due to the inception of a national political dialogue in which, in an uneven but active way, several regions have taken part. This outcome has also been made possible by the adoption of a wide interpretation of the EWM mechanism which has allowed the regions to voice their concerns not only on matters completely devolved to them, but also on issues which would have in any case a repercussion on them. The second positive externality, despite different attitudes toward EU affairs, is that the consultation of regional councils has enhanced the cooperation among them and, unlike Spain, strengthened the role of the Conference of the Presidents of regional parliaments. The third positive externality is the strengthening of the national parliamentary process in EU affairs. The introduction of the EWM has triggered a strong form of vertical inter-parliamentary cooperation which has resulted in more parliamentary deliberation and more participation in EU affairs from a parliament which previously did not use to properly scrutinise EU draft proposals. Finally, the current constitutional reform will change the composition of the Senate in favour of a large representation of members of regional councils. If the reform is approved, it is clear that the avenues for regional intervention on EU affairs will further multiply. Fasone concludes that the position of regional councils has at least partially been restored in the Italian constitutional system as a result of the implementation of the EWM.

[27] Fasone has already engaged with this topic in 'Towards new Procedures between State and Regional Legislatures in Italy, Exploiting the Tool of the Early Warning Mechanism' (2013) 5 *Perspectives on Federalism* 122.

Werner Vandenbruwaene and Patricia Popelier examine the most complex case of intertwining between the national and regional levels, that is, Belgium. The logic of Belgian federalism permeates the procedural set-up of subsidiarity scrutiny[28] which entails exclusivity. It is for this reason that Belgium issued Declaration 51 to the Lisbon Treaty stating that regional and communities' parliaments also count as components of the national parliamentary system. Given the number of devolved competences in the Belgian context, such an arrangement clearly empowers the sub-state parliaments as primary actors in subsidiarity review. In order to make subsidiarity review effective in such a pluralist constitutional system, a cooperation agreement among the seven legislative assemblies was signed in 2005 and then modified in 2008. However, because of a number of what Vandenbruwaene and Popelier define as 'endogenous' and 'exogenous' factors, the functioning of subsidiarity scrutiny has been anything but smooth and effective. A close qualitative analysis of reasoned opinions and practice of the Political Dialogue shows that in general, subsidiarity review is understood by all parliaments in a wide political sense, even though it is not possible to deduce a single shared meaning of its content.

The third part of the volume focuses on the analysis of the EWM as used in many of the 28 Member States. A selection of Member States was necessary and it has been made according to certain criteria. The four largest Member States were included by virtue of their role in EU law-making and their value as peculiar constitutional models. The other Member States are grouped according to regional spheres around the Visegrád group and the Scandinavian countries. Belgium, given its peculiar constitutional arrangement and the importance of its regions and communities has been placed in the second part.

This third part opens with a chapter by Anna Jonsson Cornell on some of the most active and highly praised legislative assemblies: the Nordic parliaments. Cornell pays attention to both the similarities and differences between the Swedish *Riksdag*, the Danish *Folketing* and the Finnish *Eduskunta* under three different aspects: constitutional context; procedural aspects of the use of the EWM; and conceptions of the principle of subsidiarity. Referring to Cooper's typology, she concludes that at the constitutional level the differences are more relevant than the similarities because these three parliaments understand 1) the principle of subsidiarity, 2) their role in EU law-making, and 3) the function of the EWM, all in substantially different ways.

In the following chapter, Nicola Lupo examines the Italian approach to the EWM in light of the different experiences of the two chambers of the parliament. His analysis, nested in the wider 'Euro-national Parliamentary System',[29] is centred

[28] Vandenbruwaene and Popelier had already explored the federal organisation of the Belgian subsidiarity scrutiny in 'The Subsidiarity Mechanism as a Tool for Inter-Level Dialogue in Belgium: On "Regional Blindness" and "Cooperative Flaws"' (2011) 7 *European Constitutional Law Review* 221.

[29] A Manzella and N Lupo (eds), *Il Sistema parlamentare Euro-nazionale* (Torino, Giappichelli, 2014).

on both formal and informal elements. The two parliamentary chambers have not yet formalised the procedures for the EWM, but their practice is reconstructed by Lupo by accounting for the influence of the political system, and analysing the reasoned opinions issued until now and other documents mostly produced by the EU policies committees. Lupo concludes that the Italian approach to the EWM results in a view of subsidiarity review as political (rather than formal or legal), dynamic, and generally geared toward the support of the national interest. The two chambers tend to conceive both the EWM and the Political Dialogue in an individualistic way, placing more emphasis on the relation between each national parliament and the Commission rather than on inter-parliamentary cooperation.

France offers a rather distinct case in the application of the EWM because of its semi-presidentialist form of government. Angela Tacea shows how the peculiar French constitutional culture affects the workings of the EWM. The two chambers do not cooperate, and their subsidiarity review is impacted by different political horizons. As happens in other countries, the Senate enjoys more independence from the government and this independence has been strengthened when the election of the lower house has been made to overlap with election of the President of the Republic. Apart from the institutional design, there are other reasons behind the divide between the two Chambers. Traditionally, the lower house has been more pro-European and has conceived the EWM as an instrument in the hands of Euro-sceptics. This is reflected in the less frequent use of the EWM by the Assemblé Nationale, which has mostly adopted reasoned opinions in support of the position of the government. Contrary to this attitude, the Senate has seen in the EWM an opportunity to move beyond the dynamic between government and parliament and, as a consequence, to carve out a new role for itself.

Just as the French parliamentary use of the EWM is heavily influenced by its constitutional design and culture, the same is valid for another important constitutional model: the UK.[30] Adam Cygan's analysis is conducted within the framework of political accountability, usually conceived as the cornerstone of the British model of constitutionalism.[31] This shapes the way in which both Houses undertake subsidiarity review. In fact, both Houses tend to put more emphasis on and resources in parliamentary scrutiny because it is deemed to be more effective than subsidiarity review. As a consequence of this scepticism, it is no wonder that the UK parliament is among the strongest advocates of the introduction of a red card in the EWM. Even though committees are supposed to operate in a less partisan way than the plenary, one can still detect an influence of the Westminster model over the operation of the House of Commons. The fusion of the legislature with

[30] For a reconstruction of the three main European constitutional models (France, UK, Germany) from a US-based perspective, see B Ackerman, 'Three Paths to Constitutionalism' (2015) 45 *British Journal of Political Science* 704.

[31] Cf A Tomkins, *Public Law* (Oxford, Clarendon Press, 2003). Cygan has already worked on a comparison between the British and the German model of scrutiny in *National Parliaments in an Integrated Europe: An Anglo-German Perspective* (Dordrecht, Kluwer, 2002).

the executive makes the opinions of the House of Commons closer to the positions adopted by the national government, while the House of Lords can afford a more autonomous role. This factor, together with the lack of proper and structural communication, explains the difference in the numbers of reasoned opinions sent by the two Houses.

In her chapter on Germany and Austria, Katrien Auel investigates the differences and the reasons behind the decline of interest in the EWM in both countries after what had been an enthusiastic start. Overall, the German and the Austrian parliaments have been less active than the average of the EU parliaments and their contribution is decreasing. Auel reviews how both parliaments use the EWM and the Political Dialogue, with an analysis based on sociological institutionalism. Hence, parliamentary and constitutional cultures play a central role in explaining the norms and values of active parliamentarians. The German and Austrian political systems are still marked by strong party discipline, which represents a disincentive for MPs. In the German case, the Bundestag also perceives itself as exogenous vis-à-vis the European legislative process and it does not consider its task to be holding EU institutions accountable. Both parliamentary majorities tend to agree with the position sketched out by the governing coalitions. Moreover, after initial engagement, in both countries there is a growing sense of a lack of effectiveness of the EWM and the Political Dialogue, due to the absence of press coverage for this activity and the more general difficulty of reaching the electorate. Hence, and despite the actual material capacity to handle a complicated procedure like the EWM, there is no strong incentive to engage with that instrument.

In the final chapter of this part, Katarzyna Granat reconstructs the functioning of the EWM in two neighbouring countries: the Czech Republic and Poland. Both countries are instantiations of asymmetrical bicameral systems with strengthened EU affairs committees. While apparently very similar in constitutional terms, the actual performances of both parliaments are rather different in practice. Granat undertakes a close analysis of the Polish and Czech parliaments by looking at the debates, their reasoned opinions and their participation in the Political Dialogue. Intriguingly, in both countries Protocol no 2 has been interpreted in a wide sense and subsidiarity review has been understood as more than a legal and formal check upon Commission's proposals. Moreover, both parliaments tend to adopt reasoned opinions by unanimity and through a plenary vote, while the level of participation seems not to be determined by EU-friendly positions. In terms of substance, the Polish reasoned opinions assess the material and procedural aspects of the subsidiarity principle while the Czech parliament emphasises the possible violations of fundamental rights. Granat explains the differences in the use of the EWM and the Political Dialogue as a consequence of the procedures put into place for the application of these instruments and, often, the limited resources available to both parliaments.

The last chapter, by Cornell and Goldoni, serves a two-fold aim: to sum up the findings of the previous chapters and to illustrate what directions the future of the EWM might take and with what consequences for national parliaments.

Beginning from the premise that the political context does not allow for a definitive judgment on the effectiveness of the EWM, this chapter draws upon the main continuities and discontinuities in the various experiences of regional and national parliaments. It also engages with the potential future development concerning the EWM, from the red and the green card to the forums of inter-parliamentary cooperation. Overall, the suggestion is that there is still room for parliamentary politics, and in particular national parliamentary politics, in EU law-making.

Part I

Subsidiarity Review—Goals Achieved and Future Challenges

2

Is the Early Warning Mechanism a Legal or a Political Procedure? Three Questions and a Typology

IAN COOPER

I. Introduction: Legal or Political? A Highly Instructive Question

Is the Early Warning Mechanism (EWM), in which national parliaments check the legislative proposals of the European Union (EU) for their subsidiarity compliance, essentially a legal or a political procedure? This is a difficult question that reasonable people, both academic observers and political practitioners, disagree over how to answer. The nature and purpose of the EWM has always been ambiguous and contested: this was true when it was originally conceived in the European Convention (2002–03) and when it was codified in the Treaty of Lisbon (2009), and it has continued to be so as the EWM has been worked out in practice. The role of national parliaments in the EWM has been likened on one hand to a Council of State, conducting an advisory 'legal review' of EU legislation,[1] and on the other to a 'virtual third chamber', a political body with the power to intervene in the EU's legislative process.[2] Even after the EWM has been in operation for five years, it is not obvious which description is closer to the truth.

This question is also, as it turns out, highly instructive: the simple legal-versus-political dichotomy covers a number of inter-related debates, and an analysis of these gives us a more nuanced overview of the competing interpretations of the

[1] P Kiiver, *The Early-Warning System for the Principle of Subsidiarity: Constitutional Theory and Empirical Reality* (Abingdon, Routledge, 2012) 126–33.

[2] I Cooper, 'The watchdogs of subsidiarity: national parliaments and the logic of arguing in the EU' (2006) 44 *Journal of Common Market Studies* 283. I Cooper, 'A "virtual third chamber" for the European Union? National parliaments after the Treaty of Lisbon' (2012) 35 *West European Politics* 441. I Cooper, 'Bicameral or tricameral? National parliaments and representative democracy in the European Union' (2013) 35 *Journal of European Integration* 531.

EWM. This question is inextricably linked to the deeper, normative question of whether the principle of subsidiarity, around which the EWM revolves, is fundamentally a legal or political concept. Most of this chapter is devoted to 'unpacking' this debate, which reveals three distinct questions. First (section II), should subsidiarity and the EWM be studied by legal scholars or political scientists? A review of the literature shows that these disciplines approach the subject in different, but complementary ways. A second question (section III) is: should subsidiarity and the EWM be implemented by legal or political institutions? A historical review shows that the implementation of the principle of subsidiarity in the EU has always been primarily the responsibility of political institutions. The EWM is an innovation only in that it brings in a new bunch of political institutions, national parliaments, as subsidiarity watchdogs. The European Court of Justice (ECJ) has the authority to interpret the relevant subsidiarity provisions of the EU treaties, but it has never substantially exercised it. The third question (section IV) is: do subsidiarity and the EWM entail a legal or a political mode of reasoning? The answer depends on one's understanding of the principle of subsidiarity, both in itself and as it relates to adjacent treaty principles (proportionality, conferral) and, at a further remove, political concerns (policy effectiveness, political expediency).

Building upon this analysis, a typology (section V) is presented in which there are not just two but *three* broad approaches to the EWM—one 'legal' and two 'political'. These are ideal types (although exemplified by certain participants, in parentheses below), and each depends on a different understanding of subsidiarity. The first approach is *Legal Rule-Following* (Commission, Finnish *Eduskunta*), in which subsidiarity is a quasi-legal rule whose requirements may be clearly ascertained. National parliaments defer to the Commission's interpretation of subsidiarity, based on a system of rigorous impact assessment. If national parliaments have other concerns about a proposal (eg proportionality, policy substance), they raise them in the Political Dialogue rather than the EWM. The second approach is *Political Bargaining* (Danish *Folketing*, Dutch *Tweede Kamer*), in which subsidiarity is an endlessly flexible concept which may be interpreted so as to allow or prohibit almost any course of EU action. National parliaments use the EWM when they see it is in their political interest to oppose an EU measure. They will seek to build a coalition to achieve a yellow or orange card. The third approach is *Policy Arguing* (Swedish *Riksdag*, UK House of Commons), in which subsidiarity is a vague but nevertheless useful concept. The EWM enables a policy argument between the Commission and national parliaments concerning whether and how the EU should legislate in particular circumstances. To be clear, the point of this section is to sketch out the three approaches, using certain parliaments as illustrative examples,[3] not to comprehensively categorise all the national parliaments;

[3] Empirically, I drew liberally from the trove of useful information, both country-specific and comparative, to be found in C Hefftler, C Neuhold, O Rozenberg and J Smith, *The Palgrave Handbook of National Parliaments and the European Union* (London, Palgrave Macmillan, 2015), as well as the various contributions to this volume.

furthermore, throughout the chapter I refer to some EU legislative proposals to illustrate my points—in particular the two proposals that were the targets of the first two yellow cards—but no attempt is made to provide a comprehensive legislative history of the EWM. Finally, the chapter concludes (section VI) by pointing out that the EWM remains a contested procedure in that the participants cannot agree on the social rules governing it. However, the Commission has recently signalled that it may be open to a more explicitly political EWM in the future.

II. Are Subsidiarity and the EWM Best Studied by Legal Scholars or Political Scientists?

First of all, should subsidiarity and the EWM be studied by political scientists or legal scholars? This is, in context, a foolish question, given that the growing body of literature on this subject—including, of course, the many exemplary works within this volume—features scholars from both disciplines. It would be a mistake to assume that legal scholars would automatically adhere to a narrow, legalistic approach to the EWM, and that political scientists would favour a broader, more explicitly political, approach. In fact, the existing scholarship on the EWM does not fit this pattern, as a 'narrow-vs.-broad' debate may be discerned within both disciplines. For example, the authors of one legal commentary on the first use of the 'yellow card'—in the case of the 'Monti II' Regulation on the right to strike—argued that the national parliaments went beyond their role by raising objections that were not strictly based on subsidiarity concerns; they argued that the proposal was clearly compliant with subsidiarity, implying in effect that the yellow card was a misuse of the EWM.[4] Other legal theorists, however, have written approvingly of the 'political approach'[5] that was evident in the case of the first yellow card and of national parliaments' 'creative' use of the subsidiarity framework.[6] Political scientists, too, differ in whether they envisage subsidiarity review under the EWM in broad or narrow terms. From one perspective that adopts a flexible understanding of subsidiarity, the EWM could lessen the democratic deficit by giving national parliaments greater influence at the EU level, so that they become a 'virtual third chamber' for the EU.[7] Against this view, others have argued that the EWM will not

[4] F Fabbrini and K Granat, '"Yellow card, but no foul": the role of the national parliaments under the subsidiarity protocol and the Commission proposal for an EU regulation on the right to strike' (2013) 50 *Common Market Law Review* 115.

[5] M Goldoni, 'The Early Warning System and the Monti II regulation: the case for a political interpretation' (2014) 10 *European Constitutional Law Review* 90.

[6] M Bartl, 'The Way We Do Europe: Subsidiarity and the Substantive Democratic Deficit' (2015) 21 *European Law Journal* 24.

[7] I Cooper, 'A "Virtual Third Chamber"' (n 2 above).

reduce the democratic deficit, in part because violations of subsidiarity are rare occurrences, and that national parliaments would be well advised to focus their attention elsewhere in order to increase their influence in the EU.[8] These examples show that disciplinary affiliation does not determine an author's attitude towards the correct use of the procedure.

There is, however, a deeper and more pervasive difference between the two disciplines that emerges from their respective methodologies. These methodologies lead them to address quite different questions, which naturally yield different kinds of results. On the whole—at the risk of generalising—legal scholars who study the EWM are interested in how it will affect the legal and constitutional order of the EU. When considering a specific case—eg a yellow card—they tend to engage in a textual analysis of the reasoned opinions of the national parliaments, in order to compare their reasoning to that of the Commission. Political scientists, by contrast, are more interested in how the EWM will affect political outcomes. They are less interested in the substantive content of reasoned opinions; rather, they are more likely to see the EWM as a political tool, and to ask under what circumstances it is likely to be wielded by national parliaments and what effect it may have. The contrast between the two disciplinary approaches is vividly on display in their respective analyses of the *Monti II* yellow card: whereas legal scholars debate the relative merits of the opinions of the national parliaments and the Commission,[9] political scientists analyse the tools of inter-parliamentary coordination that were activated in order to make the yellow card happen, in addition to debating the political importance of the outcome.[10]

In general, these two disciplinary approaches are complementary, in that each one has its respective strengths, and insofar as one may have weaknesses or blind spots these may be compensated for by the strengths of the other. For example, it seems that political scientists' disciplinary perspective allows them, on the whole, to adopt a more flexible understanding of subsidiarity within the context of the EWM. Legal scholars tend to emphasise the narrow scope of the EWM which, whether they like it or not, they perceive as intractable.[11] Even those who regret such narrowness, expressing a belief that the role of national parliaments in EU policy scrutiny should be expanded beyond mere subsidiarity control, do not see a way out of the conundrum—at least short of treaty change. They do not see what seems obvious to political scientists: that the EWM is a tool which national

[8] P De Wilde, 'Why the Early Warning Mechanism does not alleviate the democratic deficit' (2012) Maastricht: *OPAL Online Paper* No 6/2012. T Raunio, 'Destined for irrelevance? Subsidiarity control by national parliaments' *Elcano Royal Institute, Working Paper* 36/2010 (Madrid, 2010).

[9] F Fabbrini and K Granat '"Yellow card, but no foul"' (n 4 above). M Goldoni, 'The Early Warning System and the Monti II regulation' (n 5 above).

[10] I Cooper, 'A yellow card for the striker: national parliaments and the defeat of EU legislation on the right to strike' (2015) 22 *Journal of European Public Policy* 1406.

[11] G Davies, 'Democracy and Legitimacy in the Shadow of Purposive Competence' (2015) 21 *European Law Journal* 15–16. G Davies, 'Subsidiarity: The Wrong Idea, in the Wrong Place, at the Wrong Time' (2006) 43 *Common Market Law Review* 67–68.

parliaments may adapt for their particular purposes, and that they may reinterpret subsidiarity in a way that allows them to challenge an EU legislative proposal on other grounds, such as legal basis, proportionality, and policy effectiveness. As it happens, this is the approach to the EWM which many national parliaments have taken, as discussed below.

Another strength of the political scientist's method is that the rigorous comparison of national parliaments' approaches to the EWM, often using quantitative methods, may yield unexpected insights. For example, it is often assumed that it is the 'strong' parliaments—those considered to have the most institutional capacity to scrutinise their own governments—that would be most likely to extend their influence to the EU level by, for example, participating in the EWM. Conversely, it is sometimes posited that 'weak' parliaments would be more likely to participate because, having little national-level influence over their own governments' conduct of EU affairs, they would instead focus their attention on EU-level procedures such as the EWM. However, an empirical analysis of the recent use of the EWM shows with bracing clarity that neither supposition turns out to be true: 'There was no correlation, negative or positive, between the institutional strength of the chambers and the number of opinions they sent within the EWM or the Political Dialogue.'[12] Evidently, it is not enough that national parliaments are able to act, but they also must be willing. Further studies have attempted to go beyond institutional capacity to inquire whether the variation between national parliaments' propensity to participate in the EWM may be explained according to incentive-related factors, such as party-political contestation or the salience and urgency of draft legislative acts,[13] or public opinion regarding the EU.[14] Yet such quantitative methods, so beloved of political scientists, cannot analyse more subtle differences in the approach of national parliaments to the EWM, including contrasts in their legislative cultures and in their normative interpretation of subsidiarity.[15] To fully understand such differences requires a qualitative methodological approach, such

[12] K Auel, O Rozenberg and A Tacea, 'Fighting Back? And, if so, how? Measuring Parliamentary Strength and Activity in EU Affairs' in Hefftler et al, *The Palgrave Handbook of National Parliaments and the European Union* (n 3 above) 86.

[13] K Gattermann and C Hefftler, 'Beyond Institutional Capacity: Political Motivation and Parliamentary Behaviour in the Early Warning System' (2015) 38 *West European Politics* 305. Perhaps the most significant finding of this study (at 322), though one not emphasised by the authors, is that the likelihood that any one chamber will pass a reasoned opinion under the EWM rises sharply if a large number of other chambers have already done so (statistically, the probability is 21% higher if 10 other chambers have passed a reasoned opinion than if none have done so). This suggests that many parliaments are more likely to pass a reasoned opinion if they think a yellow card is likely, in line with what I call a 'political bargaining' approach to the EWM (see section V, below.)

[14] C Williams, 'Issuing Reasoned Opinions: The Determinants of Usage of the Early Warning System' (2015), ms, European University Institute, *European Union Politics*, 25 February 2016: eup.sagepub.com/content/early/2016/02/25/1465116516633301.full.pdf+html.

[15] One legal scholar undertook an analysis to see whether the type of scrutiny system employed by a parliament (centralised, decentralised, or mixed) affected its level of activity in the EWM, but she found no robust relationship. K Granat, *National Parliaments and the Policing of the Subsidiarity Principle* (PhD Dissertation, European University Institute, Florence, 2014) 160–61.

as is commonly employed by legal scholars—as well as some political scientists—that entails a close, substantive reading of texts, such as the reasoned opinions of the national parliaments.

In lieu of a one-dimensional continuum separating 'strong' from 'weak' parliaments in varying degrees, there have been attempts both by legal scholars and political scientists to develop typologies that classify national parliaments according to their differing approaches to EU affairs generally or the EWM specifically. One political science study identified 'modes of parliamentary activity in EU affairs' with which to identify five groups of parliaments/chambers according to which type of activity they emphasise in EU affairs, which are: Scrutinisers (scrutiny in committee), Debating arenas (plenary debates), Policy shapers (mandates and resolutions), Commission watchdogs (Political Dialogue and EWM), and Scrutiny laggards (none). It is the fourth of these that is most relevant for scholars of the EWM, because a parliament/chamber that aspires to be a 'Commission watchdog' will invest its resources in EU-level engagement at the expense of domestic scrutiny. Unfortunately, this study did not yield results specific to the EWM, because to arrive at their measure of EU-level engagement the authors combined each parliament/chamber's number of reasoned opinions under the EWM with its number of contributions under the Political Dialogue, which tend to be more numerous.[16] As a result, the only 'Commission watchdogs' they identify are the Portuguese parliament and the Italian Senate, both of which have been particularly active in the Political Dialogue but not in the EWM.

One legal scholar, Philipp Kiiver, produced a typology of four kinds of parliaments/chambers, classified specifically according to how they approach the EWM: the Literalists, who faithfully adhere to a narrow check of the subsidiarity compliance of a legislative proposal, as required by the treaty (including, eg the two Dutch chambers and the French *Sénat*); the Pseudo-co-legislators, who ignore the formal limits of the EWM and treat it as a policy consultation (including, eg the German Bundesrat and the UK House of Lords); the Pre-emptors, who generally decline to participate in the EWM but choose to react instead to EU consultation documents (eg the Nordic parliaments of Denmark, Sweden and Finland); and the Absentees, who tend not to participate in the EWM at all (mostly parliaments in Southern and Eastern Europe).[17] There is much to quibble with in this typology, including whether the parliaments/chambers cited as examples belong in these categories. For example, the three Nordic parliaments, which Kiiver puts together in the same category, have in practice acted very differently in the EWM. Measured by the numbers of reasoned opinions passed, the Swedish *Riksdag* has been by far the most active parliament in the EWM, whereas the Finnish *Eduskunta* has been

[16] During the period examined, 2010–12, there were more than eight times as many Political Dialogue contributions (1324) as reasoned opinions (161). The latter were overshadowed by the former, despite being accorded double weight by the study's authors. Auel et al, 'Fighting back?' (n 12 above) 71, 76.

[17] P Kiiver, *The Early-Warning System* (n 1 above), 136–39.

among the least active, and the Danish *Folketing* has been close to the average.[18] It is argued below (section V) that these three parliaments, while similar in many other ways, actually exemplify three very different approaches to the EWM. Moreover, the two Dutch chambers and the French *Sénat*—which Kiiver calls Literalists—raised objections to the EPPO proposal which were roundly rejected by the Commission for going beyond the scope of the subsidiarity review.[19] To be fair, Kiiver's typology was speculative, based not on an analysis of the EWM in operation but on an analysis of the subsidiarity tests that were conducted by COSAC between 2004 and 2009, prior to the entry into force of the Treaty of Lisbon. During the COSAC tests the Dutch chambers did take a Literalist approach (similar to what I call Legal Rule-Following in my own typology) but since then they have changed their methods, leading to 'a politicisation of the process, whereby reasoned opinions are increasingly used to support or undermine a policy'.[20] (In my own typology, below, I classify the *Tweede Kamer* as an exemplar of the Political Bargaining approach.) Another problem is that, in practical terms, it may be difficult to distinguish Literalists from Absentees: both types will seldom issue reasoned opinions, but for different reasons—the former out of respect for the narrow scope of the EWM, and the latter due to a lack of capacity, lack of interest, or both.[21] But my principal complaint about this typology is that it fails to capture the most salient differences between the approaches of national parliaments to the EWM, which is a reflection of their disparate approaches to the norm of subsidiarity (see section V).

III. Should Subsidiarity and the EWM be Implemented by Legal or Political Institutions?

A more practical question concerning the EWM is whether it is and/or ought to be implemented by legal institutions (eg courts) or by political institutions (eg parliaments). This is closely related to the question of whether the principle of subsidiarity itself should be interpreted primarily by legal or political institutions. The second question pre-dates the first, because subsidiarity was introduced into

[18] I Cooper, 'The Nordic parliaments and the EU' in C Grøn, P Nedergaard and A Wivel (eds), *Still the other European Community? The Nordic Countries and the European Union* (Abingdon, Routledge, 2015) 104. See also the chapter by A Jonsson Cornell, this volume.

[19] Commission Communication of 27 November 2013 (COM(2013) 851 final) 5.

[20] A-L Högenauer, 'The Dutch Parliament and EU Affairs: Decentralizing Scrutiny' in Hefftler et al, *The Palgrave Handbook of National Parliaments and the European Union* (n 3 above) 261.

[21] For example, the Estonian parliament's low level of participation in the EWM may be attributed in part to its 'pro-European stance' but also to a 'lack of resources and staff'. P Ehin, 'The Estonian Parliament and EU affairs: A Watchdog that does not Bark?' in Hefftler et al, *The Palgrave Handbook of National Parliaments and the European Union* (n 3 above) 524.

EU law in the Maastricht Treaty (1992), long before the EWM was first devised by the European Convention (2002–03) as a system that would delegate the role of subsidiarity watchdogs to a set of political institutions, the national parliaments. During the intervening decade, subsidiarity was a subject studied more by legal scholars than by political scientists, and the scholarship focused most often on the role of the European Court of Justice in subsidiarity control.[22]

However, it should be noted that even during this period the official EU position was that the primary responsibility for ensuring subsidiarity compliance lay with the EU's political institutions, and not with the ECJ. It is true that while the Maastricht Treaty codified the principle in Article 3b TEU, it said little about how and by whom it should be implemented. But after a negative referendum result in Denmark threw the ratification of Maastricht into doubt, European leaders seized on the treaty's subsidiarity provisions as a means to prove to the public that the EU would respect the autonomy of the Member States and exercise its powers with self-restraint. To this end, they developed a set of substantive and procedural guidelines for the implementation of subsidiarity and proportionality which were appended to the European Council conclusions in Edinburgh (1992), and eventually incorporated into a protocol attached to the Amsterdam Treaty (1997). The procedural guidelines are addressed to the political institutions of the EU:

> [The] Amsterdam protocol … sets out detailed *procedural* guidelines which require the political institutions to give due consideration to subsidiarity and proportionality at each stage of the legislative process—that is, whenever a measure is initiated, amended or adopted. The Commission, as the institution which formally proposes legislation, must do four things: it must consult widely before proposing legislation, justify the relevance of its proposals with regard to subsidiarity, minimize the financial and administrative burdens of legislation and submit an annual report to the other institutions on the implementation of Article 3b (Art. 9). The European Parliament and the Council of Ministers, in turn, are enjoined to consider Commission proposals, as well as any suggested amendments, for their compatibility with Article 3b (Art. 11).[23]

The Amsterdam protocol was silent on the role of the ECJ in the implementation of subsidiarity. However, there is little doubt that the ECJ has the authority to interpret the principle, insofar as it is incorporated into the EU treaties and is, consequently, justiciable.

Subsidiarity after Maastricht was implemented as a 'norm of self-limiting governance' intended to change the legislative culture of the EU so that it legislated less often (subsidiarity per se) and in a less intrusive manner (proportionality). It was not a separation-of-powers, 'checks and balances' system in which an over-zealous legislative branch would be restrained by the countervailing power of the judicial branch; rather, the legislative branch (which in this context includes the Commission, with its formal right of initiative) was expected to reform itself from within.

[22] See eg A Estella, *The EU Principle of Subsidiarity and its Critique* (Oxford, Oxford University Press, 2002).

[23] I Cooper, 'The Watchdogs of Subsidiarity' (n 2 above) 285–86.

Many have interpreted the ECJ's steadfast refusal to exercise a robust review of EU legislation for its compliance with the principle as a sign that subsidiarity has been ineffective. However, arguably the relevant test of subsidiarity's post-Maastricht effectiveness is not whether it was used in judicial review but whether it had an impact on the EU's legislative output. From this perspective, in retrospect, did it work? The Commission, for its part, insisted that it made a difference. In its annual reports on the application of the principles of subsidiarity and proportionality, published under the rubric of 'Better Lawmaking', it cited a year-on-year decline in the number of Commission proposals for new legislation during this period—the number fell by more than half between 1990 and 2002—as evidence that a changed legislative culture had taken hold in the EU.[24] Indeed, there was a concomitant decline in the overall volume of EU legislation over the same period, which could be taken as evidence that subsidiarity was having an effect.[25]

However, whatever the practical impact of subsidiarity after Maastricht, it was perceived as inadequate; for this reason, part of the mandate of the European Convention was to improve the implementation of the principle of subsidiarity. The Convention created a 'Working Group' on subsidiarity, which directly addressed the question of whether a new subsidiarity control mechanism should be 'legal' or 'political' in nature, for example by determining which kinds of institutions—judicial, technical, or political—should be involved in its implementation:

> [The] working group on subsidiarity considered but ultimately rejected subsidiarity review mechanisms of a largely technocratic or judicial nature. These included: the creation of a new, *ad hoc* body to monitor the application of the principle of subsidiarity; the appointment within the Commission of a 'Mr or Mrs Subsidiarity'; the creation of an ad hoc chamber within the ECJ responsible for questions of subsidiarity; and an *ex ante* judicial mechanism to scrutinize an EU legislative act after it is adopted but before it enters into force. These mechanisms were found unsuitable because the working group agreed that subsidiarity is 'a principle of an essentially political nature' … which should be monitored by political institutions.[26]

In place of a judicial or technocratic solution, the Convention quite deliberately devised the EWM as a system involving political institutions, making national parliaments into subsidiarity watchdogs. That much is obvious. Moreover, they are political institutions with a particular bias: they may be expected, on balance, to favour an interpretation of subsidiarity that restrains the actions of the EU. This is because when the EU takes action in policy fields where competence is shared with the Member States, this necessarily encroaches on national parliaments' own field of action. It is fair to presume, then, that national parliaments were chosen not

[24] See the Commission report of 12 December 2003, *Better Lawmaking 2003* (COM(2003) 770 final) 31.

[25] I Cooper, 'Subsidiarity and Autonomy in the European Union' in L Pauly and W Coleman (eds), *Global Ordering: Institutions and Autonomy in a Changing World* (Vancouver ONT, UBC Press, 2008) 234.

[26] I Cooper, 'The Watchdogs of Subsidiarity' (n 2 above) 290–91.

as disinterested arbiters but precisely because they have an interest in promoting certain kinds of outcomes.[27]

From this perspective the EWM marks a change in the EU's approach to subsidiarity, bringing it closer to a 'checks and balances' system. Unlike the post-Maastricht approach, which attempted to change the EU's legislative culture from within, the EWM empowers a group of external political actors as a restraining force. Of course, by this standard it is quite a weak 'check' on EU legislation. That was especially true of the version that emerged in the Constitutional Treaty, which was merely advisory. As originally designed, national parliaments' only means of intervention in the EU legislative process was a 'yellow card', wherein one-third of them (with a voting system adjusted to allow for bicameralism) could force the review of a legislative proposal that allegedly violated the principle of subsidiarity; this was (and is) effectively advisory because the proposing institution, usually the Commission, is not required to withdraw the proposal but may instead amend it or maintain it unchanged. In the transition to the Treaty of Lisbon, the EWM was strengthened to also include the possibility of an 'orange card': if a majority of national parliaments raise subsidiarity-based objections to a proposal, this triggers a vote in the EU's two legislative chambers, either of which may immediately vote to reject it (by a vote of 55 per cent of the members of the Council, or by a majority of votes cast in the EP). The addition of the orange card still did not give national parliaments a veto over EU legislation—it is not a 'red card'—but it did nonetheless increase their influence within the EU legislative process, insofar as their intervention could lead to the rejection of a proposal if another of the principal EU institutions might be persuaded to agree. National parliaments would only need to convince the Commission to withdraw the proposal, or either the Council or the European Parliament (EP) to vote it down. Arguably, empowering national parliaments in this way made them EU-level actors in their own right, and collectively a 'virtual third chamber' for the EU. For the present discussion, the point to emphasise is that the addition of the 'orange card' reinforced the political nature of the EWM, insofar as it left the ultimate decision over a contested proposal in the hands of political institutions—ie the Commission, which despite its technocratic pedigree is a thoroughly political institution, and the Council and the EP, the two bodies which together constitute the 'EU legislator'.[28]

Up to this point we have not discussed the ECJ—obviously a legal, rather than political, institution—which is also ascribed a role by the treaty in subsidiarity

[27] A Dashwood 'The Relationship Between the Member States and the European Union/European Community' (2004) 41 *Common Market Law Review* 368.

[28] It has previously been argued that national parliaments are now collectively in a position something like that of the EP in the 1980s, with influence in the legislative process of the EU but lacking a veto over the final outcome. I Cooper, 'A "Virtual Third Chamber"' (n 2 above) 448–49. From this perspective the first successful use of the yellow card, which prompted the withdrawal of the targeted Monti II Regulation, represents an '*Isoglucose* moment' for national parliaments, analogous to the first occasion when the EP succeeded in forcing the other EU institutions to consider its opinion. In fact, a closer historical analogue is the Benzene Directive of 1988, the first legislative proposal to fail in part due to opposition from the EP. I Cooper, 'A Yellow Card for the Striker' (n 10 above) 1420–21, 1423 fn.

control. My description of the EWM as a procedure that only involves 'political' institutions requires a certain sleight of hand, in that it depends on defining the EWM as the procedure set out only in Articles 6 and 7 of Protocol no 2 (TEU/TFEU). The role of the ECJ is set out in Article 8, which states that, the ECJ

> shall have jurisdiction in actions on grounds of infringement of the principle of subsidiarity by a legislative act, brought ... by Member States, or notified by them in accordance with their legal order on behalf of their national Parliament or a chamber thereof.

Since Maastricht it had been widely accepted that the ECJ had jurisdiction over the judicial interpretation of the relevant subsidiarity provisions of the treaty; the innovation in this article is to state that such actions may be brought by a Member State 'on behalf of' its national parliament or a chamber thereof. This gives national parliaments the standing of 'indirect semi-privileged applicants' before the ECJ—indirect because they must bring the action of annulment via their governments, and semi-privileged because it only concerns one of their institutional prerogatives, subsidiarity control.[29]

For this provision of the treaty to have practical consequences, two things must happen. First, national parliaments must bring actions—or, more precisely, they must request that their governments bring actions—to the ECJ challenging the subsidiarity compliance of EU legislation. Secondly, the ECJ must prove willing to seriously consider such challenges. The first of these seems quite likely to happen sooner or later, particularly in the case of an EU legislative proposal that has passed into law despite the subsidiarity-based objections of one or several national parliaments. However, the second occurrence is much less likely, given the ECJ's reluctance to touch the issue. Imagine, for a moment, the circumstances: if the legislation in question were passed by the ordinary legislative procedure, this would presumably mean that the Commission, Council and EP had all broadly supported the measure—support which implies that all three have endorsed the measure's compliance with subsidiarity. The ECJ would be accused of rampant judicial activism if it were to take the side of a disgruntled national parliament to, in effect, overrule the considered opinion of the three principal political institutions of the EU.[30] Historically, the ECJ has also been extremely reluctant to disapply an EU law for lacking a legal basis in the EU treaties, even though its authority to do so is unequivocal, and the legal principle at stake—that of conferral—is relatively clear. In the case of a subsidiarity-based challenge, both its authority and the principle at stake would be much more ambiguous.

This example raises a broader question that is central to this debate: under the rules of Protocol no 2, who has final authority over the application of the

[29] K Granat, *National Parliaments and the Policing of the Subsidiarity Principle* (n 15 above), 188. This author performs a systematic comparison of the national parliaments' arrangements for ex post subsidiarity review, finding that 'parliaments that are perceived as strong scrutinisers have been granted much more independence in the subsidiarity action' (at 188).

[30] A Toth, 'A Legal Analysis of Subsidiarity' in D O'Keeffe and P Twomey (eds), *Legal Issues of the Maastricht Treaty* (London, Chancery, 1994) 48.

principle of subsidiarity—political institutions or legal institutions? Within the EWM—by which I refer simply to the system of reasoned opinions, yellow cards, and orange cards—the application of the principle of subsidiarity is entirely in the hands of political institutions, although no single institution has final interpretive authority. In the first instance it is a dialogue—or more pointedly, an argument—between the Commission and the national parliaments: the institution proposing new legislation, almost always the Commission, must justify the proposal with respect to subsidiarity; national parliaments may respond with reasoned opinions challenging the Commission's justifications; and the Commission must respond to national parliaments with further justifications of its position. In the case of a yellow card, the Commission must choose whether to maintain, amend, or withdraw the proposal; if it chooses to maintain or amend, the final decision on the proposal—also by implication a decision on its subsidiarity compliance—is in the hands of the Council and the EP. In the case of an orange card, if the Commission chooses to maintain the proposal, its fate then lies with the Council and the EP, either of which may immediately vote it down. In this way, the ex ante application of the subsidiarity principle is in the hands of political institutions. However, could it be said that a legal institution, the ECJ, has the ultimate say over the ex post application of subsidiarity, by virtue of its standing as the final interpretive authority of the EU treaties? Recall the example cited above. If the ECJ disagrees with the national parliament's contention that the EU law in question violates subsidiarity, it would not, as a legal institution, be asserting its own interpretation of subsidiarity over that of a political institution, the national parliament. It would be more apt to say that the ECJ would be deferring to the interpretation of subsidiarity endorsed by the principal political institutions of the EU—the Commission, Council, and EP.

IV. Should Subsidiarity and the EWM Entail a Political or Legal Mode of Reasoning?

Whereas previous questions (legal scholars vs. political scientists, political vs. legal institutions) were something of a diversion, here I think we come to the heart of the matter regarding the nature of the subsidiarity review. Even if it is conceded that the EWM is a procedure that mostly or entirely involves political institutions, this still leaves open the question of whether it entails a form of reasoning that is essentially legal or political. How should the participants in the EWM approach the problem? Some have argued that national parliaments—which are, evidently, political institutions—must nonetheless act like legal institutions when they participate in the EWM. Kiiver has said that national parliaments in the EWM engage in 'what can best be described as legal review': they 'behave in a court-like manner, accepting or at least attempting to use subsidiarity as a legal principle'.[31] On the other hand, national parliaments could approach the EWM simply as an opportunity to influence policy and legislative outcomes at the EU level, as participants in a 'virtual third chamber'.[32]

Here I will set aside certain procedural questions concerning the nature of the subsidiarity review, such as whether inadequate justification of a measure should itself be treated as a subsidiarity breach, or whether the parts of a legislative package should be considered separately or together. Rather, I wish to focus on the most important substantive questions that arise in the EWM. What is the nature of the subsidiarity norm? What is its relationship to the 'adjacent' treaty principles of proportionality and conferral?[33] What is its relationship to the broader political principles of policy effectiveness and political expediency? And is it justifiable for national parliaments to raise these other issues in their reasoned opinions under the EWM?

A. Subsidiarity

First of all, what is the nature of the principle of subsidiarity? What is, as it were, its ontological status? This has been the subject of a great deal of philosophical rumination, as subsidiarity has origins in the social teachings of the Roman Catholic Church and deeper roots in European thought, extending back to Thomas Aquinas and even Aristotle.[34] But here we will focus on the concept as it is commonly used in the constitutional parlance and political practice of the EU—where it remains deeply contested. Perhaps the first question to ask is, is subsidiarity determinate? Is it possible to discover, with some degree of certainty (or at least confidence) exactly which potential actions of the EU are permitted or proscribed by subsidiarity? Some find it to be an endlessly malleable concept so open to interpretation that it could allow almost any course of action to be either prohibited or permitted (or even required). The opposing view is that subsidiarity, at least as it is defined in the EU treaties, is relatively straightforward and concrete. A middle view is that subsidiarity is 'vague but not meaningless', whose requirements are not self-evident but may be discovered and elaborated through a rational, analytical process (such as an impact assessment) or even through an interpretive and/or adversarial process, such as the EWM.

[31] P Kiiver, *The Early-Warning System* (n 1 above), 76.

[32] I Cooper, 'A "Virtual Third Chamber"' (n 2 above).

[33] Kiiver refers to conferral and proportionality as principles that are 'adjacent' to subsidiarity, and he argues convincingly that—even from a strictly legal point of view—it is justifiable for national parliaments to include them in their grounds for review under the EWM. P Kiiver, *The Early-Warning System* (n 1 above) 23, 97–100.

[34] C Millon-Delsol, *L'Etat subsidiaire* (Paris, Presses Universitaires de France, 1992).

This leads to the question of whether the subsidiarity is a 'legal' norm or something different—a 'political' norm, for lack of a better term. This question also concerns its relationship to the adjacent principles of conferral and proportionality. It will be recalled that EU actions are governed by these three principles, first codified in the Maastricht Treaty. In theory the EU legislator is required to ask three consecutive questions before legislating: First (principle of *conferral*), does the EU have the legal power, conferred by the treaty, to take action in a given circumstance? Secondly (principle of *subsidiarity*), is EU action appropriate in this instance? Thirdly (principle of *proportionality*), are the means chosen the least burdensome required to achieve the purpose? It is possible to view all three principles as similar in kind, as legal principles that demarcate, in progressively finer detail, the boundary that separates the EU's field of competence from that of the Member States.

Yet a different perspective is that the latter two principles are different in kind from the first: that even after it is determined that the EU has the *power* under the treaty to act, it is still subject to certain constraints concerning whether it *should* do so (subsidiarity) and, if so, to what extent (proportionality). Even if EU action is *legal*, it is not necessarily *appropriate*. The idea that the latter two principles are different from the first was underlined in the Lisbon Treaty, when it stated, 'The limits of Union competences are governed by the principle of conferral. The use of Union competences is governed by the principles of subsidiarity and proportionality'. Subsidiarity and proportionality could be seen as together comprising a 'norm of self-limiting governance' placing normative limits on the actions of the EU: in fields where competence is shared between the EU and the Member States, the EU should only take action when necessary (subsidiarity); and in all fields, it should act in the least intrusive way (proportionality). In other words, the EU has some political discretion in the manner in which it uses its legal powers, and it ought to do so with self-restraint. Looked at in this way, the boundary separating the EU's field of competence from that of the Member States is not a precisely demarcated borderline but rather an indistinct *frontier* insofar as EU action may or may not be warranted under particular circumstances—indeed, the actions of the EU may expand and recede in response to changing circumstances.[35]

Arguably, the decision of whether and how to legislate involves a different kind of reasoning from the determination of whether a legal basis for such legislation exists. It involves political judgement to decide whether it is preferable for action to be taken at the EU level or left to the Member States. If so, then it is not only the case that the EWM chiefly involves political institutions, as pointed out above, but also that these should adopt a political form of reasoning within it. National

[35] One section of the Subsidiarity Protocol to the Amsterdam Treaty says: 'Subsidiarity is a dynamic concept and should be applied in the light of the objectives set out in the Treaty. It allows Community action within the limits of its powers to be expanded where circumstances so require, and conversely, to be restricted or discontinued where it is no longer justified' (Art 3).

parliamentarians need not think and act 'in a court-like manner'. Rather, they need only think and act like legislators. If this analysis of subsidiarity is correct, it would also justify the ECJ's reticence with respect to subsidiarity: its reluctance to police the principle may be read simply as deferring to the judgement of the EU's political institutions as to how it should be interpreted and implemented.

Another question concerning subsidiarity is whether this principle can be separated from, or is inextricably linked to, related principles that are used as criteria by which to judge an EU legislative proposal, which are: proportionality, conferral, policy effectiveness, and political expediency. This is a philosophical question concerning the ontological status of subsidiarity, but it also has practical implications for the EWM. The European Commission insists that the EWM should be confined to the principle of subsidiarity, and that if national parliaments wish to raise objections on these other grounds they should do so through the Political Dialogue.[36] The position of at least some national parliaments, whether stated explicitly or implied in their reasoned opinions, is that it is legitimate to raise these other concerns because they are so closely related to subsidiarity that they are an intrinsic part of the review of a measure's subsidiarity compliance. From this perspective, the correct understanding of subsidiarity is as a principle with a broad scope that to some extent encompasses these other concerns which become, by extension, elements of the review process under the EWM. However, each of the four above-mentioned criteria entails a somewhat different argument for its inclusion. Let us examine them one by one.

B. Proportionality

Proportionality is the 'sister principle' to subsidiarity in EU law: the two are paired together in the Lisbon Treaty's 'Protocol [no 2] on the Application of the Principles of Subsidiarity and Proportionality'. Indeed, the Protocol stipulates that, 'Each institution shall ensure constant respect for the principles of subsidiarity and proportionality' (Article 1), and that, 'Draft legislative acts shall be justified with regard to the principles of subsidiarity and proportionality' (Article 4). But when setting out the specifics of the EWM (Articles 6–7) and appeal before the ECJ (Article 8), proportionality is excluded and subsidiarity is the sole principle at issue in the national parliaments' reasoned opinions or any further action of the Commission, the EU legislator (Council and EP) or the ECJ.

[36] Procedurally, the Commission does not contest the substantive content of reasoned opinions when counting them as 'votes' under the EWM. For example, even though it regarded many of the reasoned opinions in response to Monti II and EPPO as off-point, the Commission acknowledged that a yellow card had been passed in both cases. However, when giving a substantive response in the context of the EWM, it disregards those elements of national parliaments' arguments that it considers to be not based on subsidiarity.

There is logic to this exclusion. In the simplest terms, the subsidiarity question is either/or: to claim that a legislative proposal violates subsidiarity is to allege, in effect, that no legislation is needed. By contrast, to claim a proportionality violation is to object to the proposal in its current form—as overly intrusive or burdensome—but at the same time to agree, in effect, that some legislation may be necessary. Confining the review to subsidiarity makes it easier to treat all reasoned opinions as equivalent, as votes against a legislative proposal to be tallied towards a yellow or an orange card. To include proportionality would turn the system into a dialogue, with national parliaments offering constructive criticism as to how the legislation should be improved.[37] By this logic, objections purely on proportionality grounds should be excluded from the EWM and made in the context of the Political Dialogue.

However, there are cracks in this logic. The Protocol states that, when faced with a yellow card, the Commission (or other proposing body) must review the proposal, after which it has three options: it may decide 'to maintain, amend or withdraw the draft' (Article 7(2)). However, if national parliaments object purely on subsidiarity grounds—arguing that no legislation is needed—then surely the Commission should only have *two* options, either to maintain or withdraw, because the reasoned opinions would provide no guidance as to how to *amend* the proposal.[38] What this example suggests is that the distinction between subsidiarity and proportionality is not nearly so clear-cut. Indeed, some have noted that the treaty's definition of subsidiarity also includes an element of proportionality, stating that, 'the Union shall act only if *and in so far as* the objectives of the proposed action cannot be sufficiently achieved by the Member States' (Article 5(3) TEU, emphasis added).[39] Some national parliaments agree. The Swedish *Riksdag*'s Committee on the Constitution has stated that the above wording implies that subsidiarity control also includes aspects of proportionality; in a concrete example, the *Riksdag*'s Committee on Transport and Communications submitted a reasoned opinion on proportionality grounds, stating among other things that the proposal (on high-speed electronic communications networks) should have employed a less intrusive legislative instrument—a directive instead of a regulation.[40] However, the Commission maintains that such arguments are out of place in the EWM; such was its response, in the case of the second yellow card, to the French *Sénat* which had passed a reasoned opinion expressing approval for the creation of a European Public Prosecutor's Office but questioning certain elements of the proposal.[41]

[37] I Cooper, 'The Watchdogs of Subsidiarity' (n 2 above) 300–302.

[38] I Cooper, 'The Watchdogs of Subsidiarity' (n 2 above) 301–2.

[39] P Kiiver, *The Early-Warning System* (n 1 above) 99–100.

[40] H Hegeland, 'The Swedish Parliament and EU Affairs: From Reluctant Player to Europeanized Actor' in Hefftler et al, *The Palgrave Handbook of National Parliaments and the European Union* (n 3 above) 434.

[41] Commission Communication of 27 November 2013 (COM(2013) 851 final) 5, 10. On the Commission response to the Swedish reasoned opinion on EPPO, see A Jonsson Cornell, this volume.

C. Conferral

As noted above, the question of whether the EU has the legal power to take action is different in kind from whether such action is appropriate in a given circumstance: whereas conferral governs the 'limits' of Union competences, subsidiarity (along with proportionality) governs their 'use' (Article 5(1) TEU). It has been argued that if a legislative proposal does not have a correct legal basis in the EU treaties then it also, by definition, violates the principle of subsidiarity; by extension, it is perfectly valid for a national parliament to allege a breach of the principle of conferral in a reasoned opinion under the EWM.[42] On the other hand, it may be argued that while national parliaments are well-equipped for the task of subsidiarity control, they do not have the expertise to assess the legal basis of a legislative proposal in comparison either to the ECJ or the EU's political institutions.[43]

However, it is not always possible to draw a neat line separating the principles of conferral and subsidiarity. Many supposed that the introduction of subsidiarity into the EU treaty would lead to a wholesale reordering of competences between the EU and the Member States. Indeed, the Laeken Declaration, which set out the mandate of the European Convention, seemed to conflate conferral and subsidiarity when it tasked the Convention to examine the role of national parliaments, asking among other things whether they should 'focus on the division of competence between Union and Member States, for example through preliminary checking of compliance with the principle of subsidiarity?'[44] Because most EU competences are shared with the Member States, when the EU takes action in those areas it is to some extent staking out new territory along the frontier that separates the two spheres of competence. The fact is that many national parliaments review the legal basis of EU legislative proposals as part of their review under the EWM. On the other hand, the Commission 'has thus far never been materially influenced by the legal basis arguments raised by national parliaments'.[45]

A concrete example demonstrates some of the difficulties of separating the review of a measure's subsidiarity compliance from that of its legal basis. The Monti II Regulation regarding the right to strike, the object of the first yellow card, received 12 reasoned opinions from national parliaments, with at least 10 of them also raising objections concerning its legal basis.[46] The Commission had grounded the proposal in Article 352 TFEU, the 'flexibility clause', which gives the EU the power to legislate if action 'should prove necessary, within the framework of the policies defined in the Treaties, to attain one of the objectives set out in the Treaties, and the Treaties have not provided the necessary powers'. The Commission

[42] P Kiiver, *The Early-Warning System* (n 1 above) 98.

[43] K Granat, *National Parliaments and the Policing of the Subsidiarity Principle* (n 15 above) 88–90. F Fabbrini and K Granat, '"Yellow card, but no foul"' (n 4 above) 122–24.

[44] European Council, 'Laeken Declaration on the Future of the Union', 15 December 2001.

[45] K Granat, *National Parliaments and the Policing of the Subsidiarity Principle* (n 15 above) 262–63.

[46] ibid, 258–60.

justified its use of this 'catch-all' provision on the grounds that even though the treaty does not empower the EU to pass legislation to regulate the right to strike—it is excluded from the relevant treaty article—the ECJ had decided that this right was nevertheless subject to EU law, and may be abridged if it conflicts with the economic freedoms of the internal market. When a proposal is based on Article 352, questions related to its compliance with the principles of conferral and subsidiarity respectively are difficult to disentangle. Whereas conferral concerns the *limits* of EU competences and subsidiarity concerns their *use*, this distinction breaks down when the flexibility clause is employed, because its *use* has the effect of redefining the *limits* of the legislative competence of the EU.

D. Policy Effectiveness

A broader question to be asked is whether it would be legitimate for national parliaments to use the EWM to object to EU legislative proposals on more explicitly political grounds. The principles of conferral and proportionality are 'adjacent' to subsidiarity in the sense that the three of them appear together in Article 5 TEU as consecutive tests of the appropriateness of EU legislation; they are closely related to subsidiarity, even though observers disagree as to whether it is valid for national parliaments to invoke them in their reasoned opinions under the EWM. But all three of these principles could be construed as representing narrow, technical questions that are far removed from the primary concerns of national parliaments, ie the content of the proposal and its political implications. However, I believe it is too vague to put all 'political' objections into a single, general category. Here let us make an important distinction between objections to an EU proposal based on doubts about whether it will achieve its stated objective (policy effectiveness) and objections based on the values and/or interests of the parliaments or parliamentarians concerned (political expediency).

Policy effectiveness is simply the principle that legislation should be designed to achieve its stated purposes. Far from being a legal or technical question, the policy effectiveness criterion is focused squarely on the substantive content of a proposal. Now, is this criterion a valid ground for a national parliament to submit a reasoned opinion under the EWM? An objection to a legislative proposal on these grounds would not primarily be about competence, but rather a claim that it is fundamentally misconceived or unworkable. In a way it would be similar to a proportionality objection, in that the parliament in question could agree with the policy ends that the measure is supposed to achieve, but disagree with the means chosen to achieve it; however, rather than claiming that the proposal is too burdensome or intrusive, the parliament would be saying that it is ill-designed. In an EWM with a narrow scope, such as is favoured by the Commission, such an objection would be out of bounds. Yet if one looks carefully at the relevant treaty provision it seems to require that a legislative proposal must meet the test of policy effectiveness in order to be compliant with the principle of subsidiarity. After all, it is commonly interpreted as containing two separate tests, those of 'insufficiency' and 'comparative effectiveness':

> Under the principle of subsidiarity, in areas which do not fall within its exclusive competence, the Union shall act only if and in so far as the objectives of the proposed action cannot be sufficiently achieved by the Member States, either at central level or at regional and local level, but can rather, by reason of the scale or effects of the proposed action, be better achieved at Union level [Article 5(2) TEU].

These two tests, which are inter-related, stipulate that EU action should take place only when Member State action is insufficient and the objectives of the proposed action can be 'better achieved' at EU level. Needless to say, if a proposed EU action fails the test of policy effectiveness, then it also fails the 'comparative effectiveness' test, and thus does not comply with the principle of subsidiarity.

But is not almost any proposed EU action likely to be far more effective than a patchwork of Member State laws? In response, let us look again at the case of the Monti II Regulation. One of the common complaints (among many) of the national parliaments in their reasoned opinions was that this proposal simply would not work. They said, in effect, that it was logically incoherent, and for this reason would not achieve the stated objective of the legislation, which was to 'clarify' the law regarding the right to strike. To understand their point, we must delve into the substance of the proposal. The legislation was a response to ECJ decisions (*Viking*, *Laval*, and others)[47] dealing with situations where labour unions had taken collective action targeting cross-border businesses—where, in other words, the right to strike was in conflict with internal market freedoms (the freedom of establishment and the freedom to provide services). The ECJ recognised the right to strike but declared that it was not absolute, and must give way to internal market freedoms in certain circumstances. The Commission intended to remedy the resulting legal uncertainty by regulating the right to strike with positive EU legislation, without fundamentally altering the legal status quo established by the ECJ decisions. And so the Commission proposed the Monti II Regulation, which included language (Article 2 of the proposal) intended to explain that the right to strike and internal market freedoms co-exist, and that each 'shall respect' the other:

> The exercise of the freedom of establishment and the freedom to provide services enshrined in the Treaty shall respect the fundamental right to take collective action, including the right or freedom to strike, and conversely, the exercise of the fundamental right to take collective action, including the right or freedom to strike, shall respect these economic freedoms.[48]

[47] Case C-341/05 *Laval un Partneri Ltd v Svenska Byggnadsarbetareförbundet and others* [2007] ECR I-11767; Case C-438/05 *International Transport Workers' Federation and Finnish Seamen's Union v Viking Line ABP and OU Viking Line Eesti* [2007] ECR I-10779.

[48] Commission, 'Proposal for a Council Regulation on the exercise of the right to take collective action within the context of the freedom of establishment and the freedom to provide services', 27 March 2012 (COM/2012/0130) 18.

This Solomonic pronouncement—the crux of the Monti II proposal—recognises that these two fundamental values co-exist, implicitly in tension with one another, but it does not state which should take precedence over the other.[49]

The complaint of many national parliaments was in effect that the Monti II Regulation was misconceived, insofar as it would not achieve its stated objective of clarifying the relationship between the right to strike and the economic freedoms of the internal market. The Danish *Folketing* stated that the provision 'does not provide further clarity'[50] regarding the relationship between these two principles, a sentiment echoed later in the reasoned opinion of the Dutch *Tweede Kamer*.[51] The Luxembourg *Chambre des Députés* remarked that in Article 2, 'the two general principles seem to neutralize each other'.[52] The Latvian *Saiema* noted that the text is 'not unmistakably clear and definite', citing Article 2 as an example.[53] The Maltese Parliament wrote: 'The Regulation does not clarify'.[54] Some parliaments explicitly connect subsidiarity with policy effectiveness, making clear that the measure fails the subsidiarity test *precisely because* it would not achieve its stated goal: for example, the Finnish *Eduskunta's* reasoned opinion stated that the proposal 'fails, in its current wording to meet its goal of clarifying the current legal situation (the *Laval* and *Viking Line* cases). Consequently, the proposal is contrary to the principle of subsidiarity and proportionality'.[55]

Probably the most cogent critique along these lines came from the Swedish *Riksdag*. The reasoned opinion is worth quoting at length:

> The key provision of the proposal is Article 2 that basically states that the exercise of economic freedoms should be consistent with the exercise of the right to collective action, including the right to strike, and vice versa. The Riksdag has difficulty seeing how the proposal, in its current state, contributes to the clarification of the relationship between liberties and rights that is the proposal's purpose according to the explanatory memorandum. The Riksdag cannot see either that the regulation would create greater legal certainty in this regard. Nor can the Riksdag see how the proposal would be 'reducing tensions between the national industrial relation systems and the freedom to provide services' which is stated as essentially the basis of the proposal. It is thus difficult to see how the proposal could help achieve any of the objectives referred to in the Treaty, which is a prerequisite for the flexibility clause to be used.[56]

[49] A spirited defence of the Monti II proposal is put forward by anonymous authors, writing pseudonymously as The Adoptive Parents, who were involved in its drafting. The Adoptive Parents, 'The Life of a Death Foretold: The Proposal for a Monti II Regulation' in M Freedland and J Prassl (eds), *Viking, Laval and Beyond* (Oxford, Hart Publishing, 2014) 95.

[50] Reasoned Opinion of the *Folketing*, 3 May 2012, p 1. All the reasoned opinions of national parliaments on Monti II can be accessed from the relevant page on the IPEX website: www.ipex.eu/IPEXL-WEB/dossier/document/COM20120130.do (accessed 15 November 2015).

[51] Reasoned Opinion of the *Tweede Kamer*, 22 May 2012, p 1.

[52] Reasoned Opinion of the Luxembourg *Chambre des Députés*, 15 May 2012, p 1.

[53] Reasoned Opinion of the Latvian *Saiema*, 18 May 2012, p 3.

[54] Reasoned Opinion of the Maltese Parliament, 22 May 2012, p 6.

[55] Reasoned Opinion of the Finnish *Eduskunta*, 15 May 2012, p 1.

[56] Reasoned Opinion of the Swedish *Riksdag*, 11 May 2012, p 2.

The *Riksdag* focused on the 'policy effectiveness' criterion as it is implicit in Article 352 (the flexibility clause), but its reasoning could just as easily be applied to the test of comparative effectiveness in Article 5(2) TEU.

It should be emphasised that an objection on the basis of the policy effectiveness is different both from an objection on principle to any EU action, and from a purely political objection that the proposal runs against the interests and/or values of the parliament involved.[57] Many on the left would have preferred that instead of attempting to balance the right to strike with the economic freedoms, the legislation had simply asserted that the first takes precedence over the second; certainly, such a formulation would reflect the political preferences of some parliamentary chambers, but it would also be more likely to clarify the legal situation, which would make for more coherent legislation that would be, by extension, compliant with subsidiarity. This seems to have been the position of the French *Sénat*, which stated in its reasoned opinion that in order to make the proposal comply with subsidiarity, Article 2 should be redrafted to state *only* that the exercise of the freedom of establishment and the freedom to provide services respect the fundamental right to collective action, including the right to strike.[58] However, even if the proposal were redrafted in this way its effectiveness would still be uncertain, because ordinary legislation cannot necessarily overturn the decisions in *Viking* and *Laval* which were based on the ECJ's interpretations of the relevant provisions of the EU treaties. For this reason, the European Trades Union Congress actually proposed changing the EU treaties to add a Social Progress Protocol stating clearly that the right to strike takes precedence over the economic freedoms.[59] Of course, this would involve a far more burdensome legal instrument than Monti II, a treaty amendment rather than a regulation, and thus would tend in the opposite direction from the principle of proportionality. Even so, such a proposal would arguably be more likely to meet the test of policy effectiveness insofar as it would bring clarity to the relationship between the right to strike and the economic freedoms.

E. Political Expediency

There is yet one more general reason that a national parliament might use the EWM to raise objections to an EU legislative proposal—if it is judged to

[57] Fundamentally, the question of policy effectiveness is an empirical question, even if it is laden with normative concerns; in this, it is distinct from the wholly normative question of whether a particular policy outcome is desirable or morally worthy. This was noted in a previous work, which stated that the EWM 'would in part be an argument about the empirical nature of the world, concerned with objective facts (are the actions of the Member States in a particular area insufficient?) and with cause-and-effect relationships (will the proposed EU action actually achieve its intended purpose?)': I Cooper, 'The Watchdogs of Subsidiarity' (n 2 above) 298.

[58] Reasoned Opinion of the French *Sénat*, 22 May 2012, p 3. The original text reads as follows: 'Pour être conforme au principe de subsidiarité, l'article 2 devrait être rédigé de la façon suivante: "L'exercice de la liberté d'établissement et de la libre prestation des services énoncées par le traité respecte le droit fondamental de mener des actions collectives, y compris le droit ou la liberté de faire grève"'.

[59] Commission, 'Proposal for a Council Regulation' (n 48 above) 5, 7.

contravene the values and/or interests of a majority of its members. Theoretically, such an argument could be 'purely political', entirely separate from the principles of conferral, proportionality, and even policy effectiveness. Let us suppose, for the sake of argument, that a national parliament agreed that the EU had the legal power to take action in a given area (conferral), that the proposal in question was proportionate to the ends sought (proportionality) and likely to achieve its stated goal (policy effectiveness), but still objected to it on ideological grounds and/or because it ran against the interests of an important constituency, however defined. In such a case, the parliament could even agree that some EU action is indeed necessary (thus passing the subsidiarity test, narrowly defined) but disagree with the particular course of action chosen. In such circumstances the parliament could be inclined to use the EWM simply as a political tool with which to oppose the measure. Of course, the Commission's view is that such opposition should instead be channelled through the Political Dialogue. But the parliament may prefer to use the EWM after observing that the Commission is more likely to take their concerns seriously if they are put formally in a reasoned opinion rather than a contribution to the Political Dialogue. Certainly, in the case of a yellow card the Commission is legally required to respond to national parliaments' concerns, though not necessarily to accede to them. Now, would it be illegitimate for a national parliament to 'knowingly' object to an EU legislative proposal on purely political grounds—under, as it were, false pretences?

Even if it seems to violate the letter of the EU treaties, a purely political approach to the EWM is defensible—certainly on pragmatic grounds, but also even on the grounds of democratic legitimacy. Pragmatically, national parliaments might justify their actions by noting that they are only doing their job to the best of their ability by making use of every tool at their disposal, in defence of the values and/or interests of their constituents. They might argue, also pragmatically, that they should make maximal use of the limited powers bestowed on them by the EU treaties; this has been, in effect, the strategy of the European Parliament over decades, allowing it to parlay its initially limited powers into significant influence—and, eventually, much more substantial powers. Furthermore, they could argue that the democratic legitimacy of the EU is enhanced by the increased involvement of national parliaments in its legislative process via the EWM; this, again, is similar to the arguments made historically in order to justify the European Parliament's use of its powers to the maximum. After all, a large part of the rationale for giving national parliaments a direct role in EU politics was that this would somehow reduce the democratic deficit. The design of the EWM was, at the very least, ambiguous as to whether its main purpose was to improve the democratic legitimacy of the EU or the subsidiarity compliance of EU legislation.[60] By these standards a national parliament would be justified even in a wilful misuse of the EWM to achieve purely political goals.

[60] I Cooper, 'The Watchdogs of Subsidiarity' (n 2 above).

Yet in practice it is difficult to separate purely politically-motivated objections to a proposal from those based on a sincere belief that does not comply with the principle of subsidiarity. If a national parliament is convinced that a proposal is truly odious, contravening the core values or interests of its constituents, then it will be loath to accept that it passes the test of 'necessity' and is consequently subsidiarity-compliant. It is difficult to identify empirical cases where it can be said with certainty that a parliamentary chamber adopted a reasoned opinion for purely political motives, merely using subsidiarity as a pretext. This is true even in cases where it seems obvious to some commentators that the legislative proposal at issue unquestionably complies with subsidiarity. The subsidiarity-compliance of the Monti II Regulation was taken as self-evident by the Commission—which initially declined even to respond individually to the arguments of national parliaments—and other observers, because it dealt with cross-border issues that could only be regulated at the EU-level.[61] Similarly, the proposal to create the EPPO was thought by many to easily pass the subsidiarity test, given that this body—whose creation is clearly authorised by the treaty—must by definition be an EU-level entity. If these proposals are taken to be self-evidently subsidiarity-compliant then the implication is that the actions of national parliaments in passing reasoned opinions are brazenly political, and in effect a misuse of the EWM. Yet in both these cases many national parliaments at least managed to muster cogent arguments to make the case that the proposal in fact ran afoul of subsidiarity.

What this section has shown is that the ontological status of subsidiarity remains contested and this has practical effects for the EWM. National parliaments often disagree with the Commission (and among themselves) as to how to define subsidiarity, both in itself and in its relationship to a number of related principles. National parliaments have at various times used these other principles—proportionality, conferral, policy effectiveness, and political expediency—as a basis for their objections to EU proposals in their reasoned options. It is important to acknowledge that justifications may be found both for a narrow EWM, focused strictly on subsidiarity, and for a broad EWM that also may include these other principles. However, even within the latter 'broad' approach it is also important to distinguish between a position maintaining that subsidiarity, as a concept, is so flexible that it is essentially meaningless, and one in which subsidiarity is still a useful concept in that it is 'vague but not meaningless'. In the first of these, the distinction between subsidiarity and these other principles collapses, so that an objection on subsidiarity grounds is effectively indistinguishable from an objection on the grounds of political expediency. In the second, subsidiarity is still a distinct principle, while it overlaps with the principles of proportionality, conferral and policy effectiveness (but not political

[61] See the letter from Commissioner Maroš Šefčovič to national parliaments, 12 September 2012. The Adoptive Parents, 'The Life of a Death Foretold' (n 49 above). F Fabbrini and K Granat, '"Yellow card, but no foul"' (n 4 above).

expediency). Looked at in this way, we may discern three approaches to the EWM based on whether one conceives of subsidiarity as definite, elastic or ambiguous.

V. Three Approaches to the EWM: Legal Rule-Following, Political Bargaining, and Policy Arguing

The forgoing analysis has brought to the fore many of the complex questions that are subsumed within the debate over whether the EWM is fundamentally a legal or a political procedure. In the remaining pages I will build upon the previous analysis in order to construct my own typology of approaches to the EWM. I posit that rather than there being merely two approaches—legal and political—it is more useful to conceive of three: one 'legal' approach and two different 'political' approaches. This builds on an analysis that was published a decade ago, based on the version of the EWM in the Constitutional Treaty, years before it was strengthened (with the addition of the orange card) in the Treaty of Lisbon and finally put into practice; that analysis speculated that if and when the EWM came into force, it could take shape either as a system in which national parliaments merely use it as a tool to oppose legislative proposals that they dislike (now referred to as 'political bargaining'), or a system in which national parliaments engage in a constructive argument with the Commission over when and how the EU should legislate (now referred to as 'policy arguing').[62] Now that the EWM has come into operation, these two approaches (both of which are broadly 'political') may be glimpsed in the actions of some of the parliamentary chambers participating in the EWM. Yet there is also a third, broadly 'legal' approach, approved most notably by the Commission and certain other parliamentary chambers, in which the participants set out to ascertain how subsidiarity should be applied in a given circumstance, and then put it into practice (which I will call 'legal rule-following'). Each of these three approaches depends on its own particular understanding of subsidiarity. Looking back, what is perhaps most surprising is that even after five years of being in operation, the EWM has still not 'taken shape' as one type of system or another, as there remains profound disagreement among the participants as to its nature and purpose. What follows is an attempt to map out this disagreement.

Some points of clarification should be made before describing this three-way typology in detail. First, the use of the term 'approaches' may imply that I am aiming to categorise the various parliamentary chambers according to their actions in the EWM. Yet, strictly speaking, these three are not traits or attitudes that inhere in individual actors; rather, they are modes of interaction, and are inherently social.

[62] I Cooper, 'The Watchdogs of Subsidiarity' (n 2 above).

This typology is based on a theory developed by Thomas Risse,[63] in which there are three logics of social action governing different social situations, each of which employs a different form of rationality, leading to the adoption of a different kind of behaviour: the logic of appropriateness (normative rationality, rule-following behaviour), the logic of consequences (instrumental rationality, bargaining behaviour) and the logic of arguing (argumentative rationality, arguing behaviour).[64] These are ideal types, and any real-life social situation will involve a mixture of these three logics and their concomitant forms of rationality and behaviour. This is also true of the three approaches to be outlined here, each of which may be glimpsed at various times in the real-life interaction of the participants in the EWM. Indeed, this is a large part of the reason why, even after five years, there is still no consensus on how the participants in the EWM should conduct themselves or what they should expect it to accomplish. The reason that confusion continues to reign in the EWM is that the participants do not agree on what kind of interaction it is, and what social rules should apply.

The three approaches—legal rule-following, political bargaining, and policy arguing—are sketched out here (see Table 1). Each approach entails a different understanding of the principle of subsidiarity, its relationship to other related principles and its normative implications. The differing interpretations of subsidiarity have practical consequences for how national parliaments interact with the Commission and with one another. While I will not attempt to categorise all national parliamentary chambers according to the three approaches, I will give examples of EWM participants that come closest to each of them.

A. Legal Rule-Following

In the first approach, subsidiarity is a (quasi-) legal rule, and the purpose of the EWM is to enable the EU to legislate in a manner that complies with it. The practical requirements of subsidiarity for EU legislation are definite: if they are not self-evident, they are at least determinable, in the sense that they may be discovered through a rational process—such as the Commission's elaborate systems of consultation and impact assessment. Subsidiarity is also clearly separable from the related principles of conferral, proportionality, policy effectiveness and political expediency. As a result national parliaments can and should narrow the substantive focus of the EWM to subsidiarity only; if they wish to raise objections to an EU proposal based on these other principles, they must do so through the Political

[63] T Risse, 'Let's Argue! Communicative Action in World Politics' (2000) 54 *International Organization* 1.

[64] My previous work predicted that the EWM would be a contest between the logic of consequences and the logic of arguing; it treated the logic of appropriateness as a 'background condition' rather than a separate approach in its own right: I Cooper, 'The Watchdogs of Subsidiarity' (n 2 above) 297. Here all three are presented as equally plausible social logics for the EWM.

Table 1: Three Approaches to the EWM

Approach to the EWM	Legal Rule-Following	Political Bargaining	Policy Arguing
Logic of Social Action	Logic of Appropriateness	Logic of Consequences	Logic of Arguing
How clear are substantive requirements of subsidiarity?	Definite: Self-evident, or determinable through process of consultation, impact assessment	Elastic: Very unclear—Open to multiple, competing interpretations	Ambiguous: Somewhat unclear—may be clarified through the process of EWM itself
Subsidiarity vis-à-vis related principles?	Separate (other concerns raised in Political Dialogue)	Continuous (including with Political Expediency)	Overlapping (with Conferral, Proportionality, Policy Effectiveness)
National parliaments see Commission as…	Partner	Adversary	Interlocutor
Relationship among national parliaments	Disregarding	Coalition-building	Persuading
Ideal result of NPs' intervention	Intervene to prevent manifest errors	Become veto-players on salient issues	Reshape proposals, improve public policy
Exemplary Actors	Commission, Finnish *Eduskunta*	Danish *Folketing*, Dutch *Tweede Kamer*	Swedish *Riksdag*, UK House of Commons

Dialogue, or address their concerns to their respective governments who act as the representatives of the Member States in the Council. Because subsidiarity is a narrowly-defined principle, and the Commission has internal expertise in determining its requirements, in practice it will be a rare occurrence for there to be an EU legislative proposal that violates it. Therefore, the EWM should in practice be seldom used, activated only on those rare occasions where the Commission has made a manifest error in its reasoning with respect to subsidiarity. On those occasions, the national parliaments can use their reasoned opinions to helpfully point out the error to the Commission, acting much like a Council of State, using the EWM much like a legal ex ante check on the constitutionality of a legislative proposal. In doing so, each national parliament will in general focus on the legislative proposal and its dialogue with the Commission—which it views more as a partner than an adversary—and disregard the opinions of other national parliaments.[65] In this approach, national parliaments act solely in an individual capacity and do not form a collective. They are nothing but a 'phantom collective', and if a yellow card occurs it will not be the result of inter-parliamentary coordination but merely 'a coincidental sum of unrelated events'.[66]

It seems clear that this is the approach to the EWM favoured by the Commission. The Commission has consistently favoured a EWM focused solely on subsidiarity, narrowly defined. To this end, the Commission has, within the EWM context, been dismissive of objections raised by national parliaments in their reasoned opinions that are not, in the Commission's eyes, strictly subsidiarity-related. Are there also some national parliamentary chambers that favour such an approach? For many chambers, it is difficult to say: whereas a great number of them only rarely pass a reasoned opinion to raise objections to an EU legislative proposal, such inactivity may simply reflect a lack of capacity to intervene rather than a sincere belief that all other such proposals are subsidiarity-compliant. However, some parliamentary chambers have shown that they have the capacity to act but do not do so. One example is the Finnish *Eduskunta*, which is consistently ranked as among the 'strongest' parliaments in the EU; however, the *Eduskunta* is primarily focused on controlling the Finnish government's position on EU affairs, and it generally refrains from participating in the EWM and other forms of inter-parliamentary cooperation. Moreover, it adheres to a narrow interpretation of subsidiarity and rejects the use of the EWM as a means to voice political opposition to EU proposals.[67] This means, in effect, that the *Eduskunta* supports the 'legal rule-following' approach to the EWM. This could also be said of those chambers that most actively participate in the Political Dialogue, such as the Portuguese parliament[68] and the Italian *Senato*,[69] but rarely pass reasoned opinions under the EWM. These chambers obviously have the capacity to communicate their views to the Commission, but they choose to act informally through the Political Dialogue rather than through the EWM, thus implicitly recognising the boundary between the principle of subsidiarity and other principles which may be construed as 'related' under the EWM.

[65] The EP seems be of a similar opinion: its Constitutional Committee (AFCO) expressed the view that 'the control of subsidiarity was not a collective exercise, but an individual one of every Parliament/ Chamber'. COSAC 22nd Biannual Report, 4 November 2014, p 38.

[66] P Kiiver, *The National Parliaments in the European Union: A Critical View on EU Constitution-Building* (The Hague, Kluwer Law International, 2006) 162, 164.

[67] T Raunio, 'The Finnish Eduskunta and EU: The Strengths and Weaknesses of a Mandating System' in Hefftler et al, *The Palgrave Handbook of National Parliaments and the European Union* (n 3 above) 416.

[68] D Jančić, 'The Portuguese Parliament and EU Affairs: From Inert to Agile Democratic Control' in Hefftler et al, *The Palgrave Handbook of National Parliaments and the European Union* (n 3 above) 379–80.

[69] S Cavatorto, 'Italy: Still Looking for a New Era in the Making of EU Policy' in Hefftler et al. *The Palgrave Handbook of National Parliaments and the European Union* (n 3 above) 222–23. See also the chapter by N Lupo, this volume.

B. Political Bargaining

In the second approach, subsidiarity is an elastic concept with no fixed meaning. In practical terms, it can be employed to justify almost any position in favour of or in opposition to EU action in a given circumstance. This means that it is not possible to differentiate between subsidiarity and the related principles of conferral, proportionality, and policy effectiveness. Moreover, a reasoned opinion raising subsidiarity objections will be indistinguishable from one that is based on political expediency alone. In other words, national parliaments will simply adopt reasoned opinions in response to EU legislative proposals that they oppose for political reasons, using subsidiarity as a pretext. National parliaments will prefer to use the EWM rather than the Political Dialogue because it offers them greater leverage in the EU's legislative process, and the division between the two channels of communication with the Commission relies on a meaningless distinction between subsidiarity and other concerns. National parliaments will tend to see the Commission as an adversary. Also, they will be intensely interested in what is going on in other parliamentary chambers, counting votes under the EWM. In the case of a proposal they find objectionable, they will seek to build a coalition of chambers in opposition, with the aim of gathering enough votes under the EWM to achieve a yellow card or an orange card. In such cases the national parliaments would most closely resemble a 'virtual third chamber' in which they seek to maximise their legislative leverage on salient issues, making them a collective 'veto-player'—or something close to it—in the EU's legislative process.

While no national parliamentary chambers perfectly exemplify this approach to the EWM, two that come close are the Danish *Folketing* and the Dutch *Tweede Kamer*. Both of these parliaments take an explicitly political approach to the EWM and both have at times acted strategically to rally other national parliaments to oppose a legislative measure with the specific goal of achieving a yellow card.[70] While the Danish parliament is not one of the most active participants in the EWM—the number of reasoned opinions it passes is actually close to the average—the *Folketing* was the first chamber to pass one in opposition to the Monti II Regulation, and after that it deliberately set out to persuade other parliaments to do the same, raising the issue with them at an inter-parliamentary meeting that took place in Copenhagen during the eight-week review period.[71] Similarly, the *Tweede Kamer* tried to persuade other national parliaments to oppose the proposal for the creation of the EPPO, raising the issue with them at an unrelated inter-parliamentary meeting that took place in Vilnius during the eight-week review period.[72]

[70] Another chamber that has at times actively encouraged other parliaments to take part in the EWM is the Czech Senate. M Hrabálek and A Strelkov, 'The Czech Parliament and European Integration' in Hefftler et al, *The Palgrave Handbook of National Parliaments and the European Union* (n 3 above) 501–3.

[71] I Cooper, 'A Yellow Card for the Striker' (n 10 above) 1411–14.

[72] ibid, 1423 fn.

However, even some parliaments or chambers that only rarely participate in the EWM may also adopt this approach. Many may participate only selectively because they have decided that such a course of action is in their political interest. They may calculate that in most cases, even if they find an EU legislative proposal objectionable, it is not worth their time to pass a reasoned opinion because a yellow card is highly improbable. Yet on those rare occasions when the level of opposition reaches the point that a yellow card is within reach, they may judge it worthwhile to pass a reasoned opinion in the final stages of the process. An example of this kind of approach may be found in the actions of certain parliaments in the case of the Monti II yellow card. A detailed reconstruction of the timing and sequence of the various reasoned opinions in that case reveals an interesting pattern. Relatively early in the eight-week review period, most of the parliaments/chambers that made a political decision to pass a reasoned opinion were those that had most frequently done so in the past. However, most of the reasoned opinions which came in the final week before the deadline—and which proved decisive in providing the necessary votes to reach the yellow card threshold—were passed by parliaments/chambers that had hitherto rarely or never passed a reasoned opinion under the EWM.[73] This 'band-wagoning' occurred only at the point when it became apparent that the 'vote count' was nearing the threshold for a yellow card, and that the participation of the additional parliaments/chambers would indeed make a difference. The pattern revealed in this episode accords with the more general finding that, on the whole, any given parliament or chamber is more likely to pass a reasoned opinion objecting to a proposal if many others have already done so,[74] reflecting its increased incentive due to the prospect of a successful outcome, ie a yellow card. This dynamic shows that even among the majority of parliaments/chambers that have seldom passed reasoned opinions, there may be many adherents of the political bargaining approach.

C. Policy Arguing

The third approach occupies a middle ground between the other two regarding the norm of subsidiarity. In this approach subsidiarity is neither definite nor elastic, but rather ambiguous. As a concept it is vague but it is not meaningless, and it can prove useful in critically analysing a prospective action of the EU. A similar point may be made concerning subsidiarity's relationship to other, related, principles: it is neither neatly separable nor indistinguishable from them; rather, it remains a distinct concept, but it overlaps heavily with the related principles of conferral, proportionality and policy effectiveness. As a result, according to this approach (and unlike the legal rule-following approach) it is legitimate for a national parliament to raise, within the EWM itself, objections to an EU legislative proposal

[73] ibid, 1414–17.
[74] K Gattermann and C Hefftler, 'Beyond Institutional Capacity' (n 13 above) 322.

on the basis of these other concerns when they are closely related to subsidiarity concerns; such objections need not be relegated to the Political Dialogue. However (unlike the political bargaining approach), objections based purely on political expediency should be excluded from the EWM, although objections that are more broadly 'political' will often be included. According to this approach, the role of national parliaments is to put forward arguments to fundamentally challenge the justifications put forward by the Commission (or other proposing body) that a given EU legislative proposal is indeed necessary and appropriate, and thereby subsidiarity-compliant. The Commission is neither a partner nor an adversary, but rather an *interlocutor* in an argument over whether (subsidiarity) and how (proportionality) the EU should legislate in a given circumstance. National parliaments are not indifferent to one another's positions, but they are less concerned with building a coalition of like-minded chambers to pass a yellow or orange card than with persuading their peers to add their voices to the argument with the Commission over whether the proposed legislation is appropriate in a given circumstance. In order for the argument to be constructive, each side would need to listen to the other and be open to persuasion. Ideally, the involvement of national parliaments would result in the reshaping of legislative proposals in a way that improves public policy. If the EWM were to develop along these lines it would also resemble a 'virtual third chamber', but one in which the principal activity is policy deliberation rather than legislative bargaining.

The Swedish *Riksdag* is the parliamentary chamber that best exemplifies this approach;[75] the UK House of Commons is another possible example.[76] The *Riksdag* has produced by far the greatest number of reasoned opinions among the national parliaments of the EU. This reflects, in part, peculiarities of its internal arrangements.[77] In the *Riksdag*, responsibility for vetting EU legislative proposals and drafting reasoned opinions lies not with its European Affairs Committee but with 15 sectoral committees, which means that the workload is shared out and their policy expertise is brought to bear; moreover, Members of Parliament examine every legislative proposal without preselection by parliamentary administrators. The *Riksdag* also feels free to raise objections within the EWM on other grounds than (narrowly-defined) subsidiarity, such as conferral, proportionality, or (as argued above in the case of Monti II) policy effectiveness. The *Riksdag* does not raise these other issues in the Political Dialogue, in part because, according to its own internal rules of procedure, any opinions pertaining to EU legislative files

[75] See A Jonsson Cornell, 'The Swedish Riksdag as Scrutinizer of the Principle of Subsidiarity' (2016) 12 *European Constitutional Law Review* (forthcoming).

[76] The House of Commons 'is primarily concerned with the legal aspects of the subsidiarity control mechanism, in contrast to some parliaments which appear to use the EWM to highlight legislation they do not like or which breaches proportionality, something that is not covered by Lisbon. The House of Lords, given the policy-oriented structure of its Sub-Committee system, takes a more longitudinal interest in the overall direction of EU policy'. A Huff and J Smith, 'Westminster and the European Union—Ever Increasing Scepticism?' in Hefftler et al, *The Palgrave Handbook of National Parliaments and the European Union* (n 3 above) 323. See also the chapter by A Cygan, this volume.

[77] H Hegeland 'The Swedish Parliament and EU Affairs' (n 40 above) 432–36.

must be channelled through the EWM. But although it is very active in passing reasoned opinions under the EWM, the *Riksdag* is less inclined than some other parliaments—such as the *Folketing* or the *Tweede Kamer*—to reach out to other parliaments to try and build a coalition to achieve a yellow or orange card.[78]

VI. Conclusion: It Takes Two to Tango

Even after it has been in operation for five years, the EWM remains an essentially contested procedure: the participants—mainly national parliaments and the Commission—do not agree over its nature and purpose. The EWM does not yet have a settled 'social logic'. While the disagreement is often described as a debate between a legal and a political interpretation, it has been argued here that there are fundamentally three different approaches to the EWM, one legal (legal rule-following) and two political (political bargaining and policy arguing). Each of these approaches relies on its own understanding of the nature of subsidiarity and its relationship to associated principles, and of the relationship of national parliaments with the Commission and with one another. While these three potential social logics of the EWM are ideal types, certain participants may be identified as exemplars of each of the approaches. The Commission, in particular, exemplifies the legal rule-following approach, insofar as it insists that the EWM should be focused solely on the principle of subsidiarity, narrowly defined, and that any other concerns should be channelled through the Political Dialogue. And while the Commission has generally been *procedurally* responsive to the concerns of national parliaments—responding individually, in writing, to each opinion—it rarely or never concedes any *substantive* point regarding subsidiarity. This is illustrated by the Commission response to the two yellow cards under the EWM. In the first case, the Commission withdrew the Monti II Regulation, but it insisted that the reason was not the concerns of national parliaments about subsidiarity but rather the lack of political support in the Council and the EP.[79] In the second case, the Commission maintained the EPPO proposal unchanged, dismissing as outside the scope of the EWM the concerns raised by national parliaments that were not based on a narrow definition of subsidiarity. In both cases the yellow card left the Commission seemingly unshaken in its conviction that its own interpretation of subsidiarity was essentially correct.

The second approach,that of political bargaining, is exemplified by those parliaments—such as the Danish *Folketing* and the Dutch *Tweede Kamer*—which promote the use of the EWM as a political tool that national parliaments can use to enhance their influence in EU affairs. These chambers may even seek the achievement of a yellow card as an end in itself, independently of the substance of the

[78] I Cooper, 'The Nordic parliaments and the EU' (n 18 above).

[79] I Cooper, 'A Yellow Card for the Striker' (n 10 above) 1420.

proposal at hand, as a demonstration that the system works.[80] Such a strategy may be read as a reasonable response to the Commission's position: if a national parliament perceives that the Commission is unwilling to entertain any opposing arguments regarding subsidiarity, then it may decide that its most effective move is to pass a reasoned opinion under the EWM, which (unlike the Political Dialogue) legally obliges the Commission at least to respond to their concerns, if not to accede to them.

In the third approach, national parliaments raise thoughtful objections to EU legislative proposals with the intention of instigating a constructive argument with the Commission over whether and how the EU should legislate. A decade ago this author thought, perhaps in an idealistic flight of fancy, that this would be the best possible outcome of the EWM: it would result in improved public policy and more subsidiarity-compliant EU legislation.[81] Some parliamentary chambers, most notably the Swedish *Riksdag*, participate in the EWM in a way that suggests they seek such an argument with the Commission. However, such a constructive argument has not come about for the simple reason that the Commission has not been willing to engage in one. The problem, in short, is that 'it takes two to tango'.

More recently, there has been some indication that the Commission may be willing to consider changing its approach towards national parliaments, subsidiarity and the EWM. The number of reasoned opinions from national parliaments grew steadily year-on-year between 2010 and 2013, but then fell sharply in 2014.[82] This reflected in part a diminishment in the overall number of new legislative proposals in 2014, due to the EP elections and the anticipated installation of the new Commission. But it also reflected the fact that the new Commission promised increased respect for subsidiarity and far fewer new legislative proposals than what had previously been the norm. If this continues, the reduced output of EU legislative proposals will likely mean that there will be fewer reasoned opinions from national parliaments. In addition, the new Commission included for the first time the position of a 'First Vice-President' whose role, in part, is to act as a legislative gate-keeper, responsible for the application of subsidiarity. One month after taking office, this First Vice-President, Franz Timmermans—who is also responsible for inter-institutional relations, including relations with national parliaments—spoke at the COSAC meeting in Rome, saying the following:

> I think that the Commission should be more proactive in coming to national parliaments whenever there is an issue that is of importance related to Europe in national

[80] Prior to the first yellow card, an EU expert at the *Tweede Kamer* told an interviewer, 'we want to be a pioneer in the issuance of a yellow card. It does not really matter what topic. It is just to test the system, how it works and what the Commission does': A-L Högenauer, 'The Dutch Parliament and EU Affairs' (n 20 above) 262.

[81] I Cooper, 'The Watchdogs of Subsidiarity' (n 2 above).

[82] According to the Commission's Annual Reports on the application of the Principles of Subsidiarity and Proportionality, the total numbers of ROs in each of the first five years of the EWM were: 36 (2010), 65 (2011), 71 (2012) 88 (2013), and 21 (2014). Commission, 'Annual Report 2014 on Subsidiarity and Proportionality, 2 July 2015. I Cooper, 'A Yellow Card for the Striker' (n 10 above) 1423 fn.

> parliaments. If national parliaments take the trouble to scrutinize European proposals, and they then flag a yellow card, the Commission should respond … And it should not respond along bureaucratic lines, it should respond in a political way. Because we all know that sometimes a yellow card is raised because there is a problem with subsidiarity or proportionality, and sometimes a yellow card is raised because there is more a problem with the content of a proposal. And then to dismiss that on procedural grounds I think is not the attitude the Commission should take. We should engage and explain in the national parliaments why we have decided to take a certain initiative. We should take on board the criticism formulated in national parliaments.[83]

These remarks, which signal an openness to a more political approach to the EWM, were greeted warmly by the assembled national parliamentarians. At the time of writing, it is still early in the life of the new Commission, which has not yet been faced with a yellow card. As a result, it is too soon to tell whether this change in tone will result in an overall change in the social dynamics of the EWM.

[83] Remarks of Franz Timmermans, 1 December 2014. Transcribed by the author.

3

Reconstructing the EWM?

JÖRGEN HETTNE

The national parliaments' role has been emphasised in the debate on how to best design a more democratic European Union. In this chapter, several proposals which aim to improve the Early Warning Mechanism (EWM) for this purpose will be discussed. It has been argued that the yellow card should be converted into a binding red card, which gives national parliaments the possibility of stopping unwanted proposals on EU legislation from the Commission. It has also been argued that a so-called green card, which gives national parliaments an opportunity to propose new EU legislation or the withdrawal or amendment of existing unwanted legislation, should be introduced. The new European Commission took office on 1 November 2014, with a number of structural changes including the creation of a First Vice-President, a responsibility given to the former Dutch Foreign Minister, Frans Timmermans. The First Vice-President wants to ensure that every Commission proposal respects the principles of subsidiarity and proportionality. If the Commission pays more attention to the principle of subsidiarity and treats it more as a political commitment than a constitutional barrier (a constitutional dialogue), it is possible that the demand for strengthening the control of national parliaments in the EWM will dissipate. The new Commission's high level of interest in the principle of subsidiarity also means that this is an excellent moment to evaluate the present mechanism and to present some ideas on how subsidiarity can better be respected in the Union.[1]

I. Introduction

The principle of subsidiarity was introduced as a tool to keep under control the distribution of powers in the EU, where the competences are shared between the

[1] This chapter is partly based on a European Policy Analysis from the Swedish Institute for European Policy Studies (SIEPS): J Hettne, 'Making Sense of Subsidiarity and the Early Warning Mechanism—A Constitutional Dialogue?' (*European Policy Analysis* 2014:9), available at: www.sieps.se/sites/default/files/2014_9epa%20eng%20A4%20korr9.pdf.

Union and the Member States. The principle should ensure that the EU uses its powers and resources for the right things. The preservation of domestic regulatory power and only limited supranational involvement, in a supplementary or complementary capacity, can also be seen as a manifestation of the spirit of subsidiarity.[2] However, it is obvious that states can have different views on what the EU should do and what should be left to domestic regulatory power. In a Union composed of 28 governments and a directly elected European Parliament, there will always be different preferences for what the Union should achieve. The needs of European integration will, furthermore, vary over time, as was demonstrated in the aftermath of the financial crisis,[3] when the Union developed an agenda for economic governance, which was unimaginable before the crisis. With this diversity of opinions and the dynamic character of the integration process, it is clear that a vague and non-binding principle of subsidiarity does not have much effect. The principle must have concrete content and be binding. This is already the case as a result of the Maastricht Treaty, through which the general principle of subsidiarity was inserted in the founding Treaties for the first time. The principle will, it is thought, point to the most efficient level for decision-making (national or European) in situations in which the competence of the Union is not exclusive.

However, the outcome of the subsidiarity test depends heavily on how the objectives are expressed in the proposed legislative acts. Since EU cooperation is designed to find common solutions to transnational problems, legal review as a constitutional barrier has often been considered to be fairly weak. The case law from the Court of Justice of the European Union (the Court of Justice) indicates that if an action complies with the Treaties and is linked to their aims, that action can under hardly any circumstances be contrary to the principle of subsidiarity, ie it will not be rendered unconstitutional by legal ex post control.[4] Professor Derrick Wyatt has explained this development by arguing that the interpretation and application of the principle of subsidiarity includes a large element of policy assessment and political judgement, and allows 'the EU institutions to present almost any proposal for EU wide action as having an objective which can be better achieved at EU level than at national or sub national level, and that is precisely what they do'.[5]

[2] See A Dashwood et al, *Wyatt and Dashwood's European Union Law*, 6th edn (Oxford, Hart Publishing, 2011) 115.

[3] ibid, 116.

[4] See, for example, Case C-377/98, *Netherlands v European Parliament and Council*, EU:C:2001:523, Case C-491/01, *R v Secretary of State for Health, ex parte British American Tobacco (Investments) and Imperial Tobacco*, EU:C:2002:741, Joined cases C-154/04 and C-155/04, *The Queen (on the application of Alliance for Natural Health and Nutri-Link) v Secretary of State for Health*, EU:C:2005:449 and Case C-58/08, *The Queen (on the application of Vodafone Ltd and Others) v Secretary of State for Business, Enterprise and Regulatory Reform*, EU:C:2010:321. For a discussion of the case law, see, for instance, A Biondi, 'Subsidiarity in the Courtroom' in A Biondi, P Eeckhout and S Ripley (eds), *EU Law after Lisbon* (Oxford, Oxford University Press, 2012) 213 ff.

[5] Professor Derrick Wyatt QC, Brick Court Chambers, *submission of evidence* to the Report from the UK Government: *Review of the Balance of Competences between the United Kingdom and the European Union; Subsidiarity and Proportionality* (December 2014) see p 54. Available at: www.gov.uk/review-of-the-balance-of-competences, accessed on 30 May 2015.

Against this background, the Lisbon Treaty sharpened the political ex ante control and made national parliaments the primary supervisors in the pre-legislative stage.[6] From a democratic legitimacy perspective, no institutions can, of course, be more appropriate to carry out the subsidiarity review than the national parliaments, as the powers used by the Union come from them. Thus, the Lisbon Treaty introduced the EWM that gave national parliaments, collectively, a right to challenge the legislative initiatives of the EU in the light of the principle of subsidiarity. The idea of enhancing the political ex ante control is sound, but the present construction is, in my view, based on two incompatible objectives. On the one hand, the parliamentary control is supposed to be political and, therefore, broader than the judicial review carried out by the Court of Justice. On the other hand, the control is framed in the same way as the control exercised by the Court of Justice, and the Court also has the last say when it comes to the ultimate meaning of subsidiarity. This implies that the national parliaments, if they respect the limits of their mandate, are forced to take a position on relatively complex legal questions, which to a large extent inhibits their ability to consider the broader political and constitutional issue, namely whether a proposal is something to which the EU should give priority within its limited powers and resources. The strict legal barriers that frame the EWM, and the non-binding nature of the reasoned opinions resulting from it, have, in general, not been appreciated. Several national parliaments have now presented proposals that aim to strengthen the subsidiarity review and make it more binding,[7] but they do not seem to take full account of the present institutional balance in the EU and the principal differences between ex ante political review and ex post judicial review. This brings us to the complex nature of the principle of subsidiarity, which will be discussed next.

II. The Nature of The Present System

Even when the principle of subsidiarity was first introduced through the Maastricht Treaty, the principle was cut into two parts: the first as a broader political objective, and the second as a binding provision working as a legal barrier against the misuse of Union competences. The current system suffers from this inherent conflict of objectives. The scrutiny by national parliaments is based on the legal definition

[6] See A Dashwood et al, *Wyatt and Dashwood's European Union Law* (n 2 above) 119.

[7] See, for instance, the Dutch Parliament, *Ahead in Europe: On the Role of the Dutch House of Representatives and National Parliaments in the European Union* (2014), available at: www.government.nl/documents-and-publications/notes/2013/06/21/testing-european-legislation-for-subsidiarity-and-proportionality-dutch-list-of-points-for-action.html, accessed on 30 May 2015. See also the abovementioned report from the UK Government: *Review of the Balance of Competences between the United Kingdom and the European Union; Subsidiarity and Proportionality* (2014), n 5 above, and the report from the Danish *Folketing*: *Twenty-three Recommendations—to strengthen the role of national parliaments in a changing European governance* (European Affairs Committee, 2014), available at: renginiai.lrs.lt/renginiai/EventDocument/6fa11f98-fc15-4443-8f3f-9a9b26d34c97/Folketing_Twenty-three%20recommendations_EN.pdf, accessed on 30 May 2015.

of subsidiarity in Article 5.3 TEU. At the same time, the national parliaments are expected to consider the principle of subsidiarity in a broader political perspective. In the protocol on proportionality and subsidiarity[8] (the Protocol) it is stated that all decisions should be made as closely as possible to the citizens. The Swedish Committee on the Constitution believes that this means that the EWM is a commitment that follows from the Treaty and is intended to enhance the democratic legitimacy of the decision-making process in the Union.[9]

This inherent conflict of objectives has created both uncertainty and debate on what should be encompassed in subsidiarity reviews by the national parliaments. Several parliaments, including the Swedish Parliament, have, for example, emphasised that it is unreasonable that the review outlined in the Protocol should distinguish between subsidiarity and proportionality and that the Protocol only allows for a limited review on issues regarding subsidiarity *stricto sensu*. With the support of parts of the doctrine,[10] the Swedish Parliament has argued that a proportionality test is included in the subsidiarity review, and that national parliaments therefore have reason to rule on proportionality concerns in their opinions with regard to the principle of subsidiarity. This question came into the spotlight when the Commission, in a Communication, rejected certain arguments from national parliaments because they did not correspond to the Commission's interpretation of what is covered by the term 'subsidiarity'.[11] Some national parliaments have reacted strongly to this attitude, because they believe that a reasoned opinion on subsidiarity from a national parliament cannot be ignored by the Commission on such formal grounds. The Commission should not be entitled to dismiss arguments from a national parliament for the sole reason that, according to the Commission, those arguments do not have their origin in Article 5.3 TEU. Thus, the EU Committee of the House of Lords stated in its 2013–14 report on the role of national parliaments in the European Union that 'the Commission should make an undertaking that, when a "yellow card" is issued, it will either drop the proposal in question, or substantially amend it in order to meet the concerns expressed'. It suggested that the aim should be to focus the procedure not on whether the concerns were consistent with the Commission's own interpretation of subsidiarity

[8] Treaty on European Union, Protocol No 2.

[9] Konstitutionsutskottets utlåtande 2013/14:KU45, *Granskning av kommissionsrapporter om subsidiaritet och proportionalitet m.m.*, 26 (Opinion from the Committee on the Constitution on reports from the Commission concerning subsidiarity and proportionality). Available at: www.riksdagen.se/sv/Dokument-Lagar/Utskottens-dokument/Betankanden/Granskning-av-kommissionsrappo_H101KU45, accessed on 30 May 2015.

[10] See, inter alia, P Kiiver, *The Early Warning System for the Principle of Subsidiarity: Constitutional Theory and Empirical Reality* (London, Routledge, 2012) 99 f, K Lenaerts and P Van Nuffel, *European Union Law*, 3rd edn (London, Sweet & Maxwell, 2011) 144 f, T Tridimas, *The General Principles of EU Law*, 2nd edn (Oxford, Oxford University Press, 2006) 176 and J Hettne, 'Subsidiaritetsprincipen: Politisk granskning eller juridisk kontroll?', (SIEPS, *European Policy Analysis* 2003:4), p 20 f ('The Principle of Subsidiarity: Political Scrutiny or Legal Review?').

[11] COM(2013) 851 on the review of the proposal for a Council Regulation on the establishment of the European Public Prosecutor's Office with regard to the principle of subsidiarity, in accordance with Protocol No 2.

but on what should be altered to address the concerns expressed by a large number of national chambers.[12] The Swedish Committee on the Constitution notes, in this context, with some emphasis, that it follows from Article 6 of the Protocol that each national parliament, within eight weeks, may send a reasoned opinion to the presidents of the European Parliament, the Council and the Commission stating 'why it considers that the draft in question does not comply with the principle of subsidiarity'. According to the Swedish Committee, the Protocol does not give any room for the body proposing the draft legislation unilaterally to disregard some of the reasons that the national parliaments have put forward as the basis for their opinions. Thus, the Commission should not have any superior right to determine which arguments fall within the scope of the principle of subsidiarity but should, as follows from Article 7 of the Protocol, take account of the reasoned opinions issued by the national parliaments.[13]

One might think that this discussion is about legal details, but it underlines the inherent conflict of interests that characterises the present system. This conflict needs to be resolved if the legitimate aim of strengthening democracy in the EU decision-making process is to be achieved.

The current mechanism can therefore be described as political control of a constitutional nature within a very narrow legal framework. In the following, I will discuss what can be done to rectify this, both within the current regulatory framework and through changes to this framework. First, however, it is necessary to take a closer look at the present mechanism and the proposals for reform that have been put forward.

III. Cards in the Hands of National Parliaments

A. The Yellow Card

The EWM is, in short, constructed to operate as follows. The national parliaments receive a draft legislative act. It is then possible for them, within eight weeks, to lodge a reasoned opinion of why they consider that the draft in question does not comply with the principle of subsidiarity. If the opinions that are submitted represent at least one-third of all the votes allocated to the national parliaments (ie 19 of a total of 56 votes), then the draft *must be reviewed* (the yellow card). The threshold is one-quarter of votes in the case of a draft legislative act submitted on the basis of Article 76 TFEU in the area of freedom, security and justice.

[12] House of Lords European Union Committee, *The Role of National Parliaments in the European Union*, 9th Report of the Session 2013–14 (2014). Available at: www.publications.parliament.uk/pa/ld201314/ldselect/ldeucom/151/151.pdf.

[13] Konstitutionsutskottets utlåtande 2013/14:KU45 (n 9 above) 27.

After such review, the Commission or, as the case may be, another institution may decide to *maintain, amend or withdraw the proposal.* If it chooses to maintain the proposal, the Commission or the other institution shall, in a reasoned opinion, justify why it considers that the proposal complies with the principle of subsidiarity. Accordingly, the yellow card can be seen as a recommendation from a certain number of national parliaments that a certain proposal should be taken off the table. However, it has no binding effect on the institution (normally the Commission) requiring it to actually alter or withdraw the proposed act.

B. The Orange Card

If the ordinary legislative procedure is supposed to be used, which will be the case for the majority of the proposals from the Commission, a special rule applies if reasoned opinions from *at least a simple majority of the votes allocated to the national parliaments* claim that a proposal for a legislative act does not comply with the principle of subsidiarity. In such a case, the proposal must not only be reviewed; if the Commission chooses to maintain the proposal, the issue of subsidiarity must also be considered by the Union legislator (the Council and European Parliament). If, by a majority of 55 per cent of the members of the Council or a majority of the votes cast in the European Parliament, one of these institutions is of the opinion that the proposal is not compatible with the principle of subsidiarity, the proposed legislative act will not be given further consideration. This is called the orange card, as it is not a veto right for the national parliaments but a right to formally involve the Council and the European Parliament at a very early stage in the legislative procedure.

C. The Proposed Red Card

Against this background, it has been suggested that the Union should introduce a so-called 'red card' to allow a certain number of national parliaments to definitively block new Commission proposals or retroactively annul existing legislation. The British thinktank *Centre for European Reform* (CER) has proposed a mechanism under which the Commission would withdraw a legislative proposal if half of all national parliamentary chambers voted against it on subsidiarity grounds. CER suggest that the advantage of a 'red card' system would be to enhance the powers of national parliaments, thus increasing accountability.[14] This was also supported by the thinktank *Fresh Start*, which specifically searched for options for

[14] CER, Can National Parliaments Make the EU More Legitimate?, available at: www.cer.org.uk/insights/can-national-parliaments-make-eu-more-legitimate (2013), accessed on 30 May 2015, and C Grant, How to Build a Modern European Union (October 2013). Available at: www.cer.org.uk/sites/default/files/publications/attachments/pdf/2013/rp_119-7927.pdf, accessed on 30 May 2015.

a new UK-EU relationship before the Brexit referendum. It considered the red card as an option to change the relationship between national parliaments and the Commission, particularly in light of the Commission's continuation of the European Public Prosecutor's Office (EPPO) proposal, which will be commented on below.[15] Politically, the change from an orange card to a red card has mainly been supported by the UK Government. In its reply to the Lords inquiry on national parliaments in the EU, the UK Government said that a sufficient threshold of national parliaments should have the power to block a proposal if they found that it violated subsidiarity. It considered that this would assure national parliaments that their positions would have an effect on the legislative process.

An alternative or additional approach that has been advocated is that the yellow card should be treated in effect as a red card, with the Commission undertaking to reconsider its proposal. Among those advocating this was former Netherlands Foreign Minister, Frans Timmermans, and now First Vice-President in the European Commission.[16] Such a unilateral undertaking from the Commission, it is thought, should not need any formal change in the Protocol.

D. The Proposed Green Card

In the debate, the term green card has also appeared. So far this term does not always have the same meaning, but it signifies that the parliaments should not only have negative powers which can be used to halt the process, but also powers of a more positive nature in order to give a green light to a certain proposal or more importantly the power to propose new legislation. The question of a green card has been raised by the Dutch *Tweede Kamer* and the Danish *Folketing* The intention behind these proposals is to allow national parliaments to propose new policies or legislation to the Commission, including amending or repealing existing EU laws.[17] The House of Lords EU Committee has agreed that in principle there should be a way for a group of likeminded national parliaments to make constructive suggestions for EU policy initiatives, which may include reviewing existing legislation. It suggested that this would echo the role that the European Parliament has when it adopts initiative reports under Article 225 TFEU. Moreover, in order not to intrude on the Commission's formal right of initiative, the Committee suggested that it could work through a Commission undertaking to consider such suggestions carefully, and either act on them or explain why not.[18]

[15] See Fresh Start, 'Mandate for Reform', (November 2013) available at: www.eufreshstart.org/downloads/mandateforreform.pdf, accessed on 30 May 2015.

[16] See 'Monnet's Europe Needs Reform to fit the 21st Century', *Financial Times*, 14 November 2013.

[17] See Clingendael and CEPS, *From Subsidiarity to Better EU Governance: A Practical Reform Agenda for the EU* (2014). Available at: www.clingendael.nl/sites/default/files/Clingendael%20CEPS%20From%20Subsidiarity%20to%20Better%20EU%20Governance.pdf, accessed on 30 May 2015.

[18] House of Lords European Union Committee, Report HL 151 of Session 2013–14, *The Role of National Parliaments in the European Union* (2014). Available at: www.publications.parliament.uk/pa/ld201314/ldselect/ldeucom/151/151.pdf, accessed on 30 May 2015.

IV. How 'Legal' Should the Political Control Be?

The different proposals boil down to the important question of the nature of the subsidiarity review and how legally binding it reasonably can be at this early stage of the legislative procedure. It must be underlined that a change of the present EWM towards a red veto card would obviously influence the division of powers in the Union. This is the reason why national parliaments, when the Protocol was drafted, were not given a stronger influence over the EU legislative process than the influence described above (yellow card and orange card).[19] National parliaments have a right to highlight the fact that there are serious doubts as to whether a proposal from the Commission (or exceptionally from another institution) complies with the principle of subsidiarity. The ultimate decision on the legislative act must, however, be adopted by the political institutions of the Union. If the national parliaments were to be given greater influence in the form of a veto right, the present institutional balance would change. The European Parliament and the Council would then have no opportunity to take a position on subsidiarity, and the independent role of the Commission in safeguarding the long-term goals of the Union would be affected.

A further question of importance is whether the national parliaments, when taking part in the EWM, are suitable as veto holders. The issue at stake, subsidiarity in accordance with Article 5.3 TEU, is an obviously legal or even a constitutional question, and parliaments will always be political bodies, and should, it is submitted, not act as anything else. If it was a constitutional veto process that was intended by the EWM, a council of national constitutional courts or supreme courts would have been a better option. It has been argued by Philipp Kiiver that such a role for national parliaments is not impossible.[20] However, even if I were to agree with Kiiver that the mechanism set up is, on its surface, similar to the function carried out by the national council of a state, like the French *Conseil d'Etat* or the Swedish *Lagrådet*, it seems highly problematic to attribute such a legal or constitutional function to an international council composed of all the national parliaments in the Union. Even if some national parliaments have developed the competences and skills to carry out this function, usually through an increased involvement of civil servants, it does not appear to be the desired way forward. One should also add that the institution that has the last say on questions regarding subsidiarity is the Court of Justice. A council of states would possibly try to

[19] It should be noted that the European Convention's working group that was tasked with reviewing subsidiarity monitoring discussed the introduction of a 'red card' that would allow a sufficient majority of national parliaments to block a Commission initiative. The aim was to ensure that any new monitoring mechanism would have real teeth. However, in their final report the group agreed that any improvements to subsidiarity monitoring should not block decision-making, or make the process more lengthy or cumbersome, and as such the 'red card' idea was not taken forward (Working Group I on the Principle of Subsidiarity, Conclusions CONV 286/02 (2002)).

[20] P Kiiver, *The Early Warning System* (n 10 above) 126 ff.

compete with the Court of Justice as regards the final meaning of subsidiarity, but that would be a peculiar and unreasonable situation, especially if the council were composed of national parliaments, and it would in any case be incompatible with the role given to the Court of Justice in the EU Treaties. Political bodies like parliaments are not designed to give authoritative rulings on constitutional issues, and it does not help that the EWM is based on the collective actions of a number of parliaments. A development in which the position of a certain group of parliaments or chambers, usually from a minority of the Member States in the Union, can issue a legal opinion that in practical terms has the same legal value as a judgment of the Court of Justice seems hazardous.

This is illustrated by the controversial decision from the Commission to go ahead with the proposal to create a European Public Prosecutor's Office (EPPO), even though a group of national parliaments considered the Commission proposal to be in conflict with the principle of subsidiarity.[21] The Treaty clearly foresees the creation of this office. Article 86 TFEU provides that in order to combat crimes affecting the financial interests of the Union, the Council, by means of regulations adopted in accordance with a special legislative procedure, may establish a European Public Prosecutor's Office from Eurojust. The Council is to act unanimously after obtaining the consent of the European Parliament. Hence, there is a clear legal basis for this development, but a unanimous decision from the Council is required. Moreover, the treaty also foresees the possible lack of support from some Member States for such a development and underlines the possibility of enhanced cooperation. Article 86 continues by stating that, in the absence of unanimity in the Council, a group of at least nine Member States may request that the draft regulation be referred to the European Council. In that case, the procedure in the Council is to be suspended. After discussion, and if a consensus is obtained, the European Council, within four months of this suspension, is to refer the draft back to the Council for adoption. Within the same time-frame, if there is no consensus, and if at least nine Member States wish to establish enhanced cooperation on the basis of the draft regulation concerned, they are to notify the European Parliament, the Council and the Commission accordingly. In such a case, the authorisation to proceed with enhanced cooperation referred to in Article 20(2) and Article 329(1) TFEU will be deemed to be granted, and the provisions on enhanced cooperation will apply.

It is not difficult to guess that the Commission had the option of enhanced cooperation in mind (at least as an alternative option) when it initiated the process of creating the EPPO, a process that led to the negative reaction from several national parliaments.[22] However, if the objection from this group of national

[21] See proposal for a Council regulation on the establishment of the European Public Prosecutor's Office, COM/2013/0534 final. A total of 19 votes from parliaments in 11 Member States objected on subsidiarity grounds.

[22] See Commission Communication: COM(2013) 851 on the review of the proposal for a Council Regulation on the establishment of the European Public Prosecutor's Office with regard to the principle of subsidiarity, in accordance with Protocol No 2.

parliaments against the EPPO *had to* be respected, this would not only remove the power of the Council and the European Council to decide on the issue, but it would also eliminate the possibility of the Court of Justice having a say on the validity of any decision on the creation of the EPPO.

It follows from all this that the EWM should continue to be a warning mechanism and not a veto mechanism. Otherwise, the present institutional balance in the Union would change dramatically.

V. Should National Parliaments Have the Same Impact in All Areas?

In the debate regarding the strengthening of the role of national parliaments, another question which has been raised is whether the threshold for a yellow or orange card should be lowered. A question which seems important to address in this context is whether national parliaments should have the same impact in all areas. If the objective is to enhance democratic legitimacy, it seems rational that national parliaments should be given more influence in areas where they have significant powers according to their national constitutional orders. For instance, in most countries a large part of the Single Market *acquis* is implemented through regulations adopted by governments or even at lower levels. Is it reasonable that the parliaments should have a substantial influence over these issues, if they do not have it in their national systems? Even if the national constitutional orders are different in the various Member States, there is a sufficient amount of common ground to make it possible to identify areas under EU law where it is rational that parliaments should have bigger influence than in others. In these areas there are stronger reasons to strengthen the control, by lowering the threshold for the yellow card. There is already an indication of such a development in the existing Protocol. It is sufficient that a quarter (and not a third) of the national parliamentary chambers are submitting reasoned opinions in order to generate a yellow card in the area of justice and home affairs. In this area powers have relatively recently been transferred to the Union, which in turn is due to the fact that these powers belongs to the core competences of the national parliaments in the Member States' constitutional systems, eg powers which cannot easily be delegated to the government. This is particularly true as regards criminal law. This line of reasoning could be extended and have a greater impact on the thresholds in the EWM.

To a large extent, the thresholds for the yellow card could follow the rules of decision-making in the EU treaties. Member States have been reluctant to entrust EU-institutions with decision-making powers based on qualified majority voting in some areas, even if these areas, from a purely economic perspective, seem apt for European integration. Hence, there is national constitutional resistance, based on arguments related to national sovereignty rather than economic rationality, which explains that the EU can only adopt legislation by unanimous decisions in an area such as direct taxation. Furthermore, it is, against this background, understandable that a development that is not fully anticipated and requires the use of the flexibility clause requires unanimity in the Council in accordance with Article 352 TFEU. In this case, it is also stated that the Commission shall draw national parliaments' attention to such proposals. Thus, legal bases in the Treaties stating that the Council must act unanimously on a proposal from the Commission are typical areas in which national parliaments in general have a particular interest in controlling that the principle of subsidiarity is respected. The same applies to the recent and rapid developments in the area of economic policy, as this has implications for national public finances and the national state budget. As the Commission in its recent reports has emphasised, this is an area where direct dialogue with national parliaments is especially important and necessary to increase legitimacy in the European Union.[23]

There are therefore reasons not only to expand the 'quarter rule' to areas where the EU Treaties require unanimity in the Council, but also where a proposal concerns an area of special importance for the national parliaments such as fiscal and economic policy.

VI. How Limited in Scope Should the Subsidiarity Review Be?

It is noticeable that the scrutiny of national parliaments under the EWM is limited in several respects. First, it is only a draft *legislative act* that can be scrutinised by the national parliaments, not a *non-legislative act* (ie an act under the TFEU that is not derived from a legislative process, such as a delegated act or an implementing act adopted by the Commission). It is thus important to verify which pieces of legislation constitute legislative acts. It follows, for example, from the TFEU that a request to amend the Statute of the Court of Justice is a draft legislative act,[24] but some important acts adopted under the chapters on competition policy and social policy are not legislative acts.[25]

Secondly, as has been mentioned earlier, a national parliament can only comment on why it considers that a draft is inconsistent with the principle of subsidiarity. National parliaments are not invited to comment on whether a proposal

[23] See, for instance, COM(2013) 565 final, Report from the Commission—Annual report 2012 on relations between the European Commission and national parliaments, p 8.

[24] According to Article 3 of the Protocol: 'For the purposes of this Protocol, "draft legislative acts" shall mean proposals from the Commission, initiatives from a group of Member States, initiatives from the European Parliament, requests from the Court of Justice, recommendations from the European Central Bank and requests from the European Investment Bank, for the adoption of a legislative act'.

[25] See A Dashwood et al, *Wyatt and Dashwood's European Union Law* (n 2 above) 85.

appears to be incompatible with the principle of conferral or the principle of proportionality, even though these two principles obviously have the same context (the distribution of powers between the EU and the Member States), as illustrated by Article 5 TFEU, where these three principles are expressed together. Furthermore, there is no explicit provision for national parliaments to object if they believe that national identity has been violated, within the meaning of Article 4.2 TEU. It is therefore understandable that the subsidiarity review is considered, by several national parliaments, to be a blunt instrument of control, because the principle of subsidiarity is isolated from these other, related principles.

Indeed, in many cases subsidiarity completely misses the point. The judgement to be made under the principle of subsidiarity is not about the objective pursued but about whether the pursuit of that objective requires Union action.[26] Thus, the principle of subsidiarity does not (on its own) provide a method of balancing the interests of the Member States and the Union. Instead it raises the question of who should implement objectives that are already agreed.[27] In fact, it has proved virtually impossible to challenge a harmonisation measure which has the objective of improving the Single Market, in the light of the subsidiarity principle. In these cases, the Court has pointed out that when the objective pursued by the measure is harmonisation, which is necessary in order to prevent differences between national laws causing obstacles to movement or distortions of competition, it is manifestly the case that Member States alone cannot act.[28] Accordingly, subsidiarity in its strict sense has no relevance to those measures whose aim is to create the uniformity necessary for the Single Market. Nevertheless, this is the area where the principle has been claimed to have its biggest impact (shared competences). Where uniformity is necessary, only the Union will be able to act.

Against this backdrop, it is not surprising that several parliaments have argued that an element of proportionality is part of the principle of subsidiarity. Moreover, subsidiarity and proportionality have frequently been conflated in impact assessments, and many national parliaments have considered subsidiarity checks ineffective if proportionality is not included.[29] The two concepts are clearly closely related, and explicitly extending the procedure to include proportionality would

[26] See opinion of Advocate General Maduro in Case C-58/08, *Vodafone Ltd and Others*, EU:C:2009:596 (n 4 above), para 30.

[27] See G Davies, 'Subsidiarity: The Wrong Idea, in the Wrong Place, at the Wrong Time' (2006) 43 *Common Market Law Review* 63, 69.

[28] See eg Case C-491/01, *British American Tobacco (Investments) and Imperial Tobacco*, EU:C:2002:741 (n 4 above), para 182.

[29] See, for instance, Dutch Parliament, *Ahead in Europe: On the Role of the Dutch House of Representatives and National Parliaments in the European Union* (2014), the above-mentioned reports from the UK Government: *Review of the Balance of Competences between the United Kingdom and the European Union; Subsidiarity and Proportionality* (2014), the Danish *Folketinget: Twenty-three Recommendations—to strengthen the role of national parliaments in a changing European governance* (European Affairs Committee, 2014) (n 7 above) and the Swedish Parliament: Konstitutionsutskottets utlåtande 2013/14:KU45, *Granskning av kommissionsrapporter om subsidiaritet och proportionalitet m.m.*, 26 (n 9 above).

avoid sterile disputes about whether a particular concern about a proposal falls under one heading or the other.[30] It has been argued that the fact that previous reasoned opinions and yellow cards covered other matters such as proportionality and competence shows that national parliaments have incentives, and the ability, to protect those matters too, and/or that it is impractical to split these off from subsidiarity in political, if not in legal terms.[31] Hence, the Dutch Parliament has suggested that it should be possible for reasoned opinions to cover proportionality and the choice of legal basis.[32]

In the light of this discussion and what has previously been stated, it is submitted that the EWM should be seen as a political dialogue regarding constitutional issues (a constitutional dialogue), and not as a veto system. Besides subsidiarity, such dialogue should include issues related to the principle of conferral (legal basis), proportionality and respect for national identity.

VII. Should the National Parliaments Have a Collective Right of Initiative?

Something should also be said about the proposal to give the national parliaments some kind of right to propose or remove Union legislation. The 'green card' should especially be considered against the background of the Netherlands' action of removing unwanted but existing legislation at EU level.[33] A green card would theoretically move the power of initiative from the Commission to a group of national parliaments. However, it has not been presented as a binding obligation on the Commission to go forward with such proposals, but rather as an obligation to explain why unwanted legislation shall continue to be in force (see the discussion above). It can safely be stated that the Commission is not best placed to take the initiative to clean up legislative failures and mistakes in the European integration process. The Commission is the engine of this process which, by its

[30] House of Lords European Union Committee Report HL 151 of Session 2013–14 *The Role of National Parliaments in the European Union*, para 77. Available at: www.publications.parliament.uk/pa/ld201314/ldselect/ldeucom/151/151.pdf, accessed on 30 May 2015.

[31] Senior European Experts Group, *submission of evidence* in above-mentioned report from the UK Government: *Review of the Balance of Competences between the United Kingdom and the European Union; Subsidiarity and Proportionality* (2014).

[32] See, for instance, the Dutch Parliament, *Ahead in Europe: On the Role of the Dutch House of Representatives and National Parliaments in the European Union* (2014), available at: www.houseofrepresentatives.nl/sites/default/files/news_items/ahead_in_europe_tcm181-238660_0.pdf, accessed on 30 May 2015.

[33] See the proposal from the Dutch Government: *Testing European legislation for subsidiarity and proportionality—Dutch list of points for action*, available at: www.government.nl/documents-and-publications/notes/2013/06/21/testing-european-legislation-for-subsidiarity-and-proportionality-dutch-list-of-points-for-action.html, accessed on 30 May 2015.

nature, is moving in one direction, namely forward. This kind of initiative, attributed to national parliaments, can therefore be healthy for the Union and does not seem incompatible with the integration model which the EU currently represents. Removing legislation can, however, only be done through the procedure required for the adoption of the same kind of legislation, which normally means a qualified majority in the Council and the involvement of the European Parliament as co-legislator. The Union legislator will therefore always ultimately decide on the matter. The right to propose new legislation does not seem controversial. The Treaty already provides similar rights for the European Parliament (Article 225 TFEU) and the Council (Article 241 TFEU) and the Treaty of Lisbon introduced in addition the citizens' initiative which put an obligation on the Commission to take into consideration a proposal that 1 million EU citizens from a certain number of member countries support (Article 11.4 TEU). It would not upset the present institutional balance in the Union if national parliaments had a similar opportunity.

VIII. Bring the Court in Earlier?

If the proposed distinction between political and legal control is accepted, the subsidiarity review becomes more efficient. National parliaments become involved at a deeper level. At the same time, the EU constitutional order is preserved, with the European Parliament and the Council as legislators and the Court of Justice as the ultimate arbitrator.

If such an arrangement meets resistance from the national parliaments because of its non-binding nature, there is still one option available that would not upset the institutional balance of the Union.

What might be appropriate, as an alternative to a red card, is to create an opportunity for the Court of Justice to have a role earlier in the process. At present, Article 8 of the Protocol expressly confers upon the Court the jurisdiction to hear actions based on the principle of subsidiarity for the *annulment of legislative acts* of the Union that are brought by Member States or notified by them 'in accordance with their legal order' on behalf of their national parliaments or a chamber thereof. This constitutes ex post judicial review.

However, it seems possible to construct also an ex ante legal review whose effect would be similar to the control exercised by national constitutional courts in many Member States. If a certain number of parliaments have serious doubts about the compatibility of a proposal with the constitutional principles of the Union and the Commission declares that, regardless of the objections raised, it will go forward with it, they would collectively be able to initiate such a preliminary examination before the Court of Justice, in the same way as is possible when the Court examines international agreements that the Union is intending to conclude with third countries or international organisations.

According to Article 218.11 TFEU, a Member State, the European Parliament, the Council or the Commission may obtain the opinion of the Court of Justice as to whether a proposed agreement is compatible with the Treaties. When the opinion of the Court is adverse, the proposed agreement may not enter into force unless it is amended or the Treaties are revised. That provision has the aim of forestalling the complications that would result from legal disputes concerning the compatibility of the Treaties and international agreements that are binding upon the EU.[34] A similar provision regarding whether a proposed legislative act is compatible with the principle of subsidiarity, and possibly with other related constitutional principles, could be added to the Protocol.

To bring in the Court earlier obviously needs further consideration. For instance, it must be decided how many parliaments or chambers are needed to support a request for an opinion and when this should be possible. It seems reasonable that the thresholds for requesting the opinion of the Court should be the same as for a yellow card (one-third or one-quarter of the votes depending of the legal base for the proposal) but not necessarily based on votes from the same national parliaments/chambers that collectively invoked the yellow card. It also seems reasonable that the Commission should have the possibility to review its proposal and give reasons for its position, before the Court is involved, and that a condition for bringing the matter to the Court should be that the Commission has not chosen to withdraw its proposal. For practical reasons, it is furthermore appropriate that the request to the Court is formally lodged by the Commission, on behalf of the national parliaments, if the relevant threshold is met. To extend the possibility to proposals from other institutions appears unnecessary in light of the objectives discussed above for reconstructing the EWM.

The mere presence of such a possibility for the national parliaments would probably put further pressure on the Commission to take subsidiarity seriously during the EWM.

IX. Conclusions

To make the subsidiarity review by national parliaments the instrument that it was intended to be—a necessary counterweight to the increased competences of the EU—it should be wider and should include the main constitutional principles of the Union. If we accept that the national parliaments, regardless of the names they give to their subsidiarity reviews, are engaged in politics, there is no reason to restrict their control to the principle of subsidiarity in the strict sense. The EWM should be seen as a political dialogue regarding constitutional issues

[34] See Opinion 2/94, EU:C:1996:140, para 3; Opinion 1/08, EU:C:2009:739, para 107; and Opinion 1/09, EU:C:2011:123, para 47.

(a constitutional dialogue), and not as a veto system. Besides subsidiarity, the national parliaments should be able to consider the principles of conferral (legal basis), proportionality and the respect for national identity,[35] which are issues that are closely linked to the principle of subsidiarity.[36] National parliaments should therefore be engaged in a wider constitutional review without any unnecessary and troublesome legal barriers framing their control at the outset. It should be seen as a special form of political dialogue that, in contrast to the broader Political Dialogue,[37] focuses on issues relating to the division of competence between the Union and its Member States.

Against that background, the choice of a yellow card and not a red veto card was reasonable. Similarly, the addition of an orange card did not change the logic by disturbing the institutional balance in the EU. Neither the yellow card nor the orange card makes the national parliaments veto players, and both leave the legislative triangle between the Commission and the Council/European Parliament intact. If the reasoned opinions of a certain number of parliaments are followed by these institutions, the constitutional balance in the Union is not shifted. The same can be said about the proposed right of initiative (the green card). As long as this initiative is not binding on the Commission, it can be a healthy contribution to the present system. Finally consideration should also be given to lowering the threshold for a yellow card from a third to a quarter of the EWM votes when the EU Treaties require a unanimous decision in the Council and when a proposal concerns an area of special importance for the national parliaments, such as fiscal and economic policy.

A wider control or dialogue could also be combined with a new role for the Court of Justice, giving the Court power to rule on constitutional issues beforehand if a certain number of parliaments so requested. This would mean a strengthening of the current controls that respect the institutional balance in the Union, as the Court of Justice is clearly the final arbiter when it comes to these issues.

A wider, ex ante control should be possible without Treaty changes. It is something that could be agreed on through an inter-institutional agreement between the Commission, the Council and the European Parliament. There is already an inter-institutional agreement between these three institutions regarding better law-making, which covers how these institutions should support the application of the principle of subsidiarity.[38] The additional constitutional objections that a

[35] For national identity, see Article 4.2 TEU. 'The Union shall respect the Member State's national identities inherent in their fundamental structures, political and constitutional, inclusive of regional and local self-government'.

[36] See, in particular, P Kiiver, *The early warning system* (n 10 above) 71 ff.

[37] The former President of the European Commission, José Manuel Barroso, initiated a Political Dialogue with national parliaments in 2006, which provides national parliaments with the opportunity to submit opinions or contributions on proposals and consultation documents without a time limit, the Commission guaranteeing a reply.

[38] European Council, European Parliament and European Commission, Inter-Institutional Agreement on Better Law-Making, [2003] OJ C321/1–5. New version [2016] OJ L123/1–4.

national parliament may raise in a reasoned opinion are already accepted as part of the Political Dialogue. What is requested therefore seems to be that the Commission undertakes to accept objections on constitutional issues related to subsidiarity and to treat these as objections on subsidiarity or at least not to disregard constitutional arguments presented under the heading of subsidiarity in reasoned opinions from national parliaments. In an inter-institutional agreement it should also be possible to insert a non-binding right of initiative for the national parliaments and it should not be a legal problem for the Commission to accept the extension of the lower threshold for the yellow card in certain cases, even though this is not formally provided for in the Protocol.

To bring in the Court earlier in the process and engage it in the ex ante control would, however, need Treaty changes, probably in both the Protocol and the Treaty (TFEU) itself. It would, however, not change the Union's own institutional balance and would therefore not go as far as creating a red veto card or a new competence court or similar; these latter are solutions that would raise difficult questions about the division of competence between the new body and the Court of Justice.[39]

To sum up, the overall objective should be to give a more effective voice to the national parliaments without unduly distorting the Union's own institutional balance. The desire for a broader political control on grounds related to subsidiarity should be balanced with a respect for the legal meaning of subsidiarity in accordance with Article 5.3 TEU. This should contribute to the aim of strengthening democracy in the EU decision-making process through an enhanced constitutional dialogue between the national parliaments and the Commission and a wider duty on the latter to justify its legislative initiatives.

[39] Cf the above-mentioned report from the UK Government: *Review of the Balance of Competences between the United Kingdom and the European Union Subsidiarity and Proportionality* (2014) p 97. See also Opinion 2/13 of 18 December 2014 where the Court of Justice concluded that the agreement on the accession of the European Union to the European Convention for the Protection of Human Rights and Fundamental Freedoms is not compatible with Article 6.2 TEU.

4

Mapping out the Procedural Requirements for the Early Warning Mechanism

ANNA WETTER

I. Introduction

The question of how the national parliaments view, as well as how they *ought to* view, their role within the framework of the early warning mechanism (EWM) is continuously subject to debate, and forms part of the main theme of this book. The questions refer for example to how the national parliaments should draft their reasoned opinions to ensure that they concern subsidiarity claims and nothing else, as well as to how the internal procedures for submitting reasoned opinions are organised within each Member State. There are distinct differences to be found in the reasoned opinions both in content and form but the question is whether in fact this is a concern for the EU. This question is posed in order to enable a necessary delimitation as well as to clarify the aim of this chapter. Despite the fact that it is highly relevant what goes on at the national level in terms of the scrutiny by national parliaments of proposals for legislation from the European Commission, it is necessary to also keep an eye on the more formal conditions for the subsidiarity assessments by national parliaments. The formal conditions for the subsidiarity review which are laid out in the Treaties, including its protocols, are part of EU primary law and respect for them represents a prerequisite for a smooth and accurate application of the EU legislative process.

The rules for the subsidiarity procedure are well defined in the protocols to the Treaty on the European Union (TEU) and the Treaty on the Functioning of the European Union (TFEU). The enactment of these protocols implies that at the end of the day it could be the European Court of Justice (ECJ) that will interpret the aims and purposes of the provisions concerning the EWM. However, this is not the usual procedure with regards to the EWM, since it is a common understanding that the mechanism exists to provide the national parliaments with *political* influence rather than with influence on the legal substance.

Without getting carried away by the comparison, it is possible to visualise a board game where it is necessary for the national parliaments to avoid moving their pieces further away than what is strategically motivated. If they go further, they risk being overlooked by the Commission, since they would formally go beyond their mandate, which is to alert the legislator on concerns relating to the subsidiarity review. At the same time, it is clear that the Commission has shown an increased interest in the positions taken by the national parliaments, possibly acknowledging the role they play at the domestic level.

To put it briefly, the present chapter will focus less on the differences in the content of subsidiarity examinations and on the national procedures governing their reviews, and will instead concentrate on the specific provisions in the Treaties that lay down the procedural prerequisites for the proper functioning of the EWM. In the chapter, this examination is referred to as the *procedural subsidiarity review*. While the ECJ applies a cautious approach towards the political choices made by the European legislator (reflected in its resistance to annul legislation on the ground that it infringes the principle of subsidiarity), it has criticised the EU legislator for not having paid sufficient respect to the procedural aspects of subsidiarity review, although these cases are limited in number. A selection of these judgments will be analysed in the present chapter.

II. The Evolving Participation of National Parliaments in EU Affairs

At the dawn of the EU project, there was no debate on the involvement of national parliaments in EU affairs. Instead it was clear that EU matters belonged to the exclusive competence of the executive, being the governments of the EU Member States. Although it is still very clear that the national parliaments do not form part of the EU legislature, a shift of attitude appeared in the early 1990s. A clear manifestation of this was the increased debate on the 'information gap' on EU affairs between the national parliaments and the executives at that time, leading up to the adoption of Declaration 13 of Heads of State and Government annexed to the Maastricht Treaty (1992). This declaration states that 'the governments of the Member States will ensure, inter alia, that national Parliaments receive Commission proposals for legislation in good time for information or possible examination'. The declaration thus reflects the view that national parliaments must be kept informed of what goes on at EU level and further that the EU shares responsibility with the EU Member States for ensuring the transmission of such information. In 1999, a Protocol on the national parliaments of the Member States was attached to the Amsterdam Treaty. It offered a binding arrangement for ensuring compliance with the declaration. It also broadened the scope of the Commission documents to be forwarded to national parliaments to include consultation documents. The final treaty declaration of the role of national parliaments was attached to the Nice Treaty. This declaration (No 23) invited national parliaments to participate in the debate on the future of the Union.

The most significant advance in relation to the role played by national parliaments is, however, the result of the work by the Convention on the Future of Europe. The current role of the national parliaments is secured by EU primary law and could be seen as result of the questions posed by the Member States during the Laeken European Council in 2000. During this European Council summit, the Member States remarked that the Union suffered from problems related to its legitimacy. In the declaration it was noted that 'the national parliaments also contribute towards the legitimacy of the European project' and more debate on the role of national parliaments was requested.[1] One question which was raised was whether the national parliaments should focus on the division of competence between the Union and the Member States, for example through a preliminary checking of compliance with the principle of subsidiarity.

Responding to this mission, the Working Group (IV) of the European Convention made some recommendations on how the involvement of national parliaments could be arranged. The recommendations were incorporated into the current Lisbon Treaty protocols—the Protocol on the Role of National Parliaments in the European Union and the Protocol on the Application of the Principles of Subsidiarity and Proportionality—with only some small changes made. These protocols are described as representing a considerable advance of the earlier provisions of the Amsterdam Treaty. In effect national parliaments had now been given a real opportunity to play an important role in the policy development and legislative system of the Union through the stepping up of legal provisions governing their involvement.

Although these protocols did not become part of EU primary law until the entry into force of the Lisbon Treaty (in 2009), the Barosso Commission announced in 2006 that the Commission would, even in the absence of treaty obligations, transmit all new proposals and consultation papers directly to the national parliaments inviting them to react directly so as to improve policy formulation.[2] The current provisions in the Lisbon Treaty thus only formalise the practice of the previous Commission.

An important aspect of the Lisbon Treaty rules is that the internalisation of rules governing the participation of national parliaments produces a regime whereby the EU (and thus not only the Member States) shares the responsibility for ensuring that the information reaches the national parliaments with the

[1] See Presidency conclusions of the European Council Meeting in Laeken, 14 and 15 December 2001, p 22.

[2] The initiative to enter into a substantial political dialogue with national parliaments was announced by President Barosso on 9 May 2006 in the European Parliament during the First Joint Parliamentary Meeting on the Future of the Union, and was also reflected in the Commission Communication 'A citizens' agenda—Delivering results for Europe' (COM(2006)) 211).

Member States. In effect, the system seeks to neutralise as many differences as possible in the practice of the implementation of the EWM at national level. The system is thus believed to result in more equal rights for the EU citizens by giving them more equal opportunities to influence EU affairs through the participation of the national parliaments than would have been the case if the Member States were individually responsible. Whether the national parliaments respond to the rights given to them belongs, however, to another question. This question will be further dealt with in Parts II and III of this book.

The list of measures taken to enhance the participation of national parliaments clearly shows that, at times when the legitimacy of the Union has been seriously challenged, the Heads of State have reacted by stepping up their initiatives to involve the national parliaments in EU affairs.

III. Rights of National Parliaments

The main argument stressed in this chapter, is that since the national parliaments are (still) considered a strange bird in the EU context, mainly due to the fact that they are not part of the EU legislature, it is important to pay attention to the formal prerequisites for their participation in the decision-making process. The drafters of the Treaties and protocols have formalised the conditions that they have found necessary to enable the national parliaments to participate as intended. This section reviews the relevant articles in the Treaties and in the protocols. It considers the provisions in a chronological order, starting with the rights of national parliaments that focus on preparing them for incoming legislative proposals.

The rights of national parliaments may, on a general level, be grouped into two different categories.[3] The first category refers to the right to information of the parliaments for the purpose of enabling them to carry out an ex ante review of legislation, whereas the second category reflects provisions in the Treaties and protocols that deal with the information rights that they possess in order to exercise ex post control of the EU. The former category may further be divided into two subgroups, including on the one hand rights possessed to *prepare for* the subsidiarity examination and on the other hand rights possessed to be able to actually *carry out* the examination.

The first category, related to the ex ante review, is the most conspicuous one. A list of these rights in chronological order begins with the rights of national parliaments to receive consultation documents (ie green and white papers and communications), the annual legislative programme, as well as other instruments of legislative planning or policy (Article 12(a) TEU and Article 1 of Protocol

[3] Philipp Kiiver makes a more advanced categorisation, using four groups, see P Kiiver, *The Conduct of Subsidiarity checks of EU Legislative Proposals by National Parliaments: Analysis, Observations and Practical Recommendations*, published in 2012 with open access at: Springerlink.com, pp 535–47.

No 1 TEU/TFEU). These documents are naturally drafted and communicated by the European Commission. By taking part of the consultative documents, national parliaments are expected to be better prepared for incoming legislative proposals. This information right is also part of the recommendations by the Working Group of the European Convention. The idea is that by allowing the national parliaments to be informed at an early stage of the more long-term ideas that exist for future legislation they will prepare better subsidiarity reviews. The provisions may also be seen as recognition, by the Treaty drafters, of the fact that the national parliaments are very busy institutions that need to be informed at an initial stage of the plans for future legislation.

To enable the active involvement of the parliaments intended by the Treaty drafters, they further have the right to receive draft legislative acts from the Commission, the European Parliament, the Council and from a group of Member States if it concerns initiatives from these institutions or the Member States (Article 12(a) TEU, Article 2 of Protocol No 1 TEU/TFEU and Article 4 of Protocol No 2 TEU/TFEU). This right may be seen as a logical consequence of the Early Warning Mechanism (EWM). Furthermore, the national parliaments are entitled to requests or recommendations from the Court of Justice, the European Central Bank or the European Investment Bank for the adoption of a legislative act (Article of 2 Protocol No 1 TEU/TFEU and Article 3 of Protocol No 2 TEU/TFEU).

There are furthermore some special arrangements in the Treaties, which specifically stress the rights of national parliaments to be called upon when the proposed legislation includes sensitive matters. One such arrangement is mentioned in Article 352, commonly referred to as the *flexibility clause*. The provision states that whenever the Commission proposes legislation based on that article it should draw the attention of national parliaments to the legislative proposal. The special arrangement in this article is a bit difficult to grasp, since its *lex specialis* character could suggest that the national parliaments should not be informed in every case, at least if an *e contrario* interpretation is made. One way of viewing this is to see it as containing a symbolic meaning, stressing the point that it is of *utmost* importance (in contrast to *only* important) to involve the national parliaments when the legislature intends to use Article 352 as a legal basis, due to the 'elastic' character of this legal basis. Another way of seeing it is that the presence of a special arrangement for the subsidiarity review in Article 352 excludes the exception provided for in the Protocol, which states that the Commission may in cases of urgency, exempt the national parliaments from the subsidiarity review if it provides reasons for its decision. In my view, the latter interpretation is the most plausible, since it is difficult to believe that the ECJ would rule that a subsidiarity review is only applicable in the event that the legislative procedure refers to it specifically. It also makes sense that the Commission should not be able to circumvent the EWM in the event that Article 352 is proposed as a legal basis.

National parliaments further have the right to be notified of planned applications of the ordinary Treaty revision procedure (Article 12(d), Article 48(7) TEU and Article 6 of Protocol No 1 TEU/TFEU) and of applications of the special *passarelle* instrument in the area of family law (Article 81(3) TFEU). They are also entitled to be notified of the receipt of EU membership applications (Article 12(e) TEU and Article 49 TEU).

In relation to the provisions that envisage an ex post evaluation by parliaments, they exercise in summary six rights (addressed below). The purpose of these rights to information is both to enable them to hold their governments accountable for EU actions but surely also to communicate to the national parliaments what goes on at EU level for the purpose of initiating a public debate on possible EU shortcomings. Thus, the provisions may also help to increase the transparency of the EU, which is an important aim for the Union.[4]

The six information rights which are connected to the ex post review include that national parliaments:

(i) should be informed of the content and results of evaluations of policies in the area of freedom, security and justice (Article 12(c) TEU and Article 70 TFEU),
(ii) have the right to be informed of the proceedings of the Council's standing committee on the operational cooperation on internal security (Article 71 TFEU),
(iii) should be involved in the evaluations of the activities of Eurojust (Article 12(c) TEU and Article 85(1) TFEU),
(iv) should also be involved in the political monitoring and scrutiny of Europol (Article 12(c) and Article 88(2) TFEU),
(v) in relation to annual reports, have the right to receive those stemming from the Commission on the application of Article 5 TEU on the principles of conferral, subsidiarity and proportionality (Article 9 of Protocol No 2 TEU/TFEU) as well as reports from the Court of Auditors (Article 7 of Protocol No 1 TEU/TFEU), and finally,
(vi) are entitled to receive the amended drafts and legislative resolutions of the European Parliament and positions of the Council on draft legislative acts upon adoption of the legislation (Article 4 of Protocol No 2 TEU/TFEU).

The rights of national parliaments, which have been included in the Treaties and its protocols, reflect in my view, a serious attempt by the Treaty drafters to actually put in place a system for the national parliaments to be involved in the EU decision-making process. This system would, however, not be able to function properly unless there were duties for the EU institutions connected to the rights of the national parliaments. The next section therefore addresses the duties of the EU institutions. It is, however, limited to analysing the duties connected to the

[4] Considering the fact that the Commission's proposal for a new Regulation on access to documents seems to have reached a dead end, due to differences in opinion between the Commission and the Council, on the one hand, and the European Parliament, on the other (which to a large extent concern the right to access to legislative documents), the respect for procedural requirements seems like a small compromise.

role played by the national parliaments in the ex ante legislative review. This is explained by the fact that the chapter focuses on the Early Warning Mechanism.

IV. Rights of National Parliaments Reflected in the Duties of EU Institutions

As noted above, rights of national parliaments may be reflected in the duties of EU institutions. This implies that each of the articles reviewed in the previous section, which entitle the national parliaments to certain rights, corresponds with an obligation for the EU institutions.

First of all, ensuring respect for subsidiarity and proportionality in the legislative process is a responsibility shared by the Commission, the European Parliament and the Council. The EU institutions are obliged to respect the principle of subsidiarity (and proportionality) in their work (Article 1 of Protocol No 1 TEU/TFEU). Each draft legislative act should further be justified with regard to the principles and contain a detailed statement making it possible to appraise compliance with the principles (Article 5 of Protocol No 1 TEU/TFEU). The same article sets out some instructions for what should be included in the draft legislative acts. The statement should further contain some assessment of the financial impact of the proposal and, in the case of a Directive, of its implications for the rules to be put in place by Member States. Article 5 even establishes the procedure for carrying out these assessments. It mentions that the reasons for concluding that a Union objective can be better achieved at the Union level shall be substantiated by qualitative and, wherever possible, quantitative indicators.

Reading the instructions addressed to the Commission in its capacity as the institution with the monopoly on legislative initiative, in conjunction with the time-limit (of eight weeks) for the national parliaments to examine the compliance with the principle subsidiarity (Article 6 of Protocol No 2 TEU/TFEU), it becomes clear that, for example, the obligation to provide a detailed statement in Article 5 is explained by the fact that the national parliaments are time-limited in their review and therefore require a good basis for their review. Another challenge for the national parliaments, which also reflects duties of the communicator of the legislative proposals (which, however, is not spelled out in the Treaty text or in the protocols,) is the fact that the national parliaments in many cases, have limited insight into the subject-matter of the legislative draft. This arguably puts pressure on the quality of draft legislation.

When it comes to the drafting of legislation by the European Commission, it should first be noted that, from a historical perspective, the Commission has been relatively free to decide on its own procedures for drafting legislation. It was not until in the early 1990s that general provisions aiming at controlling the EU's governance began to appear in the Treaties, but only few of these new provisions were aimed at controlling the Commission. Instead they targeted the Council and considerably extended the Parliament's prerogative. The Commission was quite closed at the time and did not reveal much of its policy lines before they were made official through the adoption of the draft legislative acts. These factors, jointly with the critique against the Commission for having too pro-active an agenda in the late 1980s, as well as the general critique on the democratic deficit of the EU, led to an increase in the supervision of the Commission. This is most clearly reflected in the Treaty amendments made in relation to the adoption of the Maastricht Treaty, which entered into force in 1993, through which the European Parliament was given powers to scrutinise the main posts of the Commission and even force the whole Commission to resign (Title III, Article 24 Treaty on European Communities (Maastricht Treaty)). Despite the added controls on the Commission, criticism of the Commission's use of power increased during the 1990s, mainly due to the shortcomings of the Santer Commission towards the end of the 1990s.[5] This led to a period of self-reflection within the European Commission, resulting in a White Paper on European Governance, which was adopted in 2001.[6]

In 2000, the Lisbon European Council requested a roadmap for the implementation of the EU's new ambitions to make the EU 'the most competitive and dynamic knowledge-based economy in the world, capable of sustainable economic growth with more and better jobs and greater social cohesion'.[7] With this in mind, the European Council found it necessary to improve coordination between the Commission and the other institutions. It thus asked the Commission, the Council and the Member States to set out (by 2001) a strategy for further coordinated action to simplify the regulatory environment. It is against this background that the so-called Mandelkern Group took form. The French government official, Dieudonné Mandelkern, was appointed the chair of the Group which consisted of high officials from the then 15 EU Member States. The group was tasked with developing a coherent approach and submitting proposals to the ministers, including the definition of a common method for evaluating the quality of regulation.

The findings of the Mandelkern Group and the Commission's internal review of which improvements had to be made to the drafting process pointed in the same direction. Each review summarised principles that had to be respected in the drafting of proposed legislation, and in the legislative process. Although they were 'packaged' through the use of different wordings, the conclusions of both evaluations included that respect had to be paid to some leading principles, including the principles of necessity, proportionality, subsidiarity, transparency, accountability, accessibility and simplicity.

[5] For an analysis of the resignation of the Santer Commission, see A Topan, *The Resignation of the Santer-Commission: The Impact of 'Trust' and 'Reputation'*, European Integration online Papers (EIoP), vol 6, No 14, 2002, p 1.

[6] White Paper on European Governance, [2001] OJ C287/1, of 12 October 2001.

[7] See Presidency Conclusions of the European Council Meeting in Lisbon, 23 and 24 March 2000, p 2.

As noted above, the Commission is relatively free to lay out its procedures for drafting legislation. It is, however, dependent on the response it gets to its draft legislation and this fact is probably the strongest inducement for the Commission to keep developing its drafting process. As noted above, there are, however, some requirements in the Treaties which aim at producing good draft legislation. In addition Article 317 TFEU and Article 5 of Protocol No 1 TEU/TFEU state that the Commission should carry out its activities with regard to the principles of sound financial management.

The current model used by the Commission for analysing its ideas for legislation is the impact assessment. According to the Mandelkern Group, this ex ante review contributes to the quality of legislation by giving fruitful input before it is too late to withdraw proposals.[8] It is, however, important to stress that impact assessments are rarely used to decide whether or not a legislative proposal should be launched, since the decision to proceed with legislation has already been made when an ex ante review is initiated. Thus, the purpose of impact assessments is to help the Commission to formulate and manage the legislative proposals in order to optimise the conditions for achieving the pursued objectives. Impact assessments are not used in relation to all legislative proposals, due to the costs and workload they involve, but the use of them has increased in the past decade. In 2006, the Commission also launched an internal control board, the Impact Assessment Board, which is meant to evaluate the methodology used in the impact assessments as well as make recommendations on improvements. These opinions are not binding on the Commission but they are attached to the draft proposals together with the impact assessments. In 2003 and 2008 respectively, the impact assessments were made subject to the scrutiny of the Court of Auditors. The Court of Auditors found that in principle, the impact assessment tool is useful but it also found that some revisions in relation to the methodology were necessary. In 2009, new guidelines for impact assessments were adopted.[9]

The use of impact assessments is stressed in this chapter because they form part of the material which is communicated to the national parliaments. In effect, they are used by the parliaments to examine compliance with the subsidiarity principle. Thus, it is of great importance for the purpose of this chapter to consider what the Impact Assessment Board has concluded in relation to the subsidiarity principle.[10]

As noted above, the Commission is obliged to present annual reports on the compliance of the subsidiarity requirements. In the annual report from 2009, it is stressed that the Impact Assessment Board in 34 per cent of the cases had given recommendations to improve the assessments of the principles of subsidiarity and proportionality.[11] In 2010, the Board asked for improvements in more

[8] Mandelkern Group on Better Regulation, Final Report (13 November 2001).

[9] Impact Assessment Guidelines, adopted by the European Commission on 15 January 2009, SEC(2009) 92.

[10] It should be stressed in this context that the Impact Assessment Board is an internal organisation within the Commission. This will be elaborated upon in further detail in the final remarks.

[11] Annual Report from the Commission, 2009 on subsidiarity and proportionality, p 3.

than 50 per cent of the cases.[12] In 2011, the Board remarked on 43 per cent of the impact assessments whereas in 2012 the number of recommendations had decreased to 33 per cent.[13] In 2013, the number was 34 per cent.[14]

Although it may be considered a step in the right direction that the Commission publishes reports and submits its own legislative proposals to audit, it is of little consolation to the national parliaments that the Impact Assessment Board retrospectively criticises the Commission for having provided insufficient reasons for its subsidiarity examination. The following section reviews whether the rights of the national parliaments are likely to have any substantial value if a case is brought to the Court on the grounds that the EU institutions have breached their duties.

Finally, this section will elaborate on the duty to give reasons as enshrined in Article 296 TFEU. The article states that 'legal acts shall state the reasons on which they are based and shall refer to any proposals, initiatives, recommendations, requests or opinions required by the Treaties'. Another legal basis for a general duty to give reasons is found in Article 41 of the EU Charter of Fundamental Rights (CFR) which enshrines the right to good administration. While the latter provision clearly targets individuals, being the subjects which are protected under the CFR, the former includes a duty for the EU institutions to provide reasons for their decisions (as opposed to a *right* for individuals and legal entities under the CFR). Another way to put this is to note that Article 296 TFEU is broader than Article 41(2)(c) CFR, since the former has never been limited to administration.[15]

As noted above, the EWM was introduced to add legitimacy and transparency to the EU legislative process. If respected, it provides an opportunity for national parliaments—and in the long run the European citizens—to have influence over the choice on whether or not a political aim should be executed at the EU or Member State level. Nevertheless, this goal may never be achieved unless those EU institutions which are involved in the legislative process take the duty to provide reasons seriously and thus describe their motives for pushing legislation at EU level. The Swedish Parliament is one parliament which has criticised the Commission for providing no or vague reasons for its legislative initiatives.[16] As was also noted above, the right given to national parliaments to receive information regarding EU policies reflects their need to be well informed in order to be able to contribute to enhanced legitimacy for the EU.

[12] Annual Report from the Commission, 2010 on subsidiarity and proportionality, p 3.

[13] Annual Report from the Commission, 2011 on subsidiarity and proportionality, p 3.

[14] Annual Reports from the Commission, 2012 and 2013 on subsidiarity and proportionality, p 2.

[15] S Peers et al (eds), *The EU Charter of Fundamental Rights: A Commentary* (Oxford, Hart Publishing, 2014) 1074.

[16] See the Swedish Parliament: Konstitutionsutskottets utlåtande 2013/13:KU:45, Granskning av kommissionsrapporter om subsidiaritet och proportionalitet m.m., p 14.

V. What is the View of the Court of Justice on Procedural Subsidiarity Review?

Before addressing the question of the legal impact of the rights of the national parliaments in supervising the subsidiarity principle, it is necessary to recall that national parliaments do not have direct locus standi in the ECJ. Their sole opportunity to invoke proceedings for breaches of the subsidiarity principle is by turning to their governments, as enshrined in Article 8 of Protocol No 2. The procedure for how national parliaments should address their governments to complain of breaches of the subsidiarity principle should further be laid down in the national legal orders. The presence of this article stresses, nonetheless, the importance of having a legal system in place through which national parliaments may complain if the subsidiarity principle has been infringed. The argument put forward in this chapter is that the parliaments should also be enabled to put forward complaints on breaches of the procedure for examining the subsidiarity principle and thus not only if they find that the principle of subsidiarity has been infringed. If the governments do not allow such complaints from the national parliaments, the rights given to them in the Treaties and in the two protocols will, in effect, be of little use.

Before addressing the case law of the ECJ it is necessary to elaborate on what is meant by *procedural subsidiarity review*. Such review examines whether or not the conditions for a legally valid procedure concerning the material subsidiarity review are fulfilled. To illustrate this it is possible to draw again on Article 2 of Protocol No 2. The provision states that

> the Commission shall consult widely and that such consultations shall, where appropriate, take into account the regional and local dimension of the action envisaged. In cases of exceptional urgency, the Commission shall not conduct such consultations. It shall give reasons for its decision in its proposal.

The provision thus states one main rule which reads that the Commission should consult widely and take into account the regional and local dimensions of the envisaged action. In effect, if consultations have not been held and if none of the two exceptions are applicable, the prerequisite for fulfilment of the provision has not been respected.

The first exception in Article 2 provides that the Commission has discretion to decide when it is not necessary to consult on matters relating to the regional and local dimensions. This exception applies when consultation seems to have no relevance. The second exception provides that the Commission may abstain from consulting in cases of exceptional urgency, provided that it gives reasons for the abstention. A strict application of the rules in Article 2 thus implies that if consultation has not been held it implies a failure to respect the main rule. This should in effect lead to a void measure. The reason for this is that the purpose of including the requirement of consultation in the protocol is that (on top of the benefit of consultation for the Commission itself when it drafts legislation), sharing the consultation documents with the national parliaments is expected to improve the analysis of the envisaged action, by enriching it with added perspectives. The fact that national parliaments have the right to take part in consultation confirms that consultative documents are seen as being useful for them. As shown by Diane Fromage in Chapter six in this book, it is particularly difficult to involve regional parliaments in the subsidiarity review. Since Article 2 of Protocol No 2 states an obligation for the Commission to consult widely, including taking into account the regional and local dimension of the action envisaged, it is clear that it should not be easy for the Commission to refer to the exceptions. Fromage's contribution illustrates the difficulty for regional parliaments to for example meet the deadline to transmit their reasoned opinions which in Spain amounts to four weeks. She also notes that regional parliaments suffer from a lack of information. In the following section, I will discuss whether it is reasonable to conclude that measures which have been adopted in the absence of respect for the procedural requirements should be declared void. This analysis will, however, be preceded by a review of the case law of the ECJ.

The aim of this part of the chapter is to analyse how the ECJ is likely to rule, if a case was referred to it where the complainant argued that the procedures laid down in the two Protocols had been infringed. These reflections are made in light of the case law of the ECJ where the Court has ruled on similar questions. What would be, for example, the result if the Commission 'forgot' to forward consultation documents (Green Papers, White Papers and messages) to the national parliaments? Article 1 of the Protocol, which provides that such documents shall be sent to the national parliaments is expressed as a mandatory obligation to circulate such documents. Would the ECJ apply the article strictly and thus declare the act void, stressing the need to protect the national parliaments in the decision-making process? Or would it stress that the national parliaments are not part of the EU legislature and that therefore, the measures should not be disqualified?

A case from 1980 suggests that the former reasoning is most probable. In the *Isoglucose Case*, the European Court of Justice annulled an act after having established that the Commission had failed to consult with the European Parliament.[17] In this case, the ECJ ruled that the competence of the Parliament to express its views was an essential procedural requirement, which, if it were not respected, could render the act invalid. The Court further noted that the article reflects at Community level the fundamental democratic principle that people should take part in the exercise of power through the intermediary of a representative assembly.[18] The power given to the European Parliament was thus considered essential for the institutional balance alluded to already in the Treaty.

[17] Case C-138/79. Judgment of the Court of 29 October 1980, *SA Roquette Frères v Council* (*Isoglucose Case*), EU:C:1980:249.

[18] *Isoglucose Case*, ibid, p 3334.

The Court case is admittedly 25 years old and concerns the role of the European Parliament in the legislative process (however, long before the European Parliament became part of the European legislature), and thus, the institutional balance of power could possibly be seen as less vulnerable today when the European Parliament has gained increased influence. Nonetheless, some further steps have been taken since the 1980s to strengthen the involvement of the citizens. Thus, it is argued here that the case may be used in support of the argument that the role played by national parliaments in today's legislative process should be protected in a similar way. This is especially due to the fact that their participation is seen as strengthening the democratic legitimacy of the European project, similarly to the role played by the European Parliament in the 1980s. At least this is true if the matter is reflected in the Presidency conclusions of the European Council as reviewed above.

The *Vodafone Case* does not provide direct support for the argument put forward in this section, but there are some relevant aspects in both the opinion by the Advocate General and in the judgment of the Court that deserve some attention here.[19] The case concerns a reference for a preliminary ruling from the High Court of Justice (England and Wales) and touches upon the conditions for telecom operators in the European telecommunication market. The judgment, decided by the Grand Chamber of the ECJ, was adopted in 2010. The main issue in the case was whether the EU had the right to regulate prices under Article 114 TFEU (former Article 95 TEC) and, if so, to what extent and under what conditions. According to one of the complaints put forward, the so-called Roaming Regulation infringed the principle of subsidiarity.

Advocate General Maduro took his starting point in drawing attention to the usual balancing between on the one hand, the interest to provide for a proper functioning of the internal market and, on the other hand, the goal to preserve the political freedom for Member States to choose among a variety of policy options when regulating the market.[20] When assessing the subsidiarity principle, he points out that it is not the task of the Court to examine whether or not the legislature is right in its judgement of the necessity to adopt measures at EU level, but rather the role of the Court is limited to compel the legislature to take subsidiarity seriously.[21]

In this part of his opinion, Maduro criticises the legislator for not having, in a sufficiently clear manner, presented arguments in support of the necessity to harmonise price ceilings at the EU level. However, since this analysis was missing in the preparatory works he made it his own task to examine whether there was reason to harmonise prices at the EU level. He noted that there was some reason to

[19] Case C-58/08. Judgment of the Court of 8 June 2008, *The Queen, on the application of Vodafone Ltd and Others v Secretary of State for Business* (*the Vodafone Case*), ECLI:EU:C:2010:321.

[20] Case C-58/08. Opinion by Advocate General Poires Maduro, delivered on 1 October 2009, *The Queen, on the application of Vodafone Ltd and Others v Secretary of State for Business* (*the Vodafone Case*), EU:C:2009:596.

[21] The opinion by Advocate General Maduro in the *Vodafone Case*, para 30.

argue in the direction argued by the legislator, thus concluding that the act should not be annulled because it did not infringe the principle of subsidiarity.[22]

According to Maduro, the legislator should have a rather wide discretion to decide on policy choices but it has to provide objective arguments on why the choices made do not infringe the principle of subsidiarity.

The ECJ did not bother much about the subsidiarity claim. It did, however, annul the regulation on the basis that it infringed the principle of proportionality. Neither did it follow the path of the Advocate General, urging the legislature to pay more respect to the principle of subsidiarity. What is more interesting in this judgment is the ECJ's reference to the impact assessment when it examines whether or not the measures adopted in the regulation infringed the principle of proportionality. In this part of the judgment, the Court in its examination refers to the conclusions made in the impact assessments. The ECJ thus used the impact assessment as *travaux préparatoires*, which is rather unusual in the EU context. This use of impact assessments is relevant for the argument put forward in this chapter, as it implies that impact assessments may play a crucial role in the interpretation of EU law. This highlights the importance that the Commission keeps developing its drafting methods for European legislation.

In another case, the *Deposit Guarantee Case*, dating back to 1997, Germany claimed, among other things, that an act should be annulled because the legislator had failed to justify how the legislation was in conformity with the principle of subsidiarity.[23] It is a particularly interesting case, since Germany had made no claims that the principle of subsidiarity had been infringed, but it blamed instead the legislator for having failed to state the reasons. In that case, the Court ruled that it was sufficient that the recitals showed that the legislator had considered whether it was necessary to adopt the legislation. It further noted that it is not a requirement that the principle is expressly motivated.[24]

VI. Looking Ahead—How is the EWM Best Protected?

The case law reviewed in the above section provides little evidence to support the argument that the ECJ would be open to annulling EU legislation which has been adopted in disrespect of the procedural requirements for the EWM. While the *Isoglucose Case* supports the argument stressed in this chapter, both the opinion of Advocate General Maduro in the *Vodafone Case* and the judgment in the *Deposit-Guarantee Case* point to the opposite direction. Both in the opinion and in the judgment, it was acknowledged that the EU legislature had failed to state the

[22] ibid.

[23] Case C-233/94, *Germany v European Parliament and the Council* (the *Deposit-Guarantee Case*, Judgment of the Court of 13 May 1997, EU:C:1997:231.

[24] ibid para 28.

reasons for compliance with the principle of subsidiarity. But instead of annulling the legislation, the Advocate General and the Court engaged in their own subsidiarity reviews. Such approach is of little use for national parliaments, whose role in the legislative process will be sacrificed. Nonetheless, it is important to stress that in none of the cases did the provisions of the Lisbon Treaty apply. Thus, it is still possible that the ECJ will protect the role of national parliaments in future cases brought to it.

The arguments in support of why the ECJ should protect the role of the national parliaments are the following:

First, if the ECJ would accept (ie not declare an act void) that the subsidiarity review examination is 'hidden' in the recitals of the draft proposal, as done in the case from 1997, it would mean that the ECJ does not fully observe the rights to information that are expressed in the protocols. Since the protocols acknowledge the fact that national parliaments are generally disconnected from the underlying discussions leading to draft legislation, it is a logical consequence to not accept legislation which has been prepared in disrespect of their right to be fully informed of the decisions.

Secondly, arguably, the duty to provide reasons (Article 296 TFEU) and the principle of good administration (Article 41(1)(c)), could support the argument. While only the duty to provide reasons is applicable to the European institutions in their legislative business, adding a further responsibility in line with the principle of good administration on the EU legislature would contribute to stressing the unique nature of national parliaments in the EU legislative process. Arguably, the comparison is not unreasonable since the development of the rights of individuals in EU law and the development of rights of national parliaments have moved in a similar direction Just as the rights of individuals have increased through a gradual process, national parliaments are increasingly given more rights. In principle, good administration is a requirement for a transparent, effective and independent management of all aspects related to the work of the EU institutions in their relation with individuals. Respect for the principle is an important starting point for the system of accountability to work effectively. This is of utmost importance when dealing with the lives of individuals, but in light of what is argued in this chapter, it is also important for safeguarding the role of national parliaments in EU affairs. Thus, for the point of argument, the ECJ should look into the possibility to establish a general principle that protects the role of national parliaments in the legislative process and which goes beyond the duty to state reasons in Article 296. The reason for this is that Article 296 seemingly does not suffice, as it does not acknowledge the special role played by national parliaments in the legislative process, instead applying generally to all decision-making involving all EU institutions. Arguably, the Protocol on the application of the subsidiarity and proportionality principle, which emphasises the special role of national parliaments, creates the necessary legal basis for moving in this direction.

This might be seen as too ambitious a suggestion, but in view of the many declarations made by the Heads of State stressing the importance of coming to terms with the EU democratic deficit, not to mention the democratic ideal established in the TEU, such principle might be necessary to make the point that the ECJ looks seriously upon the respect for democratic principles. After all, all which is brought into question here is how national parliaments should be given a fair chance to examine the principle of subsidiarity; thus there is no request for increased power made here.

Finally, there is another argument in support of the recommendation that the ECJ should effectively safeguard the role of national parliaments in the decision-making process. The approach could help the ECJ to keep its cautious approach to the subsidiarity principle, also after the adoption of the Lisbon Treaty, which formalised the EWM and the procedure governing it. By taking the procedural requirements seriously, meaning keeping open the possibility of even annulling legislation, which has been adopted in breach of the procedural requirements, the ECJ could maintain its cautious line and thus maintain the view that the material aspects of subsidiarity are for the legislature to assess.

As a final note in this section, the question of how cases of this kind may be brought to the ECJ will be touched upon. As noted above, the national parliaments do not have locus standi in the ECJ; hence it has to be the governments that refer the cases to the Court. Whether or not the governments will agree to bring this type of case in front of the Court will depend on all kinds of considerations including the position they had in the legislative process and their need for support from the national parliaments. Nonetheless, it should be stressed that one of the reasons for introducing the EWM was to involve the national parliaments more in EU affairs. Some of the chapters in this book show that, in some Member States, it is a slow process to create procedures for involving the national parliaments. Eventually, the national parliaments are however expected to be more involved. It is arguably in the interest of the governments to show that they, at least, are not fighting against this development.

VII. Final Remarks

This chapter has discussed and stressed the importance of according respect for the new role of national parliaments in the legislative process. In light of the function of the principle of subsidiarity, it is somewhat understandable that the ECJ has taken a cautious attitude towards annulling legislation for violating the principle. It is perhaps true that the judiciary is not in the right position to evaluate political choices. What no one would object to, however, is that the judiciary is in fact tasked to ensure a correct application of legislation. Seen in this light, it is very difficult to argue that the legislation, which has been adopted in breach of the procedural requirements, should not be declared void by the ECJ. However, due to the limited role played by the national parliaments in the EU decision-making process, and having regard to the fact that they have no direct influence over the outcome of legislation, it is perhaps still possible to question the argument made in this chapter. Would the annulment of legislation not lead to the result that national parliaments are given more influence than was intended by the Treaty drafters? Seeing it this way would however imply that the role of national parliaments is not considered in the larger context of the democracy debate that has emphasised the legitimacy of the EU, at least, since the Maastricht Treaty was signed.

As stressed in this chapter, the impact assessments of the Commission are subject to regular criticism from the Commission's own internal control board. As shown, the current Impact Assessment Board keeps asking for improvements on, in particular, the review of the subsidiarity principle. A good development is however that since July of 2015, the Impact Assessment Board has been composed of an independent Regulatory Board.[25] If this will result in improved subsidiarity examinations by the Commission, this solution might be an alternative to the suggestion made in this chapter. This naturally depends, however, on whether this new Board will be successful in its review of the Commission's impact assessments. In this context, it may be stressed that it is Article 5 of Protocol No I TEU/TFEU, obliging the Commission to state reasons, that is most likely to be infringed by the Commission in its relations with the national parliaments.

Furthermore, as also stressed in this chapter, if the present case law of the ECJ as well as the opinion by Advocate General Maduro were to be applied in a case where complaints on the procedural subsidiarity review are put forward, it would weaken the role of the national parliaments in the EU decision-making process. The reason for this is that this case law suggests that a defective subsidiarity review by the Commission (which is passively accepted by the EU legislature) will lead the ECJ to conduct its own subsidiarity examination, which should then be seen as compensating for the defect in the preparatory documents. As already stressed, such retrospective examination will be of little use for the national parliaments when the eight weeks have passed for their period of review. Only if the ECJ were to annul the legislation would the national parliaments be given a fair chance to exercise their rights properly.

The main reason for the ECJ to use its power to annul legislation adopted in violation of the procedural requirements for the subsidiarity examination, is, however, to show by example that the EU legislature looks seriously at the legislative process, and that the EU institutions actually take seriously their many agendas and strategies for reform and better regulation. This could even be seen as a contribution to the general EU aim of increasing its legitimacy.

To sum up this chapter, national parliaments have been given a role in the EU decision-making process with the prerogative that they may contribute to strengthening the legitimacy of the EU. Their role is partly protected by the presence of procedural requirements in the Treaties and protocols. Since the Impact

[25] Decision of the President of the European Commission on the establishment of an independent Regulatory Board, C(2015) 3263 final.

Assessment Board keeps recommending further improvements to the subsidiarity examinations by the Commission (*read* 'keeps criticising'), and since the ECJ and (at least) one of its Advocate Generals avoid putting the EU legislature in its place, it is fair to conclude that the rights of national parliaments are not sufficiently protected today.

Perhaps the concerns expressed in this chapter may sound distant to any parliamentarian who reads this text, which brings me to the last point of this chapter. National parliaments are still struggling to find their role in the EU decision-making process. They should be supported by the EU institutions, in light of how the role of national parliaments has been described by the European Council in several documents, as well as by the European Convention in the early 2000s. While it seems reasonable to draw the conclusion within an internal system, for example by the ECJ, that the role played by national parliaments is not so important that legislation passed in breach of Protocols No 1 and 2 should be annulled, it is possible that this conclusion would be drawn without looking at the bigger picture of how the role of national parliaments is protected in the practice of the EU institutions. Similarly, the Commission may find that the duty to state reasons is less important since the legislation may be reviewed ex post by the Court of Justice. Seen in this light, it is necessary that each EU institution that is given the power to evaluate the role of the national parliaments in EU affairs should keep in mind the bigger picture as well as the purpose for involving national parliaments in the first place.[26] This approach corresponds well with the ECJ's general model for legal interpretation. While the ECJ often engages in a purpose-oriented interpretation of the relevant legal rules, it also seeks to embrace the broader context provided for by the EU legal order. However, considering the few cases involving the procedural subsidiarity review that are brought to the ECJ for legal examination, the EU institutions involved in the legislative process hold the primary responsibility for making sure that the rights of national parliaments in the legislative process are given effect. That aside, the ECJ should arguably be called upon by the EU institutions or by the Member States to rule on cases where serious breaches of the formal prerequisites that control the involvement of the national parliaments in the EU legislative process are suspected to have occurred.

[26] Finally, a disclaimer should be made: Since I stand without guidance on how the ECJ would rule in a case of this character, nothing said in this chapter should be interpreted as critique against the current case law of the ECJ. All arguments are thus made *de lege ferenda*.

5

Interparliamentary Cooperation between National Parliaments

BRUNO DIAS PINHEIRO[1]

I. Introduction

The role of national parliaments in the European Union (EU) has not only become an important matter of debate at the political and institutional level, but has also attracted, in recent years, a remarkable level of attention from the academic community. In both cases, the discussions have been heavily focused on the way national parliaments are perceived by other actors (institutional players and academics), and less on how those parliaments (or those involved in their proceedings) see themselves.

This chapter aims at identifying the new patterns of behaviour amongst national parliaments in their adaptation to the challenges of EU affairs, namely highlighting the consequences arising from the fact that, over the last decade, they have been accumulating a considerable experience of cooperation in conducting subsidiarity checks and in the exchange of best practice and information in fields such as the Political Dialogue and scrutiny of their respective governments. In fact, it will be argued that national parliaments are no longer merely *formal* actors in EU affairs, but are instead developing new approaches and ways of interaction between themselves, and establishing formal and informal networks to facilitate the inter-parliamentary cooperation.

Consequently, the basic questions to be addressed are, first, how can national parliaments take advantage of these developments in order to achieve a greater impact of their scrutiny work, and, secondly, how can national parliaments benefit from interparliamentary cooperation in order to gain access to more information and expertise on EU affairs. Finally, particular emphasis will be given to the consequences of this greater involvement of national parliaments, especially in terms of the positive and negative outcomes of this strengthened cooperation in the Early

[1] The views expressed here are strictly personal and do not bind or reflect in any way the political and institutional position of the Portuguese *Assembleia da República.*

Warning Mechanism (EWM). This chapter is therefore an attempt to contribute to that debate by providing insight from the standpoint of an experienced practitioner and a direct observer of these phenomena.[2] In fact, the author has been dealing with these issues as a civil servant of a national parliament since 2006; first based in a national capital as a clerk to the European Affairs Committee of the Portuguese *Assembleia da República*, then as a member of the Presidential troika of the COSAC Secretariat (2007–08) based in Brussels, and finally as the Brussels-based Permanent Representative of the Portuguese Parliament to the European Institutions (2010–14). The author had the benefit of attending all of the different formats of interparliamentary meetings since 2006, from the traditional Conferences of EU Speakers and COSAC meetings, to the recently established Interparliamentary Conference on Common Foreign and Security Policy/Common Security and Defence Policy and the Interparliamentary Conference on Stability, Economic Coordination and Governance in the European Union.

In this context, there are four methodological remarks to be made. First, the approach followed here is mostly empirical and heuristic, which is a standard technique based on professional experience to promote and develop a more in-depth knowledge of a scientific area, oriented towards problem-solving and the identification of new patterns of behaviour of the institutional actors who operate in this environment, ie, national parliaments. Secondly, from a theoretical perspective, a 'broader neo-institutionalist' approach is followed, 'which recognises that institutions are not neutral containers fulfilling certain functional needs, but interact with, and are subject to, the behaviour of individuals working with and through them'.[3] From the author's point of view, this is vitally important to understand the multi-layered environment of interparliamentary cooperation, since it comprehends not only the institutional capacities set out by legal and institutional norms, but also takes into account the incentives, peer pressure and emulation factors that drive individual and collective actors within national parliaments. Thirdly, the title of this chapter means exactly what it says: 'Interparliamentary cooperation *between national parliaments*'. The purpose is not to neglect the role of the European Parliament (EP) in this cooperation, for it is an irreplaceable pillar of it, but to put more emphasis on how the role of national Parliaments in EU affairs is inextricably linked to and affected by the degree of cooperation they are able to establish among themselves. In narrowing the perspective to the cooperation between national parliaments in EU affairs, this chapter focuses on the developments so far, highlighting some of the achievements and shortcomings of that cooperation, and attempting to draw out some patterns and trends as to how this cooperation could be further developed and strengthened.

[2] The author would like to thank his friends and colleagues Christiana Fryda, Permanent Member of the COSAC Secretariat, and Derek Dignam, Permanent Representative of the Houses of the Oireachtas to the EU, for their comments and suggestions in the preparation of this contribution.

[3] K Auel and T Christiansen, 'After Lisbon: National Parliaments in the European Union' (2015) 38 *West European Politics* 261, 264.

Finally, as far as structure is concerned, the contribution starts with a conceptual outline of interparliamentary cooperation and its main features, shedding some light on its heterogeneity and multilevel complexity.[4] It then proceeds with an analysis of a matrix of the different existing interparliamentary conferences, assessing the diverse ways in which they are organised and what role national parliaments can actually play therein. The last section is dedicated to a critical review of interparliamentary cooperation between national parliaments, identifying some of the positive developments (ie the development of the network of representatives of national parliaments in Brussels) and submitting some proposals on possible ways to improve this cooperation.

II. Interparliamentary Cooperation—A Conceptual and Systemic Approach

A. The Concept of Interparliamentary Cooperation

As the former President of the European Council, Herman van Rompuy, put it in a very clear way,

> Decisions by one national parliament—be it in Germany or Ireland, in Slovakia or Portugal—are watched all over Europe. Maybe not formally speaking, but at least politically speaking, *all national parliaments* have become, in a way, *European institutions* (emphasis added).[5]

This assumption is very relevant for this study, because it places national parliaments as actors with influence at the EU level, while simultaneously hinting that this spill-over effect of their individual actions also suggests that there is a collective dimension. In fact, the perspective adopted in this chapter considers that the adaptation of national parliaments to the challenges of EU integration, in which they have often been described as 'losers' or 'victims', has been significantly influenced by interparliamentary cooperation.

From an empirical standpoint, which stems from the personal perspective of the author of this chapter as a practitioner, interparliamentary cooperation is conceptually regarded as the set of formal and informal mechanisms of exchange of information and best practices between national parliaments on EU affairs, not only on procedures and the development of institutional capacities, but also in the debate about topics of common interest and priorities which are selected for further parliamentary scrutiny. It can be described as an ongoing process of mutual

[4] On the involvement of regional Parliaments in the EWS, please see the contribution from D Fromage, 'Regional Parliaments and the Early Warning Mechanism', Chapter 6 in this volume.

[5] Speech delivered at the Interparliamentary Committee meeting on the European Semester for Economic Policy Coordination, available at: europa.eu/rapid/press-release_PRES-12-68_en.pdf.

learning, both at administrative and political levels, which aims at increasing the level of information that national parliaments have available to them to perform their *European role* and to raise their profile vis-à-vis other institutions, namely their role in scrutinising their national governments. However, the main question that national parliaments face regarding their cooperation is the following: how can cooperation in this particular institutional system be increased to the critical levelneeded to solve certain problems?

This is why this analysis focuses only on the interparliamentary cooperation between national Parliaments. There is a parallel question which refers to the cooperation between parliaments and the EP. Article 9 of the Protocol 1 of the Treaty of Lisbon states that 'The European Parliament and national Parliaments shall together determine the organisation and promotion of effective and regular interparliamentary cooperation within the Union'.

However, the perspective adopteds that the relationship between the EP and national Parliaments has some elements of cooperation, but also many areas of competition. To be able to approach this broader interparliamentary cooperation, national parliaments should aim to increase the critical level of cooperation among them first, in order to achieve more effective results.

The European Parliament adopted, in 2014, a resolution on its relations with national parliaments (the so-called *Casini report*), which sets out a very important proposal:

> interparliamentary cooperation must seek at all times to bring the right people together at the right time to address the right issues in a meaningful way, so as to ensure that the decisions taken in the various areas of responsibility benefit from the 'added value' brought by real dialogue and proper debate.[6]

This is relevant for this analysis, because it is considered that the more national parliaments are able to cooperate and build synergies among themselves, the more they will be able to find the *right people*, able to *address the right issues in a meaningful* way for both sides of the parliamentary dimension of European integration.

The often-quoted Article 12 of the Treaty of Lisbon itself seems to follow the same two-stage approach, for it states that

> National Parliaments contribute actively to the good functioning of the Union:
>
> …
>
> (f) by taking part in the inter-parliamentary cooperation *between national Parliaments* and with the European Parliament, in accordance with the Protocol on the role of national Parliaments in the European Union (emphasis added).

[6] European Parliament resolution of 16 April 2014 on relations between the European Parliament and the national parliaments, available at: www.europarl.europa.eu/sides/getDoc.do?type=TA&language=EN&reference=P7-TA-2014-0430.

B. Interparliamentary Cooperation as a System

Interparliamentary cooperation has developed, in recent years, into a complex system of interactions between national parliaments, on the one hand, and between national parliaments and the EP, on the other. In fact, adding to the most traditional and institutionalised forms of cooperation like the Conference of Speakers of EU Parliaments or COSAC (Conference of Parliamentary Committees for Union Affairs of the EU), other *fora* have developed, such as the meetings organised by the Parliament of the Member State of the Presidency, the joint committee meetings organised by the EP, and the most recently established interparliamentary conferences on CFSP/CSDP or on Economic and Financial Governance in the EU.

Moreover, several informal formats of interparliamentary cooperation have also blossomed, such as the Visegrád Group, the meeting of Chairpersons of South European Parliaments within COSAC,[7] the COSAC Women's Forum[8] or the different side-meetings that have been organised at the margins of COSAC meetings, like the informal lunchtime session 'on the role of national Parliaments in shaping and scrutinizing EU decision-making', that was held during the COSAC meeting in October 2013, in Vilnius.[9]

From the author's perspective, it is useful to try to categorise these different layers of interparliamentary cooperation and bring some systematic coherence to a reality which is often loose and lacking in coordination. This categorisation is not exhaustive, since it leaves aside, for instance, interparliamentary *fora* that deal with third countries, bilateral meetings or meetings of European political parties, and focuses instead on those meetings, both formal and informal, that add value to the work of national parliaments in their scrutiny of EU affairs, ie, that are the essential and recurring core of the work of national parliaments. Whenever possible, we follow the definition of each interparliamentary forum given by the Guidelines for Interparliamentary Cooperation in the EU, adopted at the Conference of Speakers of the EU Parliaments, held in Lisbon on 19 to 21 June 2008.[10] The Polish *Sejm* has also elaborated a comprehensive lexicon[11] about multilateral cooperation on EU affairs, which is a valuable source of information for this exercise.

[7] For further information, please consult the founding declaration adopted in January 2014 at: www.cosac.eu/51-greece-2014/meeting-of-the-chairpersons-of-cosac-26-27-january-2014/e1-9%20Declaration%20of%20the%20Parliaments%20of%20the%20EU%20South%20Nicosia.pdf.

[8] Founding declaration available at: www.cosac.eu/50-lithuania-2013/plenary-meeting-of-the-l-cosac-27-29-october-2013/g8-3%20Declaration%20EN.pdf.

[9] The main topics for discussion can be found here: www.cosac.eu/50-lithuania-2013/plenary-meeting-of-the-l-cosac-27-29-october-2013/f9-Informal%20Lunchtime%20Session%20Suggested%20Topics.pdf.

[10] Available at: www.ipex.eu/IPEXL-WEB/dossier/files/download/082dbcc54b222e18014b53e6a34d399b.do.

[11] Available at: oide.sejm.gov.pl/oide/en/index.php?option=com_content&view=article&id=14735&Itemid=750.

The details on the composition, rules of procedure, and other features are discussed later in this chapter.

(i) *Institutionalised*[12] *Conferences of Interparliamentary Cooperation*

- *Conference of Speakers of EU Parliaments*: its first meeting was held in 1963,[13] and it gathers Speakers of the Parliaments of the EU Member States and the President of the European Parliament. The Conference oversees the coordination of interparliamentary EU activities, and meets every year in Spring;
- *COSAC (Conference of Parliamentary Committees for Union Affairs of the EU)*, established in Paris in 1989,[14] enables the regular exchange of information, best practices and views on European Union matters between European Affairs Committees of national parliaments and the European Parliament. Its plenary meetings are held every semester, preceded by a preparatory meeting of the Chairpersons of all EU Affairs Committees. It is the only interparliamentary forum mentioned in the Treaties, namely by Article 10 of Protocol 1 of the Treaty of Lisbon;
- *Interparliamentary Conference on CFSP/CSDP*, established at the Conference of Speakers held in Warsaw in 2011, it provides a framework for the exchange of information and best practices in the area of CFSP and CSDP, to enable national parliaments and the European Parliament to be fully informed when carrying out their respective roles in this policy area. The Conference replaced the Conference of Foreign Affairs Committee Chairpersons (COFACC) and the Conference of Defence Affairs Committee Chairpersons (CODACC), and held its inaugural meeting in Paphos (Cyprus), on 9–10 September 2012;
- *Interparliamentary Conference on Stability, Economic Coordination and Governance in the European Union*, which was created by a decision of the Conference of the Speakers of EU Parliaments held in Nicosia on April 2013. This Conference gives shape to what is foreseen by Article 13 of the Treaty on Stability, Coordination and Governance (TSCG), which provides for setting up a conference of representatives of the relevant committees of the EP and of national parliaments in order to discuss budgetary policies and other issues covered by the Treaty. Its inaugural meeting was held in Vilnius, on 16–17 October 2013.

[12] By 'institutionalised', we refer to those either foreseen in the Treaties or which are based on a specific political decision taken by Parliaments at the Speakers' level.

[13] For a historical overview of this Conference, please consult: www.ipex.eu/IPEXL-WEB/dossier/files/download/082dbcc54af19e11014af1d1d7770017.do.

[14] History of COSAC available at: www.cosac.eu/documents/History%20of%20COSAC%20SEPTEMBER%202014%20EN.pdf.

(ii) Regular Interparliamentary Meetings[15]

— *Joint Parliamentary Meetings (JPMs):*[16] co-organised by the EP and the national parliament of the Member State holding the Presidency, in Brussels, to discuss broad strategic issues (eg Climate Change, enlargement), which are deemed important for both sides;
— *Joint Committee Meetings*: same organisational framework as JPMs, but held at Committee level in Brussels to discuss more targeted issues, like a specific piece of EU legislation;
— *Meetings of Sectoral Committees within the Parliamentary Dimension of the EU Council Presidency:* organised only by the parliament of the Member State holding the Presidency, in the format of Committee chairs, and held in the capital of that country;
— *Interparliamentary Committee*: Meetings held on the initiative of the EP, namely by one of its Committees, to which the homologous Committees of national parliaments are invited;
— *European Parliamentary Week*: hybrid concept developed by the EP, aiming at gathering members of national parliaments and the EP in meetings to discuss economic, budgetary and social matters (eg the Annual Growth Survey, as well as the implementation of recommendations for Member States issued in the previous year). The first Parliamentary Week of the European Semester was organised in January 2013 and, in 2014 and 2015, the Inter-Parliamentary Conference on Economic and Financial Governance of the EU took place simultaneously with the European Parliamentary Week.

(iii) Informal Interparliamentary Meetings

— *Meetings of the Visegrád Group*: Composed by representatives from Poland (*Sejm* and *Senat*), Czech Republic (Chamber (*Poslanecká sněmovna*) and *Senát*) and from the Parliaments of Hungary and Slovakia. It is a forum for exchanging best practices in matters connected with membership in the European Union as well as giving an opportunity to exchange views on current issues, and to coordinate positions and take common initiatives;
— *Meetings of the Chairpersons of the European Union Affairs Committees of the Parliaments of the South*: Established within COSAC, gathering Members from Croatia, Cyprus, France, Greece, Italy, Malta, Portugal, Spain and Slovenia. It was established in Nicosia, in January 2014.[17] It convenes

[15] This section includes all the meetings which are held on a regular basis, ie which are part of the calendar of activities for each semester adopted both by the parliament holding the Presidency and by the EP, being that some are foreseen in the Guidelines for interparliamentary cooperation adopted by the Conference of EU Speakers.

[16] Which have been gradually peetering out.

[17] Inaugural declaration available at: www.cosac.eu/51-greece-2014/meeting-of-the-chairpersons-of-cosac-26-27-january-2014/e1-9%20Declaration%20of%20the%20Parliaments%20of%20the%20EU%20South%20Nicosia.pdf.

twice a year before each COSAC Chairpersons' Meeting, to discuss issues of common interest, taking into consideration the proposed COSAC agenda and any other topics forwarded by other participating parliaments. The organising parliament invites candidate countries of the South, namely the FYROM, Montenegro, Serbia and Turkey to attend the meetings of the parliaments of the EU South as observers.

— *Informal Working Group on the Possibility of Improving the 'Yellow Card' Procedure*:[18] Established following a decision taken at an informal meeting of the Chairpersons of European Affairs Committees of Parliaments of the EU Member States held in Brussels on 19 January 2015. This Group was tasked with exploring the possibility of improving the 'yellow card' procedure and of extending the deadline for reasoned opinions from eight to 12 weeks within the current Treaties. Its conclusions were presented at the LIII COSAC meeting, in Riga, on 31 May–2 June 2015.[19]

From what is outlined above, one can conclude that interparliamentary cooperation can be defined as a web of meetings and conferences, gathering together different people at different levels (Speakers, Committees of EU Affairs, Sectoral Committees, Chairpersons), in different timeframes (annually for the Speakers' Conference, every six months for COSAC, CFSP/CSDP and Economic and Financial Governance, randomly for any other format) to discuss different issues (strategic issues, European semester, topics relevant for the EP, matters of concern for national parliaments), without necessarily ensuring continuity and coherence along the multiple and heterogeneous lines that compose this web.

Therefore, it might be useful to go back to a question alluded to earlier in this contribution: how can national parliaments take advantage of these developments and of this complex web to increase the critical level of cooperation needed to address the challenges they face in their daily activity of scrutiny of EU affairs? Is interparliamentary cooperation currently shaped to allow national parliaments to obtain more information and access to the policy- and decision-making circuits at EU level? Are national parliaments benefiting from interparliamentary cooperation or are they, on the contrary, lagging behind and lost amidst so many meetings?

With regard to the EWS, for instance, it is surprising to verify that the agendas of all these meetings and conferences very rarely included a specific item related to an ongoing subsidiarity check. For instance, in the case of the eight-week period for the scrutiny of the proposal on the establishment of a European Public Prosecution Office (EPPO), the most active Parliaments (eg the Dutch *Tweede Kamer*) used the margins of the Interparliamentary Conference on Stability,

[18] More information on the work of this group is available at: oide.sejm.gov.pl/oide/en/index.php?option=com_content&view=article&id=14900&Itemid=946.

[19] A summary of the proposals can be found at: oide.sejm.gov.pl/oide/en/images/files/koferencje/kartka/Summary%20of%20the%20proposals%20tabela_EN.pdf.

Economic Coordination and Governance in the European Union held in Vilnius to try to bilaterally disseminate information and gather support for a yellow card. A more effective subsidiarity scrutiny can only be achieved through a mainstreaming of the EWS in the coordination of the activities of interparliamentary cooperation, giving it the status of a permanent agenda item, for instance, at COSAC level. This could strengthen and give political leverage to the informal exchange of information about the EWS at administrative level that occurs within the network of Representatives from national Parliaments in Brussels.

III. The Matrix of Interparliamentary Cooperation and the Influence of National Parliaments

In order to find an adequate reply to these questions, the author has developed a taxonomy of the current range of meetings in the context of interparliamentary cooperation and tries to measure the influence that national parliaments exert in each one of them. For the sake of comparison, the most relevant examples of meetings that currently take place were chosen, leaving aside ongoing developments (eg the establishment of a Parliamentary Scrutiny Unit on EUROPOL), and choosing certain criteria (legal or political basis, existence of Rules of Procedure (RoP), agenda-setting, secretariat, composition and adoption of conclusions) that allow conclusions to be drawn on the added-value and influence of national parliaments in scrutiny of EU affairs. Based on these criteria and the empirical perspective of the author, the table below is analysed further down.

The perspective adopted here considers that the influence that can be played by national parliaments stems from four main factors:

i) the Chairmanship and the place where the meeting is held;
ii) who takes the lead in the definition of the agenda;
iii) who provides the Secretariat, and
iv) the possibility of adopting conclusions or contributions, including the voting arrangements for this purpose.

To a lesser extent, the composition of delegations is also important, but for two reasons:

i) if voting is involved, an adequate balance and compromise has to be found. In this context, COSAC is a fairly good example, because national parliaments and the EP are on equal footing in terms of delegations (six Members each), which has been deemed appropriate given the scope and mission of COSAC. If the adoption of any decision is made by consensus, numbers are less relevant in that a small number of parliaments is enough to block any decision;
ii) speaking time, because the larger the delegations, the less time is available for debate.

	Legal Basis/ Background	Rules of Procedure/ Troika or Trio	Composition	Chairmanship/ Agenda/Secretariat	Outcome	Influence of national Parliaments
Conference of Speakers (EUSC)	No legal basis. Ad hoc political decisions to convene meetings between 1963 and 1999, when it was decided to hold at least one meeting a year.	Yes: Guidelines for the Conference of EU Speakers. Informal trio: the current, previous and the subsequent Presidencies of the EUSC.[20]	Speakers of all NPs and the EP President	Chaired by the Speaker of the Country holding the Presidency of the Conference. The Presidency prepares a draft of the agenda, after consulting the trio. Secretariat provided by the Presidency.	Presidency is responsible for preparing its Conclusions to be adopted by **consensus**.	***Moderate.***
COSAC	Article 10 of Protocol 1 of the Treaty of Lisbon	Yes, last amended on 4 August 2011. Troika: Composed of the national Parliaments of the Presidency, the preceding Presidency, the subsequent Presidency, and the EP	Delegations of 6 members per Parliament, including the EP.	Chaired by the Chairperson of the EU Affairs Committee of the Parliament holding the EU Presidency. Meets every six months, in the capital of that country.	Adopts Conclusions (internal) and Contributions (addressed to the EU Institutions). Prepared by the Presidency, in consultation with troika.	***Moderate high.***

[20] According to Article 3 of the Stockholm Guidelines for the Conference of Speakers of EU Parliaments, 'The parliament of the member state holding the Presidency of the Council of the European Union in the second half of a calendar year will normally hold the Presidency of the Conference of Speakers of the EU Parliaments and organise the meeting of the Conference of Speakers in the first half of the following calendar year'.

				Draft agenda prepared by the Presidency Parliament, after consulting the members of troikas. Secretariat foreseen by Article 9 of the Rules of Procedure: composed of officials from the Parliaments of the Presidential Troika, and a Permanent Member who assists the Presidency Parliament and coordinates the Secretariat's activities.	Voting (article 7.5): consensus **or** a **qualified majority** (at least 3/4 of the votes cast.	
Interparliamentary Conference on CFSP/CSDP	Decision of the EUSC in Warsaw, on 20–21 April 2012.	Yes, adopted at the first Conference in Cyprus, in September 2012.	6 Members per national Parliament and 16 Members of the EP.	Conference is presided over by the Presidency Parliament, in close cooperation with the EP.	Conference may by **consensus** adopt non-binding conclusions on CFSP and CSDP matters.	***Moderate.***

(*Continued*)

	Legal Basis/ Background	Rules of Procedure/ Troika or Trio	Composition	Chairmanship/ Agenda/Secretariat	Outcome	Influence of national Parliaments
				Agenda drafted by the Presidency Parliament, in cooperation with the trio. The Secretariat is provided by the Presidency Parliament, in close cooperation with the EP and with the previous and next Presidency Parliaments.		
Interparliamentary Conference on Economic and Financial Governance in the EU	Article 13 of the Treaty on Stability, Coordination and Governance in the Eurozone, together with the decision of the EUSC on 21–23 April, in Cyprus.	**No rules of procedure adopted yet.**[21] General principle: troika composed of the current,	Delegations from the relevant committees of the national Parliaments and the EP.	In the 1st semester of each year, held in Brussels and co-hosted and co-presided over by the Presidency Parliament and	The Presidency Parliament may present non-binding conclusions on the outcome of the meeting.	***Moderate low.***

[21] For further information on the state of play concerning the adoption of Rules of procedure, please consult the Conclusions of the EUSC in Rome, held in April 2015: www.ipex.eu/IPEXL-WEB/dossier/files/download/082dbcc54ce35cd0014ce64535e5028a.do. We refer here to the general principles stated in these Conclusions.

		preceding and following Presidency Parliaments and of the EP	The composition and size of delegations shall be determined by each Parliament	the EP. In the 2nd semester, held in the Member State holding the Presidency and presided over by the Presidency Parliament. Agenda drawn up by the Presidency Parliament in close cooperation with the Presidential Troika. Secretariat provided by the Presidency Parliament.		
Interparliamentary Committee Meetings	Foreseen by the Guidelines on Interparliamentary cooperation, labelled as Meetings of Sectoral Committees	No rules of procedure or troika/trio. Set up entirely up to the organising Parliament, either the National Parliament of the Presidency or the EP.	Chairpersons or their representatives at Committee level.	Entirely up to the organising Parliament, either the national Parliament of the Presidency or the EP.	No conclusions, in general.	*Moderate; high if held in the capital.* *Low if held in the EP, in Brussels.*

In fact, to shape the debates in a balanced way, ie, to foster an exchange which addresses issues relevant for national parliaments and not only for the EP, cooperation between national parliaments should, in theory, focus on these factors and develop the conferences where its influence is moderate or moderate high.

In a scale that would have three main levels (high, moderate and low) and two intermediate (moderate high and moderate low), the perception is that within COSAC the influence of national parliaments can be considered as moderate high, for the following reasons: the Presidency Parliament holds a considerable room for manoeuvre in defining the agenda, ie topics and guests, and in the chairing of the meeting itself, through steering the debates. Moreover, the Presidency Parliament is assisted by the COSAC Secretariat in all its tasks, which performs its duties under the political responsibility of the COSAC Presidency and the Presidential Troika in each semester. Moreover, the COSAC Secretariat, where national parliaments are preponderant, is the only Permanent Secretariat in interparliamentary cooperation. The results of its work are of considerable importance to national parliaments, not only in streamlining the procedures of COSAC itself but also the knowledge-enhancing output it produces (ie Bi-annual Reports of COSAC, background documents). Finally, the influence of national parliaments in COSAC is higher with regard to the Contribution adopted, not only because it is drafted by the Presidency Parliament, but also because, if consensus is not reached, a voting procedure follows and no single delegation alone can block adoption. Given that the Contribution adopted by COSAC is sent to the EU institutions, ie the European Commission, Council and EP, which are invited to react to points raised therein, national parliaments have been using this tool to 'gain accessto' certain dossiers, calling for a reply from the institutions.

One very clear example was the process that followed the initial reaction of the European Commission to the first yellow card adopted by national parliaments on the so-called Monti II[22] proposal for a regulation: the Commission first reacted by announcing to the EP and to the Council that it would withdraw the proposal, claiming that it

> did not find that the principle of subsidiarity had been breached. However, having regard to the views expressed and the state of play of the discussions among relevant stakeholders, the Commission decided, on 26 September 2012, to withdraw the proposal.[23]

This could at first sight look like the position of national parliaments was weak, as the European Commission had not, at that stage, provided any reply directly to those Chambers who had issued reasoned opinions. However, those national parliaments which held like-minded positions on the issue gathered to propose

[22] Proposal for a Council regulation on the exercise of the right to take collective action within the context of the freedom of establishment and the freedom to provide services.

[23] Official statement available at the EC website at: ec.europa.eu/dgs/secretariat_general/relations/relations_other/npo/subsidiarity_en.htm#yellowtriggered.

an amendment to the agenda of the COSAC meeting held immediately after that, in Nicosia (14–16 October 2012), calling upon 'the European Commission to provide individual responses to the Reasoned Opinions submitted and reasoning for why it considers that the principle of subsidiarity has not been breached'.[24] The European Commission then reconsidered its initial stance and conceded it would 'provide individual responses to the reasoned opinions received from national Parliaments'[25] on Monti II.

The Conference of EU Speakers has gained more visibility in recent years, especially after the entry into force of the Treaty of Lisbon. This is due first to the need of having a Summit that gives an impulse to interparliamentary cooperation, setting guidelines and taking decisions on how to shape and develop this cooperation. Another reason for this greater visibility lies in the enhancement of the role of national parliaments in the EU itself, which motivates Speakers to engage and to take part in this process. However, and despite the fact that it is chaired, hosted and organised by a national parliament, the experience appears to be that consensus-driven decisions tend to undermine the influence of national parliaments. The EP appears to have a de facto veto right in all decisions. The hard-fought process of establishing an interparliamentary conference on CFSP/CSDP, in which the discussions had lasted for more than a year, mostly focused on the size of delegations, and was a good example on how this consensus-driven approach can paralyse interparliamentary cooperation.

The influence of the Interparliamentary conference on CFSP/CSDP was considered moderate, since national parliaments have the initiative in the remit of all the relevant factors (Chairmanship, agenda, secretariat and draft conclusions), but with two significant obstacles: any conclusions have to be adopted by consensus; but, more importantly, the composition of delegations (6 MPs and 16 MEPs) has turned this Conference into a heavy and lengthy exercise, very often not targeted enough in terms of topics, with little time for debate amongst parliamentarians.

On the other hand, concerning the Interparliamentary Conference on Stability, Economic Coordination and Governance in the European Union, the absence of concrete rules of procedure is hampering the influence of national parliaments, for it leaves the Conference—which deals with matters of the utmost importance for national parliamentarians, like the European semester or fiscal consolidation—in a grey zone: it exists, it meets, but produces no concrete outcome. Additionally, the fact that it is hosted in the EP in the first semester, within

[24] Point 6.4 of the Contribution of the XLVIII COSAC, available at: www.cosac.eu/48-cyprus-2012/plenary-meeting-of-the-xlviii-cosac-14-16-october-2012-nicos/h8-CONTRIBUTION%20OF%20THE%20XLVIII%20COSAC.pdf.

[25] Reply of the European Commission to the Contribution of the XLVIII COSAC, available at: www.cosac.eu/48-cyprus-2012/plenary-meeting-of-the-xlviii-cosac-14-16-october-2012-nicos/k1-reply%20to%20the%20COSAC%20contribution%20Nicosia.pdf.

the European Parliamentary Week, leaves national parliaments in a more fragile position, since the proceedings are led almost entirely by the EP and its relevant Committees.

Finally, as far as meetings of sectoral committees are concerned, it could be argued that we are facing two opposite worlds: if sectoral committee meetings are held in the Member State holding the Presidency, within its parliamentary dimension (eg meeting of Chairpersons of Committees dealing with Justice and Home Affairs), the influence of national parliaments is moderate to high: there are usually no conclusions, but the composition (only Chairpersons), as well as the power to determine the agenda and shape the debates around concrete issues or legislative files, are highly influential.

By contrast, if these sectoral meetings are convened and organised solely by the EP in Brussels, the influence of national parliaments is low; they have no say on the agenda, the speaking time is rather limited and often the issues covered are rather more in the sphere of the interest of the EP in a specific field than of the concrete interests of national parliaments (eg meetings on very broad topics such as the priorities on Justice and Home Affairs or on the role of EU Parliaments in global governance are undoubtedly interesting, but have limited potential to add value to the concrete scrutiny work carried by national parliaments back in their capitals).

To conclude this section, it is submitted that these assumptions, which ultimately might be contested and subject to further discussion, are of an empirical nature, based mostly on conclusions drawn by the author through participation in these Conferences, observation of their proceedings and evaluation of their effects on national parliaments. The critical perspective adopted is due to the fact that the effectiveness of interparliamentary cooperation between national parliaments, which is the scope of this study, is inextricably linked to the influence they perceive they can actually have in these *fora*.

IV. The Present and the Future of Interparliamentary Cooperation Between National Parliaments—Trends and Proposals

Interparliamentary cooperation between national parliaments, even though still incipient and in need of further development, is a dimension of the role of national parliaments in EU affairs that cannot be overlooked. A careful analysis of the recent trends and behaviours of national parliaments allows us to identify some creative initiatives from national parliaments, outside the scope of the matrix outlined in the previous section, but with the potential to strengthen their role in that framework.

At this stage, it is worth quoting the Chairwoman of the European Affairs Committee of the Danish Parliament, Eva Kjaer Hansen:

> On inter-parliamentary co-operation, there is still room for improvement. There are a number of 'inter-parliamentary' bodies that bring together members of national parliaments and the EP, COSAC being the most important. There is also a conference on the CSDP and the fiscal stability treaty set up a conference in article 13 that will gather MPs and MEPs to scrutinize the operation of the treaty and discuss wider economic issues. There has been a lot of talk produced at these meetings, but turning that into useful input for European decision-making is now crucial. We must reduce these long and inefficient meetings with too many participants, redundant speeches, too little genuine political debate and few ground-breaking decisions. *Instead, we have to be operational, innovative and solution-oriented.* National parliaments could be organized into clusters of shared interests and common themes to ensure a more constructive impact on European decision-making (emphasis added).[26]

The choice to quote this excerpt is made mainly because of the sentence which is highlighted: national parliaments, in their cooperation, have to be *operational*, ie practical and functional, *innovative*, ie with the capacity to invent new approaches, and *solution-oriented*, ie able to identify obstacles and seek ways to overcome them. This is the main trend we would like to highlight: national parliaments, while striving to fulfil their European role, are not stagnating as neutral containers merely complying with the functional prerogatives enshrined in the Treaty and foreseen by the Political Dialogue. They are interacting with each other, subject to the behaviour of other institutional actors working with and through them. Therefore, they should be seen in the broader neo-institutionalist approach that we have referred to in the introduction (section I).

In fact, national parliaments nowadays engage not only with their traditional and most obvious counterparts (national governments and the EP), but also among themselves and with the European Commission, in a constant learning process that should lead to a consistent search for the operational, innovative and solution-oriented ways to strengthen their role in EU affairs. In this context, the other trend that can be identified, and which is particularly welcome, is a shift in the motivation that drives this cooperation, ie gradually evolving from a combination of efforts to produce a negative output by blocking proposals on the basis of a breach of the subsidiarity principle in a 'subsidiarity-obsessed' way; to a new dynamic process that actively, proposes new paths and solutions.

The initiative of the Danish Parliament, adopted on the eve of the European elections of May 2014, called *Twenty-Three recommendations to strengthen the role of national parliaments in changing European governance*[27] is a milestone in the

[26] Available at: europesworld.org/2014/02/24/why-the-eu-must-boost-the-powers-of-national-mps/#.VX35uPnF8QE.

[27] Adopted in January 2014, available at: renginiai.lrs.lt/renginiai/EventDocument/6fa11f98-fc15-4443-8f3f-9a9b26d34c97/Folketing_Twenty-three%20recommendations_EN.pdf.

debate about the role of national parliaments in the EU and, specifically, on the paths toward, and solution-oriented ideas about, interparliamentary cooperation between national parliaments. In fact, it encompasses not only a diagnosis of many of the systemic shortcomings that national parliaments face, such as how to 'design a democratic framework that matches the EU's increased role and powers regarding economic governance while still respecting the prerogatives of national parliaments', but also proposes one concrete proposal (in a total of 23) for each weakness it has identified.

For the purpose of this contribution, the merits and limitations of the 23 proposals will not be reviewed. Instead the focus will be on those considered to have the potential, as yet untapped, to increase the effectiveness of interparliamentary cooperation among national parliaments.

One of the most important ideas put forward in this chapter is the right for national parliaments to table ideas and proposals, which means that their role is not only to act as the guardians of the subsidiarity principle, blocking and delaying draft laws, but also as proactive players in a constructive sense. This is what came to be known as the 'green card' for national parliaments, or their right to invite the European Commission to table legislative proposals either to create new legislation or to amend existing laws. According to the concrete proposal,

> The Institutions of the European Union allow a number of national parliaments meeting a threshold of 1/3 of all national parliaments to invite the European Commission to table a legislative proposal either to create new legislation or to amend existing. If such a request is submitted to the Commission, the Commission is obliged to respond adequately to the request and give its reasons for taking or not taking that action.[28]

Another idea, which is not entirely new, but which needs to be streamlined, is the pre-selection of proposals from the Commission's Annual Work Programme, aiming at encouraging national parliaments to draw up a list of prioritised proposals from the Commission's Annual Work Programme before 31 January following the publication of the Programme.[29] In the conceptual approach to interparliamentary cooperation, we have alluded to the purpose of 'bring(ing) the right people together at the right time to address the right issues in a meaningful way', evoked in the Casini report. For this endeavour, it is suggested that

> national parliaments invite the Conference of EU Speakers to adopt a code of conduct on good inter-parliamentary meetings, encouraging parliaments to clearly justify the purpose of the inter-parliamentary meetings they are hosting and specify what should be their outcome.[30]

National parliaments are also developing formats for cooperation on the margins of the official interparliamentary conferences, namely around what this

[28] Proposal 1 of the Twenty-Three Recommendations (n 27 above), p 2.
[29] Proposal 8, p 5.
[30] Proposal 13, p 8.

Danish paper calls *clusters of interest*, which are meetings in small informal sessions organised along shared interests (eg a specific legislative proposal, like the European Public Prosecutor's Office or the Transatlantic Trade and Investment Pact. The proposal tabled suggests that

> Parliaments organize small scale informal meetings along shared interests between groups of national parliaments on topical EU policy issues … with clear purpose and common understanding of what their outcome should be. They could serve the purpose of either coordination, exchange of views or simply mutual inspiration on issues of particular interest to clusters of parliaments.[31]

Meetings of this sort were held in Copenhagen on 11 March 2013 on 'The Role of National Parliaments in a more Integrated Financial, Budgetary and Economic Policy Framework' and on 21 October on 'free movement and national welfare systems'.

One of the most controversial but noteworthy proposals, of which the practical arrangements and implications are yet to be explored, is the idea that the COSAC Secretariat could assist national parliaments and the EP in preparations for the Interparliamentary Conference on Common Foreign and Security Policy/Common Security and Defence Policy and for the Interparliamentary Conference on Stability, Economic Coordination and Governance in the European Union. This would lead to a greater and more effective coordination between the different formats of interparliamentary cooperation, but would also help promote synergies in terms of the exchange of information and avoid unnecessary duplications, namely of the topics discussed or the conclusions approved.

These proposals, besides showing how national parliaments (or at least some of them) are reflecting on their role in EU affairs and the cooperation among themselves, also demonstrate how operational, innovative and solution-oriented they can be. Regarding the latter, some current developments are worth mentioning here.

First, following up on the initiative of the Danish Parliament in tabling its 23 recommendations on the role of national parliaments in changing European Governance, a group of 29 Chairpersons of EU Affairs Committees of different national parliaments addressed a letter to Jean-Claude Juncker, then President-designate of the European Commission, about the cooperation with national parliaments. In this letter,[32] sent on 30 June 2014, the signatories

> call on the new European Commission to set up a working group, to include national parliamentarians and representatives of the EU institutions, to look at the role of national parliaments in the EU. The task of the working group should be to draft an action plan on ways to strengthen the role of national parliaments in the European Union.

[31] Proposal 14, p 8.

[32] The full letter is available at: www.parliament.uk/documents/lords-committees/eu-select/Role%20of%20national%20parliaments/Joint-letter-to-President-Juncker.pdf.

The letter refers explicitly to the Danish initiative, suggesting that the abovementioned working group could be tasked with the following mandate:

> How can we design a democratic framework that matches the European Union's increased role and powers regarding economic governance, while still respecting the prerogatives of national parliaments? How can national parliaments contribute actively to the good functioning of the EU? How can we ensure that European citizens do not regard themselves as alienated from European decision-making?

Despite the fact that the European Commission has so far not replied to this letter, a couple of important developments took place. First, the new European Commission led by Jean-Claude Juncker declared that a new partnership should be forged with national parliaments. In fact, in the mission letter that the President of the European Commission sent to his First Vice-President, Frans Timmermans, in charge of Better Regulation, Interinstitutional Relations, the Rule of Law and the Charter of Fundamental Rights, Juncker stated that

> I want all Commissioners to commit to a new partnership with national Parliaments: they deserve particular attention and I want … important proposals or initiatives to be presented and explained in national Parliaments by Members of the Commission. This should also allow us to deepen the country-specific knowledge within our institution and to build mutual understanding and effective channels of communication between the national and the European level.[33]

The same was highlighted in the mission letters to all Commissioners, paving the way for a new approach that national parliaments must now seize.

Secondly, in this light, a very important initiative took place in June 2015. At the LIII COSAC plenary meeting held on 2 June 2015 in Riga, the Latvian Presidency included a point in the agenda to discuss the *Future of the Parliamentary Scrutiny of the European Union Affairs.* To guide this discussion, the Latvian Presidency presented a focus paper,[34] which acknowledges that despite 'a constant constructive exchange of initiatives and new ideas … when it comes to reaching an agreement on new procedures or the improvements to the existing ones, we often find it difficult to reach consensus'. Therefore, based upon the idea that national parliaments 'have accumulated much practical experience in the conduct of subsidiarity checks, political dialogue, the scrutiny of the respective governments and interparliamentary cooperation' this paper voices the most important question:

> What conclusions can we draw at this point and what are our ambitions for the future? Have national parliaments taken full advantage of all the available opportunities and instruments? Have we outgrown the role of guardians of the subsidiarity principle and are we now ready for a more proactive involvement?

[33] Mission letter to First Vice-President, in charge of Better Regulation, Interinstitutional Relations, the Rule of Law and the Charter of Fundamental Rights, sent by Jean-Claude Juncker on 1 November 2014, available at: ec.europa.eu/commission/sites/cwt/files/commissioner_mission_letters/timmermans_en.pdf.

[34] Available at the COSAC webitse: www.cosac.eu/53-latvia-2015/plenary-meeting-of-the-liii-cosac-31-may-2-june-2015/d1-9%20Focus%20paper.pdf.

Under the general heading of *Future of the Parliamentary Scrutiny of the European Union Affairs*, the debates that took place on the second day of the LIII COSAC meeting were focused on three main topics:

1) 'The national Parliaments' involvement in EU decision-making: state of play and overview of existing instruments', addressing the following issues: What has been the most successful aspect of the parliamentary engagement in EU affairs so far? Which aspects were the most disappointing? In which areas are improvements needed?
2) 'Green card: Towards an enhanced political dialogue' will aim at shifting the focus towards a more constructive and proactive attitude of national parliaments to EU policy-making. The 'green card' is perceived as an excellent opportunity for the willing parliaments to play a proactive rather than a merely reactive role.[35] The questions debated were: Are parliaments really willing and ready to play a proactive role in the EU agenda setting process? If so, should COSAC endorse the 'green card' as a new form of political dialogue? Can we commonly define this possible process of a 'green card' mechanism?
3) 'The European Commission's multi-annual work programme and the role of parliaments', which is linked to the discussions around the summary of national parliaments' priorities compiled on the basis of the Commission's work programme for 2015. The purpose of this debate was to take this one step further, encouraging an early involvement, analysing the following issues: What is the best way forward with the scrutiny of the Commission's annual work programmes? Is there potential for the national parliaments to eventually become involved in shaping the Commission's multi-annual work programme?

This discussion led to specific references under point 2 on Parliamentary Scrutiny of EU Affairs in the Contribution adopted by COSAC:[36]

> 2.2. COSAC emphasises that there is a general willingness of national Parliaments to play a stronger role in the EU through full and efficient use of the existing mechanisms,

and

> 2.4. … COSAC notes that the 22nd Bi-Annual Report indicated that a majority of the responding Parliaments would be favourable to the creation of new tools enabling parliamentary involvement and cooperation without formal Treaty amendments. In this context, COSAC acknowledges that there is broad support from the Parliaments for initiatives, such as introduction of the 'green card', also referred to as 'the enhanced political dialogue'.

[35] For further insight on the green card, please see the contribution from J Hettne, 'Reconstructing the Early Warning Mechanism', Chapter 3 in this volume.

[36] Contribution adopted by the LIII COSAC meeting, available at: www.cosac.eu/53-latvia-2015/plenary-meeting-of-the-liii-cosac-31-may-2-june-2015/h1-9%20FINAL-Contribution_Riga_02-06-EN.pdf.

Finally

> 2.5 COSAC invites the European Commission to support the Parliaments' willingness to play a more proactive role and to engage with both the existing and new forms of cooperation in full compliance with the applicable provisions of the existing EU treaties … in the spirit of its previously announced commitment to *forging a new partnership with national parliaments* (emphasis added).

As a follow-up,

> 2.13. COSAC invites the Luxembourgish Presidency to set up a working group on Strengthening the political dialogue by introducing a 'green card' and improving the reasoned opinion procedure ('yellow card').

In the aftermath, the UK House of Lords took the initiative of launching a 'pilot green card' with a concrete proposal on food waste. The EU Select Committee of the House of Lords adopted a proposal in this regard on 9 June 2015 and its Chairman subsequently sent a letter to all Chairpersons of EU affairs Committees, inviting them so co-sign it.[37] Regardless of the outcome that this specific pilot exercise might achieve, what is relevant for this study is the innovative and solution-oriented cooperation national parliaments are developing, giving shape to a new approach and struggling to raise their *political profile* vis-à-vis the other institutional actors, corresponding to some extent to what Herman van Rompuy meant when considering that 'at least politically speaking, all national parliaments have become, in a way, European institutions'.[38]

This spirit is clearly present in the abovementioned letter sent by the UK House of Lords to all national parliaments: national parliaments 'do not seek to infringe upon the Commission's right of initiative, but to complement it … they do not seek to challenge the existing role of the European Parliament, or the duties of the co-legislators in agreeing legislation' but they ask instead that 'given that a large number national parliaments have come together in support of this proposal, that the Commission should give *it due weight*, and respond appropriately' (emphasis added). National parliaments are therefore claiming their right to be considered with due political weight as European actors. It is too early to assess whether or not they will succeed, but the momentum is definitely here to be tested: only the unfolding of all these events will tell whether national parliaments will be able to seize it.

The final point to be made relates precisely to a very important tool of interparliamentary cooperation among national parliaments which paves the way for this momentum: the network of representatives of national parliaments in Brussels.

[37] This letter is available at the EU Select Committee at: www.parliament.uk/documents/lords-committees/eu-select/green-card/green-card-letter-to-np-chairs.pdf. The full debate and report was also made available at: www.parliament.uk/business/committees/committees-a-z/lords-select/eu-select-committee-/news-parliament-2015/green-card-food-waste/.

[38] Speech delivered at the Interparliamentary Committee meeting on the European Semester for Economic Policy Coordination, available at: europa.eu/rapid/press-release_PRES-12-68_en.pdf.

As mentioned earlier, almost all parliaments are currently represented in Brussels, based at premises provided by the EP, from which they develop their work of gathering information, developing networks of contacts and promoting exchange of good practice and parliamentary procedures, as well as being focal points for the liaison with the various European institutions. These members of national parliaments' staff, despite their independent professional activity, work closely together, on a daily basis, and meet weekly at the so-called Monday Morning Meetings (MMMs), used to informally discuss internal issues, such as matters of subsidiarity and technical preparation of interparliamentary meetings, and exchange information on the proceedings taking place in other parliaments. Representatives of EU institutions are often invited to attend these meetings in order to provide information and updates on specific proposals or portfolios. According to Ian Cooper[39]

> [t]he most basic role of these civil servants from the home parliament, is as conduits of information, telling people back home what is going on in Brussels and vice versa. But theirs is also an interpretive role, in both directions: they view events in Brussels through a parliamentary lens, reporting back home with an eye to what national parliamentarians care about; and they interpret and explain events in their home parliaments for their colleagues in Brussels. Having this group in place makes it possible for a national Parliament to know, in real time, the state of play in other Parliaments

of any topic, legislative proposal or specific dossier.

The first parliament to appoint a permanent representative in Brussels was the Danish *Folketing* in 1991,[40] followed by the Finnish *Eduskunta* in 1995 and the Italian *Camera dei Deputati* in 1998. It is interesting to note that the first two parliaments who took the decision of being permanently represented in Brussels are two of those traditionally seen as having the strongest systems of scrutiny, since they have the power to mandate their governments for negotiations in the EU Council of Ministers.

The 11th Bi-annual Report of COSAC,[41] presented in May 2009 at the COSAC meeting in Prague, devoted a chapter to the role of the representatives of national parliaments in Brussels, setting out some of the reasons behind the decision of parliaments to send a representative to Brussels. For example, the Finnish *Eduskunta* identified as the main reason the need for access to information by Parliament, so that it could perform its oversight functions of government action (note: this country joined the EU on 1 January 1995 and made the decision to be represented in Brussels in the spring of that year). When an assessment was made of the decision in 2008, the two main reasons for its continued existence were the flow of information, as well as the political significance of a permanent presence in

[39] I Cooper, 'A yellow card for the striker: national parliaments and the defeat of EU legislation on the right to strike' (2015), 22 *Journal of European Public Policy* 1406.

[40] Mr Peter Juul Larsen, whom we thank for all the wisdom and knowledge transmitted during the Portuguese presidency in 2007.

[41] www.cosac.eu/documents/bi-annual-reports-of-cosac/b9-11br.pdf.

Brussels. For its part, the Danish *Folketing* decided to establish an office in Brussels to improve and supplement the information to and from the EU, and to establish a mechanism for exchanging information among parliaments. The UK House of Commons office in Brussels

> should not simply be a post-box nor again just a glorified protocol office. It is in no way a replication of UKREP28: its prime purpose must be to act as a forward observation post for the House, and to act as the eyes and ears of the European Legislation Committee acting on the House's behalf.

In 1999, the French *Sénat* decided to create a permanent administrative office in Brussels so as to get access to 'a rapid and complete information at all stages about issues discussed in Brussels' and 'to be able to intervene "upstream" into the EU decision-making process so that the position of the French Sénat can be expressed as soon as possible, before the decision-making process is completely set in motion' as well as 'to alert the authorities of the EU about the concerns of the French citizens'. The Portuguese Parliament, in turn, pointed out that the main reasons to appoint a permanent representative to the EU were to benefit from the information network in Brussels, as well as having the ability to transmit positions or the work of the Parliament in EU affairs. Furthermore, the Portuguese Parliament felt the 'the need for access to additional, diversified and up-to-date information to provide qualitative support for systematic assessment of scrutiny of the legislative and non-legislative initiatives of the European Commission and of the European decision-making process'.

This topic is outside the scope of this study and would itself merit a separate academic analysis and reflection. However, it is worth pointing out that the steady establishment and development of a group of representatives of national parliaments in Brussels is gradually being perceived as part of a valuable working relationship at administrative level, which could help foster the development of the role of national parliaments at EU level and the ownership of EU affairs at the national level. On this specific point, the author's perspective is that this network is one of the most valuable assets for the interparliamentary cooperation among national parliaments, which should be further enhanced and developed. It still has a considerable degree of untapped potential, especially in the context of new initiatives like 'the green card'. Furthermore, it could serve to build the necessary bridges at administrative and technical levels that would facilitate the political contact and interactions that the interparliamentary cooperation must encompass.

V. Concluding Remarks

More generally, and on a concluding note, the first remark to make is that new patterns and behaviours are arising among national parliaments in their adaptation to EU affairs. As Auel and Christiansen put it, 'over time the victims of integration (national Parliaments) have learned "to fight back" and obtained new opportunities for participations in domestic European policy-making',[42] which means that even if it was 'a slow and uneven process', they have accumulated much practical experience in the conduct of subsidiarity checks, Political Dialogue, scrutiny of the respective governments and interparliamentary cooperation. In fact, while striving to fulfil their European role, national parliaments are no longer stagnated as neutral containers merely complying with the functional prerogatives enshrined in the Treaty and in their internal constitutional orders, but are instead interacting with each other and are being influenced by the behaviour of other institutional actors.

As far as interparliamentary cooperation is concerned, Auel and Christiansen refer to it as a dynamic that builds on, but goes 'beyond the traditional and highly formalised mechanisms such as COSAC or the Conference of Speakers', because while 'such long-standing institutions have been upgraded in the context of the Early Warning Mechanism, informal relations between parliaments have become more widespread and more important'.[43] This has fostered collaborations between elected members, and also between parliamentary administrations (eg the network of Permanent representatives of national Parliaments in Brussels) in a process to facilitate information exchanges or the coordination of activities in the context of the EWS, for instance.

This chapter is an attempt to contribute with proposals and ideas to the debate on whether national parliaments are benefiting from interparliamentary cooperation to obtain more information and access to the policy- and decision-making at EU level, by providing some insight from the standpoint of an experienced practitioner and a direct observer of these phenomena. Therefore, the subjective conclusion that one can draw at this stage hints at the fact that the development of interparliamentary cooperation has served not only those parliaments in the 'avantgarde', with more sophisticated scrutiny systems and greater resources, that are looking for support from others in order to achieve a greater impact (eg the pilot green card initiative by the UK House of Lords or the *champions of subsidiarity* in the *Monti II* yellow card), but also those parliaments usually referred to as 'scrutiny laggards' who seek to obtain more access to information or expertise through interparliamentary cooperation.

In this complex and multi-layered system of interaction, national parliaments are regarded as potential dynamic actors which are called on to contribute actively to a wider cooperation. Consequently, the more national parliaments are able to cooperate and build synergies among themselves, the more prepared they will be

[42] K Auel and T Christiansen, 'After Lisbon' (n 3 above).
[43] ibid 276.

to find the *right people*, able to *address the right issues in a meaningful* way for both sides of the parliamentary dimension of European integration.

But how can national parliaments take advantage of this development and of this complex framework to increase the critical level of cooperation needed to address the challenges they face in their daily activity of scrutiny of EU affairs? From the author's perspective, national parliaments, in their cooperation, have to be *operational*, ie practical and functional, *innovative*, ie with the capacity to invent new approaches, and *solution-oriented*, ie able to identify obstacles and seek ways to overcome them, exerting an enhanced influence in the overall process of policy- and decision-making at EU level.

In this context, interparliamentary cooperation between national parliaments should be seen within what some Auel and Christiansen call the 'incentives and driving forces of parliamentary actors',[44] ie the motivation of parliaments to use the institutional opportunities of interparliamentary cooperation to maximise their benefits in the scrutiny of EU affairs. Auel and Christiansen refer to two different sets of motivations with this regard: a) the electoral and career benefits that parliamentarians expect from their EU-related activities; and b) the chance of having a policy impact. In a context of asymmetric access to information, interparliamentary cooperation between national parliaments offers them access to a wide range of sources and interactions that have the potential to maximise the benefits of their involvement in EU affairs.

Against this background, the other trend which we find particularly welcome is a shift in the motivation that drives this cooperation, ie gradually moving from a combination of efforts to produce a negative output by blocking proposals on the basis of a breach of the subsidiarity principle in a subsidiarity-obsessed way, but, most importantly, by actively ex ante proposing new paths and solutions. Therefore, initiatives like the *Twenty-Three recommendations to strengthen the role of national Parliaments in changing European governance*, the pilot green card or the coordination and exchange of information and proceedings regarding the European Commission's multi-annual work programme are important steps to increase that critical amount of cooperation national parliaments need to take full advantage of all the available opportunities and instruments and to outgrow the role of guardians of the subsidiarity principle towards a more proactive involvement.

To conclude, while acknowledging that the EWM is a very important legal tool available to national parliaments, for it gives them a specific role in the EU decision-making process, it should not, however, prevent them from engaging in the policy-making process. In fact, scrutiny of EU affairs by national parliaments is a dynamic process that encompasses several dimensions beyond the eight-week period dedicated to subsidiarity. Therefore, the proposals submitted here, not-

[44] ibid 269.

withstanding the fact they need further discussion and elaboration, aim at contributing to a debate that places national parliaments as active, innovative and European actors with due political weight in the context of EU governance. There are many differences between national parliaments, their motivations, strengths, institutional capacities, incentives to cooperate, or event distinct objectives within that cooperation. Nevertheless, 'at a time when national parliaments have arrived in "Europe" and are there to stay',[45] the assessment of interparliamentary cooperation is an ambitious field of research for the future, not only for academics but hopefully also for practitioners.

[45] ibid 277.

Part II

Regional Parliaments

6

Regional Parliaments and the Early Warning System: An Assessment and Some Suggestions for Reform

DIANE FROMAGE*

I. Introduction

With the entry into force of the Lisbon Treaty in 2009, the regional dimension of the European integration process was strongly reinforced, in article 4 TEU especially. Indeed, in spite of the creation of the Committee of the Regions following the approval of the Maastricht Treaty, the Treaties had referred to the regional dimension of the integration process mostly in reference to the cohesion policy. Since 2009 however, article 4.2 TEU establishes that 'The Union shall respect the equality of Member States before the Treaties as well as their national identities, inherent in their fundamental structures, political and constitutional, *inclusive of regional and local self-government*' (emphasis added). Hence, this sub-national component of the Member States is linked to the constitutional identity in the Treaty.[1] Additionally, and most importantly for the topic of this chapter, the principle of subsidiarity, contained in the European Treaties since the Treaty of

* I am thankful to the participants of the seminar 'Los parlamentos regionales y el Sistema de Alerta Temprana: balance y perspectiva 5 años después de Lisboa', organised at the Pompeu Fabra University of Barcelona on 2 June 2015 and to those of the panel on 'The EU Post-Lisbon and After the Crisis: Challenges for the EU, National and Regional Levels of Government' organised in the framework of the Social Issues for Social Sciences—9th Max Weber Fellows' June Conference at the European University Institute (Italy) on 10 June 2015. I am further particularly indebted to the editors, to Cristina Fasone and to the parliamentary administrators who agreed to take part in the survey I conducted in September and October 2015. Of the 74 regional parliaments existing in the EU, 15 participated and have inspired the present analysis: three from Austria, one from Belgium, eight from Germany, one from Italy and two from Spain.

[1] See on this relationship: C Fasone, 'Regional legislatures in the early warning mechanism. When the national (constitutional) identity affects the cooperation among parliaments in EU affairs' *Federalismi.it*, 28 January 2015, pp 1–30.

Maastricht, now also specifically mentions the regional and local dimensions, as article 5.3 TEU reads, since 2009:

> Under the principle of subsidiarity, in areas which do not fall within its exclusive competence, the Union shall act only if and in so far as the objectives of the proposed action cannot be sufficiently achieved by the member states, either at central level *or at regional and local level*, but can rather, by reason of the scale or effects of the proposed action, be better achieved at Union level (emphasis added).

The regional and local dimensions shall further be taken into account by the EU Commission when preparing its impact assessments (articles 2 and 5 Protocol no 2). With these additions, the system of multilevel governance in the EU is now (at least formally) complete. Regions may also, of course, voice their opinions and concerns in the Committee of the Regions but the number and heterogeneity of its members make frequent efficient actions through this means unlikely.

In parallel to this recognition of the regional and local levels, national parliaments were granted particular importance in the new Treaties, such importance being visible in the attribution of a series of rights of information and participation, contained mainly in article 12 TEU, among which is their ability to control the respect of the principle of subsidiarity in the framework of the EWS. This inclusion was performed with the aim to improve the democratic deficit in the EU.[2] Such faculty was extended to regional parliaments too, although the relevant Treaty provision is far from being free of any controversy. This derives from the fact that Article 6 Protocol no 2 simply states that 'It will be for each national Parliament or each chamber of a national Parliament to consult, *where appropriate*, regional parliaments with legislative powers' (emphasis added).[3] Eight Member States have regions with legislative competences—Austria, Belgium, Finland, Germany, Italy, Portugal, Spain and the United Kingdom—and therefore, they had to provide an interpretation of this provision. Although this chapter does not aim at examining the detail of how Member States have adapted in order to allow for regional participation,[4] but rather questions the role of regions in this framework

[2] C Panara, *The sub-national dimension of the EU. A legal study of multilevel governance* (Heidelberg, Springer, 2015) 112.

[3] The French, the German, the Italian and the Spanish versions are also far from being clearer, as they respectively state: 'Il appartient à chaque parlement national ou à chaque chambre d'un parlement national de consulter, *le cas échéant*, les parlements régionaux possédant des pouvoirs législatifs'; 'Dabei obliegt es dem jeweiligen nationalen Parlament oder der jeweiligen Kammer eines nationalen Parlaments, *gegebenenfalls* die regionalen Parlamente mit Gesetzgebungsbefugnissen zu konsultieren'; 'Spetta a ciascun parlamento nazionale o a ciascuna camera dei parlamenti nazionali consultare *all'occorrenza* i parlamenti regionali con poteri legislativi'; and 'Incumbirá a cada Parlamento nacional o a cada cámara de un Parlamento nacional consultar, *cuando proceda*, a los Parlamentos regionales que posean competencias legislativas' (emphasis added).

[4] This question has been thoroughly analysed in two studies prepared for the Committee of the regions: D Bourdin and G Vara Arribas, *The Role of Regional Parliaments in the Process of Subsidiarity Analysis within the Early Warning System of the Lisbon Treaty* (Brussels, Committee of the Regions, 2011) and P Schmitt, T Ruys and A Marx, *The Subsidiarity Early Warning System of the Lisbon Treaty—the Role of Regional Parliaments with Legislative Powers and Other Subnational Authorities* (Brussels, Committee of the Regions, 2013). See also C Fasone, 'Italian Regional Councils and the Positive

on a conceptual level, it should be mentioned that of these eight states, only one—Austria—has a parliamentary chamber composed solely of representatives of the regional parliaments. Indeed, in Belgium, for instance, the Senate is composed of 50 Senators delegated from the Communities and Regions and of 10 Senators designated on the basis of the results of the elections of the House of Representatives. In Germany, representatives of the regional governments—and not the regional parliaments—make up the *Bundesrat*, whereas in Italy and in Spain, in spite of the extended competences which the regions own, they are not represented as such in the Senate (Italy)[5] or form only a minority (Spanish Senate). As we will see in the second section of this chapter, this does not mean that regional parliaments cannot effectively participate in the Early Warning Mechanism (EWS) in the Member States other than Austria, but this indirect participation will necessarily require the establishment of formal or informal procedures of participation. For this and other reasons explored in this chapter, regional participation in the EWS can be uneasy, and six years after the entry into force of the Lisbon Treaty is still characterised by instability. This raises the issue of the desirability of the systematic participation of regional parliaments in this framework and of the possibility to consult other regions with no legislative competence in the spirit of subsidiarity taken in the broader framework of the Political Dialogue. Their participation in this informal dialogue with the EU Commission could indeed contribute to enhancing participatory democracy, by hosting public debates on EU matters that are often considered to be contributing to the European democratic deficit.[6] Besides, some regions with no legislative competences do have indirectly elected assemblies too. In sum, this highlights the need to reflect on the role of regions in the EU and a potential need for reform in order to guarantee the democratic character of the EU and stop the erosion of the citizens' trust in the European project.[7]

II. The Participation of Regional Parliaments with Legislative Competences in the Early Warning System

An overview of the situation in terms of the possibilities opened to the regional parliaments with legislative competences is first in order, six years after the entry

Externalities of the Early Warning Mechanism for National Constitutional Law' (Chapter 8) and W Vandenbruwaene and P Popelier, 'Belgian Parliaments and the Early Warning System' (Chapter 9), both in this volume.

[5] A reform of the composition of the Italian Senate is, however, in preparation in June 2016. See further on this reform C Fasone, 'Italian Regional Councils and the Positive Externalities of the Early Warning Mechanism for National Constitutional Law', Chapter 8 in this volume.

[6] O Cramme and SB Hobolt, 'A European Union under stress' in O Cramme and SB Hobolt (eds), *Democratic politics in a European Union under stress* (Oxford, Oxford University Press, 2015) 8.

[7] Erosion evidenced by Cramme and Hobolt, *A European Union under stress* (n 6 above) 3.

into force of the Lisbon Treaty. Indeed, as has been mentioned in the Introduction, only in Austria are the delegates from the parliaments of the *Länder* components of one of the two national legislative chambers. In the other Member States, regions can also be represented in the higher chamber but other members of the same chambers may be designated on another (sometimes territorially defined) basis, as is for instance the case in Spain where 'The Senate is the House of territorial representation' (article 69-1 Spanish Constitution).

A. Formal and Informal Possibilities of Regional Participation

Despite these differences, some formal and informal mechanisms have been developed in order to allow for the participation of regional parliaments in the EWS, although the binding character of the opinions expressed by regional legislatures is not always in accordance with the actual competences held by regions. This issue can have several dimensions. In the worst case, the opinion defended by regional parliament(s) can be fully ignored by the national parliament—which, according to the Treaties, has the two votes allocated to that specific Member State—even if it has (or they have) exclusive competences in the domain affected by the European legislative proposal. Even in such circumstances, they may not even be consulted. In this respect, important differences exist among the eight Member States that have regions with legislative competences.

For instance, the German *Bundesrat*—composed of delegates of the regional governments—always has one of the two votes attributed to Germany in the framework of the EWS, even when the proposal at stake does not affect competences of the *Länder* (article 11-1 Responsibility for Integration Act). Note that the regional *parliaments* are not mentioned as such in any of the laws allowing for the participation of the chambers in EU affairs; the *Bundestag* and the *Bundesrat* are, in fact, the only addressees of these three laws which are the Responsibility for Integration Act, the Act on Cooperation between the Federal Government and the German Bundestag in Matters Concerning the European Union and the Act on Cooperation between the Federation and Länder in European Union Matters.[8]

By contrast, in Spain, the parliaments of the Autonomous Communities will, in the end, always depend on the final decision made by the Joint Committee on European Affairs which is common to both parliamentary chambers. The Law of modification of Law 8/1994, through which the Joint Committee on European Affairs is regulated for its adaptation to the Lisbon Treaty (Law 24/2009), merely foresees that regional parliaments will have four weeks to transmit their opinions to the Joint Committee. These opinions will then be taken into account—but they are not binding—and annexed to the reasoned opinion prepared by the

[8] The regional parliaments were also not mentioned in the Lisbon decision of the Federal Constitutional Court (2 BvE 2/08).

Joint Committee, if the Joint Committee considers too that there is a breach of subsidiarity (article 6-2 and 6-3 Law 24/2009). If this is not the case, the regional opinion is simply ignored and not sent to the EU institutions by the Joint Committee. Therefore a reasoned opinion issued by a regional parliament is by no means binding or even determinant in the Joint Committee's assessment, even if the European legislative proposal affects exclusive competences of the region that has transmitted an opinion. In fact, regional opinions have almost never triggered an ad hoc analysis of the principle of subsidiarity by the Joint Committee.

A similar situation exists in Italy, although recent developments have reinforced the relationship between Senate and regions and, hence, the regional influence.[9]

In Portugal, the two regional assemblies can be heard by the European Affairs Committee to whom they can submit their opinions. Where the regional and the national opinions differ, the national one shall prevail but the regional opinions will be attached to the national one when it is sent to the EU institutions.[10] This procedure was followed, for example, in the framework of the reasoned opinion that the Portuguese Parliament submitted on the Proposal for a Directive of the European Parliament and of the Council on the approximation of the laws, regulations and administrative provisions of the Member States concerning the manufacture, presentation and sale of tobacco and related products (COM(2012) 788 final). In this case, the Portuguese Parliament submitted its reasoned opinion to which it attached, among others, an opinion of the Assembly of Açores also concluding that a breach had occurred and an opinion of the Assembly of Madeira which did not find there was any issue of subsidiarity.

The situation of the British devolved assemblies is somewhat different. In the House of Lords, 'If a potential subsidiarity issue is detected, some or all of the devolved assemblies *may* be alerted, at staff level, on a case-by-case basis' (emphasis added).[11] Hence, the devolved assemblies depend first of all on the House of Lords' decision to consult them—or not. No indication as to how their opinions are then treated is given. In the House of Commons, the situation is slightly more beneficial for the devolved assemblies since a detailed, yet informal, procedure has been defined. As for the Commons European Scrutiny Committee, it does not filter the proposals, as it 'considers that it would not be in a position to act on behalf of the regional parliaments spotting what for them might be objectionable

[9] See Cristina Fasone's contribution in this volume. Also: L Bartolucci, 'In attesa del "nuovo" Senato, un canale di collegamento più fluido con i Consigli regionali negli affari dell'Unione europea' (2014) 3 *Osservatoriosullefonti.it* and C Fasone, 'In attesa della riforma costituzionale, alcune recenti evoluzioni nella 14ª Commissione del Senato sui raccordi tra Stato, Regioni e Unione europea' (2015) 1 *Forum di Quaderni costituzionali Rassegna*.

[10] P Schmitt et al, *The Subsidiarity Early Warning System of the Lisbon Treaty* (n 4 above) 78.

[11] House of Lords, European Union Committee, Annual Report 2009, Appendix 8 'Committee procedures for a reasoned opinion on subsidiarity'. See more generally on the subsidiarity scrutiny by the UK Parliament: A Cygan, 'Parliamentary Scrutiny of EU Affairs by the UK Parliament: The Primacy of Ministerial Accountability', Chapter 13 in this volume.

proposals'.[12] Therefore, it requires the devolved assemblies to find and examine the EU legislative proposals and warn it in case they have objections. Additionally, a devolved assembly that has previously raised issues of subsidiarity should be allowed to express its opinion on the draft reasoned opinion prepared by the European Scrutiny Committee.[13] Where this is not possible because the opinion has already been submitted to the plenary, or where the Scrutiny Committee disagrees with the devolved assembly's views, it is invited to submit its opinion to the Committee so that it is forwarded to the Government.[14] Thanks to this access that regions have to the British government—whose voice arguably counts more in the Council than that of the House of Commons in the framework of the EWS—they, at least, have the guarantee that their opinion will eventually be taken into account which is not the case of the Italian and the Spanish regions for example. The British devolved assemblies do not make a frequent use of their right, though. One explanation for this may lie in the fact that the regional and the national governments regularly cooperate and therefore it may not be needed for the devolved assemblies to issue any reasoned opinion, especially as the unity of the British position in EU matters is granted particular importance.[15]

By contrast, the situation of the only existing regional parliament of Finland, the Åland Parliament, is particularly protective since its reasoned opinion—issued within a period of six weeks—will then be examined in the Grand Committee of the national parliament and attached to the communication transmitted to the EU Commission, even if the Finnish national parliament decides not to issue a reasoned opinion itself.[16] In fact, the regional parliament can be at the origin of the scrutiny procedure—which is not automatic and can be requested by the Grand Committee, the appropriate committee and the regional parliament which all are forwarded the EU legislative proposals. In case the Åland Parliament requests it, the Grand Committee is in fact obliged to conduct a subsidiarity check.[17]

In Belgium, regions and communities can actually use the votes available to the Federal Parliament in the framework of the EWS. The complex system existing strictly attributes the votes to the competent parliament(s) in accordance with the draft inter-parliamentary cooperation agreement organising the participation

[12] COSAC, 'Annex to the 13th biannual report of COSAC: National Parliaments' replies to the questionnaire' (2010) 492.

[13] In the House of Commons, reasoned opinions are always submitted and approved in plenary.

[14] COSAC, 'Annex to the 13th biannual report of COSAC' (n 12 above) 492.

[15] As remarked by David Melding, Member of the Welsh Parliament: 'Within the UK, engagement with the European Union is considered part of foreign policy and as such remains a reserved competence of the UK Government. Therefore, direct relations between the UK and the EU Institutions, in theory, are the preserve of the UK Government'. D Melding, 'Role of sub-National Parliaments in the EU', paper presented at the conference 'Parlamenti nazionali e Unione Europea nella governance multilivello' held at the Italian Chamber of deputies on 15 March 2015, p 3.

[16] This obligation derives from art 59a of the Act on the Autonomy of Åland. Finland-Åland REGPEX profile available at: extranet.cor.europa.eu/subsidiarity/maps/pages/Regions.aspx?Region=FIAL (last consulted: 25 May 2015).

[17] Schmitt et al, *The Subsidiarity Early Warning System of the Lisbon Treaty* (n 4 above) 42.

of the regional and community parliaments in the application of the subsidiarity scrutiny mechanism, which never entered into force but is de facto generally applied.[18] As a consequence, a regional parliament can be attributed directly one of the two Belgian votes.

B. Common Features in the Mechanisms Designed at Regional Level

The elements mentioned so far actually concern the possibility for the regional opinions to be taken into account *at national level* since, as has been underlined in the introduction, the regional parliaments have not been guaranteed any independent right of participation in the Treaty. Nonetheless, in order for this participation to be possible in the first place, regional parliaments ought to design internal procedures too. Although this analysis does not aim at examining each and every single mechanism existing within the 74 regional assemblies, some distinctive elements can be highlighted.[19]

First, the pace with which all regional assemblies have adapted varied widely. In Spain, for instance, the contemporary revision process of the Statutes of Autonomy (regional constitutions) was used in order to anchor the subsidiarity check and allow for regional participation early on—before this was even possible at national level in fact.[20] In contrast, in Germany the adaptation of (some of) the Landtage was much slower and took place in 2010–11,[21] and the same applies to the Belgian regional parliaments as, for instance, the Brussels-Capital region parliament still had not defined any procedure in 2013.[22]

Secondly, another distinctive element of regional parliaments in this framework is the high frequency of the changes in the internal procedures designed in some States, at least where no guarantee exists at national level. In the Catalan Parliament, for instance, the practice has evolved and the legal services do not produce systematic reports on each EU legislative proposal as they used to after the entry into force of the Lisbon Treaty. In fact, the personalities of the deputies involved

[18] See also Patricia Popelier's and Werner Vandenbruewene's contribution on Belgium, Chapter 9 in this volume.

[19] These mechanisms have been examined in several studies among which: V Cuesta López, 'El escrutinio de los asuntos europeos por los Parlementos británicos : la participación de las Asambleas Legislativas de Escocia, Gales e Irlanda del Norte en el control del Principio de Subsidiariedad' in JI Navarro Méndez (ed), *Parlamentos regionales europeos y principio de subsidiariedad* (Madrid, Aranzadi, 2014). See also n 4 above.

[20] AM Carmona Contreras, '¿Hacia la europeización de los parlamentos autonómicos? Reflexiones al hilo del Mecanismo de Alerta Temprana' (2012) 16 *Revista d'Estudis Autonòmics i Federals* 141, 153.

[21] G Abels, 'Sub-national Parliaments in a Multi-Level Parliamentary System—Reform Processes in the German Länder in the Post-Lisbon Era' (2012) UACES Conference, Passau, 3–5 September 2012, p 13. The required reforms have now been fully implemented though. A Buzogány and J Häsing, 'Europäisierung des deutschen Landesparlamentarismus ? Zur Rolle der Landtagsverwaltungen' (2015) 46 *Zeitschrift für Parlamentsfragen* 128, 137.

[22] P Schmitt et al, *The Subsidiarity Early Warning System of the Lisbon Treaty* (n 4 above) 34.

have a strong influence on the importance that the subsidiarity check will assume in that Parliament.[23] The Parliament of the Basque country also contemplated modifying the practice according to which it approves a resolution on each and every single European legislative proposal it receives but, so far, no reform has been approved. The Assembly of Castilla y León also changed the identity of the organ in charge of the subsidiarity check; first it was the EU Affairs Committee, but from 2011 onwards it was changed to the Presidency Committee.[24] Also in Wales the Assembly modified its procedure in the framework of a general mainstreaming of EU affairs among the committees of the Assembly launched in 2011. As a result, the dedicated European and External Affairs Committee was abolished and the Constitutional and Legislative Affairs Committee now plays a central role in the examination of the respect of the principle of subsidiarity.[25] As mentioned, one element that may contribute to these changes may be the lack of a formal guarantee. Deputies who are unsure that their opinion will be considered may prefer to dedicate their efforts to other more fruitful tasks which are, additionally, likely to be more important for their re-election. Only committed Europeans could find the participation in the EWS attractive per se.

In addition to these variations in the adaptation of the eight Member States whose regions have legislative powers, some elements common to all regional parliaments in fact invite reflection as to the desirability of a regional participation in the EWS or, at least, the frequency with which this participation should take place.

III. Is a Systematic Regional Participation in the EWS Desirable in the Current Context?

Several elements of a practical nature especially indicate that the participation of regional parliaments in the EWS as it now stands may, in fact, not be desirable at this stage or that it should be strictly targeted on the legislative proposals that seriously affect the interest of the regions in question.

A. Timeframe for Regional Participation

One of the elements that speak in favour of a strictly targeted regional participation is linked to the time constraints the EU Treaties impose for the subsidiarity

[23] This is, however, not a specificity of the regional level since, in Spain too, at the national level the activity of the Joint Committee is closely linked to the activism of some of its members.

[24] L Seseña Santos, 'La participación de las Cortes de Castilla y León en los asuntos europeos' in P Andrés Sáenz de Santa María and JI Ugartemendia Eceizabarrena (eds), *El Parlamento europeo: ¿esta vez es diferente?* (Guipúzcoa, IVAP, 2015) 277.

[25] Melding, 'Role of sub-National Parliaments in the EU' (n 15 above) 4.

check. National parliaments have eight weeks at their disposal to perform their control. As a result, regional parliaments—which, except from the German ones,[26] depend on their national counterparts—need to perform their control within a few weeks if they want their opinions to be taken into account. Several Member States have established a deadline for the regional parliaments to transmit their reasoned opinions, ranging from four weeks in Spain (article 6-2 of Law 24/2009) to six weeks in Finland and Portugal. On the other hand, neither Italy, nor the United Kingdom—where, as mentioned, regional parliaments are not directly represented in a national legislative chamber—has defined any timeframe for regional participation, although in Italy according to Law 234/2012, regional parliaments have 30 days to transmit observations to the state government, like regional governments (article 24-3). This has led the Italian regional parliaments to sometimes submit their opinions on the respect of the principle of subsidiarity after the national chambers have already transmitted theirs to the EU institutions.[27]

Arguably, whereas some kind of common timeframe, or at least efficient communication and cooperation, between the regional and the national levels is necessary in order for the national parliament to be able to take the regional stance into account, a too strict and short deadline, as for instance the one existing in Spain, may in fact hamper regional participation. On the other hand, the absence of any time-limit could prove problematic were a regional parliament to submit a reasoned opinion, whose justification or content would diverge from that of the national chamber, at the very last moment. This is, in fact, a real risk existing in the British system. Therefore, it would be best for regional and national legislatures to cooperate and communicate at each stage of their procedures effectively, at least during the eight-week period allocated for the subsidiarity check but preferably also in advance, for instance when the national parliament examines the Commission's annual work programme, as has been the case in Italy with the Senate in 2015.[28] Even if the national parliament does not examine the Commission annual work programme in order to define its priorities in terms of subsidiarity,[29] regional parliaments should do it, and ideally in the framework of a common exercise among regional legislatures. For instance, there is currently room for improvement in Belgium in this respect. The Belgian regional parliaments are

[26] German parliaments depend on their regional governments whose delegates form the *Bundesrat*. Actually, the opinions expressed by the regional parliaments need not always be taken into account and, when they are, they are not always binding on the governments. F Wittreck, 'Wächter wider Willen—Probleme der Beteiligung von Parlamenten am europäischen Integrationsprozeß auf Bundes- und Landesebene' (2011) 2 *Zeitschrift für Gesetzgebung* 122, 133. However, some regional parliaments may mandate their governments. Abels, 'Sub-national Parliaments in a Multi-Level Parliamentary System' (n 21 above) 352.

[27] C Fasone, 'Towards new Procedures between State and Regional Legislatures in Italy, Exploiting the Tool of the Early Warning System' (2013) 5(2) *Perspectives on Federalism* E-122.

[28] Session held on 26 February between the European Affairs Committee and the regional parliaments.

[29] Several chambers, such as the French National Assembly and the German *Bundestag*, in fact do not proceed to such a prioritisation.

indeed involved in the examination of the Commission annual work programme when it is examined by the Federal Advisory Committee on European Affairs of which 10 members are delegated from the Senate. But this organ is also composed of deputies of the House of Representatives and of Members of Parliament (MEPs). Besides, the possibility recently formulated by the Belgian Senate to use the parliamentary reserve in order to extend the eight-week deadline could potentially also be used to the benefit of regional parliaments.[30] On the other hand, it emerges from a survey conducted in Autumn 2015 among 15 regional parliaments that some initiatives exist in a similar direction in Germany, whereas this is not the case in Spain.

B. The Absence of Horizontal Cooperation

The absence of an efficient horizontal cooperation among regional parliaments within the same Member State is also one of the further difficulties that exist in this framework. This is not true of all of them, since the Austrian *Länder* even distribute the different policy areas among themselves on a yearly basis; that is to say that at the beginning of the year, they all come together, proceed to the distribution and then each *Land* monitors the area it has been attributed.[31] This division of responsibilities arguably takes place at the executive level but parliaments and governments cooperate largely. Additionally, as already mentioned, the Italian regions set priorities in the framework of the National Conference of Regional Legislatures that they then shared with the Senate.[32]

In contrast, no such cooperation exists in Belgium, in Spain or in the UK, at least formally. In Spain, any attempt in this direction is particularly unlikely, as a climate of distrust exists among the Autonomous Communities and has been recently reinforced by the aspiration to independence of Catalonia especially. Regions have different traditions and identities, are not used to cooperating and when they do, it is at the executive level. As in Italy, a conference composed of the Presidents of the regional assemblies does exist in the form of COPREPA (*Conferencia de los Presidentes de los Parlamentos Autonómicos*). However, their role in this framework is rather limited; even the attempt to introduce a common standardised document to examine the question of the respect of the principle of subsidiarity failed, since it is not used by all regional parliaments. What makes it even more difficult is the fact that the Spanish regions have different competences and also different interests linked to their geographical locations for instance, although the latter is true

[30] This proposal is currently under discussion. Information report on the transposition of European Law into Belgian Law published on 18 May 2015, p 141.

[31] Schmitt et al, *The Subsidiarity Early Warning System of the Lisbon Treaty* (n 4 above) 19f.

[32] *Conferenza delle Assemblee legislative regionali.* See more detailed on this point C Fasone, 'Italian Regional Councils and the Positive Externalities of the Early Warning Mechanism for National Constitutional Law', Chapter 8 in this volume.

of other non-Spanish regions too. A similar situation can be observed in Belgium where the regions' desire for autonomy is too strong to allow them to cooperate.[33]

In fine the asymmetrical nature of the British, German and Italian regionalised states can be an obstacle to an effective horizontal cooperation. The German regional parliaments, on the other hand, have opted for an intermediate solution and have created a common mailing-list through which they will typically exchange information. This informal means of communication in fact satisfies a large part of the actors involved,[34] and could already be a step in the right direction if the other regional parliaments were to use it as a source of inspiration.

C. Regional Parliaments' Lack of Information

A further difficulty derives from the deficit of information from which regional parliaments suffer. Indeed, their situation is even less satisfying than that of national parliaments as only a minority of them are represented directly in Brussels.[35] This issue has led, for instance, several German regional parliaments to open an office in Brussels but not all of them can afford it, and their added-value remains to be seen.[36] Additionally, while the Catalan Parliament did send one administrator to Brussels, this presence was discontinued already after one year.[37] Besides, filtering all EU documents for those parliaments that receive all legislative proposals without them being selected on the basis of their competence—as is for example the case in Italy, Spain or the UK—necessarily requires expertise in EU matters and the availability of material and human resources, in particular if the subsidiarity check has to be conducted within a very limited period of four weeks, as is the case in Spain. Even where regional parliaments do not face such a temporal constraint, they will need important resources, especially in terms of qualified personnel, and the differences in this sense among the different regions surely contribute to the significant variation in the frequency of their participation. This is the case in Germany, where certain *Länder* such as Baden-Württemberg, North-Rhine-Westphalia and Bavaria have a long tradition of active participation in EU matters and others, such as Saarland, have difficulties in participating at all.[38]

[33] See further on Belgium: W Vandenbruwaene and P Popelier, 'Belgian Parliaments and the Early Warning System' Chapter 9 in this volume.

[34] Buzogány and Häsing, 'Europäisierung des deutschen Landesparlamentarismus ? Zur Rolle der Landtagsverwaltungen' (2015) 46 *Zeitschrift für Parlamentsfragen* 128, 135.

[35] This is for instance the cases of Bavaria, Baden-Württemberg and Wales.

[36] Abels, 'Sub-National Parliaments in a Multi-Level Parliamentary System' (n 21 above) 17.

[37] M Palomares Amat, 'El Parlamento de Cataluña y la Unión Europea' in P Andrés Sáenz de Santa María and JI Ugartemendia Eceizabarrena (eds), *El Parlamento europeo: ¿esta vez es diferente?* (Guipúzcoa, IVAP, 2015) 269. See on the parliaments' representations in Brussels and their utility as sources of information: BA Dias Pinheiro, 'Interparliamentary Cooperation between National Parliaments', Chapter 5 in this volume.

[38] This lack of human and material resources was, for example, noted by the MP Isolde Ries during the conference 'Strengthening the Role of Regional Parliaments in EU affairs. Challenges, Prac-

Arguably, not all regional parliaments have decided to restrict their participation to those EU legislative proposals that affect their areas of competence and hence will need to filter the proposals received first.[39] However, they will still need important resources to scrutinise the even higher number of proposals resulting from this absence of filter.

The weakness from which regional parliaments suffer in this area also poses the question of their relationship with their regional governments in this framework, since regional governments are usually better represented at EU level. Some regional parliaments, such as for instance those of the Salzburg, Voralberg and Mecklenburg-Vorpommern regions, never receive any subsidiarity assessment from their regional governments, whereas others, such as the Upper Austrian parliament and the parliament of Sachsen-Anhalt, systematically do. By contrast, the Welsh Assembly is seeking to reinforce its link to its government by requesting it to send its position on relevant dossiers for Wales but has, so far, been unsuccessful in this attempt.[40]

Whereas regional parliaments should try to benefit from this governmental expertise, this might prove difficult, first because as it happens at national level, regional parliaments may be tempted to simply trust and follow their regional governments' opinion without exercising any critical judgement.[41] In practice, the opinions adopted by the parliament can therefore be those of the government and *in fine* such a tendency does not contribute to the 'Europeanisation' of regional parliaments either.[42] It is evident that the parliament will tend to support the government stemming from its majority but it is also desirable that the parliamentary minority can express its opinion. The predominance of the regional executives over the regional legislatures, or even their 'monopoly',[43] should be avoided as

tices and Perspectives' held on 2 July 2014 in the Committee of the Regions. Proceedings, available at: cor.europa.eu/en/events/forums/Documents/2214%20proceedings%20regional%20parliaments%20indd%2026-09.pdf (last accessed: 5 December 2014).

[39] Out of the 15 regional parliaments surveyed in 2015, it is interesting to note that the parliaments of Baden-Württemberg, Saxony, Emilia-Romagna, Wallony-Brussels, the Basque Country and Catalonia have declared that they first filter the proposals received on the basis of their competence, whereas the Parliament of Thuringia examines proposals based on its competence or on the interest they represent for the region, and the other eight do not discriminate and can analyse any proposal independently of their competence in the affected area.

[40] Melding, 'Role of sub-National Parliaments in the EU' (n 15 above) 8.

[41] This has happened at national level in Germany for instance, where the regional ministers tend to follow the assessment provided by the Federal government. P Becker, 'Die Subsidiaritätsprüfung in Bundestag und Bundesrat—ein Rechtliches oder ein Politisches Instrument?' (2013) 23 *Zeitschrift für Politikwissenschaft* 5, 24.

[42] In reference to the Catalan case, see Palomares Amat, 'El Parlamento de Cataluña y la Unión Europea' (n 37 above) 270 but this can be extended to all regional parliaments.

[43] R Hrbek, 'Die europapolitische Rolle der Landes- und Regionalparlamente—zur Einführung' in P Straub and R Hrbek (eds), *Die europapolitische Rolle der Landes- und Reigonalparlamente* (Baden-Baden, Nomos, 1998) 11.

far as possible.[44] Secondly, as is now clear, certain celerity is required and the risk therefore exists that regional governments simply transmit an analysis, prepared on the basis of a standardised model by their administration, to the parliament instead of providing it with a true political analysis, as happens in the Basque Country. Hence, some prior selection appears, yet again, to be particularly needed. The regional governments, but also the regional legislatures, should cooperate closely in limited cases of particular regional interest.

D. The Absence of Effective Coordination among Regional Parliaments at European Level

In addition to these difficulties existing at national level, regional parliaments are confronted with the absence of coordination or cooperation among regional legislatures at the European level.[45] They do regularly come together in the framework of the Conference of European Regional Legislative Assemblies (CALRE). Nonetheless, this Conference, which meets only a few times per year, cannot be the place of regular and efficient cooperation in the field of subsidiarity among the 74 regional assemblies with legislative competences. Rather, it should serve for the exchange of information and best practices.

With this objective in mind, it would be interesting for CALRE to circulate in advance of its meetings questionnaires to be filled in by all regional parliaments, following the practice now established by COSAC, which has proved to be a useful source of information for the public but also for national parliaments themselves. Moreover, it should act for the reinforcement of the RegPEX platform through which regional parliaments are supposed to share their opinions in the field of subsidiarity. Additionally, if national parliaments do put in place the system of alert (proposed during the meeting of IPEX users held in January 2015) following which national parliaments would receive an automatic email alert as soon as eight national parliaments have indicated that they have concerns regarding the respect of the principle of subsidiarity in one and the same proposal,[46] regional parliaments should be included in this mailing-list too.

[44] Predominance highlighted in Spain by Laura Seseña Santos: Seseña Santos, 'La participación de las Cortes de Castilla y León en los asuntos europeos' (n 24 above) 273 and in a comparative perspective, D Fromage, 'Les Parlements dans l'Union Européenne après le Traité de Lisbonne. La participation des parlements allemands, britanniques, espagnols, français et italiens' (Paris, L'Harmattan, 2015).

[45] In addition to CALRE and the Committee of the Regions mentioned here, another forum for cooperation among regional parliaments existed in the form of the Network of Regional Parliamentary European Committees (NORPEC) between 2002 and 2005. This initiative, that brought together the EU affairs committees of the regional parliaments, was discontinued since.

[46] This idea was voiced by Ms Maria João COSTA, Permanent Representative of the Portuguese Assembly of the Republic in Brussels, during the first IPEX users Conference held in Copenhagen in January 2015. IPEX users Conference Report, p 2.

The idea to involve regional parliaments through COSAC has also been expressed[47] but takes place so far only to a very limited extent. In fact, CALRE was represented at the COSAC plenary meeting held in Rome at the beginning of December 2014 but it was not invited at the following plenary meeting organised in Riga at the beginning of June 2015. It therefore appears that it may be the fact that the COSAC presidency was held by Italy and that at the same time the CALRE presidency was in the hands of the regional parliament of Lombardy that allowed contacts to be established. In any event, even if for instance it can be useful for CALRE to send its conclusions and its annual work programme to COSAC, any attempts of closer cooperation appear to be particularly difficult to establish as COSAC already faces its own challenges and hence CALRE may spend some of its precious time in this effort with little hope that any effective outcome is achieved, in the short term at least.[48]

Furthermore, regions have the opportunity to express their concerns in terms of subsidiarity through the Committee of the Regions and its Subsidiarity Monitoring Network. However, here too there are many obstacles to effective participation of the regions. The Committee of the Regions does not participate, as such, in the EWS. It can express its concerns when it is consulted and can bring a case ex post before the CJEU. Its margin of action is thus rather limited. Additionally, the diversity of its members in terms of both interests and (institutional) nature—ranging from associations of municipalities, provinces, regions even to national high chambers—is likely to make the approval of any common position particularly difficult. Potentially, the most viable option would be that of an action before the CJEU on procedural grounds if the Commission did not respect its obligation to take the regional and the local dimensions into account in its impact assessment. It remains to be seen, though, whether in such a case the CJEU would be willing to sanction the Commission as it has, in a previous case, recognised the existence of a tacit compliance with this obligation.[49]

E. Regional Parliaments and the Shortcomings of the EWS

Finally, it should be noted that regional parliaments face the same problems as national parliaments, although sometimes in an even more acute manner. They are first of all linked to the absence of a clear and common definition of the principle of subsidiarity. In particular, some national parliaments consider that the principle of proportionality should also be examined, as it is contained in the principle of subsidiarity, in spite of the fact that Protocol no 2 clearly excludes

[47] CALRE 2015 Programme, p 4.

[48] See on the functioning of COSAC the dedicated chapters in C Fasone and N Lupo (eds), *Interparliamentary cooperation in the composite European Constitution* (Oxford, Hart Publishing, 2016).

[49] Case C-233/94, *Germany v Parliament and Council* [1997] ECR I-2405.

proportionality from the EWS.[50] As a consequence, national—and, potentially, regional—parliaments express their opinions on different bases and the risk exists that the EWS is activated by very diverse opinions, which in turn makes the EU Commission's task more difficult at the time of reacting to the opinions received. In fact, the Commission usually accepts all reasoned opinions designated as such by national parliaments and only examines whether they are actually addressing a breach of subsidiarity when the threshold for the EWS's activation is close. It therefore remains quite free in its assessment notwithstanding the fact that the political consequences are not the same if it ignores a yellow card or if it simply ignores a series of reasoned opinions. This vagueness could therefore also provide it with an acceptable ground to indirectly easily dismiss a yellow card, or at least to maintain its draft proposal without any changes. In order to tackle this issue, a majority of national parliaments have recently expressed their wish to issue informal guidelines on how to draft reasoned opinions and contributions in the context of the Political Dialogue.[51] Such an initiative, if it were to be successful,[52] could create a common basis helpful to national as well as regional parliaments in their task of control.

On the other hand, European legislatures are confronted with a lack of justification by the Commission, which often limits itself to underlining the transnational dimension of the issue addressed without necessarily entering into the two dimensions inherent to the principle of subsidiarity: a goal cannot be achieved at Member States level and can, simultaneously, be better achieved at EU level.[53] This, in fact, can even amount to a subsidiarity breach.[54]

Finally, the EWS guarantees little to parliaments in the end, although their participation in it is particularly time-consuming and demands many resources. Such a failure to take both of these dimensions into account is so because the thresholds required for the activation of the System are barely reachable and because, even when they are, the EU Commission remains free to act as it sees fit as it can maintain, modify or withdraw the proposal (article 7.2 Protocol 2). Therefore, if the incentive for national parliaments to participate is not always clear, it is even less so for regional parliaments which, in most cases and as highlighted above, also and primarily depend on their national parliament to be heard.

[50] COSAC, '18th Bi-annual report on the report developments in European Union procedures and practices relevant to parliamentary scrutiny' (2012) 1.

[51] COSAC, '23rd Bi-annual report on the developments in European Union procedures and practices relevant to parliamentary scrutiny' (2015) 29f.

[52] Three years after the entry into force of the Lisbon Treaty, national parliaments were much more reluctant to establish a common definition of subsidiarity and no attempt was finally made in this direction. COSAC, '18th Bi-annual report on the report developments in European Union procedures and practices relevant to parliamentary scrutiny' (2012) 1.

[53] COSAC, '16th Bi-annual report on the report developments in European Union procedures and practices relevant to parliamentary scrutiny' (2011) 7.

[54] P Kiiver, 'The Conduct of Subsidiarity Shecks of EU Legislative Proposals by National Parliaments: Analysis, Observations and Practical Recommendations' (2012) *ERA Forum* 535, 545.

In this context, and with so many obstacles for efficient participation of regional parliaments in the EWS, the will of the politicians involved plays a determining role and explains why, in some cases, the regional participation in this framework, be it through the submission of reasoned opinions or of simple opinions, varies widely and is unstable over time.[55] Against this background, regional participation can be considered desirable only when an important regional interest is at stake, hence resembling the practice established by the British regional assemblies rather than that of the Spanish ones, in the immediate aftermath of the entry into force of the Lisbon Treaty at least. Indeed, regional parliaments should not miss the opportunity the EWS opens to them to use yet another avenue to be heard at European level. But a systematic participation in the EWS should be avoided in light of all the above.

This somewhat unsatisfactory situation for regional parliaments invites, in any case, reflection as to the role they should play in the EWS and in the EU in general, and as to the need of a reform.

IV. The Role of Regions in the EU and a Need for Reform

Given all the obstacles evidenced in the preceding analysis, and especially in the previous section, it is legitimate to wonder whether the scope of the participation of regional parliaments should not, at least, be extended to the Political Dialogue with the EU Commission. This already happens in Italy (article 9 Law 234/2012) but in the other Member States, given the fact that the Political Dialogue has not been anchored in any legislative act—and rightly so in my opinion, given its informal nature—regional parliaments are formally limited to participation in the EWS, although some German parliaments de facto participate.[56] Arguably, the entrenchment of the Political Dialogue in a legal act at national level can be protective of the national and regional legislatures as their right to participate is then strictly guaranteed. Additionally, after almost a decade of Dialogue between national parliaments and the Commission, it seems that this initiative originally put into place in order to compensate for the failure of the Constitutional Treaty is set to remain. Nevertheless, other elements, such as the consistent delay of the EU Commission in providing its answers, or the recent diminishing participation of some parliamentary Chambers,[57] actually speak against such an entrenchment in

[55] This is also true of the national level as mentioned, however to a lesser extent as the incentive to participate is higher for national chambers which do have a vote contrary to the regional parliaments.

[56] Only the parliament of Sachsen-Anhalt declared it cannot participate.

[57] For instance, the number of contributions submitted by the Portuguese Assembly or by the Italian Senate diminished significantly between 2012 and 2013. European Commission, 'Annual Report 2012 on Relations between the European Commission and National Parliaments', COM(2013) 565, p 9 and European Commission, 'Annual Report 2013 on Relations between the European Commission and National Parliaments', COM(2014) 0507, p 10.

a legal act. Rather, regional participation in the Political Dialogue should indeed be permitted but on a strictly informal basis and always through the national parliamentary channel.

Such an extension of the regional parliaments' prerogatives is particularly needed since, for instance in Spain, the strict limitation to a negative role, with the absence of guarantee already underlined above, has led to a certain frustration and loss of interest by regional parliamentarians after five years;[58] only two regional parliaments have actually remained very active after 2011.[59] The number of contributions submitted by regional parliaments has diminished from 80 in 2010 to 22 in 2011 and was slightly higher in 2012 (34), though still amounting to less than half the number in 2010.[60] In this context, José Tudela considers that 'After a first euphoric period, the participation of subnational parliaments in the Early Warning System … of the Treaty of Lisbon has become an administrative process carried out by legal advisers'.[61]

Some regions also contemplated the possibility of transmitting their reasoned opinions to the EU institutions directly, independently of the procedure existing at national level, and some Austrian and German regional parliaments already do so; the latter since 2012. This development was in fact welcomed by the Presidents of the German *Landtage* in 2014 and they considered that it should be further extended.[62] This developing practice—however still limited to fewer than 10 opinions per year—poses problems of sustainability and of transparency that cannot be neglected. The former issue is because the EU Commission already faces great difficulty in its attempt to answer all national (reasoned) opinions effectively, both in terms of delay and of content.[63] The latter problem, on the other hand, lies in the fact that, given the absence of any institutional or legal framework for this practice, the Commission has absolutely no obligation in terms of transparency. It therefore publishes neither the opinions it receives nor the answers it provides. The relationship between the Commission and parliaments is already complex and opaque enough to the citizenry that it is unnecessary to worsen the current situation even more as this would, in an attempt to improve democracy, in fact make the EU's actions even less democratic in its citizens' eyes.

58 On Catalonia: Palomares Amat, 'El Parlamento de Cataluña y la Unión Europea' (n 37 above) 267 and on Castilla y León: Seseña Santos, 'La participación de las Cortes de Castilla y León en los asuntos europeos' (n 24 above) 283. On the reduction of the number of regional contributions: JÁ Camisón Yagüe, 'La Asamblea de Extremadura y el control del principio de subsidiariedad a través del Mecanismo de Alerte Temprana' (2011) 14 *Revista d'Estudis Autonòmics i Federals* 264, 285.

59 J Tudela Aranda, 'The Spanish Autonomous Parliaments participation in the European decision making process', paper presented at the conference 'Parlamenti nazionali e Unione Europea nella governance multilivello' held at the Italian Chamber of deputies on 15 March 2015, p 12.

60 V Navarro Marchante, 'El control del principio de subsidiariedad en la práctica: la actividad de la Comisión Mixta para la Unión Europea y del Parlamento de Canarias' in JI Navarro Méndez (ed), *Parlamentos regionales europeos y principio de subsidiariedad* (Madrid, Aranzadi, 2014) 114.

61 Tudela Aranda, 'The Spanish Autonomous Parliaments Participation' (n 59 above) 3.

62 Declaration adopted by the Conference of the Presidents of the *Länder* in June 2014, p 3.

63 COSAC, '16th Bi-annual report Developments in European Union Procedures and Practices Relevant to Parliamentary Scrutiny' (2011) p 6 and statements during the COSAC plenary meeting held in Rome in December 2014.

On another level, some had predicted that

> the involvement of regional assemblies in the subsidiarity control could become a useful way of accelerating Europeanisation process of subnational political élites, bridging the gap between the regional politics and EU policies which, in the long run, could help overcome the long-lasting 'deparliamentarisation' at the subnational level.[64]

Such Europeanisation was, indeed, particularly necessary as regional parliaments, even more so than national parliaments, long remained outside of the European integration process both due to the original 'regional blindness' of the EU and due to the fact that Member States were reluctant to allow regions to participate. In fact, Member States often delegated the exclusive competences of their regions to the EU without their approval.[65] Additionally, regional parliaments, especially, developed an interest for EU affairs and, consequently, institutional structures for their participation, only more recently. Indeed, some have considered that the EWS's ultimate goal was that of integrating EU affairs in the daily parliamentary tasks while, in doing so, bringing EU affairs closer to the MPs and, ultimately, to the citizens.[66] It would therefore be particularly unfortunate if regional parliaments ceased to participate in this field due to the shortcomings of the EWS and the limited scope it offers them. Instead, mechanisms to allow for their involvement and consultation should be developed at national level so that the national opinions expressed in the framework of the Political Dialogue also mirror regional preferences.

On the other hand, if the regional participation in the EU is to take place on a content-level and not solely on the basis of subsidiarity—and this would be in line with the original intention to reinforce democracy in introducing the EWS—and if the national level is to centralise the regional opinions, it can be argued that also the other regions which do not have legislative competences could systematically be consulted provided that regions implement 70 to 80 per cent of EU legislation.[67] Indeed, in the EU, 'regions with legislative powers seem to have a slightly stronger position [with respect to that of other subnational governments] due to their unique role as the implementers of EU legislation',[68] although this

[64] K Boronska-Hryniewiecka, 'Regions and subsidiarity after the Treaty of Lisbon: overcoming the "regional blindness"?' in M Cartabia et al (eds), *Democracy and subsidiarity in the EU. National parliaments, regions, civil society in the decision-making process* (Bologna, Il Mulino, 2013) 352.

[65] This danger was identified early on by certain German *Länder*. But even they had to wait until the approval of the Single European Act to enjoy recognition in this framework. On this attempt by certain *Länder* to gain rights of participation at the time of the approval of the ECSC Treaty, see: U von Alemann and C Münch, 'Nordrhein-Westfalen in Europa—Eine Region im Spannungsfeld zwischen regionaler Identität und Europäischer Integration' (2002) *Jahrbuch der Heinrich Heine Universität* 293, 295.

[66] Palomares Amat, 'El Parlamento de Cataluña y la Unión Europea' (n 37 above) 267.

[67] T Christiansen and P Lintner, 'The Committee of the Regions after 10 Years: Lessons from the Past and Challenges for the Future' (2005) 1 *EIPASCOPE* 7, 10.

[68] F Hendriks, A Lidström and J Loughlin, 'Local and regional democracy in European politics' in JM Magone (ed), *Routledge Handbook of European Politics* (Abingdon, Routledge, 2015) 411 in reference to the analysis of R Scully and R Wyn Jones. R Scully and R Wyn Jones (eds), *Europe, Regions and European regionalism* (Basingstoke, Palgrave Macmillan, 2011).

may be truer of certain regions, like the German *Länder*, than of others, such as the Italian ones.

The regions with legislative competences, whose assemblies are directly elected, represent a political will separate from the national one. Yet other regions have elected regional councils too, such as France for example. And, in fact, some of them, such as for instance the Bulgarian and the Cypriot regions, can express their concerns in matters of subsidiarity in the framework of larger consultation procedures,[69] whereas others, such as the Croatian ones, remain excluded.[70] In the spirit of subsidiarity, of multilevel governance[71] and of democracy, with the latter being so dear to the EU leaders,[72] it appears desirable to clarify this situation and invite all regions to participate in the EU integration process through the Political Dialogue. Of course they can already be actively involved in the consultation procedures existing at EU level, but it would be positive for them to know that their opinion is expected and valued. At a time where Eurosceptic movements keep expanding and do often start at local level, it is necessary to build, eventually, an effective bridge between the different levels of governance existing in the EU where the Committee of the Regions has failed so far.

The Presidents of the German regional parliaments pronounced themselves in favour of a closer relationship to EU institutions by arguing that their more intensive participation in the European integration process reinforces the democratic legitimacy of the European decisions, allows for the inclusion of regional interests and regional particularities and reinforces the acceptance of European politics.[73] But it can be legitimately argued that the involvement of the regions with no legislative competences would have equal benefits for democracy in the EU.

Additionally, the inclusion of the 74 regional parliaments with legislative competences only may also have been, to a certain extent, the result of particular circumstances. As underlined by Nicola Lupo, the creation of this new category had to do with the way in which interests are organised.[74] Regions with a larger autonomy, which had remained unsatisfied with the Committee of the Regions, created a new association (the Conference of Regions with Legislative Powers—REGLEG) and

> decided to find their element of identification in the fact of being able to exercise 'legislative powers'. This criterion, although founded more on the holding of formal powers—their qualification as legislative being decisive—than on substantial autonomy, allowed the involvement in this association of the most active entities.[75]

[69] Schmitt et al, *The Subsidiarity Early Warning System of the Lisbon Treaty* (n 4 above) 135.

[70] ibid 132.

[71] On this concept: Panara, *The sub-national dimension of the EU* (n 2 above) 46f.

[72] On the original silence of the Treaties on this issue see: N Lupo, 'National and Regional Parliaments in the EU Decision-Making Process, After the Treaty of Lisbon and the Euro-Crisis' (2013) 5(2) *Perspectives on Federalism* E1, E4.

[73] Declaration adopted by the Conference of the Presidents of the *Länder* in June 2014, p 3.

[74] Lupo,'National and Regional Parliaments in the EU Decision-Making Process' (n 72 above) 13.

[75] ibid.

This author also notes the inclusion of the vocabulary used by CALRE in the Treaty since it refers to 'regional parliaments' and does not maintain the national denominations of these assemblies, ie *Landtage* in Germany, *Consigli regionali* in Italy etc.[76] Therefore, the reference to 'regional parliaments with legislative competences' could—and should probably—be interpreted widely.

Bearing this in mind, and combining it with the fact that regions implement most of the EU legislation and with their long absence in EU affairs, the desirability of regional participation in the EU integration process is not in itself to be questioned. Rather, there is a need for reflection as to the effectiveness and, in the end, the sense it makes for regional parliaments to participate systematically in the EWS, as it currently stands, in the light of all the existing difficulties highlighted here. It is useless to create yet more heavy and inefficient mechanisms for the participation of European regions in the European integration process. Rather, the multilevel cooperation has to be developed in a spirit of efficiency which would replace the current situation in which regions—with or without legislative competences—are led to knock at all—national and European—doors in order to be heard, with often a lack of guarantee and eventually a misuse of their scarce resources.

Regional parliaments with legislative competences should hence only participate in the EWS in limited cases of particular political importance, whereas all regional assemblies should be given the possibility to express their opinion, through their national parliament, in the framework of the Political Dialogue.

[76] ibid 14.

7

A New Player in the 'Multi-Level Parliamentary Field'. Cooperation and Communication of Regional Parliaments in the Post-Lisbon Scenario

KAROLINA BOROŃSKA-HRYNIEWIECKA

I. Introduction

The latest studies of parliamentary activity under the Early Warning Mechanism (EWM) allow us to see it in a new light, as a Europeanisation and multi-level governance mechanism which increases mutual interdependence between various institutional actors in the European Union (EU).[1] Surely, this tool has given rise to more cooperative forms of governance and policy-making, linking the national parliamentary arenas with the EU level. In this sense, the EWM constitutes an additional legislative transmission belt between the European Commission and the Member States' parliaments who, through scrutinising EU draft legislation, legitimise or question EU action. The European Parliament (EP) has also opened itself to the feedback of national chambers and is currently receiving all reasoned opinions coming from national parliaments within the framework of the EWM.[2] Such a state of affairs encourages conducting comparative studies and developing explanatory frameworks regarding the actual impact of the EWM not only on the national parliamentary mobilisation but also on the subnational parliaments

[1] G Vara Arribas, 'The Early Warning System in Motion' in G Abels and A Eppler (eds), *Subnational Parliaments in an EU Multi-level Parliamentary System: Taking Stock of the Post Lisbon Era*, Foster Europe—International Studies Series vol 3(Innsbruck, Studienverlag, 2015); K Borońska-Hryniewiecka, 'Democratizing the European Multi-Level Polity? A (re-)assessment of the Early Warning System' (2013) 16 *Yearbook of Polish European Studies* 167–88; G Vara Arribas and D Bourdin, *The Role of Regional Parliaments in the Process of Subsidiarity Monitoring within the Early Warning System of the Lisbon Treaty* (Committee of the Regions, 2011).

[2] Borońska-Hryniewiecka, 'Democratizing the European Multi-level Polity?' (n 1 above) 181.

which have been explicitly recognised in the Lisbon Treaty as a separate category of democratic institutions.[3]

The EU-oriented activities of subnational (regional) parliaments provide a relatively new and uncharted area of research.[4] Cases of subnational parliamentary activity have been analysed in single-country studies and mostly from a legal perspective.[5] Apart from the few comparative attempts to account for the patterns of parliamentary mobilisation under the EWM,[6] the topic of regional parliaments and their involvement in EU affairs is still a rather fragmented and under-developed field of study. Moreover, the existing theoretical framework for studying parliamentary representation in the EU seems to overlook the subnational dimension. In their conceptualisation of a 'multilevel parliamentary field', Crum and Fossum de facto limit their analysis to two-level relations between the European Parliament and the national chambers.[7] In other words, the EU-oriented activity of regional parliaments is a research field where many questions remain unanswered.[8] One of them relates to the potential impact of the EWM on the multi-level parliamentary relations in the EU, which this chapter attempts to address.

This contribution builds on a premise that if the input legitimacy of the EU is to be comprehensively evaluated, the analysis should also include the subnational dimension of the European parliamentary democracy. Consequently, this chapter provides a comprehensive overview and analysis of the cooperation and communication patterns among regional parliaments and other EU institutional actors within the framework of the EWM. To this end, section II of this chapter explains the scope and relevance of regional parliamentary engagement in EU policy-control. Section III proposes a typology of inter-parliamentary relations in the EU

[3] Article 6 of the 'Protocol no. 2 on the application of the principles of subsidiarity and proportionality' attached to the Treaty of Lisbon states 'it will be for each national Parliament or each chamber of a national Parliament to consult, where appropriate, regional parliaments with legislative powers'.

[4] P Bursens, F Maes and M Vileyn, 'Playing the Next Level of the Multilevel Parliamentary Game. Let's Add Subnational Parliaments to the Scene' (2012) *Political Studies Association Specialist Group on Territorial Politics*, Brussels; G Abels, 'Adapting to Lisbon: Reforming the Role of German Landesparlamente in EU Affairs' (2013) 22 *German Politics* 353.

[5] G Heggie, 'The Scottish Parliament and the EU Constitution: Moving Beyond the Principle of Partnership' in P Kiiver (ed), *National and Regional Parliaments in the European Constitutional Order* (Groningen, Europa Law Publishing, 2006); M Palomares Amat, 'La participación del parlamento de Cataluña en la aplicación y el control del principio de subsidiariedad' (2011) 33 *Revista de Derecho Comunitario Europeo* 19; AM Carmona Contreras, 'Hacia la europeización de los parlamentos autonómicos? Reflexiones al hilo del mecanismo de alerta temprana' (2012) 16 *Revista d'estudios autonòmics i federals* 141.

[6] For example: K Borońska-Hryniewiecka, 'Differential Europeanization? Explaining the Impact of the Early Warning System on Subnational Parliaments in Europe' (2016) 8 *European Political Science Review* (forthcoming).

[7] B Crum and JE Fossum, 'The Multilevel Parliamentary Field: a Framework for Theorizing Representative Democracy in the EU' (2009) 1 *European Political Science Review* 249.

[8] T Raunio and A Wright, 'Holyrood and Europe: an Incremental Response to Deparliamentarization' (2006) 16 *Regional & Federal Studies* 281; Vara Arribas and D Bourdin (n 1 above); K Borońska-Hryniewiecka, 'Subnational Parliaments in EU Policy Control: Explaining the Variations Across Europe', *RSCAS Working Papers* 38/2013: www.cadmus.eui.eu/bitstream/handle/1814/27156/RSCAS_2013_38.pdf?sequence=1.

and presents contextual factors which might account for the various patterns of regional parliamentary cooperation strategies. The final section illustrates them in a cross-country comparison (section IV). The findings presented in this empirical section are based on document analysis and interviews conducted among regional parliaments in five EU Member States (Germany, Spain, Italy, Belgium the United Kingdom).[9]

II. Regional Parliaments in the Post-Lisbon Scenario

The theoretical and empirical relevance of adding regional parliaments to the picture have normative as well as efficiency-related explanations. First of all, there are 74 subnational parliaments with legislative powers which can be found in eight important EU Member States: three federal (Austria, Belgium and Germany), two regionalised (Spain and Italy), one devolved (the UK) and two unitary states (Portugal—Madeira and Azores; and Finland—Åland Islands). They are legitimate and directly-elected institutions representing the 'multiple demoi' of the EU.[10] The Special Eurobarometer (307/2009) 'The role and impact of local and regional authorities within the European Union' revealed that while only one-third of Europeans tend to trust their national governments, half of the citizens express trust towards their regional and local authorities. The same survey showed also that the majority of Europeans feel that public authorities at the subnational level are not sufficiently taken into account in EU policy-making. These findings imply that EU citizens not only entrust regional authorities with significant scope of political responsibility, but they also expect regional responsiveness to the possibility of being consulted on EU-related issues.

Moreover, as there is an extensive overlap between regional and EU competences in various policy areas and regional parliaments implement over 70 per cent of EU legislation and programme,[11] their knowledge of EU policies affects the quality and timeliness of the legal transposition. Acting closer to the people, regional parliaments are also able to better capture social demands and represent them along the EU decision-making process.

Last but not least, regional parliaments generate significant costs for the public budgets of states. For instance, the maintenance of 17 Spanish autonomous assemblies costs yearly over €380 million, almost three times the budget of the

[9] As regards the gathered data, the questionnaires were completed by 36 out of 61 regional parliaments (the response rate of 59%): 8 German, 9 Spanish, 12 Italian, 4 Belgian and 3 parliaments of the UK in the years 2012–13.

[10] A Benz, 'Linking multiple demoi. Inter-parliamentary relations in the EU' (2011) 1 *Institut für Europäische Verfassungswissenschaften, IEV-Online* 11: deposit.fernuni-hagen.de/2856/1/benziev-online2011nr1.pdf.

[11] T Christiansen and P Lintner, 'The Committee of Regions after 10 Years. Lessons from the Past and Challenges for the Future' (2005) 1 *EIPAScope* 7–13: aei.pitt.edu/5940/1/scop05_1_2.pdf.

Spanish Congress and Senate.[12] Just to compare, the Scottish Assembly alone costs taxpayers €83 million each year. So there is a fair reason to have a closer look at how regional parliamentary roles are evolving in the context of EU governance.

In this regard, Protocol no 2 on the Application of the Principles of Subsidiarity and Proportionality annexed to the Treaty of Lisbon recognises, for the first time, regional parliaments with legislative powers as a separate category of representative institutions and grants them the right to participate in the so-called EWM for subsidiarity control. The Protocol leaves it, however, to the discretion of national parliaments to decide whether to consult regional assemblies as well as to determine the criteria for the selection and inclusion of regional contributions in the national chambers' reasoned opinions. In this sense, the importance of regional assemblies in the operationalisation of the effective scrutiny of EU policy is inextricably related to the willingness of national-level institutions to channel and consider regional opinions.

Empirical evidence shows that the Lisbon Treaty provisions have induced new institutional dynamics in decentralised polities, and are creating new patterns of interactions between national and subnational parliaments. Studies reveal that in the majority of countries possessing legislative regions, appropriate regulations at the national level have been established to ensure subnational participation in the EWM.[13] Regional parliaments receive EU legislative acts, from which they can select those affecting their competences to be scrutinised in relation to subsidiarity and proportionality compliance. At the regional level, almost all Spanish *parlamentos autonómicos* have already incorporated the new provisions for EU policy control into their legal order and accordingly adjusted their parliamentary rules of procedure to participate in the EWM. On the other hand, the majority of German *Landtage* and the Italian *consigli regionali* are still in the process of institutional reorganisation.[14]

Comparative research shows that the nature and scope of regional mobilisation in EU affairs varies between the countries, but there are also considerable intrastate variations which illustrate the different institutional capacities and preferences of EU regions.[15,16] With respect to the inclusion of the regional voice in the national reasoned opinions, the evidence is mixed but some positive trends can be observed in Spain and the UK, where the reasoned opinions issued by the *Cortes Generales* and the British Houses of Parliament respectively acknowledge the reports of regional parliaments.[17]

[12] R Perez, 'Cada escaño autonómico cuesta 319.210 euro', *ABC.es*: www.abc.es/20120122/espana/abci-escanos-201201220315.html.

[13] Arribas and Bourdin (n 1 above); Borońska-Hryniewiecka (n 5 above); Abels (n 4 above); A-L Högenauer, 'All by themselves? Legislative Regions and the Use of Unmediated Access to the European level' (2014) 6 *European Political Science Review* 451.

[14] Borońska-Hryniewiecka (n 1 above).

[15] Borońska-Hryniewiecka (n 6 above).

[16] ibid.

[17] On the basis of questionnaires conducted at the Welsh and Scottish Assemblies, August 2012 and sources from IPEX Inter-Parliamentary EU Information Exchange Platform (IPEX database) available at: www.ipex.eu.

The domestic EWM mobilisation of regional parliaments is complemented by the different parliamentary cooperation strategies in the wider context of EU affairs. The remaining part of this chapter focuses on these relations and their underlying dynamics.

III. Types of Inter-Parliamentary Relations and Their Contextual Factors

Within the framework of the EWM or in a broader context of EU affairs, regional parliaments might engage in interactions with other institutional actors for several reasons. First, they aim at gaining the necessary expertise related to particular, territorially-salient policy sectors and their EU regulation. As 'latecomers' in the process of European integration, they also seek to acquire the necessary experience *in* and knowledge *of* the specificity of European policy-making. To this end, they often cooperate with more experienced regional executives, or with resourceful regional parliaments from other regions. Secondly, they want to stay informed about EU policy developments in order to be able to voice their opinions about the potential economic, social or environmental impact of the proposed legislation at the regional level. In this case, they tend to use their regional offices in Brussels or liaise with the Committee of the Regions (CoR) as an intermediary between the regions and EU institutions. Finally, regional parliaments seek coalitional empowerment in order to exert influence on the EU legislative process. Here, they might rely on cooperation within transnational networks of regional parliaments with legislative powers, committed to raising the level of active participation of these regions in EU policy formation.[18]

In order to systematise the analysis, we should distinguish between two broader types of inter-parliamentary relations. The first one includes horizontal relations among regional parliaments which might be further divided into intra- and extra-state relations. While the first subcategory refers to contacts with regional parliaments of the same state, the latter refers to contacts with regional parliaments of other Member States. Regional parliaments can also engage in horizontal relations with other institutional actors such as regional governments or non-governmental organisations. The second type of parliamentary relations includes vertical interactions between levels of governance. They also have their intra- and extra-state dynamics: whereas the first one relates to contacts with the national parliamentary chamber(s), the latter relates to relations with EU institutions such as the Commission, European Parliament or the CoR. These vertical relations might be mediated through facilitating institutions, such as the seat of the regional office in

[18] Compare: O Costa, S Stavridis and C Dri, *Parliamentary Dimensions of Regionalization and Globalization. The Role of Inter-Parliamentary Institutions* (Basingstoke, Palgrave Macmillan, 2013) Part II and Part III.

Brussels. Both horizontal and vertical relations might be further divided into formal and informal, as well as political and technical, cooperation. While the former differentiation is based on the existence or absence of some form of formalised agreements, the second one depends on whether the interaction is carried out by administrative staff or political members of regional parliaments.

It is important to observe that the different categories of parliamentary relations do not necessarily entail cooperation. For the purpose of this chapter cooperation is understood as *an active engagement and exchange of resources (ie information, expertise, support) between the actors.* As will be shown, empirical data reveal that in many cases, the relations among regional parliaments and other actors, though formalised, are in fact under-used and remain passive.

Similarly to the general level of regional mobilisation in EU affairs, regional strategies of EU-oriented inter-parliamentary cooperation depend on various factors.[19] One of the most important factors is the domestic institutional context in which regional parliaments operate.[20] It can be further broken down by several different variables such as the type of decentralisation and distribution of competences in a state; the position of regional governments in domestic governance arrangements; the existence of formal provisions for inter-institutional cooperation; or the character of socio-political cleavages.

As regards the first variable, in line with the literature on territorial mobilisation, it is assumed that higher levels of devolution result in stronger subnational mobilisation in EU affairs which, in turn, generates more intense inter-parliamentary cooperation.[21] Taking for granted that parliaments quite often depend on their governments in terms of administrative resources and expertise, the position of a regional executive as an independent variable might either successfully facilitate, constrain or even block effective regional parliamentary participation in the EWM. In case of legislative-executive relations, if regional governments act as gatekeepers to national-level decision-making or are used to monopolise EU-related information, regional parliamentary powers become severely restricted and limited to rubber-stamping executive decisions. Ambitious regional parliaments might, therefore, seek external assistance and liaison in cooperation with regional parliaments of other Member States or EU institutions. Yet, it might happen that weak regional parliaments, limited in their capacity by their executive chambers, might simply remain inactive and not engage in any kind of inter-institutional

[19] For the overview of some factors affecting regional parliamentary mobilisation inside the EWM see: Borońska-Hryniewiecka (n 6 above).

[20] C Jeffery, 'Sub-National Mobilization and European Integration: Does it Make any Difference?' (2000) 38 *Journal of Common Market Studies* 1; G Marks, R Haesly and H Mbaye, 'What do Subnational Offices Think they are Doing in Brussels?' (2002) 12 *Regional and Federal Studies* 1, C Rowe *Regional Representations in the EU. Between Diplomacy and Interest Mediation* (Basingstoke, Palgrave Macmillan, 2011).

[21] G Marks, F Nielsen, J Salk and L Ray, 'Competencies, Cracks, and Conflicts: Regional Mobilization in the European Union' (1996) 29 *Comparative Political Studies* 164; B Hocking, 'Regionalism: An International Relations Perspective' in M Keating and J Loughlin (eds), *The Political Economy of Regionalism* (London, Frank Cass, 1997).

cooperation due to lack of motivation or resources. In the same vein, in states where regional governments enjoy a privileged institutional position in EU affairs, inter-parliamentary relations may play an altogether weaker role. A case in point is the German *Landtage*, which tend to underuse their EU participatory rights due to executive domination and are not very active in inter-parliamentary fora.

The existence of formal provisions for regional participation in the EWM concerns primarily the right of subnational parliaments to timely information, consultation and decision-making. Such rules are usually set up at the national level, and vary across Member States.[22] In line with the rational choice approach, it is assumed that the existence of such legal resources will encourage regional parliamentary engagement in the scrutiny of EU legislation as well as entering into cooperative relations with other institutional actors. On the other hand, lack of formal provisions for cooperation between the regional and national parliaments might push regional players to seek external access to EU institutions.

With respect to political cleavages, strong divisions along the centre-periphery line might be expected to weaken the vertical domestic cooperation while inter-regional domestic polarisation might encourage regional parliaments to seek external allies. On the other hand, regional parliaments with the same party majorities are likely to work together to support each other's stances on EU policy dossiers. Cultural distinctiveness might also play a role in inter-parliamentary cooperation patterns in the sense that regions representing ethnic minorities might liaise with each other in order to pursue a common EU-oriented agenda.

Other important factors behind parliamentary relations are obviously the financial, administrative or expertise-based resources of regional parliaments. Some authors find that a region's financial and economic position (measured by the size of the regional budget or regional GDP respectively) influences the scope and quality of subnational mobilisation in the EU.[23] The importance of resources has been empirically confirmed with regard to regional influence in Brussels, especially to the activity of regional representation offices and territorial interest associations.[24]

The last two, and quite often overlooked, factors which might affect inter-parliamentary cooperation are the attitude of members of regional parliaments towards the EU as well as the exposure to Europeanisation. With respect to the former, a sceptical position on the part of politicians towards the regional leverage in the EWM will decrease their willingness to engage in inter-institutional

[22] Vara Arribas and Bourdin (n 1 above).

[23] T Börzel, 'Towards Convergence in Europe? Institutional Adaptation to Europeanization in Germany and Spain' (1999) 37 *Journal of Common Market Studies* 573; J Blatter, M Kreutzer, M Rentl and J Thiele, 'Preconditions for Foreign Activities of European Regions: Tracing Causal Configurations of Economic, Cultural, and Political Strategies' (2009) 40 *Publius: The Journal of Federalism* 171.

[24] C Jeffery, 'Regional Information Offices in Brussels and Multi-Level Governance EU: A UK-German Comparison' (1996) 6 *Regional & Federal Studies* 183; Marks et al (n 21 above); C Moore, 'The Impact of Devolution on EU Level Representation: British Regional offices in Brussels' (2007) 17 *Regional & Federal Studies* 275.

cooperation. The same effect might paradoxically be achieved by a strong pro-European orientation when the EWM is perceived as a pure veto mechanism. On the other hand, for regional politicians with strong EU-oriented ambitions, gaining coalitional empowerment vis-à-vis their national counterparts will be one of the priorities under the new treaty provisions. Finally, the level of Europeanisation also plays a role. In this regard, the common-sensical expectation would be that the longer the EU membership, the stronger the traditions of inter-parliamentary relations in EU affairs. Yet, the length of EU membership should not be confused with its intensity. The evidence reveals that some regional chambers with relatively short experience of the EU have developed greater awareness, engagement, and internal specialisation in the field of European affairs than their older counterparts.

IV. Cross-Country Overview

A. Spain

The Spanish regional assemblies are among the most active in terms of their participation record under the EWM.[25] The majority of them have incorporated the new provisions for subsidiarity control into their legal order either by amending their statutes of autonomy or by changing the parliamentary rules of procedure.

The Spanish system of territorial power distribution is characterised by the competitive nature of centre-periphery relations and weak intergovernmental coordination.[26] Yet, such pattern does not project itself on the regional parliamentary level. Spanish regional legislatures tend to communicate among themselves and to focus more on the domestic parliamentary channels of cooperation rather than to seek external influence. Several factors are behind this trend.

One of the reasons for a quite effective adjustment within the EWM as well as an increased inter-parliamentary cooperation among *comunidades autónomas* (autonomous communities) might be the existence of national-level regulation guaranteeing regional participation in the EU subsidiarity scrutiny procedure.[27] Law 38/2010 grants regional parliaments information and participation rights and establishes a direct link between the national and regional-level legislators via the so-called Joint Commission of the Congress and Senate for the EU. Law 38/2010 establishes that once received by the Spanish Congress, the EU draft legislative proposal is automatically sent to regional parliaments without any prior selection. Autonomous parliaments are then given four weeks to elaborate an opinion

[25] Varia Arribas and Bourdin (n 1 above); Borońska-Hryniewiecka (n 1 above).
[26] T Börzel, *States and regions in the European Union* (Cambridge, Cambridge University Press, 2002).
[27] Law 38/2010.

on the compliance with the principle of subsidiarity. They may draw up a report if they consider that, first, regional competences are affected, and secondly, the principle of subsidiarity has been violated. Although the Joint Commission is not obliged to take into account regional opinions, the analysis of the IPEX database reveals that regional feedback is taken into account at the national level and passed on to the European Commission. Some regions, however, are not satisfied with the way their voice is treated at the national level and complain that the formalisation of vertical inter-parliamentary relations has not yet translated into genuine inter-parliamentary cooperation.[28] In order to remedy this weakness, some positive steps forward might be observed in the form of joint technical sessions and training organised between the lawyers working for regional and the national parliament.

With respect to the vertical extra-state cooperation, autonomous parliaments remain quite passive. Only seven of them are partners of the Subsidiarity Monitoring Network[29] of the CoR and occasionally upload their opinions via the regional REGPEX database. Nor, due to lack of resources, do autonomous parliaments maintain direct contacts with EU institutions, except the CoR.

The horizontal intra-state relations cooperation among Spanish regional parliaments has recently been developing. In this regard, in 2011, the Conference of Presidents of the Spanish Autonomous Parliaments (COPREPA) issued a handbook facilitating elaboration of regional opinions within the EWM.[30] They are also working on the development of a standardised questionnaire for the evaluation of the European Commission's legislative proposals which would make it easier for the less experienced regional assemblies to effectively contribute to the EWM. Moreover, an inter-parliamentary online communication network *Red_Parlamenta* has been established to facilitate the exchange of scrutiny information.

Finally, the majority of Spanish parliaments systematically collaborate with their executives, thus gaining valuable expertise (Cantabria, Basque Country, Canary

[28] The data extracted from IPEX reveal that reasoned opinions issued by *Cortes Generales* acknowledge reports of regional parliaments. Yet, the Law 38/2010 regulating the work of the Mixed Commission under the EWM establishes that the opinions of regional assemblies would be passed on to EU level only if the Commission declares infringement of the subsidiarity principle concerning the legislative proposal. In other words, when it comes to establishing the binding force of the regional negative appraisal, it will only be taken into consideration when the Commission deems it advisable to do so, ie if it serves to strengthen its point of view.

[29] The Subsidiarity Monitoring Network established in 2007 includes parliaments and governments of regions with legislative powers, local and regional authorities without legislative powers and local government associations in the European Union. It is also open to CoR national delegations and chambers of national parliaments. It serves as a platform of cooperation and exchange of experience among subnational authorities in subsidiarity-related issues. The Spanish regional parliaments who are the partners of the SMN are: Asturias Legislative Assembly, Basque Regional Parliament, Canary Islands Regional Assembly, Catalan Regional Parliament, Extremadura Regional Assembly, Galician Regional Parliament, Navarre Regional Parliament.

[30] AM Carmona Contreras, 'Hacia la europeización de los parlamentos autonómicos? Reflexiones al hilo del mecanismo de alerta temprana' (2012) 16 *Revista d'estudis autonòmics i federals* 141, 165.

Islands, La Rioja, Galicia). Some respondents have observed that as a result of the EWM, communication between the executive and legislature has improved in the area of European affairs and is increasingly based on mutual assistance.[31] On the one hand, governmental experience is used by the parliaments to help build the necessary 'EU sensibility', and on the other hand, since the analysis of subsidiarity is fundamentally a political evaluation,[32] regional executives 'see it [as] crucial to submit EU projects to a parliamentary debate involving all the political parties'.[33]

In terms of horizontal extra-state cooperation, the majority of regional parliaments opt for participation in transnational networks of collaboration such as CALRE[34] instead of relying on individual bilateral contacts.

To conclude, in terms of the horizontal inter-parliamentary relations in Spain, intra-state cooperation seems to be stronger than the extra-state. In the vertical dimension, only intra-state formal relations between regional parliaments and the Spanish *Cortes* have been established, but the actual quality of cooperation still leaves much scope for improvement.

B. Germany

While German *Länder* are among the most active regional authorities in EU policy-making, their parliaments (*Landtage*) have been for a long time considerably marginalised in the sphere of European affairs. They lag behind some of the newer legislative regions' parliaments like the British or Spanish, which have deployed a much more proactive approach to developing opportunities for action at the EU level. European integration, together with centralisation of German federalism, has clearly worked in favour of (de-) parliamentarisation at the subnational level.[35] This has affected the participation of *Landtage* in domestic EU policy-making, including the EWM as well as the patterns of their inter-institutional cooperation. The problem of German *Landtage* is that to be able then to effectively network and cooperate with each other as well as with external institutional actors, they need to renegotiate their controlling function over regional

[31] In fact, regional executives in Spain have been granted the possibility to voice subsidiarity-related concerns before the Joint Committee of Senate and the Congress of Deputies (Law 38/2010).

[32] See Jörgen Hettne's Chapter 3 in this volume.

[33] Interview: Basque Parliament, 26 May 2010.

[34] CALRE (Conference of European Regional Legislative Assemblies) is a network of Presidents of regional parliaments with legislative powers from eight EU Member States. Its aim is to minimise the democratic deficit at the regional parliamentary level and to contribute a forum for exchange of knowledge and information between regional and national parliaments as well as the EP.

[35] M Bauer, 'Europaausschüsse—Herzstück landesparlamentarischer Beteiligung in Angelegenheiten der Europäischen Union?' in *Jahrbuch des Föderalismus* (Baden-Baden, Nomos, 2005) 632; S Kropp, 'Federalism and Subnational Parliaments—a Delicate Relationship?' Paper presented at the International Workshop 'Subnational Parliaments in an EU Multi-level Parliamentary System' (Eisenstadt, November 2011).

governments. Although *Landtage* have recently been active in politically reclaiming their position, several contextual factors hamper the process.

First, the voice of the *Länder* in the EWM is mediated through the federal second chamber, the *Bundesrat*. Since the latter is fully composed of representatives of *Länder* governments, they perform the EU-controlling function which the Lisbon Treaty assigns to parliamentary actors. In this way, the *Landtage* remain significantly marginalised in the EWM. Secondly, due to the absence of national-level provisions granting *Landtage* participation and information rights under the EWM, the effective parliamentary scrutiny depends to a great extent on the nature of parliaments' relations with subnational executives. Yet, in Germany, in contrast to the Spanish case, the cooperation between the regional executives and legislatures is not a well-established practice. Regional governments, as natural protagonists in EU policy-making, tend to monopolise expertise and have only recently been pressured to share information with their legislatures.[36]

In the absence of national-level incentives to get involved in the EWM, the domestic inter-parliamentary cooperation is rather weak. Moreover, the effectiveness of networking is viewed sceptically in light of diverging interests and capacities of the German *Länder*. Although the distribution of power is symmetric, the reality illustrates that there are intra-state differences between the *Landtage*, especially as regards resources. A large majority of *Landtage* lack the necessary administrative capacities to conduct effective scrutiny and consequently to have a stake in liaising with other institutional actors. One of the potential vehicles for strengthening inter-parliamentary coordination could be the Conference of *Landesparliaments Presidents*. But due to its weak power base and the non-binding nature of its declarations it serves more as a forum for political discussion. As regards more technical cooperation, in 2011 the German *Landtage* established formal cooperation at the working level in order to facilitate the exchange of EU-subsidiarity matters.[37]

As regards extra-state relations, the horizontal transnational cooperation has been institutionalised with the Austrian regional parliaments, whose privileged position within the domestic governance structure made them more experienced in EU affairs than their German counterparts. The more resourceful *Länder*, such as Bavaria or Baden-Württemberg, systematically cooperate with stronger parliaments of other Member States. Another example of quite active transnational parliamentary cooperation is the participation of four German regional parliaments in the Baltic Sea Parliamentary Conference, which gathers parliamentarians from 11 national and regional parliaments.[38] Although not strictly of EU

[36] G Abels, *Sub-National Parliaments in a Multi-Level Parliamentary System—Reform Processes in the German Länder in the Post-Lisbon Era*, Conference paper presented in Passau, 3 September 2012.

[37] Based on interviews with representatives with *Landtage*, September–December 2012.

[38] The Baltic Sea Parliamentary Conference (BSPC) was established in 1991 as a forum for political dialogue between parliamentarians from the Baltic Sea Region. It aims at raising awareness and opinion on issues of current political interest and relevance for the region. It includes parliaments from Germany, Poland, Sweden, Estonia, Russia, Latvia, Finland, Iceland, Denmark and Greenland.

character, the Conference deals with European issues affecting the interests of Baltic Sea Regions.

As a result of lack of formal provisions for communication between the subnational and federal legislators, no direct, vertical parliamentary cooperation exists.

In case of vertical extra-state relations, the parliaments of Bavaria, Baden-Württemberg and North-Rhine Westphalia established their offices in Brussels in order to be informed, often well before the legislative scrutiny takes place, about any significant policy developments which might affect regional interests. They also remain in systematic contact with the European Commission, which is an exception in the EU. *Landtage* of Bavaria and Baden-Württemberg send their opinions under the EWM directly to the Commission, bypassing the national level. According to *Länder* representatives, the Commission takes regional feedback into consideration.[39] On the other hand, less resourceful *Landtage* express a rather permissive consensus towards the status quo and seem to rely on the 'voluntary underuse of their participatory rights'.[40]

To conclude, the German executive-dominated system of multi-level governance results in weak horizontal intra-state parliamentary cooperation and a stronger networking outside of the domestic framework. As for the vertical relations, the intra-state parliamentary channel is non-existent, and the extra-state is asymmetrically used only by the three strongest Land parliaments.

C. Italy

Although Italy belongs to the founding states of the EU, its regional councils (*consiglii regionali*) in general have long presented quite a low level of EU-oriented activity.[41] The Italian case, however, is also one which has been evolving most markedly in recent times. Since the introduction of the EWM by the Lisbon Treaty, the Italian regional dynamics have been characterised by an increasing—though unevenly—regional parliamentary mobilisation, especially regarding inter-institutional cooperation and platform building.

According to regional respondents, the willingness of regional councils to establish their own subsidiarity monitoring procedures depends to a great extent on the readiness of the national level to cooperate with regional chambers within the EWM. Yet, for a long time, Italian regions had not received the necessary stimulus from Rome. Until late 2012 there was no specific regulation at the national level transposing Lisbon Treaty provisions for subsidiarity control into the domes-

[39] According to the statement made by the representative of Baden-Württemberg at the Committee of the Regions' conference: 'Strengthening the role of regional parliaments in EU affairs: challenges, practices, and perspectives', Brussels, 2 July 2014.

[40] Bauer, 'Europaausschüsse—Herzstück landesparlamentarischer Beteiligung' (n 35 above).

[41] See, for an overview, Chapter 8 by Cristina Fasone in this volume.

tic context and, consequently, no established formal cooperation between the national and regional legislators under the EWS. Vertical inter-parliamentary relations regarding ex-ante EU policy control were limited to informal exchanges of views between some more proactive Italian regions such as Marche, Toscana or Emilia-Romagna and the Italian Senate. They have usually been mediated by civil servants rather than members of parliament who, in general, expressed a lack of interest and willingness to undertake EU policy scrutiny. This deficit of national-level provisions was compensated for by a law on domestic participation in EU affairs (*Legge 24 dicembre 2012, n° 234*). This law strengthens the role of regional parliaments in the creation of EU legislation by giving them the opportunity to send observations applicable to the principle of subsidiarity to the Senate and the Chamber of Deputies.

Over the last two years, the inter-parliamentary communication deficit has been gradually compensated for by the Conference of the Presidents of the Italian Regional Assemblies.[42] This body acts as a coordinator and facilitator of inter-parliamentary cooperation and information exchange in European affairs in its vertical and horizontal dimensions. In the first case, the Conference's role is to mediate communication between the regional councils and the Senate as well as the Chamber of Deputies. In the second one, it provides a platform of learning and EU-oriented training for the regional councils. In this vein, the Conference's important function is acting as a Europeanisation agent in the domestic parliamentary field. In 2010, the Conference established an internal body of cooperation among the Presidents of parliamentary Commissions on EU Affairs, which functions as a 'political table' where some of the more active regional councils might establish common positions on particular EU dossiers.

Due to limited resources and lack of EU experience, regional councils limit their cooperative contacts to the domestic arena. Transnational horizontal cooperation is quite weak and is conducted within some broader networks such as the aforementioned CALRE. The more resourceful ones are active partners of the CoR's Subsidiarity Monitoring Network (SMN) where they occasionally upload their regional reasoned opinions. Italian regional councils have also no direct relations with EU institutions; their opinions are sporadically forwarded to the Commission through the Senate.

In general therefore, Italian regional councils focus on the domestic area of inter-parliamentary cooperation both in its vertical and horizontal dimensions. This cooperation is gradually developing thanks to the role of facilitating institutions and formalisation of national-level provisions for regional participation in the EWM.

[42] *Conferenza dei Presidenti delle Assemblee legislative delle Regioni e delle Province autonome.*

D. Belgium

Belgium represents a paradoxical case where institutionally strong regional parliaments reveal the lowest level of interest in participation in the EWM.[43] According to the Declaration No 51 on the national parliaments signed in December 2008, the six Belgian regional chambers jointly have the right to cast one subsidiarity vote under the EWM in the sphere of the so-called mixed affairs, and two votes in case of exclusive competences. Theoretically then, Belgian regional assemblies function on an equal footing with the national parliament. However, since no agreement has been reached on how to effectuate the Declaration No 51, the participation capacities of the regional chambers remain only presumed. Due to institutional standstill, there is no genuine legal basis for inter-parliamentary cooperation.

Another obstacle for inter-parliamentary cooperation is the dual character of the Belgian federal system as well as strong centre-periphery cleavages. In Belgium, each governance level enjoys its own exclusive catalogue of legislative competences and cannot overrule the act of another level. As a result, Belgian parliaments are not stimulated to cooperate with each other, since they are in a way legislatively 'self-sufficient'. Moreover, the salience of EU affairs in the parliamentary work has been very low. According to empirical studies, there is little parliamentary follow-up on the proposals from EU institutions, even when they display some political relevance for Belgium.[44] At the same time, members of Belgian parliaments express, in general, a very pro-European orientation which 'makes it difficult to discuss or question Europe and European affairs under the EWM', perceived by some as a veto mechanism. As one of the Belgian respondents observed, 'for a debate in parliament you need disagreement. We need a conflict to get involved'.[45]

As regards the domestic horizontal relations, formally, there is the Conference of Presidents of the seven parliamentary assemblies, yet the cooperation record has hitherto been mainly based on exchanges of views on the incomplete inter-institutional agreement.[46] Cooperation along party lines is also very weak due to strong socio-political splits and ethnic divisions. Belgian parliamentarians are also quite sceptical about engaging in transnational networks. Some of them called the meetings organised by CALRE as nothing more than 'parliamentary tourism'. In fact, participation and activity in the works of CALRE differ from region to region depending on the regional interests and potential. The main criticisms related to the network concern the vague and imprecise declarations it makes at its annual

[43] For an in-depth analysis of Belgium federal arrangements see Chapter 9 by Patricia Popelier and Werner Vandenbruwaene in this volume.

[44] X Vanden Bosch, 'The Belgian parliaments and EU affairs: the reasons behind their limited involvement' (2014) 28 *European Policy Brief*: www.egmontinstitute.be/wp-content/uploads/2014/03/EPB-28-ENG-Parliaments.pdf.

[45] Interview, Flemish Parliament, November 2012.

[46] ibid.

meetings, the lack of clear vision on how to organise decision-making structures, as well as lack of physical representation in Brussels.[47]

As regards vertical relations between the subnational assemblies and the federal parliament, since there is no need for any consensus on the reasoned opinions under the EWM, the former have no motivation to get involved in cooperation with the national level and vice versa. Outside of the domestic framework, some members of the Flemish parliament admitted to maintaining [only?] occasional contacts with their Members of Parliament (MEPs) at the European Parliament.

To conclude, there is neither horizontal nor vertical intra-state cooperation between the various Belgian parliaments. Extra-state parliamentary relations are limited to rather sceptical involvement in the activity of parliamentary transnational networks and occasional contacts with MEPs.

E. United Kingdom

The research reveals that although the British devolved assemblies have the shortest experience of the EU, their awareness, engagement, and internal specialisation in the field of European affairs is relatively well advanced. This might be due to the fact that as young parliaments they had to face the challenge of extensive Europeanisation already at the time of their establishment. The degree of devolution in the United Kingdom (UK) is asymmetrical, but the impact of EU law on the exercise of devolved matters is considerable in each of the regions. Situated among the analysed cases, British devolved parliaments, especially the Scottish and Welsh Assemblies, locate themselves somewhere between the Spanish and German model.[48] In this sense, the informality of the British provisions for parliamentary participation in the EWM lies halfway between the formally institutionalised arrangements present in Spain and the absence of any facilitating mechanism in Germany.[49]

As regards patterns of intra-state parliamentary relations, although no formal mechanisms exist to coordinate the subsidiarity monitoring work of the UK's devolved legislatures, information is regularly shared informally between officials in Wales, Scotland and Northern Ireland in relation to proposals which may raise subsidiarity concerns. One example of institutionalised parliamentary cooperation in EU affairs is the European Affairs Committee of the British-Irish Parliamentary Assembly, which facilitates general discussions between the devolved and UK parliaments and assemblies in relation to European issues.

Similarly, in spite of the absence of institutionalised provisions for the vertical cooperation between the Houses of Parliament and the devolved legislatures

[47] Feedback gathered at the CoR conference 'Strengthening the role of regional parliaments in European affairs: challenges, practices and perspectives', Brussels, 2 July 2014.

[48] In the case of the Northern Ireland Assembly, its parliamentary experience was suspended between 2002 and 2007 due to political unrest.

[49] For an overview of the British case in the EWM see Chapter 13 by Adam Cygan.

under the EWM, direct contacts between these levels exist. In this regard, the House of Commons' European Scrutiny Committee invites the comments of the devolved assemblies on the Committee's draft opinions on matters affecting their competences. The House of Lords, on the other hand, elaborated a handbook on EU policy scrutiny, stating that if a subsidiarity issue is raised at the staff level, the EU Liaison Officer will alert the devolved legislatures in due time. Informal contacts with staff members of the UK Parliament also play an important role.

As regards extra-state cooperation, due to the informal character of domestic governance arrangements, British assemblies seek to gain external influence in European affairs through pre-legislative lobbying, networking and policy control, often bypassing the national level. The SMN of the Committee of the Regions is the preferred vehicle of communication for the Welsh and Northern Irish assemblies. In their view, the CoR's REGPEX database is a useful source of information exchange in the process of monitoring of EU legislative proposals.[50] Moreover, the Scottish and Welsh Parliaments established their offices in Brussels to keep their members informed about relevant developments in the EU's agenda. The two devolved assemblies have also started forging closer ties with MEPs and practise short secondments to the European Parliament.

V. Conclusions

The introduction of the EWM by the Treaty of Lisbon has increased the institutional awareness of the necessity to discuss EU policies with regional parliaments having legislative powers. While at the EU level, the Commission encourages national parliaments to constructively consult on its legislative proposals with their regional counterparts, the former, either for the sake of policy pragmatism or to ensure the effective implementation and compliance with EU law, are slowly adapting their domestic regulations to channel regional opinions upstream. The European Parliament also underlines the role of regional parliaments in the area of subsidiarity control and called on the national chambers to work together with them under the EWM.

These top-down motivational gestures do not, however, suffice to create meaningful regional parliamentary networking and participation in EU policy-making. The empirical evidence shows that the actual system of inter-institutional cooperation is fragmented and dispersed. Regional parliaments lack proper, horizontal as well as vertical mechanisms of information exchange and coordination which could serve to increase the coherence and technical precision of the regional opinions, but also of the potential joint positions regarding EU legislative proposals.

[50] Interviews with the Welsh and Northern Irish Assemblies, November 2012.

The reasons for cooperative deficits vary across EU Member States depending on the specific domestic institutional factors. While the Spanish autonomous parliaments reveal a higher level of mobilisation and seek to improve their intra-state communication channels, the UK devolved assemblies and stronger German *Landtage* tend to explore external routes of control over EU policy. The existence of national-level regulations in Spain as well as cooperative relations between the executives and legislatures at the regional level encourage the latter to engage in inter-parliamentary networking in order to gain influence over EU affairs. In Germany, the domination of regional executives and lack of formal provisions for regional parliamentary participation in the EWM have for a long time prevented the *Landtage* from getting involved in any inter-institutional collaboration. In the case of the more resourceful *Landtage*, a certain degree of state bypassing and EU-level capacity building can be observed. In the UK, intense Europeanisation of regional parliamentary activity, combined with an absence of formal mechanisms of inter-level coordination, has encouraged the devolved assemblies to set up networks of cooperation in Brussels. In Italy, institutional sluggishness and low resource capacity has for a long time prevented regional parliaments from networking and collaboration. The weakly Europeanised Italian regional chambers have—however—recently gained pace in institutional EU-oriented reorganisation and they are becoming more active under the EWM. They, however, prefer to rely on domestic facilitating structure as a forum for inter-parliamentary cooperation rather than to seek external coalitions. The case of Belgium is peculiar due to its dual federal character and lack of regional interest in discussing the EU. Paradoxically, due to strong Euro-enthusiasm among the regional assemblies their involvement in the EWM is minimal. Another reason for the lack of subnational cooperation is the institutional stalemate in the process of ratification of the agreement on the distribution of subsidiarity votes among all the seven Belgian parliaments, as well as strong political and territorial cleavages among the units of the Belgian federation.

Generally, inter-parliamentary cooperation in all the analysed cases leaves much scope for improvement. If we look at the functions regional parliaments perform through their various forms of activity, we could say they are still mostly guardians and controllers of their executives, while remaining weak networkers and policy entrepreneurs.[51] This is caused mainly by their lack of the necessary EU expertise as well as insufficient political engagement on the side of members of regional parliaments. For this reason, inter-parliamentary cooperation has mostly been of a technical and administrative nature with quite under-developed political dialogue.

With respect to the challenges regional parliaments are facing today, there is still a large amount of leeway regarding the tools for making their engagement more efficient, faster and meaningful under the constraints of the Euro-

[51] Compare Chapter 2 by Ian Cooper in this volume.

pean decision-making process. In order to strengthen their position in the EU institutional architecture, regional parliaments have to invest further in improving the extra-state collective channels of cooperation such as CALRE or the SMN. In this sense, the two platforms should commit more to enhance Europeanisation of regional parliaments through organising inter-institutional training, tutorials and political debates on territorially-salient EU policy dossiers. CALRE would certainly do better by setting up its office in Brussels and re-think the extension of its membership beyond the position of Presidents. The SMN, with its political infrastructure at the heart of the CoR, should take a role of better policy-entrepreneur and focus on regional parliaments, rather than governments and other local actors, as its main institutional partners.

The willingness for further Europeanisation should also come from the members of regional parliaments themselves. They have to realise that the role of their institutions has changed. Nowadays, when most policy-deals and laws are made outside parliaments, their work becomes less and less law-making *sensu stricto* and concentrates more on controlling government's activity in EU affairs and implementing EU policies. In this sense, meaningful participation in the EWM becomes a catalyst for the exercise of these tasks and prevents parliaments from being suspended in an institutional limbo. Finally, the European Commission might want to increase the political salience of inter-parliamentary cooperation by providing a stake in the form of linking the EWM at the regional level to the territorial impact assessment procedure, which takes into account the potential economic, social and environmental consequences of EU future legislation, as well as those regarding the regulatory burden for the private and the public sectors at the regional level.

8

Italian Regional Councils and the Positive Externalities of the Early Warning Mechanism for National Constitutional Law

CRISTINA FASONE*

I. The Effects of a 'European' Procedure on National Constitutional Law

The early warning mechanism (EWM) is a European procedure introduced by the Treaty of Lisbon and its protocol (no 2) on the application of the principles of subsidiarity and proportionality. It has had considerable implications for Italian constitutional law in general, and more specifically for the role of national and regional legislatures and their participation in EU affairs. This chapter argues that the EWM has produced positive externalities[1] for the Italian constitutional system.

It has done so from the perspective of regional councils. This is how the regional parliaments with legislative powers for the purposes of protocol no 2 are named according to Italian constitutional provisions and case law, which in fact forbid the use of the word 'parliament' for these legislatures, as highlighted in section II of this chapter. Regional councils, as will be pointed out in section III, had been

* The author would like to thank the organisers and the participants at the workshop on 'National Parliaments and the EU-legislative Procedure post-Lisbon: A Comparative Analysis of the Early Warning Mechanism', held at the University of Uppsala, Uppsala Forum for Democracy, Peace & Justice, on 4–5 September 2014, and Diane Fromage for their insightful comments on an earlier version of this chapter. The usual disclaimer applies.

[1] The concept of positive 'externality' is used here as it was originally framed by JM Buchanan and WM Craig Stubblebine in 'Externality' (1962) 29 *Economica* 371, as a benefit that affects a party which did not choose to incur that benefit. In the case in question, a procedure conceived at the European level to enhance the political control of compliance with the principle of subsidiarity and the democratic legitimation of EU law-making by national parliaments has proved to be highly beneficial to Italian regional councils in the domestic constitutional system, in terms of their mutual horizontal relationships, cooperation with the national parliament, and the involvement of political minorities in EU affairs.

somewhat marginalised at the national level as a consequence of the implementation and judicial interpretation of constitutional reforms in 1999 and 2001.

Article 6, protocol no 2, in the framework of the EWM[2] offered an opening to consultation of regional parliaments with legislative powers by national parliaments and this has been an opportunity for Italian regional councils for three reasons:

1) It has led to the setting up of new structural relationships with the Italian Parliament, in particular the Senate, which had never been established since the entry into force of the Italian Constitution (Externality I);
2) It has strengthened cooperation between regional councils so as to foster, wherever possible, a common representation of regional interests before the national parliament (Externality II);
3) A sort of 'alliance of legislatures', regional and national, has emerged, also representing the viewpoint of minorities within the Italian position towards the EU institutions (Externality III).

These three positive externalities are further considered in section IV of this chapter. Where appropriate, the analysis draws on a comparison with the Spanish case. Spain is the European country most similar to Italy in terms of territorial organisation of the state, and is often seen as a source of inspiration for reform of Italian regionalism.[3] The comparison aims to explore how different models of participation in the EWM have developed in the two countries in terms of the degree of involvement of regional councils in subsidiarity scrutiny in collaboration with other regional and national legislatures.[4]

One of the main findings of this chapter is the emerging practice of 'interparliamentary scrutiny' of EU legislative proposals in Italy. This inter-parliamentary scrutiny moves away from a narrow focus on the legal evaluation of the subsidiarity principle and instead embraces a more political view of the EWM as a device that indirectly fosters a more thoughtful and coordinated assessment between legislatures—at different levels of government—of the political implications and the merits of EU proposals. In order to confirm this assessment, section V of the chapter is devoted to examining two case studies: reform of the common agricultural policy and reform of the cohesion policy in 2011–12.

[2] A-L Högenauer and V Arribas, 'Legislative Regions after Lisbon: A New Role for Regional Assemblies?' in C Hefftler et al (eds), *The Palgrave Handbook of National Parliaments and the European Union* (Basingstoke, Palgrave Macmillan, 2015) 133.

[3] Regarding the territorial division of powers between regions and the state and the limits on the participation of regions in national procedures, eg the legislative process and the approval of constitutional amendments, see JM Castellà Andreu and M Olivetti (eds), *Nuevos Estatutos y reforma del Estado: las experiencias de España e Italia a debate* (Barcelona, Atelier, 2009).

[4] *cf* K Borońska-Hryniewiecka, 'A New Player in the "Multi-Level Parliamentary Field". Cooperation and Communication of Regional Parliaments in the post-Lisbon Scenario', Chapter 7 in this volume, on the different types of inter-parliamentary relations that involve regional legislatures.

II. The Constitutional Prohibition on Calling Regional Councils 'Parliaments'

Although the Italian version of Article 6, protocol no 2 uses the expression 'regional parliaments with legislative powers', Italian regional councils, the directly-elected legislative authorities in each Italian region, cannot be officially denominated as such. The Italian Constitutional Court prevented regional legislatures from changing their names to 'parliaments' in two important judgments in 2002.[5]

The controversy started when the Liguria Regional Council passed a motion stating that in subsequent documents it approved, the name regional council would be placed side-by-side with that of 'Parliament of Liguria'. The state challenged the motion before the Constitutional Court, arguing that only the institution exercising sovereign powers, the national parliament, can be called a 'Parliament'. The Court declared the motion to be in violation of the Constitution, but rejected the argument proposed by the state. It affirmed that the name 'parliament' does not derive exclusively from the exercise of sovereignty on behalf of the people: there is no identity relationship between sovereignty and the national parliament. Instead, according to Articles 55 and 67 Italian Constitution, the name 'parliament' can only be attributed to the constitutional body composed of two chambers and whose members represent the entire nation (not regional polities) without a binding mandate. Therefore, 'regional councils', as the Italian regional legislatures are denominated by Article 122 Italian Constitution, could potentially choose other names, with the one notable exception of 'parliaments'.[6]

Despite this fact, the Italian version of Article 6, protocol no 2, annexed to the Treaty of Lisbon, which was drafted years after the Constitutional Court's judgments, still refers to 'regional parliaments with legislative powers' in the context of the EWM. In other words, rather than taking national constitutional differences into account, the Italian version of the protocol neglects that according to the Italian Constitution regional legislatures cannot in fact be named 'parliaments'.[7] However, this by no means impairs the application of the protocol to the Italian regional councils, since they meet the substantive conditions for participation in the EWM via the national parliament based on the protocol: the regional dimension between the state and local government; their elective nature; and their

[5] See judgments nos 106 and 306/2002 of the Italian Constitutional Court and the case note by N Lupo, 'Tra interpretazione letterale (della Costituzione) e interpretazione contenutistica (degli atti introduttivi del giudizio): a proposito dei Parlamenti-Consigli regionali e dell'impugnazione dei nuovi Statuti' (2002) 5 *Le Regioni* 1209.

[6] For example, the regional councils of Marche and Sicily are officially named 'legislative assembly of Marche' and 'Sicilian regional assembly'.

[7] See N Lupo, 'National and Regional Parliaments in the EU Decision-Making Process, after the Treaty of Lisbon and the Euro-crisis' (2013) 5 *Perspectives on federalism* 14 and, now, Lupo, 'The Scrutiny of the Principle of subsidiarity in the Procedures and Reasoned Opinions of the Italian Chamber and Senate', Chapter 11 in this volume.

legislative authority.[8] Nevertheless, the reference to regional 'parliaments' in the Italian version of the protocol shows that its drafting has not taken the Italian constitutional constraint about the name of regional legislatures into great consideration, just as one might expect from Article 4(2) TEU.[9]

III. The (Weak) Position of Regional Councils in the Italian Constitutional Context

The regional councils established in the 20 Italian regions—15 ordinary regions and five special regions, with two autonomous provinces, Trento and Bolzano[10]—have traditionally not been powerful institutions in the Italian constitutional system. This is due to several factors. First, regional councils enjoy different statuses depending on whether they are established in a special or in an ordinary region. The special regions and autonomous provinces, and hence their councils, were set up before (like Sicily) or immediately after (like Friuli-Venezia Giulia) the enactment of the 1948 democratic Constitution and were granted an enhanced degree of autonomy from the centre by statutes approved by constitutional law, for historical, economic, geographical and linguistic reasons. By contrast, the ordinary regions and their councils were created more than 20 years later, only in the 1970s, because of a clash between the dominant party in the post-war era, the *Democrazia Cristiana*, and the opposition parties, particularly the Italian *Partito comunista*, over the shape and balance of power within the new regional arrangements.

Not only were the councils of the ordinary regions established following a considerable delay, but they were only entitled to adopt legislative norms upon delegation by the state or in the subject-matter listed in Article 117 Italian Constitution, providing that they complied (in those matters) with the fundamental

[8] The expression 'regional parliaments with legislative powers' is used in the protocol with the aim of referring to regional legislatures without providing for a solid conceptual underpinning behind the choice of the word 'parliaments' rather than assemblies, legislatures or councils. On this point, see D Fromage, 'Regional Parliaments and the Early Warning System', Chapter 6 in this volume.

[9] In particular, where Art 4(2) TEU states that the Union respects Member States' 'national identities, inherent in their fundamental structures, political and constitutional, inclusive of regional and local self-government'. For example, the words regional legislatures (*legislativi*) or legislative assemblies (*assemblee legislative*) could have been used in Article 6, protocol no 2. No Member State other than Italy poses specific constitutional limitations or preclusions on the denomination of its regional legislatures.

[10] The five special regions are: Valle D'Aosta, Trentino-Alto Adige, Friuli-Venezia Giulia, Sardegna and Sicily. Trento and Bolzano are autonomous provinces within the special region Trentino-Alto Adige and in fact most legislative powers and participation in EU affairs in this special region are delegated to the autonomous provinces.

principles fixed in national framework legislation and did not encroach upon the national interest.[11] Nor were they assigned any role in EU affairs.[12]

Furthermore, at that time the regional form of government, combined with the then electoral system, produced much political fragmentation and instability in the regional councils, which negatively impacted on the performance of the regional executives. The latter became too unstable and too conditioned by changes in the political majority in the regional councils.[13] Most regional governments did not reach the end of their five-year term, and as a consequence the regional councils were accused of being responsible for political deadlock. Against the backdrop of this status quo and aiming to produce a stable majority in regional legislatures, an amendment to the national law on the election of regional councils (law no 108/1968) in 1995 did not in fact improve the position of regional councils.[14] Nor, unlike other Member States of the European Union,[15] were—or are—the councils of special or ordinary regions represented in the national parliament.

In the view of their proponents, Constitutional laws no 1/1999 and 3/2001 should have re-shaped the balance within the regional governments, reinforcing the position of the president of the region in relation to the council and providing the latter with the role of a true legislature. Among the many implications these reforms had, one significant effect is that they reduced the gap between special and ordinary regions, both in terms of the regional form of government and of regional legislative powers. The most significant difference still remaining is related to fiscal powers, which are broader for the special regions than for the ordinary regions. The implementation of the constitutional laws of 1999 and 2001 nevertheless showed a gradual but consistent marginalisation of regional councils,

[11] National framework legislation here means legislation passed by the Italian Parliament to identify the fundamental principles of certain subject-matter provided for by Art 117 Italian Constitution, eg agriculture, which bind regional councils in the approval of relevant and more detailed legislative provisions. Compliance by regional councils with these principles is a condition for upholding the constitutional validity of the regional legislation.

[12] On EU regional 'blindness', see S Weatherill, 'The Challenge of the Regional Dimension in the European Union' in S Weatherill and U Bernitz (eds), *The Role of Regions and Sub-national Actors in Europe* (Oxford, Hart Publishing, 2005) 3–6, and M Olivetti, 'The Regions in the EU Decision Making-Processes' in M Cartabia, N Lupo and A Simoncini (eds), *Democracy and Subsidiarity in the EU. National Parliaments, Regions and Civil Society in the Decision-Making Process* (Bologna, Il Mulino, 2013) 319, 321–22.

[13] See, eg, A D'Atena, 'Il doppio intreccio federale: le Regioni nell'Unione europea' (1988) 6 *Le Regioni* 1401. At that time, the president of the region (together with the other members of the executive body), who was entitled to define the general political directions of the subnational entity, was elected by the Council from amongst its members (as in the Spanish Autonomous Communities). His mandate as president depended on the support of the majority in the Council—an Assembly with limited legislative power with the authority to adopt regulations, programmes and plans for the region, the same majority that voted for him after the election.

[14] See especially C Pinelli, 'La crisi dei Consigli regionali e i circuiti tra Stato e Regioni' in *Scritti in onore di Michele Scudiero*, vol III (Napoli, Jovene, 2008) 1777–89.

[15] Like Austria and, partly, Spain. For more details, see n 56 below.

which ultimately appeared to be—partly through their own fault—the main victims of the constitutional reforms.[16]

The president of the region is now directly elected by the people, and thus relies on an autonomous channel of legitimation rather than through the regional councils.[17] The aim of this reform was acknowledged by the Constitutional Court itself, ie to simplify the regional political systems—with the aspiration of moving from extreme fragmentation of political groups to bipolarisation—and to make the functioning of the political institutions more stable (judgment no 2/2004). Therefore, the regional councils have become far less free to determine the destiny of the regional executives compared to the past. The directly-elected president of the region now has the power to appoint and remove the other members of the regional executive, without any participation by the council. The latter still has the authority to force the president in office to resign by approving 'a reasoned motion of no confidence' (Article 126 Constitution).[18] However, removal of the president by the council through a withdrawal of confidence is definitely made unlikely by the 'joint destiny' of the two organs (*simul stabunt, simul cadent*): the removal or the resignation of the president of the region automatically leads to the dissolution of the council and vice versa. Moreover, should the dissolution of the council or the simultaneous resignation of the majority of its members occur, a new president of the region must be elected.

Concerning legislative competence, in principle Constitutional law no 3/2001 could have significantly enhanced the role of regional councils as legislatures, reversing the previous criterion of distribution of legislative competences and giving the regions the general power to legislate (Article 117.4 Italian Constitution) except in those fields reserved for the state (Article 117.2 Italian Constitution) or subject to shared competence between the state (defining the fundamental principles of the matter) and the regions (regulating the remaining issues). Of interest for our purposes is the circumstance that following this constitutional reform the

[16] See, in general, M Olivetti, *Nuovi Statuti e forma di governo delle Regioni* (Bologna, Il Mulino, 2002); V Lippolis, 'Le prospettive della riforma dei Consigli regionali e l'equilibrio della nuova forma di governo' in E Gianfrancesco et al (eds), *Il Filangieri. Quaderno 2009. Nuove regole per nuovi Consigli regionali* (Napoli, Jovene, 2010) 105–8; M Carli, 'La marginalità dei Consigli regionali: qualche suggerimento per evitarla' in P Caretti and E Rossi (eds), *Osservatorio sulle fonti 2009. L'attuazione degli Statuti regionali* (Torino, Giappichelli, 2010) 1–7; P Cavaleri, 'Ambiguità del ruolo attribuito ai Consigli regionali dai nuovi Statuti ordinari' in E Gianfrancesco et al (eds), *Il Filangieri. Quaderno 2009* (Napoli, Jovene, 2010) 337–42.

[17] On the reasons behind the institutional choice to directly elect the President of the regions, see E Gianfrancesco, 'La forma di governo regionale nella recente esperienza italiana' in JM Castellá and M Olivetti (eds), *Nuevos Estatutos y reforma del Estado* (Barcelona, Atelier, 2009) 193.

[18] Although in judgment no 12/2006 the Constitutional Court arguably denied the existence of the confidence relationship between the assembly and the President and affirmed that the relationship is based rather on 'political consonance'. See A Buratti, 'Dal rapporto di fiducia alla "consonanza politica". Rigidità della forma di governo regionale e libertà del processo politico' (2006) 1 *Giurisprudenza costituzionale* 90.

authority to legislate over the 'international and EU relations of the regions' is shared between the state and the regions, with the state adopting the framework legislation—law no 11/2005, now repealed by law no 234/2012—and each region passing its own law on EU affairs, which almost all the regional councils have now done.[19] Moreover, unlike other European countries, like Spain for example, where there is no specific constitutional reference to the European powers of the Autonomous Communities, the revised text of the Italian Constitution provides that in areas falling within their responsibilities, Italian regions and autonomous provinces—without clarifying which regional body is involved—participate in the formation and implementation of EU measures.

On the whole, however, constitutional case law has undermined the effectiveness of these new provisions on regional legislative powers, often neglecting the existence of the residual competences of the regions to the detriment of regional legislatures.[20] By contrast, through a 'creative interpretation' of Article 117 of the Italian Constitution, the Constitutional Court has expanded the legislative authority of the state. The Italian Parliament has been entitled to pass legislation on a series of issues which the Court has unilaterally placed in the brand new category of so-called 'transversal matters' (*materie trasversali*), such as protection of the environment. This category, which does not exist in the codified constitutional catalogue of legislative competences, identifies cross-sectional clauses rather than real matters, 'allowing the State to intervene in different ambits', and 'can evidently serve as a Trojan horse for the centralisation of competences'.[21] The same result has been triggered by the Court by making reference to the legal and economic unity of the Republic or to combined recourse to the principle of subsidiarity, as understood in Italian constitutional law, and the principle of legality.[22]

All the elements described above lead to the conclusion that the position of regional councils is somewhat weak in the Italian constitutional context. This is especially so when the following are taken into account: their relationship with regional executives, in particular after 1999; their constrained legislative powers; and their lack of representation in the national parliament and law-making.

[19] With a few exceptions, such as Liguria and the autonomous provinces of Trento and Bolzano. This does not imply, however, that the regional laws on participation in EU affairs are all updated in accordance with the new provisions of the Lisbon Treaty and law no 234/2012 (see section IV of this chapter below).

[20] S Parisi, 'Potestà residuale e "neutralizzazione" della riforma del Titolo V' in *Scritti in onore di Michele Scudiero*, vol III (Napoli, Jovene, 2008) 1601–2.

[21] See G Martinico, 'The Impact of "Regional Blindness" on the Italian Regional State' in E Cloots, G De Baere and S Sottiaux (eds), *Federalism in the European Union* (Oxford, Hart Publishing, 2012) 365–66.

[22] See, for example, judgment no 303/2003 of the Italian Constitutional Court.

IV. The Positive Externalities of the Early Warning Mechanism for the Italian Regional Councils

It is claimed here that the Treaty of Lisbon and the EWM are having a positive, though indirect, impact on the—so far marginal—position of regional councils in the Italian constitutional system. In the following, three positive externalities brought by the EWM for regional councils are analysed.

1) The chapter considers the setting up of a long-lasting relationship with the national parliament, and in particular with the Senate (*Senato della Repubblica*), by looking at the national procedures for implementation of the EWM and prospective composition of the Senate should the ongoing constitutional reform enter into force. To this end, it first deals with the pre-Lisbon arrangements between regional councils and the Italian Parliament; then gives an overview of the post-Lisbon executive-legislature relationships in Italy regarding EU affairs; next, examines the scope and effects of regional councils' opinions in comparison with those of the Spanish regional parliaments; and lastly considers the input from the regional councils and the Italian Senate on the use of the EWM as a tool to enhance their mutual cooperation.

2) The second positive externality considered as a consequence of the application of the EWM, and of the reduced asymmetries of Italian regionalism after 2001, is strengthened cooperation among regional councils. This development may also be beneficial in enabling the whole country to express a more coherent position on EU legislative proposals and documents (Communications, White and Green Papers, etc) under scrutiny.

3) Finally, the third positive externality examined affects participation by the (national and regional) legislatures as the institutions representing both the majority and the opposition or minorities in EU affairs. It is argued that this more broadly encompassing representation of political orientations to the EU at the national and regional levels of government has been enhanced thanks to the EWM, and has brought added value to the involvement of political minorities in European-oriented procedures.

A. Positive Externality I. Promoting a Long-Lasting Relationship with the Italian Parliament, Particularly the Senate

(i) The Weak Interaction between Italian Regional and National Legislatures under National Law before the Lisbon Treaty

Regional councils do not have any structural relationship with the national parliament under the Italian Constitution. The procedures that put the regional and national legislatures in contact have been used rarely or only once, as in the case of five regional councils putting forward a proposal for an abrogative referendum on national legislation (Article 75 Constitution); or a request for a (consultative) constitutional referendum whenever a constitutional bill, despite being passed by an absolute majority, has not been approved by a two-thirds majority of each chamber in the second vote (Article 138 Constitution).[23] By the same token, every seven years (which is the ordinary term of the presidential mandate), each regional council elects three regional delegates to sit in the Italian Parliament summoned in joint session for the election of the President of the Republic (Article 83 Constitution). These procedures have not allowed the regional councils to establish a long-standing relationship with the parliament. On the other hand, the power of legislative initiative assigned to every regional council (Article 121 Constitution), despite being regularly exercised, has not really been effective in terms of the number of (regional) bills finally approved by the parliament.[24] It is instead the State-Regions Conference, which is composed of state and regional executives, that is the main indirect interlocutor of the parliament on matters concerning national legislation. Indeed, in a series of cases when a regional competence is in question, a prior and binding agreement has to be reached within this Conference before the parliament approves a law.[25]

(ii) Executives and Legislatures in Italian Post-Lisbon Procedures on EU Affairs

Despite being delayed three years, the implementation of the Treaty of Lisbon, and its protocol no 2 in particular, was passed in December 2012 as Law no 234/2012.[26] It has created the most significant opportunity for regional councils to set up a stable relationship with the national parliament, after a series of failed attempts.[27] Law no 234/2012 eventually provided for the two chambers to consult regional

[23] On the interpretation and application of Art 138 Italian Constitution, see C Mortati, 'Concetto, limiti, procedimento della revisione costituzionale' (1952) 2 *Rivista trimestrale di diritto pubblico* 41; A Tesauro, *Istituzioni di diritto pubblico*, vol I (Torino, UTET, 1960) 269; SM Cicconetti, *La revisione della Costituzione* (Padova, Cedam, 1972); A Pizzorusso, 'Art. 138' in G Branca and A Pizzorusso (eds), *Commentario della Costituzione* (Bologna, Zanichelli, 1975) 715; and T Groppi, 'Art. 138' in R Bifulco, A Celotto and M Olivetti (eds), *Commentario alla Costituzione*, vol III (Torino, UTET, 2006) 2709.

[24] By the same token, the involvement of regional councils in the implementation of law no 42/2009 on fiscal federalism in the framework of the bicameral committee for the fulfilment of fiscal federalism (Art 3) has not represented a channel able to make the regional councils and the parliament work together. See N Lupo, 'Il procedimento di attuazione della delega sul federalismo fiscale e le nuovi sedi della collaborazione tra i livelli territoriali: commissione bicamerale, commissione tecnica paritetica e conferenza permanente', *Federalismi.it*, 2 December 2009, p 20–21.

[25] See law no 59/1997 and legislative decree no 281/1997.

[26] For details, see N Lupo, 'The Scrutiny of the Principle of Subsidiarity', Chapter 11 in this volume.

[27] The latest of these attempts, provided by Art 11 of Constitutional law no 3/2001, foresees the integration of the composition of the existing bicameral parliamentary committee for regional affairs by representatives of the regions and local authorities, according to the rules of procedure is the correct denomination of the Chamber of Deputies and the Senate and pending the approval of the constitutional reform. Whether or not it is mandatory to integrate the composition of this committee has been subject to scholarly debate. It suffices to say, however, that this provision has never been applied. See R Bifulco, 'Nuove ipotesi normative (minime) in tema di integrazione della Commissione parlamentare per le questioni regionali' (2003) 2 *Rassegna parlamentare* 339–61.

councils in the framework of the EWM (Article 8.3) and for the opinions issued by regional councils and governments to be taken into account by the Parliament within the Political Dialogue with the European Commission and the EWM (Article 9.2).[28]

As was prescribed by law no 11/2005—which the new law of 2012 repealed—it is still the national government, not the parliament, that is the authority responsible for transmitting all EU legislative proposals to the regions—to both regional legislatures and executives—through their Conferences.[29] Thus, unlike the choice made in other Member States, such as Spain—where the bicameral committee in the national parliament in charge of EU policies and subsidiarity scrutiny, the Joint Committee on EU Affairs, sends all EU draft legislative acts to the regional parliaments and receives their opinions in turn—the Italian Parliament only collects regional opinions but does not have direct avenues of interaction with regional councils before the scrutiny of EU documents starts. There is instead a preference to confirm centralised control by the national government as the main authority and contact point responsible for the flow of information and documents from the EU institutions to the national parliament and regional authorities.

Another important element of divergence with other national experiences is the fact that a 'national political dialogue' is established and that in this framework regional executives can also send their opinions to the national parliament, besides the opinions transmitted by their legislatures and regardless of whether they are formally empowered to send opinions on their own or not. At the same time, both regional councils and executives also send their opinions to the national government. In other words, national executives are put on an equal footing with regional councils regarding the comprehensive scrutiny of EU draft legislation and documents, concerning the merits of the EU measure, the choice of the legal basis and compliance with the principle of proportionality. In practice, the regions have tried to establish institutional procedures at the regional level to foster cooperation between regional councils and executives to either give precedence to the opinion expressed by the council or to force the regional executive and the council to reach an agreement on the position to be taken.[30] All these regional opinions concerning the general scrutiny of EU legislative proposals and documents have to be issued within 30 days of the transmission of the act in question.

By contrast, examination of compliance with the principle of subsidiarity, according to Article 25 (law no 234/2012), is reserved to legislatures; that is, the

[28] Indeed, this article refers to regional opinions sent both within the framework of the political dialogue and of the EWM (Art 24(3) and 25, law no 234/2012).

[29] See Art 24, law no 234/2012. There are two different conferences in place: the Conference of regions and autonomous provinces represents regional executives; and the Conference of the Presidents of regional councils represents regional legislatures. A third conference, the State-regions Conference, is the body where the national and regional executives coordinate their action, including on EU affairs.

[30] An example of a regional law giving precedence to the regional council is Abruzzo's law no 39/2014 (Art 3), whereas Marche's law no 14/2006 (Art 2) provides an example of regional legislation requiring an agreement between the regional council and the executive on a regional position.

national parliament and the regional councils. Interestingly, for this particular scrutiny no deadline has been set. Regional councils must send their opinions in due time for the purpose of the national parliamentary procedures—which in any case should be completed within eight weeks, according to protocol no 2—and must also forward them to the Conference of the Presidents of regional councils.

(iii) Scope and Effects of Regional Legislatures' Opinions in the Early Warning Mechanism. A Comparison between Italy and Spain

The destiny of regional opinions on subsidiarity, however, remains unclear.[31] This is mainly due to a lack of updated procedures in the Italian Parliament after the Treaty of Lisbon. The procedural rules of the chambers have not been amended regarding subsidiarity scrutiny—or for the other novelties introduced by the Treaty provisions and law no 234/2012—and the new experimental interpretation of the existing rules by the President of the Senate and the Committee on the Rules of the Chamber of Deputies has not been extended to the relationship with regional councils in the EWM.[32]

Regarding timing, the wording of the provision de facto leaves much discretion to the national parliament to decide on a case-by-case basis what 'due time' actually means and thus when the time has elapsed. As for the effects, some concerns can be raised. For example, no distinction between exclusive, shared and residual competence of regions has been drawn concerning the regional councils issuing 'reasoned opinions'.[33] In fact, one could argue that in the event of an EU legislative proposal only falling within the remit of regional residual competence, a reasoned opinion by a regional parliament should be taken into much greater consideration than an opinion regarding the exclusive competence of the state.

The lack of a clear reference to the relevant competence, which could be expected given the subsidiarity scrutiny undertaken, has its pros and cons for regional legislatures. On the one hand, it makes the opinions of regional councils less compelling for the national parliament, given the absence of a correspondence between the domestic state/regions division of legislative competences and the assignment of specific responsibilities by subject-matter between legislatures under the EWM. On the other hand, however, the vagueness of law no 234/2012 on this point allows

[31] See C Fasone, 'Towards New Procedures between State and Regional Legislatures in Italy, Exploiting the Tool of the Early Warning Mechanism' (2013) 5 *Perspectives on federalism* 122–55.

[32] These experimental and temporary procedures, pending a comprehensive revision of the parliamentary rules, are based on a letter from the then President of the Senate, Renato Schifani, sent on 1 December 2009 to the chairmen of the standing committees and on two opinions issued by the Committee on the Rules of the Chamber on 6 October 2009 and on 14 July 2010.

[33] According to Art 117 of the Italian Constitution, exclusive competences are those falling only within the remit of the state; concurring competences are those that require the state to define the fundamental principles of the subject-matter in a framework law while the Regions regulate the details of the matter in compliance with the state principles; and residual competences—which are very few in practice—are those remaining outside the previous two lists of competences—exclusive and concurring—which are only to be regulated by Regions.

regional councils to send their opinions on any subject-matter falling within the EWM, which also covers issues—such as cooperation on criminal matters—that are patently outside the remit of the Italian regions. Indeed, a very strict interpretation of the participation of regional councils in the EWM would have resulted in a narrower involvement of the regional legislatures. Given the case law of the Italian Constitutional Court on regional legislative competences, which has left only a few issues covered by the residual powers of the regions, such as certain local social services, the avenues for regional councils to deliver reasoned opinions in these fields would have been limited if regional councils had only been authorised to issue opinions where they enjoy a residual competence. The EU is traditionally devoid of authority to legislate on matters of social assistance or childcare, for example. By contrast, a broad interpretation of the powers of regional councils to deliver their opinions has had the effect of letting them express themselves on a wide range of issues, such as immigration, which stands as an exclusive competence of the state under Italian constitutional law but has significant repercussions at the regional level.

Notwithstanding this broad reading of the scope of regional opinions, their follow-up and the importance given to them in the national parliament have been rather modest so far, even when they engage with legislative proposals encroaching upon regional competence.[34] Apparently, the two chambers remain free to disregard regional opinions on subsidiarity without any justification, although Article 9.2, law no 234/2012, clearly states that parliamentary opinions on EU draft legislation and documents shall take into account regional opinions.[35] This is particularly important in areas of regional residual competence that perfectly match the EU shared competence—eg, agriculture, fisheries and incentives to small- and medium-size enterprises—where subsidiarity applies. Nevertheless, what can be seen as a legal obligation to consider regional councils' opinions in the EWM has until very recently never been treated as such by the Parliament.

By contrast, in Spain, where as in Italy the involvement of regional legislatures in the EWM follows a bottom-up approach, from regional assemblies to the Parliament, the incorporation of regional parliaments' opinions on subsidiarity within the national parliament's position has been observed under certain (legal and political) circumstances.[36] In its dynamic between national and regional legislatures this has anticipated some developments that in Italy have only recently occurred. For example, if a Spanish regional parliament sends an opinion on subsidiarity, the opinion is certainly mentioned in the *Informe* (report) of the Joint

[34] In Spain, likewise, on very few occasions—to be considered exceptions—has the approval of an opinion by a regional parliament triggered a procedural effect within the *Cortes Generales*. In these cases, the procedural effect has been the starting of the scrutiny procedure and the appointment of a rapporteur by the Joint Committee.

[35] Own translation of Art 9(2), law no 234/2012.

[36] See *Ley 24/2009, de 22 de diciembre, de modificación de la Ley 8/1994, de 19 de mayo, por la que se regula la Comisión Mixta para la Unión Europea, para su adaptación al Tratado de Lisboa de 13 de diciembre de 2007.*

Committee on the legislative proposal concerned. However, this is only compulsory when the subject-matter falls within the regional remit, although the reference often does not go beyond the mere citation of the regional opinion and the name of the parliament which sent it. Only when a regional reasoned opinion is issued, ie, a violation of the principle of subsidiarity has been detected, must the opinion be presented as an annex to the opinion of the Spanish Parliament. On two occasions in which the Joint Committee adopted reasoned opinions contesting a violation of the principle of subsidiarity, the opinions of the parliaments of the Canary Islands and of the Basque Country were cited, but without engaging in an in-depth examination of their contents. A paradox has been highlighted here between the negative opinion of the Spanish Parliament and those of the regional parliaments, which, by contrast, supported the EU legislative proposals.[37] The opposition between the national and the regional opinions was not made explicit; instead it appeared as if both shared subsidiarity concerns.[38] In one case, however, the reasoned opinion adopted by the *Cortes Generales* through its Joint Committee was grounded on a reasoned opinion of a regional parliament, the Basque Parliament—a case that shows the potential influence of cooperation between national and regional parliaments in the EWM. As acknowledged in the Joint Committee's opinion, the legislative proposal under scrutiny—dealing with the European statistical systems—affected a legislative competence of Autonomous Communities in Spain, according to the regional statutes of autonomy. Hence, the reasoned opinion sent by the Basque Parliament, which was also supported by the regional government, triggered the adoption of a national reasoned opinion which heavily relied on the contents of the regional one, following the constitutional allocation of competence.[39]

The codification by law of the effects of regional parliaments' opinions in the subsidiarity scrutiny carried out by the national parliament is certainly important to strengthening the position of regional legislatures in domestic procedures in

[37] See M González Pascual, *Las Comunidades Autónomas en la Unión europea* (Barcelona, Generalitat de Catalunya-Institut d'Estudis Autonòmics, 2013) 106.

[38] The Joint Committee approved two reasoned opinions on the same day, 14 June 2011. The first was contained in the Resolución de la Comisión Mixta sobre la Propuesta de Directiva del Consejo que modifica la Directiva 2003/96/CE del Consejo por la que se reestructura el régimen comunitario de imposición de los productos energéticos y de la electricidad (COM(2011) 169 Final) and cited the opinions of the Parliaments of Canarias and of País Vasco; the second reasoned opinion was approved in Resolución de la Comisión Mixta Sobre la Propuesta de Reglamento por el que se establece una cooperación reforzada en el ámbito de la creación de protección mediante una patente unitaria (COM(2011) 215 final) and, in this field, concerning the regime of translation only the Basque Parliament sent its opinion. See Diarios de Sesiones de las Cortes Generales, Comisiones Míxtas para la Unión europea, IX legislature, n° 200, 14 June 2011, pp 16–18.

[39] See Reasoned Opinion 5/2012 of the Spanish Joint Committee for EU Affairs of 12 June 2012 on the non-compliance with the principle of subsidiarity of the Proposal for a Regulation of the European Parliament and the Council amending Regulation (EC) no 223/2009 on European Statistics (text with relevance for the EEA and Switzerland), COM(2012) 167 final. The official translation into English is available at the IPEX website: www.ipex.eu.

the EWM, but it is not sufficient.[40] Likewise, political consonance between the majority in the regional parliament issuing the opinion and the rapporteur in the Joint Committee is decisive, so that the actual political circumstances can affect the outcome of the procedure and the stabilisation of the cooperation.[41]

(iv) The Input of the Regional Councils on the Use of the Early Warning Mechanism

In Italy, too, the EWM has gradually turned into a channel for establishing, step-by-step, a long-standing relationship between the national and regional legislatures, mainly as a consequence of the input provided by some regional councils and by the Senate. As the Italian procedure on the EWM is not based on consultations launched by the national parliament with regional legislatures, as Article 6, protocol no 2 might lead one to expect, but rather on the individual willingness of regional councils to be involved, the procedure has been used thanks to the commitment of nine regional councils—Abruzzo, Calabria, Friuli-Venezia Giulia, Emilia-Romagna, Lombardia, Marche, Sardegna, Umbria and Veneto—to send their opinions to the Parliament.[42] These are the councils of the regions that either at the time of the Constitutional Treaty had already started to develop regional procedures and send their opinions to the national government first and to the parliament afterwards (Emilia-Romagna, Friuli-Venezia Giulia, Marche) and those that have constantly updated their rules on the council's participation in EU affairs and in the EWM in particular (Abruzzo, Lombardia, Sardegna, Umbria, Veneto).[43] Some regional councils, like those of Friuli-Venezia Giulia and Emilia-Romagna, also stand as virtuous examples of legislatures that have been able to combine their updated legislation in the field with a consistent practice of implementation and delivery of opinions, which cannot be taken for granted. Indeed, some regional councils have passed regional legislation that takes into account both the Lisbon Treaty and law no 234/2012—Valle D'Aosta and Lazio, for instance—but they

[40] See K Borońska-Hryniewiecka, 'A New Player in the "Multi-Level Parliamentary Field"', Chapter 7 in this volume.

[41] The lack of political consonance between the regional and the national legislatures and the fact that regional parliaments in Spain can only participate in the EWM while they are excluded from the Political Dialogue have decreased the number of regional opinions delivered and the rate of participation by regional parliaments in the mechanism. See D Fromage, *Les parlements allemands, britanniques, espagnols, français et italiens dans l'UE après le Traité de Lisbonne* (Paris, L'Harmattan, 2015) and, now, D Fromage, Regional Parliaments and the early warning system: an assessment six years after the entry into force of the Lisbon treaty", SOG Working Papers 33, April 2016, 6–30.

[42] The most active regional legislatures have been those of Emilia-Romagna and Abruzzo. The regional council of Emilia-Romagna has issued on average a dozen opinions a year since 2012, although many of them refer to EU documents, like Communications from the Commission, rather than legislative proposals.

[43] See regional law (RL) of Emilia-Romagna no 16/2008; RL of Friuli-Venezia Giulia no 10/2004 as modified by RL no 13/2013; RL of Marche no 14/2006; RL of Abruzzo no 39/2014; RL of Lombardia no 17/2011 as modified by RL no 14/2014; RL of Sardegna no 13/2010; RL of Umbria no 23/2007 as modified by RL no 11/2014; and RL of Veneto no 26/2011 as modified by RL no 27/2013.

have never delivered opinions in the field of the EWM.[44] However, the remaining regional councils—the majority—have never participated in the EWM with the Parliament.[45]

Certain elements can explain this 'state of the art': the inter-institutional cooperation at the regional level; the availability of human resources able to follow procedures on the EWM in the regional councils; and expectations and perceptions about the impact of the regional legislatures' opinions at national level.[46] Indeed, the regional councils that are more engaged in the EWM are those that can rely on solid cooperation with the political and administrative structures of their regional governments in terms of exchange of information and guidance on the different dossiers scrutinised, and are those that can count on civil servants, usually working for the council's committee on EU affairs, specifically devoted to the EU and subsidiarity scrutiny. For some years, the lack of feedback received from the national government and parliament on regional opinions has also discouraged the active involvement of regional councils in the EWM. Indeed, in contrast with the practice of the European Commission to reply to every single opinion of national parliaments, the Italian Parliament (and Government) has not paid much attention to regional councils' opinions, even when transmitted in due time. The situation is now, however, gradually changing. The entry into force of law no 234/2012 and the new attitude shown by the Italian Senate towards councils have created an incentive for regional legislatures to increase the level and the quality of their participation.

(v) The Input of the Senate to Cooperation with Regional Councils on the Early Warning Mechanism

The Italian Senate is regarding the opinions of regional councils as more and more important.[47] First of all, opinions sent within the EWM to the Senate are acknowledged as regional votes on the basis of a pre-existing Senate rule (Article 138) and thus are made publicly available on the Senate's website.[48] Secondly, regional councils' opinions (votes) are often quoted within the main report or resolution dealing with subsidiarity. By way of practice, in matters of cohesion policy and of

[44] See RL of Valle D'Aosta no 8/2006 as modified by RL no 7/2014 and RL of Lazio no 1/2015.

[45] In some regions the opportunity for regional councils to be involved in the EWM and to send opinions to the national parliament is not even provided by the regional law on participation in EU affairs (see, for example, RL of Campania no 18/2008; RL of Toscana no 26/2009; RL of Puglia no 24/2011).

[46] On these elements and the nature and scope of regional mobilisation in the EWM, see K Borońska-Hryniewiecka, 'A New Player in the "Multi-Level Parliamentary Field"' and D Fromage, 'Regional Parliaments and the Early Warning System', Chapters 7 and 6 in this volume.

[47] As N Lupo, in 'The Scrutiny of the Principle of Subsidiarity', Chapter 11 in this volume, highlights, the Chamber of Deputies is much more selective than the Senate in the choice of EU legislative proposals to scrutinise, so that fewer proposals in the end complete scrutiny within the EWM and the Political Dialogue.

[48] These 'votes', according to the official translation of the Italian Senate's rules of procedure, are in fact petitions that can be proposed for consideration by the chamber from any regional council on any subject matter.

common agricultural policy, for instance, the opinions of regional councils have been cited and have contributed to forming the opinion of the Senate's standing committee on EU Policies, and in one case the document adopted by the corresponding committee of the Chamber of Deputies was based on the arguments put forward by the regional legislatures.[49] Although the committees competent on the subject-matter, which are equally involved in the scrutiny of EU legislative proposals though with different roles in the two chambers,[50] did not refer to individual regional councils' opinions and neither were regional opinions attached to the final parliamentary resolution adopted, the influence of the regional legislatures on the position of the national parliament in the EWM can be easily detected.[51]

Clear signals in the direction of strengthening the relationship between Parliament and regional councils can also be seen in recent developments in the Senate. Perhaps because of its nature as a second chamber in principle 'elected on a regional basis',[52] on 12 March 2014 the Senate Committee on EU Policies set up a subcommittee on the relationship with the regions in matters of EU affairs. This is the only permanent subcommittee established in this standing committee besides that in charge of drafting opinions—a sign of the significance assigned to cooperation between the Senate and the regions when EU law is at stake.

A few months later, on 24 September 2014, the same Committee of the Senate endorsed an inter-institutional agreement signed between the Committee and the Conference of the Presidents of regional councils to ensure better coordination between the Senate and regional councils in the EWM, in Political Dialogue and in scrutiny of the Commission's Work Programme.[53] As far as the EWM is concerned in particular, the inter-institutional agreement improves cooperation between regional councils and the Senate, as it provides for:

1) joint and coordinated selection among legislatures of the dossiers of common interest in the framework of subsidiarity scrutiny (and Political Dialogue);[54]
2) hearings of representatives of the Conference of the Presidents of regional councils' representatives in the Senate Committee on EU Policies before decisions of common concern are taken at European level;

[49] For details, see C Odone, 'La collaborazione in fase ascendente tra il Parlamento e le assemblee legislative regionali: cinque casi pratici ed alcune riflessioni', *Federalismi.it*, 3 April 2013, 13 ff.

[50] See N Lupo, 'The Scrutiny of the Principle of Subsidiarity' in this volume.

[51] C Odone, La collaborazione in fase ascendente' (n 49 above) 16–17.

[52] This is the wording of Art 57 Italian Constitution in force, although a direct link between the composition of the Senate and regional representation is currently lacking.

[53] See the resolution passed by the Senate Committee on EU Policies on 24 September 2014, Doc XXIV, no 35 and the comments by L Bartolucci, 'In attesa del "nuovo" Senato, un canale di collegamento più fluido con i Consigli regionali negli affari dell'Unione europea' (2014) 3 *Osservatorio sulle fonti online* 10 ff.

[54] See, as an example of implementation of the inter-institutional agreement, the resolution adopted by the Senate Committee on EU Policies on 4 March 2015 at the end of its analysis of the European Commission's *Work Programme 2015—A New Start*, COM(2014) 910 final, where the choice of dossier to be examined in 2015 is also based on the preference expressed in the regional councils' opinions.

3) agreement among legislatures on a standard procedure for the EWM whereby regional councils are promptly informed about the Senate Committee on EU Policies' agenda for meetings, so they can send their opinions beforehand;
4) commitment of the Senate Committee on EU Policies to include and highlight in its opinions and resolutions in the EWM (and Political Dialogue) the opinions issued by regional councils; a commitment that has always been fulfilled since.

Of the two chambers of the Italian Parliament, the Senate definitely appears more 'pro-regional', especially concerning the importance given to regional councils' opinions. In prospect, should the ongoing process of constitutional revision be successfully completed, the Senate will become, from a constitutional point of view too, the main *fil rouge* between regional councils and Parliament in the EWM.[55] Should the Constitutional Bill finally enter into force, the Senate will play a crucial role in coordination of the relationship between the EU, the state and the subnational levels of government (new Article 55 Constitution). Furthermore, regional councils will be represented in the Senate and will also be the most significant component of the newly established chamber, in an innovative fashion compared to the similar experiences of the Austrian *Bundesrat*, the Spanish *Senado* and the Belgian Senate.[56] Indeed, according to the present text of the Constitutional Bill, the new Italian Senate will be formed altogether of 100 senators: 74 regional councillors chosen by the regional councils from among their members and in proportion to the population, 21 mayors chosen in each region and autonomous province by the regional councils, and five senators appointed by the President of the Republic. Hence, if this arrangement is confirmed, the Senate will also include a representation of local authorities, but the component from regional councils will be predominant.[57] This will lead to a reframing of and potentially to an enhancement of the participation of regional legislatures in the EWM, within and outside the Senate. Depending on whether the regional councils

[55] See the Constitutional Bill no S 1429-B, *Disposizioni per il superamento del bicameralismo paritario, la riduzione del numero dei parlamentari, il contenimento dei costi di funzionamento delle istituzioni, la soppressione del CNEL e la revisione del Titolo V della parte II della Costituzione*, which has already been approved by the two chambers in two subsequent votings and whose final enactment depends of the result of the forthcoming constitutional referendum.

[56] In Austria, the 61 members of the *Bundesrat* are indirectly elected by the regional parliaments (*Landtage*). In Spain, according to Art 69 Constitution and the *ley organica del régimen electoral general*, most senators are directly elected by the people (four in each province except for the islands and their provinces) and slightly more than one-quarter of the Senate is appointed by the regional parliaments (at present 58 of 266 senators), at least one by each regional parliament plus a senator for each one million inhabitants residing in the Autonomous Community (region). In Belgium, the sixth constitutional reform of the state, accomplished in 2014, transformed the Senate into an 'Assembly of the regions', since 50 out of 60 senators are chosen by the parliaments of regions and communities from among their members. See the chapter by Patricia Popelier and Werner Vandenbruwane, 'Belgian Parliaments and the Early Warning System', Chapter 9 in this volume.

[57] See A Manzella, 'Il "nuovo" Senato' in G Gambetta (ed), *Proposte di riforma per le istituzioni e la cultura* (Bologna, Il Mulino, 2015) and P Faraguna and G Piccirilli, La legge elettorale per il nuovo Senato: un possibile vincolo all'autonomia politica regionale, Federalismi.it, –Focus Riforma costituzionale, no 16/2016, 3-7.

reach a more or less coherent position on EU legislative proposals and documents, these legislatures can either decide to act as a collective player within the new Senate and issue a joint opinion to the EU institutions or they can participate in the EWM as individual and autonomous players from a purely regional standpoint by each sending its own opinion to the national parliament and government, which then can try to mediate and find a compromise position. In other words, the avenues for regional councils to influence the domestic accomplishment of the EWM are likely to multiply.

B. Positive Externality II: Cooperation among Regional Councils—Between Individual and Collective Participation in the Early Warning Mechanism

As highlighted, Italian regional councils show very different attitudes in terms of commitment to EU affairs and engagement in the EWM. Moreover, given their geographical locations and local production and industry they do not always converge on the same policy interests. Nevertheless, the constitutional reform of 2001 provided a great input towards a legal homogenisation of the traditional asymmetries between the special and ordinary regions, first of all regarding the pool of legislative competence at the disposal of regional councils. Hence, this symmetrising trend has also paved the way to creating stable coordination between regional legislatures within the Conference of the Presidents of regional councils, which established its permanent secretariat exactly in 2001.[58] This Conference has been acknowledged as having a very significant role in EU affairs in particular. Law no 11/2005 (now repealed) treated this institutional actor as a sort of 'transmission device' between the regional councils and the national government. The government sent EU documents and legislative proposals to the regional legislatures through their Conference and received regional opinions via the Conference (at that time the Parliament was not involved in these information flows). The involvement of regional councils in the EWM resulting from the Lisbon Treaty has triggered a new coordination effort on the part of the Conference, which had already started at the time of the legislative process for the approval of law no 234/2012. This law confirms that the transmission of all EU documents and draft legislative acts to regional councils takes place through the Conference of the Presidents of regional councils. By the same token, regional councils must notify this Conference of the opinions they send to the national parliament, which is an important innovation following the Treaty revision.

[58] Cooperation among regional executives, by contrast, dates back to 1981, when the Conference of the Presidents of the regions and autonomous provinces was set up, followed by the creation of state-region-local autonomous conferences, always at the executive level. On the inter-governmental relationship between state, regions and local autonomy in Italy in a comparative perspective, see I Ruggiu, *Contro la Camera delle Regioni: istituzioni e prassi della rappresentanza territoriale* (Napoli, Jovene, 2006) 235–406.

The Conference of the Presidents of regional councils is by no means entitled to decide *on behalf of* the regional councils or to replace their action. It is simply a cooperative tool and does not impair the autonomy of each regional legislature. Although regional councils remain free to address the EWM individually, they often informally coordinate their position within this Conference or, better, they try to define together which EU legislative proposals and documents are worth examining on the basis of the annual work programme of the European Commission.

The cooperation between regional councils in the EWM through the Conference is fruitful for at least two reasons. Without preventing each legislature from expressing an opinion on whatever EU dossier it pleases, the Conference helps the regional councils to make their voices heard at the national level, in particular in the Parliament. Compared to a case where a single regional council's opinion is issued, it is much more difficult for the two chambers to disregard the regional point of view when they receive the opinions of several regional legislatures on the same EU legislative package. As the cases of the reform of the common agricultural policy (CAP) and, even more so, of the cohesion policy in 2011 demonstrate, a cohesive and strategic participation by regional councils in subsidiarity scrutiny helps make the parliamentary opinion(s) inclusive of regional positions.[59]

The second reason why the cooperation of regional councils in their Conference is useful for the purpose of the EWM is that the exchange of views and information that occurs there improves the quality of the regional opinions delivered. In particular, it fosters a more thoughtful consideration of the principle of subsidiarity when it comes to drafting opinions, which otherwise tend to mix together elements of subsidiarity, proportionality and merits in a single document without clear reference to the different grounds of assessment of the legislative proposal. Although some regional councils—of Emilia-Romagna, Friuli-Venezia Giulia, Marche and Veneto—give more careful consideration to subsidiarity scrutiny, it is often a more 'political' reading of the principle that prevails,[60] one based on the territorial impact of proposals rather than on evaluation of different regulatory options provided by the Treaty, the sufficiency of the existing regional or national intervention to fulfil the objectives of the proposed action, or the necessity of the EU measure.

All in all, the Conference has proved to be a flexible instrument in the hands of regional councils, to be exploited as a common political tool when there is a

[59] For details, see section V of this chapter below.

[60] For different understandings of subsidiarity scrutiny, see on the one hand, P Kiiver, *The Early Warning System for the Principle of Subsidiarity: Constitutional Theory and Empirical Reality* (Abingdon, Routledge, 2012) 126–32, and F Fabbrini and K Granat, '"Yellow Card, but No Foul": The Role of the National Parliaments under the Subsidiarity Protocol and the Commission Proposal for an EU Regulation on the Right to Strike' (2013) 50 *Common Market Law Review* 115–43; on the other hand, M Goldoni, 'The Early Warning System and the Monti II Regulation: The Case for a Political Interpretation' (2014) 10 *European Constitutional Law Review* 90–108 and C Fasone, 'Competing Concepts of Subsidiarity in the Early Warning Mechanism' in M Cartabia, N Lupo and A Simoncini (eds), *Democracy and Subsidiarity in the EU* (Bologna, Il Molino, 2013) 157–96.

convergence of interests, while it has mainly been used as a 'transmission belt' when there is a need to resort to individual opinions because of segmentation of regional interests.[61] In other regional states, like Spain, the Conference of the Presidents of regional parliaments (COPREPA) has not played any role in the coordination of regional parliaments' positions in the EWM, perhaps as a consequence of the (still) highly asymmetric character of regionalism and the distribution of legislative competences in that country.[62] By contrast, in Italy subsidiarity scrutiny has also revitalised cooperation between regional councils with the benefit of a gradual affirmation of the role to be played by regional legislatures working together and in close coordination with the Parliament.

C. Positive Externality III: Strengthening the Parliamentary Dimension of Participation in EU Affairs at the National Level

There is a third positive externality that the EWM has triggered in Italy at the national constitutional level. This is linked to the other two and can be found in a strengthened role of the Italian parliamentary institutions—the two chambers at the national level and the regional councils—in EU affairs. It is argued here that this development is positive because it allows the democratic institutions par excellence, those directly elected by citizens, to engage together in the scrutiny of EU legislative proposals at the national level, and wherever it is possible in terms of timing and convergences of interests to bring the Italian parliamentary position to the attention of the EU institutions. From the viewpoint of democratic deliberation, parliamentary assemblies have an advantage compared to national and regional executives. Through regional councils and the national parliament the opposition and minorities are represented in the scrutiny of EU affairs, so that decision-making is not only dominated by the majority. Indeed, this is particularly the case for EU-related procedures because the scrutiny of EU legislative proposals within the EWM is carried out primarily in committees, both in the two chambers and in the regional councils. In contrast to the floor of the House, where the divide between majority and opposition becomes evident, committees are consensual bodies where, whenever it is feasible, decisions are taken by consensus and the minorities are fully involved in negotiations and in drafting

[61] An example of the first case, in addition to the legislative package on the CAP reform (COM(2011) 630 and 631) and that on the cohesion policy (COM(2011) 615, 612 and 611), is the case of the public procurement and concession contracts (COM(2011) 897). By contrast, examples of individual participation by regional councils, with a mere formal role for the Conference, are the case of resolution no 472013 of the regional council of Abruzzo on the EU Draft Regulation establishing a legal framework for access to the port services market (COM(2013) 296) and the case of resolution no 1/2014 of the regional council of Friuli-Venezia Giulia on the EU Draft Regulation on organic production and labelling of organic products (COM(2014) 180).

[62] See S Alonso de León, 'Regions and Subsidiarity in the European Union: A Look at the Role of the Spanish and other Regional Parliaments in the Monitoring of Compliance with the Principle of Subsidiarity' (2012) 18 *European Public Law* 305–22.

opinions and resolutions. Before the introduction of the EWM, the Parliament did not scrutinise EU draft legislative acts and regional councils remained completely apart from EU affairs, which were monopolised by regional executives and their decisions on the use of the funds allotted through the cohesion policy.

The involvement of regional councils and all the political formations at the regional level has been particularly fostered by the EWM, as the Italian Constitution itself remains very vague on the issue of regional participation in EU affairs. Article 117.5 Constitution, modified by the constitutional reform of 2001, only says that 'The Regions and the autonomous provinces of Trento and Bolzano [shall] take part in the preparatory decision-making process on EU legislative acts in the areas that fall within their responsibilities', but does not add anything about which regional institutions should be involved. Indeed, until the negotiation of the Lisbon Treaty and its protocol no 2, regional councils were not considered in regional legislation as European actors to be involved in the scrutiny of EU measures.[63]

Once the Treaty of Lisbon entered into force, the full deployment of the EWM in terms of coordination among legislatures took some time. The Parliament originally perceived consultation with regional councils in the EWM as a further procedural burden, without properly taking into account the positive consequences in terms of legitimacy that could derive from the creation of a common alliance of legislatures on specific issues.[64] Similarly, a very low level of participation by regional councils could be detected. The gradual refinement of procedures between the Senate and the regional councils and cooperation between regional legislatures have certainly strengthened the role of parliamentary assemblies and the democratic legitimation of the scrutiny. However, it must be noted that, although this change has been triggered by the EWM and scrutiny of the subsidiarity principle, the vertical division of competence between Italy and the EU on the one hand, and between state and regions on the other hand, is not really the first concern for any of the parliamentary actors involved. It is instead participation in the scrutiny and the Political Dialogue at the European and national level that is valued the highest. In other words, what is considered most by the Italian legislatures is undertaking, under the European umbrella, inter-parliamentary scrutiny of EU

[63] The only exceptions were, as mentioned above, the regions of Emilia-Romagna (RL no 6/2004), Friuli-Venezia Giulia (RL no 10/2004) and Marche (RL no 14/2006). An acknowledgement of their role was provided, however, in national legislation, law no 11/2005, which allowed the transmission of regional councils' opinions to the national government. At that time, indeed, the protocol on the application of the principles of subsidiarity and proportionality annexed to the Constitutional Treaty, signed in October 2004, had already provided a reference to consultation by national parliaments of regional parliaments with legislative powers on compliance with the principle of subsidiarity.

[64] Attempts to make a Joint Committee of equally-represented senators, deputies and regional councillors' work on EU issues too have substantially failed. This Joint Committee was established by means of an inter-institutional agreement between the Presidents of the Senate and the Chamber of Deputies and the Coordinator of the Conference of the Presidents of regional councils on 28 June 2007, then modified in 2009, and also saw Italian members of the European Parliament as participants. It has been convened, however, only on very few occasions.

legislative proposals and documents coordinated between the national parliament and regional councils instead of agreeing on common standards for a strict legal assessment of subsidiarity.

V. Case Studies. The Reform of the Common Agricultural Policy and the Reform of the Cohesion Policy

Case studies of the reform of the CAP and of the cohesion policy confirm the limited significance given to strict evaluation of the principle of subsidiarity in the process of inter-parliamentary scrutiny. Often subsidiarity is not even referred to in the regional opinions sent to the Parliament, although when reading between the lines it becomes clear that concerns about compliance with this principle exist.[65] In general, collaboration between the legislatures focuses on the merits of EU legislative proposals.

Furthermore, the reforms of the CAP and of the cohesion policy highlight the different treatments reserved for the opinions of regional councils by the Chamber of Deputies and the Senate, the latter being more inclined to endorse and give visibility to regional observations in its own opinions, perhaps because of the Senate's constitutional connection with the regional level of government (Article 57 Italian Constitution).[66]

The cases of the CAP and the cohesion policy are particularly interesting because for the first time five regional councils—Calabria, Emilia-Romagna, Marche, Sardegna and Veneto, the same in both circumstances—submitted opinions on the same legislative packages.[67] On the CAP reform, although the regional legislatures sent their opinions in due time, the scrutiny was completed by the two chambers after the eight-week deadline expired, so the parliamentary opinions were considered in the framework of the Political Dialogue and not in that of the EWM. In the Senate, the Committee on EU Policies gave great prominence to the regional councils' opinions. They were cited, one by one, in the Senate Committee on EU Policies' own opinion. This Committee concurred with the substance of each regional remark, whereas the Committee on Agriculture, competent on the

[65] See, for example, Deliberation no 180/2012 of the regional Council of Umbria on the EU Draft Directive on public procurement (COM(2011) 897).

[66] See section IV of this chapter and, in particular, n 52 above.

[67] On the reform of the CAP the legislative package was composed of seven different measures: COM(2011) 625, 626, 627, 628, 629, 630 and 631. The legislative package for the reform of the cohesion policy, instead, was composed of nine regulations: COM(2011) 607, 608, 609, 610, 611, 612, 613, 614 and 615. The opinions of the regional councils did not refer to precisely the same measures in the two packages, but the scrutiny by the two chambers and the regional legislatures was done on the packages as a whole. On the scrutiny of these two packages by the regional councils, see, at length, C Odone, 'La collaborazione in fase ascendente' (2013) 7 *Federalismi.it* 15–21.

subject-matter and for the subsidiarity scrutiny, made a generic reference to the regional councils' opinions. Similarly in the Chamber of Deputies, the Committee on EU Policies endorsed and supported the views expressed in the regional opinions, without, however, giving an express acknowledgment of each regional council's individual contribution. Interestingly in terms of subsidiarity scrutiny, the fact that the opinion of the regional council of Veneto had detected—and this is very rare for regional opinions—violations of the principle of subsidiarity on the part of the draft regulations establishing rules for direct payments to farmers and support for rural development by the European Agricultural Fund for Rural Development did not trigger the approval of a reasoned opinion on the ground of subsidiarity by either chamber. They took the concerns of this regional legislature into account in their opinions but the regional subsidiarity critique did not lead to upgrading the nature of the parliamentary opinions to reasoned opinions, despite the fact that agricultural policy at national level falls within the regional remit.

The case of the reform of the cohesion policy confirms the attention paid by the Senate to inter-parliamentary scrutiny with regional councils of EU draft legislation and the little significance given in this scrutiny to strict assessment of the subsidiarity principle. In this case too, five regional councils sent their opinions to the Parliament, mainly with observations on the merits of the legislative package. Moreover, this time, soon afterwards the Conference of the Presidents of regional councils also transmitted a document to the chambers summarising the main remarks formulated by the regional councils on the EU measures in a joint contribution. This is especially important in view of strengthened cooperation between regional legislatures in EU affairs. However, on 14 December 2011, within the time-limit for the EWM, the Chamber of Deputies approved one of the very few reasoned opinions ever adopted, concerning Article 21 of the EU Draft Regulation laying down common provisions on several structural funds (COM(2011) 615 final).[68] No mention of the regional councils' opinions or of the document from their Conference—all of them in support of the proposal with a few observations—is contained in the reasoned opinion. This shows the limited room given to regional councils in the Chamber's activities on EU-related issues. By contrast, the Committee on EU Policies of the Senate not only cited in its opinion the observations brought to its attention by regional legislatures but

[68] Although this opinion is labelled as 'reasoned' it can be questioned whether what the Chamber of Deputies detected really is a violation of subsidiarity. In fact, it looks more like a violation of the principle of proportionality: what is contested in Art 21 of the EU Draft Regulation is indeed the conditionality established between fulfilment of the Partnership Contract for the use of funds and the implementation by the relevant Member States of the Council recommendations on an excessive deficit, an excessive macroeconomic imbalance, and compliance with an adjustment programme for countries receiving financial assistance. In the event that the Member State does not respond satisfactorily to the Commission's observations in this field, the Commission can decide to suspend part or all of the payments of the funds. It does not appear that subsidiarity is affected here, but rather the proportionality of the sanction applied—restriction to the use of structural funds—compared to the nature or degree of violation committed, ie of the rules on macroeconomic policy and financial assistance.

also quoted with approval passages from the Conference's document, which then became part of the Senate's position on the legislative package.

In the end, it appears that the coordination between the national parliament, particularly the Senate, with regional councils and their Conference aims to reach a common position on the political implications and the merits of EU legislative proposals rather than to put in place scrutiny tailored to check the principle of subsidiarity from a purely legal perspective.

VI. Conclusion

The EWM has produced more far-reaching effects for Italian regional councils than could have been expected from the mere introduction of an EU Treaty-based procedure.[69] After years of marginalisation deriving from the balance of powers with the executives within the regional forms of government and the gradual withdrawal of legislative competence through constitutional case law, the position of regional councils has at least partially been restored in the Italian constitutional system as a result of the implementation of the EWM.

Although today, seven years after the entry into force of the Lisbon Treaty, fewer than half of the regional councils fully participate in scrutiny of EU legislative proposals by sending their opinions to the Parliament, the EWM has at least revealed to all the regional councils a new field of activity—the usually-neglected scrutiny of EU law-making—and has strengthened their authority towards the regional executives in defining regional positions on EU policies.

Many improvements in terms of financial, human and administrative resources are still needed before every regional council is put in a condition to take full advantage of subsidiarity scrutiny. Nevertheless, it is already possible to detect the implications of the EWM for Italian constitutional law well beyond the regional domain. To some extent, this device has been used by regional councils instrumentally, not—or at least not primarily—to assess the appropriate exercise by EU institutions of their non-exclusive competence, but rather to build stable relationships based on mutual exchange and cooperation on EU affairs with other national institutions, ie regional councils and the parliament, with potential spill over effects in other areas, as the ongoing constitutional reform of the Senate seems to confirm.

Inter-parliamentary scrutiny of EU affairs is only at the beginning and it will take time before its potential is fully deployed. The involvement of regional councils in the EWM was not immediately perceived as an opportunity by the Italian

[69] Especially if this is compared with the position of authors who do not consider that protocol no 2, after the Treaty of Lisbon, in fact created an obligation for national parliaments to consult regional legislatures. See, on this point, D Fromage, 'Regional Parliaments and the Early Warning System', Chapter 6 in this volume.

Parliament, in particular by the Chamber of Deputies compared to the Senate. Furthermore, many regional councils are still reluctant or not interested in sending opinions to the Parliament, as the follow-up or the effects of their observations are not always evident or clear.

This notwithstanding, because of the 'excuse' of the EWM, regional councils are now engaged in a stable partnership with other regional legislatures if there is a convergence of interest on an EU proposal, and with the Senate, and some of them have concurred to strengthen the parliamentary dimension of Italian participation in EU affairs at the national level.

9

Belgian Parliaments and the Early Warning System

WERNER VANDENBRUWAENE AND PATRICIA POPELIER

I. Introduction

In Declaration 51 to the Lisbon Treaty, Belgium stated that the parliamentary assemblies of the regional entities within their field of competences act as chambers of the national Parliament. This way, Belgium wanted to emphasise that regional and federal assemblies are to be considered on an equal footing. This can be explained by the dual nature of Belgian federalism, marked by exclusive competences and the absence of hierarchy between legislative norms. The implementation of this principle, however, is somewhat deficient. First, there is no legal basis for an internal mechanism to translate subsidiarity opinions into the European Early Warning System (EWS). Secondly, regional parliaments in particular show little interest in the EWS. Although the federal House of Representatives, supported by an administrative unit, is more active in conducting subsidiarity analyses, all legislative assemblies mix subsidiarity analysis with Political Dialogue and consider the latter more relevant.[1] Several explanations abound, but it appears that in particular small regional assemblies are ill equipped to engage in subsidiarity checks. This is one argument that calls for the organisation of regional participation through the Senate, which was recently reformed to function as a genuine chamber of the federated entities but performed this function only partly hitherto. A second argument points out that the Belgian system, which merely gathers subsidiarity opinions without any substantive dialogue, misses opportunities to fully signify in the EWS. Nonetheless, the reformed Senate has lost all powers to intervene in international or European affairs. This brings a two-sided problem to the fore. On the one hand, it shows that the Protocol, by imposing the distribution of the bicameral Member States' votes, interferes in domestic institutional design.

[1] This is consistent with the more general observations by Jörgen Hettne, Chapter 3 in this volume, regarding the internal conflicts flowing from the implementation of political control of a constitutional nature within a very narrow legal framework.

On the other hand, it makes clear that domestic institutional reform should take a holistic approach and take into account European implications.

Belgian federalism proves an emblematic case for theories of multilevel governance. In particular, the two power-dispersing trends, upwards toward the EU and downwards toward the subnational level, seem to operate in isolation. The question of the enforcement of EU subsidiarity offers a prime example of this tension. As explained below, the resulting system of dual federalism contains a high degree of institutional complexity due to a bipolar yearn for autonomy. The operation of Protocol No 2 on the application of the principles of subsidiarity and proportionality in this tangle is no sinecure. Section II will explain the specific constraints of the operation of the EWS in Belgium. Furthermore, this contribution will analyse both the institutional set-up of the subsidiarity scrutiny by the national and regional assemblies (section III), and the content of the issued reasoned opinions (section IV). The resulting picture of the subsidiarity scrutiny in Belgium is rather bleak, due to both the federal institutional constraints, and the procedural determinants. Our conclusion distinguishes exogenous and endogenous determinants that impede the effective operation of the EWS in Belgium.

II. Subsidiarity Scrutiny and the Belgian Federal System

A. Declaration 51

EU law, and specifically Protocol No 2, leaves the question of regional involvement open with regard to the EWM. A neutral and somewhat facilitating stance allows those Member States with regional legislative bodies to draw them in, without any legal obligation.[2] Article 7 allots two votes to each national parliament, but stipulates that in case of a bicameral system, each chamber gets one of the votes. At first glance, this immediately seems to solve the question of regional participation,

[2] Some subtle nuances appear in the different language versions of the last sentence of article 6. The Dutch ('ieder parlement … raadpleegt, in voorkomend geval, de regionale parlementen met wetgevingsbevoegdheid'), the Swedish ('ska i förekommande fall') and the German versions ('obliegt es') appear slightly more forceful then the English ('it will be for each national parliament') or French ('il incombe aux') versions. The literature agrees on the lack of binding force of the phrase: C Grabenwarter, 'National Constitutional Law Relating to the EU' in A von Bogdandy and J Bast (eds), *Principles of European Constitutional Law* (Oxford, Hart Publishing, 2010) 115; JV Louis, 'National Parliaments and the Principle of Subsidiarity—Legal Options and Practical Limits' (2008) 4 *European Constitutional Law Review* 440, fn 22; D Edward and J Bengoetxea, 'Sub-state entities' in A Arnull et al (eds), *A Constitutional Order of States?* (Oxford, Hart Publishing, 2011) 37: 'This formulation does not appear to create an enforceable obligation to consult.' In particular on the different language versions, see D Edward, 'Subsidiarity as a Legal Concept' in P Cardonnel, A Rosas and N Wahl (eds), *Constitutionalizing the EU Judicial System* (Oxford, Hart Publishing, 2012) 97, fn 11.

assuming the second chamber reflects regional interests through its composition. However, in contrast to the German example, up until 2014 only a minority of the members of the Belgian second chamber—the Senate—represented regional interests. The last round of federalism reform did alter significantly the composition of the Senate, but simultaneously reduced its competences to institutional affairs only. The Belgian case does not align neatly with the requirements of the Protocol with regard to the bicameral vote distribution, either before or after the 2014 reform.

Belgian federalism aims to institutionalise and temper a dual and bipolar logic between the two main language groups, the Dutch speaking part of the population (ie Flanders) and the French speaking part. In order to mitigate a zero-sum logic that would paralyse federal decision-making, the sub-state institutional partition is not binary, but mired in complexity. Roughly spoken, the sub-state level consists of three Communities, following the language spoken (the Flemish Community, the French-speaking Community and the German-speaking Community), and three Regions (Flanders, Wallonia and Brussels). And, while the Regions neatly adjoin and make up the entire territory, the Communities overlap with regards to Brussels.[3] Legislative competences are divided between the federal state, the Regions and the Communities based on the paradigm of exclusivity. Detailed catalogues of competences in the Constitution and the Special Act on Institutional Reform (SAIR) aim at securing this exclusivity, with minor exceptions.[4] Following this logic of exclusivity, legislative norms originating from a Parliament, regardless of the level of government, are placed on equal footing. There is no need for a general rule of priority in this system.

It follows logically that Belgium issued Declaration 51 to the Lisbon Treaty, stating that

> in accordance with its constitutional law, not only the Chamber of Representatives [CoR] and Senate of the Federal Parliament but also the parliamentary assemblies of the Communities and the Regions act, in terms of the competences exercised by the Union, as components of the national parliamentary system or chambers of the national Parliament.[5]

This effectively elevates all eight chambers to the status of 'national parliament', unicameral when the issue concerns sub-state competences, and bicameral for a

[3] For a more profound introduction to the Belgian federal system, see P Popelier and K Lemmens, *The Constitution of Belgium, A Contextual Analysis* (Oxford, Hart Publishing, 2015). While outdated with regards to the last round of reforms in 2014, the following general introduction still serves as orientation: H Dumont et al, 'Kingdom of Belgium' in A Majeed, R Watts and D Brown, *Distribution of Powers and Responsibilities in Federal Countries*, A Global Dialogue on Federalism, vol 2 (Montreal and Kingston, McGill-Queen's University Press, 2006) 34–65.

[4] P Popelier and B Cantillon, 'Bipolar federalism and the social welfare state: a case for shared competences' (2013) 43 *Publius: The Journal of Federalism* 1–22.

[5] Declaration 51 of the Kingdom of Belgium on the national parliaments, 17 December 2008, [2008] OJ C306/287.

limited number of federal issues.[6] In other words: where estimations consider 70 per cent of the EU legislation to have a direct impact on the local and regional levels,[7] the federal Belgian Parliament, for most legislation within this 70 per cent, is likely to have no competence.

B. Draft Cooperation Agreements of 2005 and 2008

To effectuate the EWS, a cooperation agreement was drafted between the seven legislative assemblies in 2005. The legal basis for such a parliamentary cooperation agreement was unclear at that time.[8] Following the Lisbon Treaty, in 2008 some technical and minor adaptions were incorporated. Though not legally binding or ratified, the 2008 draft cooperation agreement functions as a guideline for the organisation of subsidiarity review.

The European Commission sends legislative proposals to the Senate, which forwards them to all other legislative assemblies. According to the cooperation agreement, parliaments who believe that a EU proposal belongs to their sphere of competence should give notice of their reasoned opinion to the other parliaments within two weeks of the Protocol's eight-week period, in order to settle possible controversies as to which entity—the federal state, the Regions, or the Communities—is competent. If legislative assemblies find a violation of the subsidiarity principle, they inform the other legislative assemblies as well as the Secretariat of the Conferences of Presidents of the seven legislative assemblies, within five weeks.

Nevertheless, during subsidiarity discussions Members of Parliament (MPs) may find that a legislative proposal affects other entities in particular. In one case, relating to the proposed Concessions Contracts Directive, the federal House of Representatives decided not to issue a subsidiarity opinion, because it considered that concessions are granted mostly in the field of regional competences, such as culture and education.[9] However, none of the regional parliaments discussed the proposal either, since the formal legal regulation of concessions pertains to the federal level.

The different opinions issued by the legislative assemblies are not discussed after issuance. Instead of establishing an institutional dialogue, the Secretariat merely gathers opinions. If one legislative parliament issues a reasoned opinion, only one

[6] Curiously, one of the exceptions to the rule of exclusivity is art 16(3) of the SAIR that allows federal substitution in case of an international judgment. While never applied in practice, the 2014 reform only gives the Senate an optional advisory role in case of a federal law based on this provision. The Senate as a chamber representing regional interests should theoretically play a larger role in this case.

[7] CoR, *The Subsidiarity Early Warning System of the Lisbon treaty—the Role of Regional Parliaments with Legislative Powers and other Subnational Authorities* (EU, November 2013) 6.

[8] P Popelier and W Vandenbruwaene, 'The Subsidiarity Mechanism as a Tool for Inter-Level Dialogue in Belgium: on "Regional Blindness" and Cooperative Flaws' (2011) 7 *European Constitutional Law Review* 204, 221–22.

[9] *Parl Doc* House of Representatives 2011–12, No 53K2155/1, 5.

vote is issued. Conversely, two votes are cast in one of the next four hypotheses. If the EU proposal concerns an exclusively federal matter, two votes are cast if both the House and the Senate enact a reasoned opinion. If only one legislative assembly has competence, this assembly can cast two votes. If the EU proposal concerns a shared competence, two votes are issued if at least one federal assembly and one regional assembly adopt a reasoned opinion. If it concerns an exclusive regional matter, two votes are issued if at least two legislative assemblies belonging to different language regimes enact a reasoned opinion. Four language regimes are discerned: a Dutch, a French, a bilingual, and a German.[10] The Secretariat of the Conference of Presidents of the seven legislative assemblies gives notice to the other legislative assemblies and the EU institutions of the bundle of reasoned opinions and the parliamentary votes.

From the above, we observe that the reasoned opinions are not compiled in a deliberative way, in order to usefully cast votes at the EU level.[11] Instead, opinions are merely gathered and the potential to contribute to a 'yellow' or 'orange' card is not fully used, as two different votes are cast without deliberation as soon as one legislative assembly has a different opinion, and only one vote is cast if only one legislative assembly was interested in discussing the proposal.

III. The Institutional Set-Up: The Differing Parliamentary Procedures and the Perspectives on EU Subsidiarity

A. The Procedures: Preparation, Drafting and Adoption of a Reasoned Opinion

Prior to and aside from the Protocol No 2, parliamentary information rights with respect to EU affairs were strengthened, and the Government was already obliged to inform the Parliament about draft EU proposals.[12] Moreover, all governments, including those from subnational entities, were obliged to take into account the advice of their assemblies regarding those proposals. These advisory opinions are not limited to, but can include, issues related to subsidiarity. For instance, while the Rules of Procedure of the Flemish Parliament distinguish between this advisory procedure and a reasoned opinion in view of Protocol No 2, this is not the case in the House of Representatives' Rules of Procedure.[13] The standing committees

[10] Note that these language regimes do not correlate to the partition between Regions on the one hand, or Communities on the other.

[11] Popelier and Vandenbruwaene, 'The Subsidiarity Mechanism' (n 8 above) 226.

[12] For instance, the Federal Advisory Committee on EU Affairs was established in 1985.

[13] Compare Art 37*bis* Rules of Procedure (RoP) of the House with Art 111 (general advice to government) and 112 (reasoned opinions on subsidiarity) RoP of the Flemish Parliament.

might mix the advice on a draft regulation in the context of the internal advisory framework, and a reasoned opinion in the context of Protocol No 2.[14]

In the House of Representatives, an Advisory Committee on European Affairs is established, consisting of 10 Members of the House and 10 Belgian Members of the European Parliament (MEPs),[15] where 'high politics' issues are dealt with.[16] An analysis centre within this Advisory Committee screens draft proposals, selects the documents that are relevant for the federal Parliament and drafts a report.[17] If the document concerns a new legislative proposal, or upon request of the president of the assembly, the president of a parliamentary committee or one-third of the members of such committee, the analysis centre will draw up a draft reasoned opinion.[18] The draft is discussed in the committee, and is considered approved by the plenary, unless one-third of the members request an actual referral to the plenary. The reasoned opinion is published in the parliamentary documents and communicated to the European Commission and the federal government. Moreover, each parliamentary committee assigns a so-called 'euro-promoter', charged with following up the documents communicated by the European Commission and the Advisory Committee on European Affairs.[19]

The Senate's rules of regulation do not provide for any procedure regarding subsidiarity opinions. Until now, the Legal Service drew up an advice on whether an EU legislative proposal fell within the Senate's fields of competence and the competent committee then decided whether it wanted to issue a reasoned opinion.

Both House and Senate make use of the possibility of consulting stakeholders or the Government's administrative services before issuing an opinion. If time is running out, opinions are even issued on the basis of a written procedure following consultations of interested parties, experts and federal government departments.[20]

At the regional level, only the Flemish Parliament, the French Community Parliament and the Walloon Parliament have inserted a provision concerning the EWS in their rules of procedure. The Parliament of the German-speaking Community has inserted a rather general provision on European Affairs.

According to the Flemish rules, each MP can initiate a draft reasoned opinion stating why the proposal does not comply with the subsidiarity principle, which

[14] Eg *Parl Doc* 2012–13, No 53K2459/1, 10: [our translation] 'MP: "The affirmative opinion of a national parliament, complemented with critical observations, can be a signal to the government to address these in the Council. The Belgian MEPs can draw from this opinion too, when discussing the legislative proposal in the European Parliament. The secretary of state confirms that he shares this point of view"'.

[15] Art 68 RoP of the House.

[16] T Delreux and F Randour, 'Belgium: Institutional and Administrative Adaptation but Limited Political Interest' in C Hefftler, C Neuhold, O Rozenberg and J Smith (eds), *The Palgrave Handbook of National Parliaments and the European Union* (London, Palgrave MacMillan, 2015) 155.

[17] See the website on EU affairs of the House of Representatives: europe.dekamer.be/index.html?language=NL (last accessed 9 June 2015)—see in general terms also M Gennart, *Le contrôle parlementaire du principe de subsidiarité* (Brussels, Larcier, 2013) 278.

[18] Art 37*bis* RoP of the House.

[19] Art 37 RoP of the House.

[20] *Parl Doc* House of Representatives 2011–12, No 53K1978/1.

is then discussed by a joint committee consisting of the Committee for European Affairs and the competent standing committee, and has to be approved by the plenary assembly.[21] Discussions are therefore more confined to the actual subsidiarity analysis.

According to the Rules of Procedure of the Parliament of the French Community,[22] a 'euro-promoter' is assigned in the Parliamentary Committee on International and European Affairs with the task to follow up European questions.[23] The administrative service of the Parliament drafts a note on the conformity of the EU proposals with subsidiarity and proportionality, either on their own initiative or upon request of the president of the Parliament, president of the Committee on International and European Affairs, the euro-promoter, or one-third of the members of a parliamentary committee. The reasoned opinion is debated and voted on in the Committee on International and European Affairs and adopted by the Conference of Presidents[24] or by the plenary assembly. The Rules of Procedure explicitly envisage a reasoned opinion on compliance with both the subsidiarity and the proportionality principles.

The Walloon Parliament has established a parliamentary committee on European Affairs, consisting of nine members of the Walloon Parliament and nine French-speaking Belgian MEPs and presided over by the President of the Walloon Parliament.[25] This committee drafts opinions for the Walloon Parliament on issues relating to the 'proper functioning of the European Union', with reference to both Protocol No 1 on the Role of National Parliaments in the European Union and Protocol No 2 on the Principles of Subsidiarity and Proportionality.[26] Hence, neither the Rules nor the actual parliamentary discussions distinguish between the two principles.

The Rules of Procedure of the German-speaking Community merely stipulate in a general manner that the regional government is obliged to inform the Parliament, and that the President of the Parliament sends the proposals to the competent standing committee, which subsequently issues an opinion to be approved by the plenary assembly. The provision does not distinguish between an advice to the federal government on the basis of Article 92*quater* SAIR, a communication in the Political Dialogue, or a reasoned opinion in the sense of Protocol No 2. However, an informal procedure took effect since October 2012, involving an analysis of EU legislative acts by a legal advisor who draws up a draft reasoned opinion, discussed by Committee I of the Parliament, and decided by the plenary assembly.[27]

[21] Art 112 RoP of the Flemish Parliament.

[22] Which calls itself 'the Federation Wallonia-Brussels'.

[23] Art 31 RoP of the French Community Parliament.

[24] This conference groups the leaders of the different political fractions in the Parliament with the leader of the assembly: see Art 7 of the RoP of the French Community Parliament.

[25] Art 48 RoP of the Walloon Parliament.

[26] Art 116 RoP of the Walloon Parliament.

[27] CoR, *The Subsidiarity Early Warning System of the Lisbon Treaty* (EU, November 2013) 36.

Table 1: Parliamentary procedures to produce an RO

Parliament	Committee	Procedure	Administrative support
House	Advisory Committee on European Affairs (mixed) Euro-promoter in standing committee	Referral to standing committee, ⅓ of committee members may refer to plenary	Analysis centre: screening, selecting and reporting drafts opinion upon request
Senate	No specific procedure	Discussion in Standing committee—adoption in plenary	Legal service prepares competence question
Flemish Parliament	Joint session of relevant standing committee and European Affairs Committee	Initiative: each MP Adoption by plenary	An individual MP is charged with drafting
Brussels Parliament	Discussion in Standing committee—adoption in plenary	No specific procedure: decision by plenary	No specific support
Walloon Parliament	Advisory committee on European Affairs (mixed)	Drafting and adopting in committee	No specific support
German Community Parliament	Standing Committee I	Decision by plenary	Legal service: draft
French Community Parliament	Standing committee on international and European affairs	Legal service can take initiative Adoption either within committee, Conference of Presidents, or plenary	Legal service

B. Conclusion

From the above it follows that the parliamentary organisation and administration with regards to the scrutiny of EU legislation is as varied within the Belgian federation as it is across EU Member States. While the size of EU staff of the Belgian

House of Representatives is below average compared to other Member States,[28] it is the best organised parliamentary administration within the Belgian federation. It conducts a first screening of EU documents, acting as a gatekeeper and adding a report on subsidiarity and proportionality questions for those documents selected for transmission to the MPs.[29] Moreover, the House's Rules of Procedures provide a fast-track procedure for the issuing of subsidiarity opinions. A Euro-promoter is appointed so as to commit MPs to EU affairs. Although in practice most Euro-promoters do not live up to the expectations related to their function, the system does promise specialisation and parliamentary attention for EU law-making.[30]

When regional assemblies are given the possibility to get involved in the EU scrutiny procedure, they are expected to build the capacity for such scrutiny.[31] This is especially the case in Belgium, where the exclusivity principle prevents the federal Parliament from interfering in matters pertaining to the sphere of Regional or Community competences. Nevertheless, most regional parliaments in Belgium are ill-equipped and hardly organised for this task.[32] Only the French Community Parliament more or less follows the Houses' model, with a fast-track procedure and the assignment of Euro-promoters, but remains lacking in administrative support. As a result, figures in section V (Table 2) show that activity of regional parliaments with regards to subsidiarity-scrutiny is low to non-existent compared to activity in the House of Representatives. Moreover, although the exclusivity principle is carried this far in no other federal EU Member State, Belgian regional parliaments are amongst the least active in EU Member States.[33]

Time pressure, task-load and insufficient resources, then, compel regional parliaments to cooperate. Subsidiarity monitoring within the Committee of Regions or CALRE has proved deficient, and the NORPEC network in which the Flemish Parliament participates seems no longer active.[34] Cooperation within the Belgian

[28] See A-L Högenauer and T Christiansen, 'Parliamentary Administrations in the Scrutiny of EU Decision-Making' in Hefftler et al, *The Palgrave Handbook of National Parliaments* (London, Palgrave MacMillan, 2015) 125. For precise data on the House's administrative staff, see T Delreux and F Randour, 'Belgium: Institutional and Administrative' (n 16 above) 158.

[29] T Delreux and F Randour, 'Belgium: Institutional and Administrative Adaptation' (n 16 above) 159.

[30] ibid 158.

[31] G Vara Arribas and A-L Högenauer, 'Legislative Regions after Lisbon: A New Role for Regional Assemblies?' in Hefftler et al, *The Palgrave Handbook of National Parliaments* (n 16 above) 140.

[32] This was also revealed in a study for the Committee of Regions, based on interviews: Leuven Centre for Global Governance, *The Subsidiarity Early Warning System of the Lisbon Treaty—the role of regional parliaments with legislative powers and other subnational authorities* (Committee of the Regions, November 2013) 39.

[33] Dept Internationaal Vlaanderen, *Subsidiariteit—het gebruik van het vroegwaarschuwingsmechanisme in de EU en in Vlaanderen*, Report (Brussels, 2014) 19–20. See also K Borońska-Hryniewiecka's Chapter 7 in this volume, where Belgium is mentioned as 'a paradoxical case where institutionally strong regional parliaments reveal the lowest level of interest in participation in the EWM'.

[34] G Vara Arribas and A-L Högenauer, 'Legislative Regions after Lisbon' (n 31 above), 146–47.

structure is also lacking. As mentioned above, in the reference period subnational parliaments were underrepresented in the Senate. Since mid-2014, the Senate represents the different subnational parliaments, but has kept only few legislative competences. The Senate, however, acquired the competence to issue so-called information reports on transversal issues. Where the recent reform forces the Senate to reinvent itself, a recommendation could be to seize upon this tool to identify problematic EU proposals and coordinate subnational subsidiarity debates.[35]

IV. Perspective(s) on Subsidiarity

Discussions in the House are prepared by the Parliament's administration, but the final selection and discussion is of a political nature. The same applies to the Senate, where the advice of the Legal Department is confined to the question of whether a legislative proposal falls within the ambit of the Senate—a question which, from now on, will almost inevitably be answered in the negative. As a result, the political evaluation outweighs the legal examination.[36]

The double nature of reasoned opinions was expressed in so many words in the Senate, where the committee members were reminded that the reasoned opinion on subsidiarity is of a legal as well as a political nature. The advice is of a legal nature in so far as it assesses whether the legislative proposal is in conformity with EU subsidiarity. This legal dimension is interpreted broadly: reasoned opinions also encompass questions of legal basis.[37] On the other hand, the opinion is of a political nature in so far as the MPs use political criteria to assess the proposal. As a result, the legislative assembly will question whether the proposal falls within the EU's competences; whether the proposal is relevant and suited for solving the problem at hand; and whether it respects the possibility for the Member States to interfere in this domain.[38] In an informative document of the House of Representatives, it is stated that the subsidiarity opinion should be interpreted in a broad way, comprising the proportionality of the proposal and its impact on Belgium.[39] Moreover, the procedure in the House of Representatives is based upon Article 37*bis* of the Rules of Procedure, which mentions that a draft advice is

[35] See the suggestion made to the Senate in their recent report on the implementation of EU law: *Parl Doc* Senate, 2014–15, No 6S131/2, 179.

[36] Some even exclude any legal dimension: 'un avis motivé … exprime un sentiment—politique forcément—quant à l'opportunité d'une réglementation européenne' F Delpérée and F Dopagne, *Le dialogue parlementaire Belgique-Europe* (Brussels, Bruylant, 2010) 19.

[37] *Parl Doc* Senate 2011–12, 5-1382/2, 3–4.

[38] ibid.

[39] www.dekamer.be/kvvcr/pdf_sections/publications/reglement/REGLEMENT_NL_062104.pdf. See also J Hettne's Chapter 3 in this volume on the relation between subsidiarity and proportionality control by the national parliaments.

issued relating to, *amongst other things*, both the principle of subsidiarity *and* the principle of proportionality. Hence, in parliamentary debates, MP's hardly differentiate between subsidiarity and proportionality review.[40]

This does not prevent the committees from discussing what is actually at stake in subsidiarity opinions. It is regularly argued why the subject-matter lends itself to EU interference and concerns are expressed regarding the impact on national legislation. However, apart from the subsidiarity opinion, and despite the Senate's explicit warning that this should not be part of the reasoned opinion,[41] observations are regularly made regarding the precise content of the draft proposal. These observations are in particular addressed to the federal government in its capacity of actor in the European decision procedure.

Moreover, the question of whether to issue a positive or a negative reasoned opinion does not merely depend upon the subsidiarity and proportionality check. In one case, a committee member expressed his concern that a negative reasoned opinion would harm Belgium's image in Europe, especially if there are indications that the thresholds in the Protocol will probably not be met.[42] A negative reasoned opinion was nevertheless issued regarding the proposed regulation, but not the proposed directive. In another case, the committee explicitly chose to formulate a positive opinion despite its concerns, but decided to convey these concerns through the Political Dialogue.[43]

V. An Analysis of the Reasoned Opinions

The several Belgian Parliaments issued 28 opinions concerning subsidiarity in the period 2010–14.[44] These discussions are mostly situated within the ambit of the Political Dialogue, but no clear distinction is drawn with the EWS-procedure. In six cases, the broader debates resulted in reasoned opinions in the EWS.[45] The federal House of Representatives is by far the most active participant with 21 opinions,[46] including four reasoned opinions.[47] The other seven opinions on

[40] See below, and T Delreux and F Randour (n 16 above) 161.

[41] *Parl Doc* Senate 2011–12, 5-1382/2, p 4.

[42] *Parl Doc* House of Representatives, 2011–2012, No 53-2068/1, p 16.

[43] *Parl Doc* House of Representatives, 2012–2013, No 53-2459/1, p 10.

[44] In the electronic databases of the parliaments we found 28 reports of debates held concerning EU legislative drafts, both in the ambit of the Early Warning System and in the ambit of the Political Dialogue.

[45] The finding of six ROs from the Belgian Parliaments over the years 2010–14 is consistent with two other sources: Department Flanders International, Report: *Subsidiarity, the use of the early Warning System in the EU and Flanders*; and K Granat, *National Parliaments and the Policing of the Subsidiarity Principle* (Firenze, European University Institute, Doctoral thesis, 2014) 152–54.

[46] *Parl Doc* House of Representatives, Nos 53-3263; 53-2910; 53-2775; 53-2689; 53-2459; 53-2452; 53-1978; 53-2221; 53-2150; 53-2155; 53-2145; 53-2068; 53-2062; 53-2048; 53-1978; 53-1970; 53-1940; 53-1507; 52-2544; 52-2536; 52-2523.

[47] *Parl Doc* House of Representatives, Nos 53-2068/1, 53-2145/1, 53-2221/1, 53-2910/1.

subsidiarity originated from four other assemblies: three from the Walloon Parliament,[48] two from the Flemish Parliament,[49] one from the Senate,[50] and one from the Brussels Parliament,[51] resulting in two more reasoned opinions, one from the Senate,[52] and one from the Flemish Parliament.[53] Although the Brussels and Walloon Parliaments both claimed a singular violation of EU subsidiarity,[54] these opinions were issued past the eight-week term.

A. Purpose of Parliamentary Opinions

In addition to the confluence between the national advisory procedure and the EWS,[55] Belgian Parliaments also make use of the Political Dialogue.[56] The fact that a similar or the same procedure is used to draft an opinion on draft EU legislation, but with differing addressees, obfuscates the picture with respect to the subsidiarity analysis. This partly explains why subsidiarity discussions are not limited to a strictly legal control of compliance with Article 5(3) TEU.[57] In general, the Belgian MP's consider the Political Dialogue more relevant precisely because it gives room for broader discussions, whereas the EWM is perceived as a 'technical and procedural mechanism'.[58]

B. Criteria

A qualitative analysis of the 28 reasoned opinions confirms the intuition that the Belgian Parliaments do not adhere to a strictly legal definition of subsidiarity as applicable in Protocol No 2.[59] In said collection of 28 Belgian reasoned opinions,

48 *Parl Doc* Walloon Parliament 2009–2010, Nos 129/1; 190/1, 631/1.

49 *Parl Doc* Flemish Parliament 2012–2013, Nos 2038/2 and 2147/2.

50 *Parl Doc* Senate 2011–2012, 1382/1. Apart from this opinion, the Senate issued another opinion to the Commission in the framework of the political dialogue, which did not in any way concern subsidiarity: see *Parl Doc* Senate, 2011–12, No 5-1329/2.

51 *Parl Doc* Brussels Parliament 2011–2012, Nos A-282/2, 282/3.

52 *Parl Doc* Senate 2011–2012, 1382/1.

53 *Parl Doc* Flemish Parliament 2012–2013, 2038/2.

54 *Parl Doc* Brussels Parliament 2011–2012, A-282/2, 282/3; *Parl Doc* Walloon Parliament 2011–2012, 631/1.

55 See above, nn 11–13 and accompanying text.

56 The so-called Barroso-initiative, see COM(2006) 211, p 9: 'The Commission wishes to transmit directly all new proposals and consultation papers to national parliaments, inviting them to react so as to improve the process of policy formulation'. This initiative was hailed by the European Council: see Point 37 of the European Council's meeting of 15 and 16 June 2006—Conclusions of the Presidency.

57 P Kiiver, *The Early Warning System for the Principle of Subsidiarity* (London, Routledge, 2012) 96–97.

58 Delreux and Randour, 'Belgium', (n 16 above) 162.

59 On the distinction between a legal and a more political conception of EU subsidiarity, see Kiiver, *The Early Warning System* (n 57 above) 72–73; M Goldoni, 'The Early Warning System and the Monti II Regulation: The Case for a Political Interpretation' (2014) 10 *European Constitutional Law Review* 90–108; W Vandenbruwaene, 'Multi-Tiered Political Questions: the ECJ's Mandate in Enforcing Subsidiarity' (2012) 6 *Legisprudence* 321–46.

three clusters of arguments can be distinguished, based on their character: legal, proportionality-related, and political. The first cluster of arguments addresses the legal criteria embodied in the EU subsidiarity principle as they arise from the text of article 5(3) TEU,[60] the case law of the CJEU,[61] and the Impact Assessment Guidelines.[62] In general terms, these legal criteria inquire into added value of action at the EU level, and the inability of Member States to achieve the objective of the measure, the transnational effects of the policy problem at hand, and economics of scale and scope.[63] The second cluster of arguments is more oriented towards proportionality, and includes such arguments as to the form of the action proposed (regulation or directive), and the cost–benefit weighing. The third cluster of arguments pertains more to the political realm. These arguments derive from notions of democratic legitimacy or sovereignty,[64] or, in a weaker form, the call for a sufficient scope for national discretion.

Our findings indicate a confluence of arguments on subsidiarity in the reasoned opinions, with a dominant role for the legal criterion of transnational effects. In total, though, legal arguments do not play a decisive role, but are often mixed together with other arguments in the debates.

C. Policy Issues

The most dominant policy issues in the 28 reasoned opinions under analysis are—unsurprisingly—economic and financial issues,[65] addressed in seven of the opinions.[66] Other returning issues concerned civil and social policy (6),[67]

[60] Essentially requiring a two-pronged test: see A Estella, *The EU Principle of Subsidiarity and its Critique* (Oxford, Oxford University Press, 2002) 94. Note that the 'old' debate on the incoherence between the two limbs of the test has disappeared due to the Lisbon rephrasing of Art 5(3), 'and can therefore' into 'but can rather'.

[61] Case C-58/08, *The Queen, on the application of Vodafone Ltd and Others v Secretary of State for Business, Enterprise and Regulatory Reform* [2010] ECR I-4999, paras 72–78; CJEU C-176/09, *Luxemburg v Parliament and Council* [2011] ECR I-3727, paras 73–83.

[62] European Commission, *Impact Assessment Guidelines*, SEC(2009) 92 at p 22, pose five questions in order to assess compliance with Art 5(3) TEU. The questions employ the substantive criteria that were developed in the Edinburgh Guidelines (resulting in the Amsterdam Protocol), and subsequently disappeared in the Lisbon version. This reallocation of the substantive criteria to the realm of soft law (IA guidelines), and away from binding primary law (Treaties and Protocol), coincides with the emphasis on political and procedural enforcement.

[63] W Vandenbruwaene, *The Legal Enforcement of the Principle of Subsidiarity* (University of Antwerp, Doctoral thesis, 2014) 145–46 and 330–33.

[64] Granat observes that national parliaments often try to weave 'national idiosyncratic elements' in a reasoned opinion on subsidiarity: Granat, *National Parliaments and the Policing of the Subsidiarity Principle* (n 45 above) 233–34.

[65] For a detailed analysis of the parliamentary reception of EMU crisis law, see W Vandenbruwaene, 'Country Report Belgium', EUI Law project Constitutional Change through Euro Crisis Law, 2014: eurocrisislaw.eui.eu.

[66] *Parl Doc* House of Representatives Nos 1507, 1940, 1970, 2048, 2062, 2068, 2452.

[67] *Parl Doc* House of Representatives Nos 1978, 2145, 2159, 2155, 1382, 2221.

Table 2: Qualitative analysis of 28 Opinions

Cluster of arguments	Criteria employed	Quantitative result	Relative out of 28 ROs
Legal criteria	Added value of action at EU level	6	21 %
	Inability of Member State	3	11 %
	Transnational effects (externalities)	7	25 %
	Economies of scale	3	11 %
Proportionality-related	Form: Regulation v Directive	6	21 %
	Cost–benefit weighing	5	18 %
	Financial and administrative burdens	1	4 %
Political criteria	Scope for national discretion	6	21 %
	Sovereignty	2	7 %
	Democratic legitimacy	3	11 %

transportation (5),[68] and environmental policy (3).[69] Economic, financial, civil and social policies are all to a large extent federal competences, while environmental issues are exclusively regional matters. This break-down along policy lines does not reflect the interests of the parliaments per se, but is constrained by their competences.

VI. Conclusions

It follows from the above that there are a number of obstacles to effective subsidiarity scrutiny in the Belgian constitutional system. They can be categorised as (A) endogenous and (B) exogenous impediments. Endogenous impediments relate to the dual setting of Belgian federalism and the lack of a forum for coordination, as well as the restricted procedural arrangement and administrative

[68] *Parl Doc* House of Representatives Nos 2459, 2689, 2775, 3263 and *Parl Doc* Flemish Parliament No 2147.

[69] *Parl Doc* Flemish Parliament No 2147, *Parl Doc* Walloon Parliament No 631, *Parl Doc* Brussels Parliament No 282.

support. Exogenous impediments are situated at EU level: the lack of guidelines for a focused subsidiarity test, as well as the detailed procedure and strict deadlines, which interfere with domestic institutional autonomy and do not provide sufficient time for a meaningful inter-level subsidiarity debate. The third conclusion addresses the political preference for the Political Dialogue over the EWM. The fourth and final point concerns the national balance of power.

A. Endogenous Determinants Impeding Effective Subsidiarity Scrutiny

(i) Federal Setting and Lack of Coordination

The dual logic of Belgian federalism precludes meaningful coordination among regional and national assemblies on the distribution and exercise of the two votes in the EWS.[70] The Senate, since 2014 a proper chamber for regional representation could act as a forum for deliberation, increasing substantive debate.[71] For instance, instead of allowing the different regions to reach opposing conclusions with regard to a subsidiarity violation, a reverse majority decision-making rule could be adopted in the Senate, resulting in a shared and uniform opinion. Such a set-up would be better aligned with the requirements of Protocol No 2.

(ii) Procedures and Administrative Support

From the empirical data in the Belgian case, the federal House of Representatives emerges as the strongest and most active participant. No stringent conclusions as to which procedural element furthers a stronger subsidiarity scrutiny can be drawn from such a small sample, although a few observations seem consistent with earlier analyses of the EWS. First, the optimal mechanism of control seems to aim at sharing responsibility for a reasoned opinion between the standing sectoral committee and a general EU or international affairs committee.[72] Secondly, the input of the legal service in the drafting stage helps the quality of the reasoning, bringing the legal cluster of arguments to the fore.[73]

[70] Popelier and Vandenbruwaene, 'The Subsidiarity Mechanism' (n 8 above) 226–27.

[71] The EWM requires coordination and cooperation both within the Member State and across: A Cygan, *Accountability, Parliamentarism and Transparency in the EU* (Cheltenham, Edward Elgar, 2013) 171;

[72] See Granat (n 45 above), 159–62. Listing pros and cons, see JV Louis, 'The Lisbon Treaty: The Irish "No": National Parliaments and the Principle of Subsidiarity—Legal Options and Practical Limits' (2008) 4 *European Constitutional Law Review* 429, 444–45.

[73] See above, table 2 (section V.B).

B. Exogenous Determinants Impeding Effective Subsidiarity Scrutiny

(i) Subsidiarity Criteria

The European Parliament has drawn attention to the need for 'guidelines [that] could be prepared, outlining criteria for reasoned opinions on subsidiarity issues'.[74] While parliamentary practice does not find itself hampered by the need to conduct a stringent and legally-oriented subsidiarity analysis, reasoned opinions and their reasoning seem indeed rather broad in their scope. Guidelines bringing together the case law of the CJEU and the Impact Assessment Guidelines could meaningfully strengthen the operability of EU subsidiarity as aimed at in the EWS, specifically with a view to using reasoned opinions in a subsequent annulment procedure under Article 263 TFEU.[75]

(ii) EWS Procedure and Regional Chambers

First, according to the set-up in the Protocol, national parliaments are free to consult regional parliaments and incorporate their views in their conclusions. While the eight-week term for a subsidiarity opinion is already short, regional parliaments are brought under even tighter time limits.[76] The operative, though not legally binding, cooperation agreement provides for a period of two weeks in which regional parliaments can give notice that they would like to issue an opinion, and in which other assemblies may contest the competence.[77] The actual time available to draft an opinion is thus even more reduced.[78]

A second point concerns the actual issuance of the vote and the reasoned opinion. While Declaration 51 elevates regional parliaments to the same standing as the national House and Senate, the Commission is not bound by this Declaration. Thus, in practice, the Flemish vote on the proposal for a directive on maritime spatial planning and integrated coastal management[79] was relayed through the Senate.[80]

[74] European Parliament Resolution of 4 February 2014 on EU Regulatory Fitness and Subsidiarity and Proportionality, (2013/2077(INI)), para 31.

[75] See on this hypothesis W Vandenbruwaene, 'What scope for subnational autonomy: the issue of the legal enforcement of the principle of subsidiarity' (2014) 6 *Perspectives on Federalism* E-45–E-73, E67–E68.

[76] G Vara Arribas and A-L Högenauer, 'Legislative Regions after Lisbon' (n 31 above) 145.

[77] Popelier and Vandenbruwaene, 'The Subsidiarity Mechanism' (n 8 above) 222.

[78] Note that in the first pilot projects carried out pre 2009, the initial time frame was six weeks for RO. Following COSAC conclusions, this was extended to eight weeks, which is still rather narrow.

[79] Commission Proposal COM(2013) 133.

[80] See the IPEX database, dossier COD/2013/0074.

Kiiver describes the former practice of labelling the opinions as 'emanating from the Belgian parliamentary system as a whole'.[81] It seems this practice has been superseded by an introductive remark referring Declaration 51.[82]

Furthermore, in the hypothetical case of an exclusive regional competence of one region, two votes should be issued. The Senate, as a regional chamber, seems a logical choice for relaying reasoned opinions, but for the House to cast a vote per regional instructions seems more troublesome. The imposition of partition of the two votes along bicameral lines in the Protocol interferes with the institutional autonomy, especially in a complex federal setting such as the Belgian one.

C. Political Dialogue

Delreux and Randour observe that 'the parliament seems to be more interested in the Political Dialogue than the EWM'.[83] They offer three principal reasons for this preference for the Political Dialogue over the EWM: first, that parliament has limited control over the governmental negotiation position either ex ante or ex post, and the Political Dialogue offers a counterweight; secondly, that the political consensus on EU affairs, combined with the high level of party discipline, yields very little interest in EU affairs. This aligns with the more general assumption in sociological literature that the more positive the attitude towards European integration, the less appropriate national parliaments' involvement in EU affairs is considered.[84] Thirdly, the Belgian House is led to believe that democratic scrutiny of EU affairs is already carried out by their colleagues in the European Parliament.[85] Indeed, out of the 21 opinions emanating from the federal House, only four[86] were genuine reasoned opinions as defined by Protocol No 2, ie containing a negative opinion on EU subsidiarity within the proper time limit.

MPs are more interested in the Political Dialogue than participation in the Early Warning Mechanism—despite the stronger enforcement tools attached to the latter. Tentatively, we observe a small increase in scrutiny of executive behaviour in EU decision-making due to the EWM and Political Dialogue. Increased awareness of EU affairs triggers national accountability. This does not extend, however, to

[81] Kiiver (n 57 above) 51.

[82] In this case: 'In accordance with Declaration 51 by the Kingdom of Belgium on national parliaments, annexed to the Treaty of Lisbon, the parliamentary assemblies of the Communities and the Regions act, in terms of the competences exercised by the Union, as components of the national Parliament. For this reason, a reasoned opinion issued by one of those parliamentary assemblies *has to be considered as a reasoned opinion of one of the chambers* of the Belgian Parliament' (emphasis added).

[83] Delreux and Randour (n 16 above) 161.

[84] C Sprungk, 'National Parliamentary Scrutiny in the European Union: The German Bundestag and the French Assemblée Nationale—Key Players or Side-Shows?', Paper presented at the EUSA Conference, Nashville TN, 27–30 March 2003, p 28.

[85] Delreux and Randour (n 16 above) 162.

[86] See n 50 above.

regional assemblies, which remain behind in the parliamentary developments following the Lisbon revision.

D. Spill-Overs: Parliaments v Executives?

The role of national parliaments under Treaty law puzzled some commentators in the beginning; after all, in parliamentary systems, parliaments 'could be expected to support their national executive'.[87] The *dédoublement fonctionnel* that transformed the national judiciary throughout the years of EU integration[88] might conceivably affect this unilaterally-dominated[89] balance of power too. It is therefore interesting to note that, albeit in this relatively small sample of opinions under study, the House of Representatives does seem to gain more confidence in its relationship to the executive, contrary to past behaviour.[90] The institutional logic of drawing in national parliaments in EU decision-making[91] prohibits a major shift in the EU institutional balance towards national parliaments, but their position in the national separation of powers role may be altered.[92] The evidence from the 28 reasoned opinions in the Belgian case suggests that this evolution seems viable at the federal level, but that the regional assemblies are lagging behind.[93] In a large number of reasoned opinions we find the simultaneous call on the national executive to observe the objections formulated in Council decision-making.

[87] This observation was specifically aimed at Art 7(3) Protocol No 2, but can easily be extended to the whole process of EWS: G Barret, '"The king is dead, long live the king": the recasting by the Treaty of Lisbon of the provisions of the Constitutional treaty concerning national parliaments' (2008) 33 *European Law Review* 66, 83.

[88] See, in general M Claes, *The National Courts' Mandate in the European Constitution* (Oxford, Hart Publishing, 2006), and specifically for constitutional courts, P Popelier, A Mazmanyan and W Vandenbruwaene (eds), *The Role of Constitutional Courts in Multilevel Governance* (Cambridge, Intersentia, 2013).

[89] D Curtin, 'Challenging Executive Dominance in European Democracy' (2014) 77 *Modern Law Review*, 1–32.

[90] Delreux and Randour (n 16 above) 168. The Belgian House of Representatives scores very low in a comparative assessment of institutional strength with regards to EU decision-making: see K Auel, O Rozenberg and A Tacea, 'To Scrutinise or Not to Scrutinize? Explaining Variation in EU-Related Activities in National Parliaments' (2015) *West European Politics* 293.

[91] P Dann, 'The Political Institutions' in A von Bogdandy and J Bast (eds), *Principles of European Constitutional Law* (Oxford, Hart Publishing, 2009) 267–69 discerns three objections: National Parliaments as mediated actors, with a dominant role for the executive, the role of confidentiality in negotiation at EU level, and the importance of consensus politics.

[92] Complementary to 'stronger' parliaments who employ scrutiny of EU affairs as a pendant of normal scrutiny of the executive, 'weak' parliaments, such as the Belgian ones, might draw from these mechanisms to heighten scrutiny of the executive. See on the stronger parliaments and executive scrutiny A Cygan, *Accountability, Parliamentarism and Transparency in the EU* (above n 73) at 54.

[93] A recent report of the Senate on the implementation of EU law calls for improvement in this domain: see *Parl Doc* Senate, 2014–15, No 6S131/2, 282, recommendations Nos 35 and 36.

Part III

The Early Warning Mechanism in National Constitutional Orders

10

Similar but Different—Comparing the Scrutiny of the Principle of Subsidiarity within the EWM in Denmark, Finland and Sweden

ANNA JONSSON CORNELL*

It has been argued that small EU Member States tend to go the great lengths to speak with one voice in Brussels in order to strengthen their bargaining positions. This seems to be the case in Finland,[1] but is not necessarily the case in Sweden. In general Sweden, Denmark and Finland are described as part of a Scandinavian system of strong parliamentarism. However, if one scratches the surface a more multifaceted picture will emerge.[2] The question that this chapter seeks to answer is why Sweden stands out in terms of the number of reasoned opinions submitted by the *Riksdag* to the EU legislature? (The Swedish *Riksdag* is the national parliament of the EU Member States that has submitted the highest number of reasoned opinions. The Finnish *Eduskunta* is in the lower ranks in terms of number of reasoned opinions submitted, and the Danish *Folketing* can be found in the middle.) In order to answer this question the implementation of Protocol (No 2) on the application of the principles of subsidiarity and proportionality to the Treaty of the Functioning of the European Union (Protocol No 2) into the national constitutional orders of Denmark, Sweden and Finland will be analysed, focusing on the scrutiny of the principle of subsidiarity. The case selection is determined by a most similar method; the determining factor being the common feature of a strong parliamentary system, including shared traits such as negative parliamentarism.

* The author would like to thank Professor Adrienne Heritiér and Dr Hans Hegeland for valuable comments and input on earlier drafts of this article, and Oscar Söderlund, research assistant.

[1] T Raunio, 'The Finnish Eduskunta and the European Union: the Strengths and Weaknesses of a Mandating System' in C Hefftler et al (eds), *The Palgrave Handbook of National Parliaments and the European Union* (New York, Palgrave Macmillan, 2015) 420.

[2] As shown by Cooper in I Cooper, 'The Nordic parliaments and the EU' in C Grøn, P Nedergaard and A Wivel (eds), *Still the other European Community? The Nordic Countries and the European Union* (Abingdon, Routledge, 2015) 104.

This chapter proposes three main explanations for the differences outlined above: 1. The relationship between the national government and legislature in EU-affairs. 2. The procedure for exercising the scrutiny nationally. 3. The material understanding of the principle of subsidiarity. The method applied is exploratory comparative. By conducting a comparison of the institutional, procedural and material aspects of the scrutiny similarities and differences can be identified. The study is based on the analysis of the national legislative framework, primarily at the constitutional level, official documents issued by national legislatures including committees and governments, and reasoned opinions sent by the Swedish, Danish and Finnish legislatures to the EU legislature. In order to fulfil the purpose of this chapter and answer the overall question raised above the following research questions will be answered:

1) What is the constitutional context within which the scrutiny takes place (the institutional perspective)? Focus will be on:
   a) The division of powers between national governments and legislatures concerning EU-affairs in general.
   b) On what level the procedure for scrutiny of the principle of subsidiarity is regulated (constitutional, ordinary laws, or something else).
2) How is the internal scrutiny procedure in the legislature conducted? Focus will be on procedural aspects, especially:
   a) The role of European Affairs Committees (EAC),
   b) The role of sectoral committees,
   c) Selection mechanisms,
   d) The role of the government,
   e) The role of the Plenum.
3) What is the material understanding/definition of the principle of subsidiarity applied when scrutinising the principle of subsidiarity in Finland, Sweden and Denmark?[3]

The chapter deals exclusively with the subsidiarity scrutiny exercised by national parliaments subsequent to a legislative proposal being sent by the EU legislator to national parliaments. However, in order to understand correctly the different approaches to the implementation of the Early Warning Mechanism (EWM) in national constitutional orders one needs to understand the overall strategy towards EU-matters, including the role of, and cooperation between, governments and legislatures. Therefore the chapter starts with a general context, outlining national strategies in EU-matters reflected in the constitutional order of

[3] In his chapter in this volume Ian Cooper develops a typology of three approaches to the EWM: legal rule-following, political bargaining, and policy arguing. This typology has some bearing on the third question asked above. It is not the purpose, however of this chapter to apply or test this typology. The purpose of this particular study is narrower and hence does not provide all the necessary empirical data and conclusions for such a purpose. See I Cooper, 'The Subsidiarity Early Warning Mechanism: Three Questions and a Typology', Chapter 2, section V in this volume.

each state. Thereafter the scrutiny of subsidiarity will be analysed taking both procedural and material aspects into consideration.

I. The Constitutional Context of the Scrutiny of the Subsidiarity Principle by National Parliaments

The division of powers between the government and the legislative assembly concerning EU-affairs has been put forward as one possible explanation for the differences between Denmark, Finland and Sweden concerning the number of reasoned opinions issued. Therefore, let us set the playing field by analysing the national constitutional framework for the relationship between the government and the legislature in the national context, focusing on EU-affairs.[4] Traditionally, and in all three states, the government has been the main actor in foreign policy matters, including EU-affairs. In Finland, this has had an impact on the design of the scrutiny process and the use of the EWM, while in Sweden it has not. In Denmark, the parliament has been fairly strong in relation to the government on EU-affairs (this point will be further elaborated below) and this might have had had an impact on the design of the scrutiny process in Denmark. For the purpose of this section, scrutiny refers to the scrutiny of EU-affairs in general; it is not limited to the scrutiny of the principle of subsidiarity.

A. Finland

It has been clearly stated that Finland only has one position on EU matters: that all positions are decided by the Finnish Parliament, *Eduskunta*, and that the government is representing this position within the EU. Therefore the *Eduskunta* should not have its own position in EU-matters. However, the Grand Committee does reserve its right to address the Commission should it benefit Finland's position in a certain matter.[5] The Grand Committee coordinates the Parliament's work on EU-affairs, except for matters of foreign and security policy. Moreover, it is the Grand Committee, not the Plenary that mandates the government on EU-affairs.[6] The mandate that the Grand Committee gives to the responsible minister before a Council meeting is not constitutionally binding, although politically, the government is depending on the support from the *Eduskunta*.

[4] Although there is an image of Sweden, Denmark and Finland being similar in terms of constitutional traditions, this is not the case. Quite the opposite; there is no Nordic constitutional model, as shown by Fredrik Sejersted. F Sejersted, 'Grunnlovens funksjon i de nordiske land' (2014) 127 *Tidsskrift for Rettsvitenskap* 535.

[5] StoUB 1/2009 rd, p 27.

[6] Raunio (n 1 above) 409–10.

The *Eduskunta* participates in the decision-making in EU-matters when provided for by the Constitution, see for example § 96 of the Finnish Constitution. The role of the *Eduskunta* in the preparation of EU matters is more closely regulated in §§ 96 and 97 of the Constitution. The Finnish scrutiny model has been designed to resemble as much as possible the procedure for scrutinising national legislative drafts.[7] According to the Finnish Constitution, § 93.2 the government is responsible for the preparation of decisions to be made within the EU and decides on associated measures, unless the legislature's approval is required. The *Eduskunta's* general right to information from the government is laid down in § 47 of the Constitution. The government keeps the *Eduskunta* informed by sharing its assessment of legislative proposals. Often, the principle of subsidiarity and correct legal basis is explicitly commented upon in the document sent to the *Eduskunta*.[8]

EU-matters are classified as E- or U-matters. U-matters include legislative proposals from the Commission that fall within the competence of the *Eduskunta*[9] and E-matters are for example Green- and White Papers and legislative proposals that do not fall under the competence of the *Eduskunta*.[10] There are important differences between U- and E-matters concerning procedure. On U-matters, the Speaker of the *Eduskunta* decides what sectoral committees should prepare the matter before it comes back to the Grand Committee. More than one committee processes the majority of U-matters. In U-matters it is mandatory for committees to forward their assessment to the Grand Committee. This is not the case concerning E-matters. Moreover, the Speaker is not concerned with E-matters; these go directly from the Grand Committee to the sectoral committees.[11] The Grand Committee formally adopts a position on U-matters before the government is informed. On E-matters, the Grand Committee normally sends the opinion of the sectoral committee directly to the government.[12] Taken together, this procedure allows for the *Eduskunta*, through the Grand Committee, to guard its legislative competence. The committees' opinions on U- and E-matters constitute guidelines for the government,[13] at the same times as these opinions often are based on the government's position paper, and expert hearings.[14]

The scrutiny of the principle of subsidiarity is integrated in the general scrutiny of EU-affairs, thus the *Eduskunta* has shown reluctance towards the EWM.[15] Moreover, the *Eduskunta* has explicitly noted that its participation in EU-affairs primarily is achieved through controlling the government. It is interesting to note

[7] StoUB 1/2009 rd, p 3. See also, Raunio (n 1 above) 409.

[8] See for example, U 25/2011 rd.

[9] See the Finnish Constitution § 80.1, and A Jyränki and J Husa, *Konstitutionell rätt* (Helsingfors, Talentum, 2015) 221–22.

[10] *Utveckling av EU-procedurerna. Betänkande från kommissionen för översyn av EU-procedurer*, Eduskunnan Kanslian Julkaisu, 3/2005, p 11.

[11] ibid, 11.

[12] ibid.

[13] ibid, 23.

[14] Raunio (n 1 above) 412.

[15] ibid, 416.

that the Grand Committee and the sectoral committees often follow the position of the government. This is partly explained by the expressed strategy to get involved as early as possible in the policy-making process at the EU-level.[16] This very strategy is likely to explain the reluctance of the *Eduskunta* to divert from the assessment already made by the government and hence the relatively low numbers of reasoned opinions. Finland has a decentralised system meaning that most of the scrutiny takes place in committees. This has also led to the effect that the role of the Plenary in EU-affairs has diminished, although it seems to have changed somewhat after the 2011 elections and the Eurozone crisis.[17] The procedural and material aspects of the scrutiny of subsidiarity within the EWM, including the role of the Plenary will be elaborated below.

B. Denmark

The formal basis for the consideration of EU-matters by the *Folketinget*, including the duty of the government to inform the European Affairs Committee (EAC) and sectoral committees, is the Danish Accession Act from 1972 (as amended) together with reports issued by the EAC.[18] Moreover, the Standing Orders of the Folketinget provide guidelines for the EAC and sectoral committees when scrutinising EU-matters.[19]

The Danish EAC is 'the primary EU-decision-making forum of parliament'.[20] The mandate and role of the EAC is not laid down in the Constitution or any other legislation. Rather it is the result of a number of political agreements between the government and the EAC, to be found in special reports by the EAC. As a result the EAC itself set the framework of its scrutiny. In general, the Danish model of scrutiny entails a centralised system. It is the (politically) binding mandate from the EAC[21] to the government, combined with minority governments that make the Danish EAC powerful. Sectoral committees are increasingly involved in the scrutiny, but they all report back to the EAC and they have no final decision on EU matters. It is, however, mandatory for them to render opinions if asked by the

16 ibid, 412–13.

17 ibid, 420.

18 More than 25 reports are adopted, making it difficult to get a complete overview. *Consideration of EU matters in the Folketing—a summary*, Ref: 05-001673-2, p 3.

19 The Standing Orders of the Folketing § 7(2).

20 MB Christensen, 'The Danish Folketing and EU Affairs: Is the Danish Model of Parliamentary Scrutiny Still Best Practice?' in C Hefftler et al (eds), *The Palgrave Handbook of National Parliaments and the European Union* (New York, Palgrave Macmillan, 2015) 276.

21 The mandate is decided by the EAC according to the rule that if it is not clear that a majority is against the mandate that position will guide the government in the Council. *Consideration of EU matters in the Folketing—a summary*, (n 18 above) Ref: 05-001673-2, p 4. Denmark, as Finland and Sweden, has a system characterised by negative parliamentarism, meaning that the government is not depending on the support of the majority. It just needs the majority not to vote against it.

EAC to do so.[22] As in Sweden sectoral committees are involved at an early stage concerning EU-matters in general.[23]

C. Sweden

The powers given to national parliaments as a result of the Lisbon Treaty and Protocol No 2 have been enacted into Swedish law by changes to the Riksdag Act (*riksdagsordningen* [RO]).[24] The *Riksdag*'s dealings with EU-matters are regulated in Chapters 7 and 9 of the RO. According to RO 9:23, the *Riksdag* is to obtain written information from the EU in accordance with the Treaties and relevant protocols. According to 10:10 of the Instruction of Government (*regeringsformen* (RF)) and RO 9:21, the government is to keep the *Riksdag* continuously informed and updated on current EU-affairs. From a procedural point of view there is a clear distinction between the political dialogue and the EWM. The scrutiny within the framework of the political dialogue is regulated in RO 7:12, 13, 17, 9:20(1), (3). Since the committees deal with these documents at a much earlier point in time compared to the EWM, matters of substance are better scrutinised and debated within this procedure. Within the context of the EWM, RO 9:20(2) is applicable. This means that the substance and material facts of the draft should not be scrutinised, which does not, of course, mean that they are not.

The Swedish EAC is formed after its Danish counterpart.[25] The Swedish government must inform and consult with the EAC before voting in the Council. The mandate given by the EAC is not constitutionally binding. The Swedish EAC focuses only on matters on the Council agenda and hence does not prepare reports to be debated by the Plenary. The main part of the scrutiny of EU-affairs takes part in the sectoral committees. The result of this scrutiny is reported to the EAC and the government. Sectoral committees themselves decide what EU-matters should be discussed with the government, while the government is obliged to consult with the EAC on the matters that fall under the EAC's mandate.[26]

D. Comparison

Finland and Sweden have chosen a decentralised model for the scrutiny of EU matters, involving sectoral committees to the fullest. A general observation is that

[22] Christensen (n 20 above) 277–78.

[23] See for example the Standing Orders of the Folketing § 7(2), and *Consideration of EU matters in the Folketing—a summary*, (n 18 above) Ref: 05-001673-2, p 22.

[24] Up till 1974, the RO held the status of a constitution. Since then it is to be found between the constitution and ordinary statutes (*lag*) in the hierarchy of norms. The Riksdag Act was changed in 2014, *Riksdagsordning* (2014:801). The new law entered into force 1 September 2014.

[25] H Hegeland, 'The Swedish Parliament and EU Affairs: From Reluctant Player to Europeanized Actor' in C Hefftler et al (eds), *The Palgrave Handbook of National Parliaments and the European Union* (Basingstoke/New York, Palgrave Macmillan, 2015) 425, 427.

[26] ibid, 429.

as a result of Sweden entering the EU, sectoral committees have gained in influence. In 1997, the RO provided sectoral committees with the power to monitor EU activities. Since 2007 the government is obliged to deliberate with sectoral committees on EU-affairs, RO 7:12(1). Hegeland has argued that this is one of the main reasons as to why the sectoral committees are the main players in the scrutiny of the principle of subsidiarity (to be elaborated in the next section).[27] In Denmark the scrutiny is centralised in the sense that it is the main responsibility of the EAC, although sectoral committees are involved.

In all three states the EAC mandates the government in EU-affairs. However, in none of the states is the mandate constitutionally binding. Still, Denmark stands out in this context in that the mandate given by the EAC cannot be disregarded by the government representative in a Council meeting. The government representative must reconnect with the Danish EAC before changing its position. The Danish model therefore potentially provides a stronger mandate and hence a stronger position for the EAC and the *Folketinget* in relation to the government than is the case in Sweden and Finland.

Concerning the regulatory framework for the scrutiny of EU-matters Denmark stands out. The scrutiny of EU-affairs, the role of the parliament etc are not regulated in the Constitution. It is mentioned very briefly in the Standing Orders of the Folketinget (which could be compared with the Swedish RO). All details are laid down in political agreements between the government and the EAC, and the Swedish RO by far exceedes them when it comes to the level of details.

In terms of strategy Finland stands out for having a clearly defined policy of speaking in Brussels with one voice only, to be voiced by the government. Although being the main actor in deciding on the content, the *Eduskunta* as a rule partakes primarily indirectly in EU-affairs. Neither Sweden, nor Denmark has a clearly stated strategy in the same sense, which at least theoretically allows a larger space for the respective parliaments to directly interact with the EU legislator. Moreover, both Sweden and Denmark have had minority governments for the time period studied, which is likely to strengthen the parliament in relation to the government. The Swedish *Riksdag* is, or at least has been, comparatively weaker in relation to the government than are its Danish and Finnish counterparts. Why this is the case it is hard to conclude from this overview, but factors likely to play an important role are the absence of a 'one voice-strategy' like the Finnish and a strong EAC like the Danish, in combination with a Swedish tradition of strong governments (irrespective of them being minority or majority governments) and weak parliaments. However, even if the sectoral committees and hence the *Riksdag* have gained in influence towards the government as a result of Sweden entering the EU, it has not caused the *Riksdag* to exercise restraint when it comes to submitting reasoned opinions within the EWM. We now turn to the second set of questions that potentially could explain why Sweden is an outlier in this context.

[27] ibid, 428, 432.

II. Scrutiny of the Principle of Subsidiarity within the EWM—Procedural Aspects

This part of the chapter is devoted to the procedural aspects of the scrutiny of the principle of subsidiarity within the EWM in Finland, Denmark and Sweden. It will focus on the following factors: 1. The role of European Affairs Committees. 2. The role of sectoral committees. 3. Selection mechanisms. 4. The role of the government. 5. The role of the Plenum. Each country's system will be analysed separately, and the section will end with a comparison between the three states, taking the factors enumerated above into consideration. The analysis is based mainly on legislation and official documents. The national scrutiny procedure within the EWM is primarily regulated by the Constitution in Finland (articles 47, 96) and the Finnish Riksdag Act, primarily by the Riksdag Act in Sweden, although the right to information is laid down in the Constitution (RF 10:10), and mainly through political agreements (EAC reports) in Denmark.

A. Finland

In Finland, the scrutiny of the principle of subsidiarity has been part of the overall scrutiny of EU legislative proposals in the Finnish Parliament since 1995. The main changes as a result of the Lisbon Treaty and Protocol No 2 are that the *Eduskunta* now has a direct channel to the EU legislator and that not only U-matters will be scrutinised by the *Eduskunta*, but also E-matters.[28] In Finland the Secretariat of the Grand Committee is responsible for information on legislative proposals arriving from EU institutions. The Secretariat makes a first selection.[29] Proposals that are likely to be the subject of subsidiarity scrutiny are filed as pending. Pending proposals are registered with the Grand Committee and relevant sectoral committees and sent to the regional parliament of Åland. The latter is mandatory, with reference to Protocol No 2 and the self-determination of Åland.[30]

A member of a sectoral committee, the Grand Committee, or of the Åland regional parliament may propose that the committee or the regional parliament asks the Grand Committee to scrutinise the proposal. Should the sectoral committee or the regional parliament decide to do so, the Grand Committee will be asked to scrutinise. Thereafter the Grand Committee takes a formal decision on whether to scrutinise or not. If the proposal comes from the Åland Parliament such

[28] *Utveckling av EU-procedurerna. Betänkande från kommissionen för översyn av EU-procedurer*, Eduskunnan Kanslian Julkaisu, 3/2005, p 45.

[29] ibid, 59.

[30] § 302 the Riksdag Act [*Riksdagsordningen*], and GrUB 9/2009 rd.

scrutiny is obligatory.[31] The scrutiny can be concerned with a legislative proposal in its totality or with parts of a proposal, for example one article of a Directive.[32] Sectoral committees must submit the conclusions from their review to the Grand Committee within six weeks from the day the proposal was registered if they want the Grand Committee to scrutinise the proposal.[33] This will be done in the form of a letter sent to the Grand Committee. According to the *travaux préparatoires* it is only in exceptional cases that a scrutiny will take place. Such scrutiny can involve expert hearings and debates in the committee.[34] These first steps of the scrutiny procedure have a six-week time frame. After this point in time the procedure of scrutiny differs somewhat depending on who initiated it. If the decision to scrutinise was initiated by the Grand Committee, the Committee can invite representatives from the government and experts to give their views on the proposal.

If reaching a conclusion that there has been a violation of the principle of subsidiarity the Grand Committee submits a draft reasoned opinion to the *Eduskunta*. This draft reasoned opinion can include the position of the government and in cases where the Regional Parliament of Åland has issued a request for scrutiny this is also included.[35] Should the Committee find that there is no violation of the principle of subsidiarity a report stating this will be submitted to the *Eduskunta*. The Plenary thereafter debates the report or draft reasoned opinion and may adopt it. Amendments can be made by the Plenary. Subsequently, the decision of the *Eduskunta* and the report from the Grand Committee will be communicated to the EU legislator in cases where a violation of the principle of subsidiarity has been found.[36]

In sum, the Grand Committee plays a crucial role in that it decides on whether a reasoned opinion should be submitted to the Plenary or not. The scrutiny of the principle of subsidiarity within the EWM is thus semi-centralised. Sectoral committees play an important role in that they can conduct their scrutiny and thereafter ask the Grand Committee to consider the issue. It is, however, the Grand Committee that decides whether to submit a draft to the *Eduskunta* or not. The government is invited to share its opinion on the matter. Moreover the Secretariat of the Grand Committee makes a first selection of proposals to be scrutinised, adding to the centralisation of the procedure. The Plenary decides on whether to submit the reasoned opinion or not. It can also add to the draft, which gives it a relatively strong position in the process, adding to the centralising traits of the Finnish system of scrutiny within the EWM.

[31] TKF 2/2009 rd, p 5, and Stora utskottets arbetsordning, §18 a mom. 2.

[32] U 25/2011 rd, p 10.

[33] Stora utskottets arbetsordning, 18 a§ mom. 3.

[34] TKF 2/2009 rd, 8.

[35] 30 § 3 mom. the Riksdag Act [*Riksdagsordningen*], Stora utskottets arbetsordning, 18 a§ 4 mom.

[36] 30 § 3 mom. the Riksdag Act [*Riksdagsordningen*], Stora utskottets arbetsordning, 18 a§ 4 mom.

B. Denmark

In Denmark the EAC is the main player in EU matters in general and this also applies to the scrutiny of the principle of subsidiarity within the EWM. In parallel with the early subsidiarity scrutiny by the committees in line with the Standing Orders of the Folketinget 7(2), the EAC pre-selects 5–10 proposals from the Commission's yearly working programme for subsidiarity scrutiny. The government is obliged to deliver an explanatory memorandum on the pre-selected proposals within a time-limit of four weeks, in which it makes an assessment of the proposal's respect for the principle of subsidiarity. Within three weeks the EAC makes an assessment as to whether a proposal should be referred to a sectoral committee. A sectoral committee thereafter has two weeks to examine the proposal's congruence with the principle of subsidiarity and report back to the EAC.[37] If a breach is found the opinion will be uploaded on IPEX and COSAC will be informed. Thereafter the EAC scrutinises the opinion of the sectoral committee. Should there be a disagreement between the EAC and the sectoral committee a meeting will be held to resolve any disagreements. Before the eight-week deadline the EAC chair will sign the reasoned opinion and forward it to the Danish government and the EU legislator.[38] The Plenary has no role in the scrutiny of the principle of subsidiarity within the EWM and the role of sectoral committees is primarily indirect, advisory and supporting.

The Danish model stands out for not involving the Plenary at all. Moreover, the Danish system involves a selection mechanism that is not applied in Finland or Sweden. The EAC has the main responsibility for the selection and the scrutiny thus making the Danish system a centralised system—the most centralised system of the three compared in this study. Sectoral committees are invited to give an opinion, in contrast to Finland where it is the sectoral committees that ask the Grand Committee to scrutinise, providing them with the main initiative to instigate a review. The government is obliged to provide its opinion. The whole procedure is regulated by political agreements and not by constitutional or semi-constitutional laws.

C. Sweden[39]

According to RO 9:20(2), it is the *Riksdag* that controls whether EU legislative proposals are in congruence with the principle of subsidiarity. According to the Swedish model, relevant sectoral committees scrutinise proposals upon referral

[37] *Report on Consideration on EU matters by the Folketing in relation to subsidiarity checks*, Report no 2, Folketinget 2009–10, 9 April 2010.

[38] www.ipex.eu/IPEXL-WEB/parliaments/institution/dkfol.do, last accessed 13 October 2015.

[39] This section partly builds on A Jonsson Cornell, 'The Swedish Riksdag as Scrutinizer of the Principle of Proportionality' (2016) 12 *European Constitutional Law Review*.

from the Chamber. The EAC is not involved in the scrutiny of the principle of subsidiarity within the EWM at all.[40] All proposals are scrutinised, no exceptions.[41] This has provoked a debate between the sectoral committees and the Committee on the Constitution, leaving the latter to conclude that there are no formal requirements as to how sectoral committees should handle the scrutiny procedure. If a committee wants to make the process more efficient by, for example, laying down a summarised procedure for drafts with no obvious subsidiarity concern, that is permissible and within the framework of the national rules for the scrutiny.[42] The secretariat for EU-affairs within the *Riksdag* Administration distributes the incoming drafts to the relevant sectoral committee.[43] The scrutiny can be partial, meaning that either the whole proposal or parts of it can be considered to be in violation of the principle of subsidiarity.

The government is obliged to share its assessment of subsidiarity within two weeks from the day a committee asked.[44] The government is obliged to provide its assessment if asked by a sectoral committee, but the latter is not obliged to consult the government.[45] This does not by definition mean that the government will provide an assessment, as was the case concerning the proposal on establishing a European Public Prosecutor's Office. The government failed to share its assessment, even though the two-week deadline was extended.[46]

Sectoral committees can ask for other committees' assessment, including the Committee on the Constitution—in the latter case, primarily concerning the interpretation of the principle of subsidiarity.[47] If a committee finds a disregard for the principle of subsidiarity it delivers a statement to the Chamber to that effect, suggesting that the *Riksdag* send a reasoned opinion to the Presidents of the European Parliament, Council and Commission. The Swedish regulation provides for a minority protection, meaning that if at least five (out of 17) committee members so require, a reasoned opinion shall be delivered to the Chamber. The Chamber will decide whether to send the reasoned opinion with a simple majority. Should the Chamber decide to send a reasoned opinion, such a decision will be executed by a written statement.[48]

[40] See above.

[41] J Hettne et al, *Subsidiaritet i EU efter Lissabon*, 45, 2013/14:KU5, p 16.

[42] 2014/15:KU5, p 17.

[43] Each of the sectoral committees has its own secretariat.

[44] RO 10:10(2).

[45] 2014/15:KU5, p 40.

[46] 2013/14:JuU13, 2013/14:KU5, 2014/15:JuU2y. As a result of the government not fulfilling its obligations according to the RO, a complaint was filed with the Committee on the Constitution within the framework of the Committee's constitutional control of the government and its ministers focusing on ministers' performance of their official duties and the handling of government business, RF 13:1. The Committee on the Constitution reached the conclusion that the government had failed to meet its obligation under the RO and that it therefore could not avoid criticism, 2013/14:KU20, pp 18–21.

[47] RO 10:3(2), 2009/10:KU2, p 14.

[48] RO 11:21(2). If the proposal is not considered to violate the principle of subsidiarity it will suffice to submit an extract from the minutes to the Chamber, according to RO 10:3(3).

In sum, the Swedish EAC has no role in the scrutiny of the principle of subsidiarity within the EWM. All proposals are scrutinised; there is no selection mechanism. Sectoral committees exercise the review. Thus the Swedish system is fully decentralised. The Plenary will adopt the draft reasoned opinion and send it to the EU legislator. The Plenary can choose to alter the draft reasoned opinion. The government is obliged to submit its assessment according to semi-constitutional law. However if it does not, there is no real sanction mechanism.

D. Comparison

The comparative analysis will proceed taking each of the factors identified above as its starting point. First the role of the EAC in each country: The EAC is the main player in EU-affairs in general in Denmark, but also concerning the scrutiny of the principle of subsidiarity. The EAC selects what proposals to scrutinise and it does so based on the Commission's working programme, although proposals can be added later. Moreover, the EAC adopts a reasoned opinion without the involvement of the Plenary and sends it directly to the EU legislator. In Sweden the EAC is not involved in the scrutiny of the principle of subsidiarity. In Finland, the Grand Committee is the equivalent to the EAC, and it plays a dominant role in the scrutiny process. It decides on whether to scrutinise or not in all cases except if the proposal comes from the Åland Regional Parliament. It also formulates reasoned opinions, which may then be formally adopted by the Plenary.

Secondly, on the role of sectoral committees: As stated above, sectoral committees are mainly advisory and supporting in the Danish scrutiny process. In Finland they have a larger role to play in that they scrutinise proposals and forward them to the Grand Committee. They are the initiators of the Grand Committee's scrutiny. In Sweden, sectoral committees are the main players. Neither the Swedish EAC nor the Committee on the Constitution are involved in the scrutiny procedure within the EWM to the same extent as in Denmark and Finland. The issue of minority protection is interesting in this context. Both Sweden and Finland has a minority protection provision laid down in the law. In Finland a minority of a sectoral committee can ask the Grand Committee to scrutinise and in Sweden a minority can put forward a reasoned opinion to the *Riksdag*. These regulations are in line with the constitutional traditions of both Sweden and Finland according to which minorities are protected in constitutional affairs in order to secure a viable political debate within the parliament.

There are also important differences on the selection mechanism. In Sweden all proposals are scrutinised. However, if it is obvious that a proposal will not raise any subsidiarity concerns it can be handled in a summarised manner. In both Denmark and Finland the EAC/Grand Committee will make an initial selection of proposals to review. This might be an important explanatory factor as to the number of reasoned opinions submitted. Concerning the role of the government, the obligation of the government to share its assessment of a proposal's congruence with the principle of subsidiarity is clearly regulated in all three states. Still, there are no real sanctions or means to force the government should it fail to do so. Finally, as regards the role of the Plenary, Denmark stands out in this context in that the Plenary has no role at all in the scrutiny process. In both Sweden and Finland the Plenary formally decides on reasoned opinions and forwards them to the EU legislator. And in both countries the Plenary can add to the draft reasoned opinions.

III. The Scope of the Review—Different Understandings of the Principle of Subsidiarity

I will now turn to the third question and focus on the material aspects of the scrutiny. In the following an analysis of the understanding/definition of the principle of subsidiarity in Finland, Denmark and Sweden will be conducted. The analysis rests on the style and wording of reasoned opinions submitted by the countries in question. Taking into account the large number of reasoned opinions submitted by the Swedish *Riksdag*, the section on the *Riksdag* will not deal with individual reasoned opinions to the extent that the low numbers of submitted opinions in Finland and Denmark allow for.

In the literature, different subsidiarity tests are suggested when it comes to the scope of the review and what it should be. Fabbrini and Granat argue for a narrow review of subsidiarity and suggest a test taking both the material and procedural aspects of the principle of subsidiarity into account. They argue that the scrutiny should focus 'exclusively [on] … the control of the principle of subsidiarity, and leave aside considerations of the legal basis, proportionality or political merits of an EU legislative proposal',[49] based on a textual, functional and structural interpretation of Protocol No 2. Goldoni calls this approach 'a strictly formalist reading',[50] and then proceeds with a contextual and teleological interpretation taking his starting point in Articles 10 and 4(2) TEU. A contextual and teleological reading of these articles allows for a broader definition of the review. Goldoni argues that 'if understood in a thin fashion as simply a question of which level should decide on what, subsidiarity is reduced to a technical exercise of competence review and it betrays, by institutional design, a pro-European centripetal prejudice'.[51] This approach would allow the EWM to become an arena for voicing national particularities worthy of protection according to national parliaments.

[49] F Fabbrini and K Granat, '"Yellow Card but No Foul": The Role of the National Parliaments under the Subsidiarity Protocol and the Commission Proposal for an EU Regulation on the Right to Strike' (2013) 50 *Common Market Law Review* 115, 121.

[50] M Goldoni, 'The Early Warning System and the Monti II Regulation: the Case for a Political Interpretation' (2014) 10 *European Constitutional Law Review* 90, 101.

[51] ibid, 102.

By so doing the communicative sphere for conflicts between the social and political is upheld by the body most suitable for this, ie national representative bodies.[52] Jančić makes an argument for a broad scope of the review to include an evaluation of the principle of conferral and the substance of the legislative proposal.[53] In contrast to the top-down and narrow perspective on the scope of the principle of subsidiarity suggested by Fabbrini and Granat, Kiiver suggests a bottom-up approach based on empirical findings.[54] By approaching the problem bottom-up and based on the analysis of the opinions of national parliaments, Kiiver reaches the conclusion that 'subsidiarity should be understood very broadly', and should include competence[55] and proportionality, but exclude substance. Concerning proportionality the 'victim is the intactness of national competence'.[56] Kiiver's definition of the scope of the review is thus narrower than the approach suggested by Goldoni and Jančić[57] respectively, although still within the broad review category.

A. Finland

Finland applies a strict understanding of the scope of review of the principle of subsidiarity to be exercised within the EWM.[58] The *Eduskunta* has declared the EWM as a 'largely illusory political process'[59] that should be referred to only in exceptional cases. This approach is mainly the result of a strategic choice of the *Eduskunta* to focus on its most important role according to national constitutional traditions, ie to control the government. Moreover, the constitutional and political approach to EU-matters is that there should be only one Finnish position at the EU-level.[60] One of the main concerns concerning the scrutiny of the principle of subsidiary is that it would distract the attention from the main task of the *Eduskunta*, ie to control the government, without rendering any political added value. Until 2015, the *Eduskunta* had submitted three reasoned opinions[61] dealing with the following legislative proposals: The Energy Efficiency Directive COM(2011) 370 final, the Council Regulation on the exercise of the right to take collective action within the context of the freedom of establishment and the freedom to provide services COM(2012) 130, and the Directive of the European Parliament and of the Council establishing a framework for maritime spatial planning and integrated coastal management COM(2013) 133.

[52] ibid, 105.

[53] D Jančić, 'The Game of Cards: National Parliaments in the EU and the Future of the Early Warning Mechanism and the Political Dialogue' (2015) 52 *Common Market Law Review* 939, 974.

[54] P Kiiver, *The Early Warning Mechanism System for the Principle of Subsidiarity. Constitutional Theory and Empirical Reality* (London, Routledge 2012) 71.

[55] Also supported by the German *Bundesrat* definition of the scope, Kiiver (n 54 above) 98.

[56] ibid, 98–99.

[57] Jančić (n 53 above) 974.

[58] TKF 2/2009 rd, 3.

[59] Raunio, (n 1 above) 416.

[60] ibid, 417.

[61] RSk 11/2011 rd, RSk 9/2012 rd, EK /2013 vp.

In the first of the three reasoned opinions the Grand Committee clarified that the scrutiny of the principle of subsidiarity is only concerned with competence issues, especially at what level measures should be decided. It argued that concerning this specific proposal it had not been proved that EU's energy efficiency goals could not be achieved by measures on Member State level, that the proposed Directive was too detailed (which would leave it inefficient in relation to its goals), and that the element of transnational activities was weak, reaching the conclusion that article 10 of the proposed Directive violated the principle of subsidiarity.[62] It is interesting to note how stringent and disciplined this Finnish reasoned opinion was, referring to at what level the EU policy goal could best be achieved and the potential added value of EU legislation. The substance of the proposal was being analysed but strictly in terms of where and whether measures would have the anticipated effect. Moreover, the reasoned opinion concluded with a paragraph stating that the Committee also found the substance of the Directive problematic but that it intended to deal with that within the 96-procedure.[63] In the Monti II case the Grand Committee underlined the weak added value of measures on the EU-level, and that the proposal did not succeed in achieving its stated goal, ie to clarify the legal position of the EU, and its relation to international- and national law. Moreover, the Commission had failed, according to the Committee, to clarify what could constitute the transnational aspect of the matter. Thus, the measure was not necessary and it did not achieve an added value related to potential transnational aspects.[64] The third reasoned opinion dealt with maritime spatial planning and integrated coastal management. Again, the Grand Committee referred to the lack of added value to be generated at the EU level and the failure of the EU to identify an added value that would justify the adoption of a Directive. Moreover, the proposed Directive would affect national competences in a manner that is contrary to the principle of subsidiarity. In addition, it would potentially have an effect on the constitutional guarantee of local autonomy concerning planning matters directly affected by the proposed Directive. Thus, the Grand Committee reached the conclusion that both the functional and the procedural objectives of the Directive are in violation of the principle of subsidiarity.[65] Again, the Grand Committee explicitly did put the burden of proof on the Commission concerning the added value that regulation on the EU level could bring.

In sum, the Finnish scrutiny test focuses on the added value with regulation on the EU level, necessity in relation to the stated goal and the strength of transnational aspects. Moreover, it explicitly puts the burden of proof on the Commission concerning the added value of regulating on the EU level. From a constitutional law perspective, the third reasoned opinion stands out in that it refers to the proposal's potentially negative effects on national constitutional law. Thus, from the above it

[62] StoUB 1/2011 rd—Ö 2/2011 rd.
[63] StoUB 1/2011 rd—Ö 2/2011 rd, p 5.
[64] StoUB 1/2012 rd, p 3.
[65] StoUB 1/2013 rd.

can be concluded that the Grand Committee adheres to the Finnish official understanding of the EWM and the scrutiny of the principle of subsidiarity within this procedure.

B. Denmark

Denmark stands out in comparison with Finland and Sweden, due to the lack of guidelines or authoritative statements as to how the principle of subsidiarity should be understood or defined within the EWM. For the purpose of this study nine reasoned opinions of the Danish *Folketing* have been analysed.[66] On 5 July 2014 the Danish EAC issues a reasoned opinion on the proposal for a Directive on the Union legal framework for customs infringements and sanctions COM(2013) 0884. The EAC declares that it does not share the view of the Commission on the issue of competence. According to the EAC the issue falls within the shared competence, and furthermore the goal, ie to make the legal framework for customs infringement more efficient, will not be achieved by the suggested measures. It is clear that the issue of sanctions is problematic for Denmark.[67] This particular reasoned opinion is rather short and not very elaborated. The style differs radically from the preceding reasoned opinion on the Tobacco Directive. In this reasoned opinion, the opinion of the minority is accounted for. Moreover, the reasoned opinion refers to the Swedish opinion, which is interesting per se and testifies to a dialogue between these two national parliaments. The main point in the Danish reasoned opinion refers to the large number of delegated acts made possible by the Directive, which might have a damaging effect on the possibility for national parliaments to safeguard the principle of subsidiarity. In contrast to the opinion on the legal framework for customs infringements this reasoned opinion is very elaborate on policy issues, probably because it involves *snus* (a form of smokeless tobacco) and its proximity to issues of health policy. Moreover, the Health Committee, which drafted the opinion, is divided along political party lines, which is probably one explanation for the principle of subsidiarity argument not being explicit, sharply defined or delimited.[68]

Again, in the reasoned opinion on the proposal for a Directive on improving the gender balance among non-executive directors of companies listed on the stock exchanges and related measures COM(2012) 614, the style and scope are different. The majority in the sectoral committee simply underlines that the goal per se is relevant and legitimate but that there is nothing preventing the matter from being regulated nationally and that national measures can solve the issue. Interestingly, the reasoned opinion communicates directly to the Danish government and other

[66] A search at Ipex.eu gives nine Danish reasoned opinions. 28 November 2015.

[67] Begrundet udtalelse om forslag om toldovertrædelser—KOM(2013) 884, 4 July 2014.

[68] The Danish Parliament's opinion on the Commission's proposal for a revision of the Tobacco Products Directive—COM(2012) 788, courtesy translation by the Danish Parliament, 3 March 2014.

Member States, encouraging them to implement gender-balancing measures (*kønskvoter*). A minority was in favour of the Directive proposal, not finding it to be in violation with the principle of subsidiarity.[69] The reasoned opinion submitted on the Regulation of the European Parliament and of the Council on the Fund for European Aid to the Most Deprived COM(2012) 130 is an interesting example of what the criticism usually forwarded by national parliaments on the insufficient subsidiarity justification of the Commission may look like. In this particular reasoned opinion the Danish EAC first concludes that the fight against poverty is best achieved by the Member States. Thereafter it turns its attention to the justification:

> Finally the Danish Parliament notes that the Commission's proposal does not contain a sufficient justification for its compliance with the subsidiarity principle. In that respect it is merely stated in recital 42 of the proposal that the objective of the regulation, namely to improve social cohesion in the Union and contribute to the fight against poverty and social exclusion, cannot be sufficiently achieved by Member States but can be better achieved at Union level. Such a justification does not fulfil the requirement in Article 5 of the Protocol on the application of the principles of subsidiarity and proportionality of 'a detailed statement making it possible to appraise compliance with the principles of subsidiarity and proportionality'.[70]

In its reasoned opinion on Monti II, the EAC declares that it does not see any need for the proposed Regulation. First, the Regulation does not, according to the EAC, provide further clarity on the matter. Secondly, there is an obvious risk that it will intervene in existing national measures, and therefore the EU should have a supporting and complimentary function only. And finally, the EU does not have the competence to legislate on existing national measures.[71] The supporting and complimentary role of the EU is also referred to in the reasoned opinion on the Globalization Fund.[72] On the proposals for a common organisation of agricultural markets the EAC, in two identical reasoned opinions, concludes that the policy goal of the Commission has shifted from being an agricultural measure to become a social policy measure and that the legal basis referred to by the Commission therefore is incorrect. It continues, arguing that even if based on the correct legal basis the proposed measure is not necessary to achieve the goal of the EU.[73]

[69] Begrundet udtalelse om en mere ligelig kønsfordeling blandt menige bestyrelsesmedlemmer i børsnoterede selskaber KOM(2012) 614, 14 December 2012.

[70] Reasoned opinion as regards the Commission's proposal for a Regulation on the Fund for European Aid to the Most Deprived—COM(2012) 617, courtesy translation by the Danish Parliament, 14 December 2012.

[71] Reasoned opinion as regards Commission proposal for a Regulation on the exercise of the right to take collective action (Monti II)—COM(2012) 130, courtesy translation by the Danish Parliament, 3 May 2012.

[72] Begrundet udtalelse fra Folketinget vedrørende Kommissionens forslag til Europa-Parlamentets og Rådets forordning om Den Europæiske Fond for Til-pasning til Globaliseringen (2014–20) KOM(2011) 608, 8 December 2011.

[73] Reasoned opinion as regards Commission proposal for a regulation establishing a common organisation of agricultural markets and on specific provisions for certain agricultural products (Single CMO), courtesy translation by the Danish Parliament, 7 March 2011, and the Reasoned opinion

Interestingly, in the first reasoned opinion of the EAC, on the deposit guarantee schemes, the EAC very briefly finds it to be in violation with the principle of subsidiarity, primarily stating that 'In the opinion of a majority in the Folketing, the proposal may in practice be a disincentive to the establishment of adequate coverage schemes in individual countries'.[74] Besides this and the fact that the mutual borrowing facility was to be compulsory, the reasoned opinion lacks any motivation as to how and why the proposal violates the principle of subsidiarity.

A pattern can be detected from the Danish reasoned opinions submitted thus far; when the *Folketinget* agrees on the policy matter, ie when no minority opinions are accounted for, the reasoned opinion is shorter and to the point. Still, in neither case is the subsidiarity argument very elaborate except for the Monti II case, which probably is the result of the national parliaments' cooperation initiated by Denmark.[75]

C. Sweden

The Swedish *Riksdag*, through the Committee on the Constitution, has recommended its sectoral committees to apply a two-step method when assessing whether a proposal is in congruence with the principle of subsidiarity.[76] The first question to be asked is whether it is possible to achieve the goals through national measures. If the answer to this question is no, the measure should be taken at the EU-level. If the answer is yes, the committee shall proceed by asking if measures at the EU-level would be better. If the answer to both questions is yes, there is no violation of the principle of subsidiarity. When considering the second question the *Riksdag* recommends that the committees take the following into account; any trans-border effects, whether measures by Member States would violate the Treaties or harm Member States' interests, and whether measures at the EU-level would bring clear advantages in terms of the effect of the proposed measure. Committees are also advised to seek guidance in the pre-Lisbon documents on the principle of subsidiarity.[77] An assessment of the legality of the proposed measure, taking the principle of conferred powers into account, constitutes an obvious starting point for the scrutiny. Once legality (correct legal basis) has been established, the substance of the matter is not to be considered.[78] The need to establish legality

as regards Commission proposal for a regulation amending Regulations (EC) No 1290/2005 and (EC) No 1234/2007 as regards food distribution to the most deprived persons in the Union—COM(2010) 486, 15 November 2010.

[74] Reasoned opinion on the European Commission's proposal for a directive on Deposit Guarantee Schemes COM(2010) 368, 10 November 2010.

[75] See for example, I Cooper, 'The Nordic parliaments and the EU' in C Grøn, P Nedergaard and A Wivel (eds), *Still the other European Community? The Nordic Countries and the European Union* (Abingdon, Routledge, 2015) 104.

[76] 2013/14:KU5, pp 13–14.

[77] 2008/09:RS4 *Tillämpningen av Lissabonfördraget i riksdagen*, p 52.

[78] ibid.

has been contested by the Committee on the Constitution in an opinion on one particular proposal, therefore the situation might be deemed unclear due to contradictionary statements in official documents.[79]

One of the main methodological concerns raised by the Committee on the Commission in the 2014 report relates to the question of whether scrutiny of the principle of subsidiarity should include a proportionality test. The Committee has declared that there is no such obligation, but that there is support in the doctrine and case law for including a limited proportionality test.[80] In more than half of the Swedish reasoned opinions from 2012 the principle of proportionality was referred to.[81] The Committee on Transport and Communications claims that the government does not include proportionality in its subsidiarity test, which, according to the Committee, causes a problem since the committees do.[82] As a response to the question 'Can a subsidiarity review include an assessment of proportionality?' the Committee on the Constitution noted that no such obligation could be read from the Treaties and its protocols. However, it also found that this very fact did not allow for an *a contrario* interpretation that it would not be allowed to do so. The Committee found that there was support for the subsidiarity review to include an assessment of the proportionality of the proposal based in the wording of article 5(3) TEU 'the Union shall act only if and in so far as'. In order to avoid any misunderstanding it underlined that assessing proportionality in this context only involves the question of at what level the measure should be taken; regional, national or EU.[83] Thus, according to the Swedish practice, a proportionality test, within the scrutiny of subsidiarity is allowed as long as it does not focus on whether the measure should be taken at all or not. It should focus solely on what level the measure should be decided at and what form of legislative act is to be adopted—a directive or regulation. This scrutiny would fall under what Kiiver has called a proportionality test where the intactness of the Members States' competence is the potential victim.[84]

Problems related to the principle of proportionality within the scrutiny of subsidiarity can also be illustrated by the Swedish reasoned opinion on the proposal on the European Public Prosecutor's Office. The Committee on Justice started out by referring to the political dialogue and the concerns that the *Riksdag* had put forward in that context. The Committee also expressed fear that the establishment of the European Public Prosecutor's Office would have far reaching consequences

[79] Compare ibid. And 2011/12:SoU18. For a recent case in which the *Riksdag* found a proposal to be in violation of the principle of subsidiarity by referring to inter alia an incorrect legal basis, 2013/14:SkU35.

[80] 2014/15:KU5, p 15.

[81] J Hettne et al, *Subsidiaritet i EU efter Lissabon*, 2013/14:RFR 10, p 50.

[82] 2013/14:KU5, p 36, 2014/15:KU5.

[83] The Committee relied on Case C-491/01, *R v Secretary of State for Health, ex parte British American Tobacco (Investments) Ltd and Imperial Tobacco Ltd*, judgment of 10 December 2002, paras 122–41, 180–85, and J Hettne, *Subsidiaritetsprincipen: Politisk granskning eller juridisk kontroll?* (Stockholm, SIEPS, Rapport nr 4/2003).

[84] Kiiver, (n 54 above) 98–99.

for Swedish legislation and Swedish authorities. In addition, it expressed concern that the powers of the European Public Prosecutor's Office could be expanded according to article 86 TFEU. It is therefore difficult, the argument went, to oversee the long-term consequences of the proposal.[85] The Committee thereafter stated that the Commission had failed to show why the goal could not be achieved by the Member States cooperating within the framework of Eurojust. Moreover, the Commission had failed to convince them why this goal would be better achieved by EU-measures. And finally, it drew the conclusion that the measure failed the proportionality test.[86] This is where the reasoned opinion turns interesting from an analytical point of view. I have argued elsewhere that the Committee makes a two-tier proportionality test.[87] First, the Committee concludes that it must be considered disproportionate to regulate at the EU-level just because some Member States are unable to uphold the desired standards concerning investigations and prosecutions of crimes against economic interests of the EU. This should be considered a proportionality test within the subsidiarity review, as understood in the Swedish context. Clearly, its purpose is to determine at what level—national or EU—the regulation should take place. The Committee then proceeds to a proportionality argument that could be considered to go beyond a limited proportionality test within the subsidiarity review. In this line of argument the Committee argues that the draft goes too far and that it exceeds what is necessary to achieve the overall goal, ie to protect the economic interest of the EU.[88] This part of the reasoned opinion addresses the substance of the proposal in a way that is not clearly referable to subsidiarity. This is an example of how broad the Swedish scope of review within the EWM can be. This particular reasoned opinion was rejected by the Commission and dismissed as being handled in the political dialogue.[89]

An analysis of the reasoned opinions submitted by the *Riksdag* up til 2013 shows that the committees do not strictly adhere to the subsidiarity test recommended by the Committee on the Constitution. Rather, they are more free in their approach and do consider other aspects than those strictly referable to the principle of subsidiarity. Questions related to such as competence, legal basis and the substance of the proposals are dealt with. This conclusion confirms the trend from early years.[90]

Sweden, in contrast to Finland has not a clearly defined understanding/definition of the scope of the review. This could be explained by several factors, for example the fact that all proposals are scrutinised, the process is fully decentralised, the fact that the Committee on the Constitution, opposite to the Finnish Grand Committee, does not review the scrutiny made by sectoral committees, and finally that the Swedish policy towards the EWM and the principle of subsidiarity is not as elaborated and clearly defined as the Finnish.

[85] 2013/14:JuU13, p 8.
[86] ibid.
[87] Jonsson Cornell (n 39 above).
[88] 2013/14:JuU13, p 9.
[89] COM(2013) 851 final, p 5.
[90] See J Hettne et al, *Subsidiaritet i EU efter Lissabon*, 2013/14:RFR 10, p 49.

D. Comparison

The Finnish understanding/definition of the principle of subsidiarity within the EWM is narrow. It would fall under the test and scope of review suggested by Fabbrini and Granat. The wording and style of the Danish reasoned opinions allow for no clear-cut conclusions as to the Danish understanding of the principle of subsidiarity within the EWM. There is a shift in the style of the Danish reasoned opinions depending on the policy issue dealt with and whether there is a minority/majority divide within the parliament on the issue at hand. The understanding/definition of the principle of subsidiarity within the EWM in Denmark falls close to Kiiver's definition. The Swedish understanding/definition of subsidiarity within the EWM as expressed in its reasoned opinions suggests that the *Riksdag* primarily views the principle as a political tool, focusing on substance, rather than as a legal tool to safeguard the competence of Member States in relation to the EU. One could argue that it falls under Goldoni's definition of the scope of subsidiarity review—it should be broad in order for it to become an 'arena for voicing national particularities worthy of protection according to national parliaments'.[91]

IV. Similar but Different—Concluding Analysis

Finland, Denmark and Sweden have chosen different ways to implement Protocol No 2 into their national constitutional orders by, for example, assigning different roles to their respective Committees on European Affairs, sectoral committees and the Plenary. First, this chapter set out to analyse the constitutional context within which the scrutiny takes place (the institutional perspective), focusing on the division of powers between national governments and legislatures concerning EU-affairs in general, and on what level the procedure for scrutiny is regulated (constitutional, ordinary laws, or something else). In all three states the parliament has a formally and constitutionally *strong* position in relation to the government in EU-affairs. In Finland, the role of the parliament in the EWM is, however, held back due to its political strategy of speaking with one voice. Alternatively, the role of the *Eduskunta* in the EWM could be understood from a holistic point of view, meaning that the EWM is applied only when needed to defend the Finnish position that has already been put forward in earlier negotiations. In Sweden, the detailed legal framework regulating the role of the parliament in the scrutiny of EU-affairs in general and within the EWM in particular, in combination with a minority government (2010–14), might have made the *Riksdag* more active within the EWM. Whether this is a result of the government and the *Riksdag* having different agendas or the Swedish government not being successful in EU negotiations in general

[91] Goldoni (n 50 above).

cannot be concluded from this study. One could argue, however, that the fact that the *Riksdag*'s participation in the EWM is regulated on a semi-constitutional level, in combination with the level of detail of the regulation, also could contribute to the activism of the *Riksdag*. In Denmark the parliament is strong in relation to the government in EU-affairs, its mandate is considered as binding, and the parliament is involved in both scrutinising and negotiating (indirectly) EU-matters at an early point. Taken together this might explain the low number of reasoned opinions submitted by the *Folketinget*. Another important explanation is that as in Finland, the *Folketinget* is involved at an early point in time, it controls the government in EU negotiations and hence it has had its say early in the drafting process. Potentially Sweden stands out in this context for having a relatively weak EAC; the mandate given by the EAC is not constitutionally or politically binding in effect. During the time of study Sweden did have a minority government, but still the activity of the *Riksdag* within the EWM was high. Differences between Finland, Denmark and Sweden as to the constitutional context within which the scrutiny takes place are due to explicit political and strategical choices, the role assigned to EACs and the strength/weakness of the parliament in relation to the government. The latter can be ascribed to both formal and informal circumstances.

The second set of questions focused on the procedural aspects of the scrutiny, especially the role of European Affairs Committees and sectoral committees, selection mechanisms, the role of the government, and the role of the Plenum. All three states have adopted different strategies when it comes to implementing the early warning mechanisms into their national constitutional orders. Sweden has opted for a decentralised model, which means that the scrutiny is conducted by sectoral committees only. In Denmark it is the joint responsibility of sectoral committees and the EAC to conduct the scrutiny. Sectoral committees are responsible for the initial review, upon the request of the EAC, while the EAC adopts reasoned opinions and sends them to the EU legislator. Thus, the Plenary is not involved. The Swedish procedure for scrutiny within the EWM is the most decentralised, taking into account that the sectoral committees are the main players. Denmark is the most centralised system taking into account that the EAC plays the main role; the Plenary is not at all involved and the sectoral committees are mainly supportive in their function. Finland is somewhere in between and could be described as semi-centralised. The Grand Committee functions as the 'controlling layer' between sectoral committees and the Plenary. There are also important differences concerning selection mechanisms. Denmark applies an elaborated selection mechanism, while all proposals are scrutinised in Sweden. In Finland, the secretariat of the Grand Committee makes a first selection. The role of the government in providing its assessment is the same in the three states. Thus, the largest differences are found as to the degree of centralisation and selection mechanisms. Sweden's decentralised system and the absence of articulated selection mechanisms could explain its high number of reasoned opinions, and vice versa concerning Denmark (clear selection mechanisms and a centralised system). However, if these were the main explaining factors Finland would have been expected to have a higher number of reasoned opinions.

We now turn to the third and final question: What is the material understanding/definition of the principle of subsidiarity applied when scrutinising the principle of subsidiarity in Finland, Denmark, and Sweden? Finland stands out in this context. Its reasoned opinions are to the point and apply a narrow and clearly defined understanding of the principle of subsidiarity. On a scale of narrow to broad Finland is followed by Denmark, which applies a slightly broader approach to the scrutiny, allowing for policy matters to be considered. Its understanding of the principle of subsidiarity is not elaborated in its reasoned opinions. Sweden stands out in the sense that the Swedish sectoral committees apply a broad understanding of the scope of the review. Its subsidiarity arguments are not as elaborated and to the point as in Finland.

Finland and Denmark differs from Sweden in that the same committees that provide the government its mandate in EU negotiations have the main responsibility for the subsidiarity scrutiny within the EWM. This is not the case in Sweden. In this sense, the Swedish EAC is weaker than its Danish and Finnish counterparts in terms of knowledge of policy issues, subsidiarity, institutional memory, expertise etc. One could argue that the fragmentation that the Swedish model entails also weakens the *Riksdag* in relation to the government in EU-matters. This study illustrates differences in constitutional and political traditions. Especially interesting is the difference between the Danish system (informal) on the one hand, and the Swedish and Finnish on the other (formal). As for political traditions or rather strategies, it is interesting to note the outspoken political stance in Finland to speak with one voice within the EU and the role that it has played for the scrutiny; something that Denmark and Sweden have not adhered to, to the same extent.

Thus, I would argue that the main explanations for Sweden being an outlier are its decentralised model for the scrutiny, the absence of clearly regulated selection mechanisms, the weak role to be played by the Committee on the Constitution[92] (especially the hesitancy of the Swedish committee on the Constitution to 'guide' the other committees in the scrutiny process from a methodological point of view), and the absence of a country-specific strategy like the Finnish 'speak with one voice'—strategy. I would also argue that these factors taken together explain the broad and political scope that the Swedish sectoral committees adopt concerning the understanding/definition of the principle of subsidiarity within the EWM. Taken together, the *Eduskunta* comes out looking more like a constitutional watchdog, as do the *Folketinget*, while the *Riksdag*, to use Cooper's typology, is engaging in political arguing with the Commission within the framework of the EWM, something that the Commission does not really appreciate.[93]

92 As elaborated in Jonsson Cornell (n 39 above).

93 I Cooper, Chapter 2 in this volume.

11

The Scrutiny of the Principle of Subsidiarity in the Procedures and Reasoned Opinions of the Italian Chamber and Senate

NICOLA LUPO

I. Introduction

National parliaments are generally institutions with a long history, strong procedural traditions and differing dynamics both externally (with their national government as well as EU institutions, and of course with the other House, in the case of bicameral systems) and internally (ie between majority and opposition and between plenary and committees). Hence, a new procedure, like the scrutiny of the principle of subsidiarity, introduced at the EU level, does not fall on a blank page. On the contrary, it is inevitably embedded in the life of each parliament, being transformed and adapted to comply—as does naturally happen in a 'composite' Constitution[1]—not only with EU requirements but also with the constraints established by each national Constitution.

That is why the way in which the EWM develops in each national parliament depends on a series of elements that are typical of each constitutional system, such as the form of government, the political and institutional culture, the approach towards European integration, the configuration of parliamentary groups and standing committees, and sometimes even the role of parliamentary bureaucracy.[2]

[1] For this expression and for its meaning see L Besselink, *A Composite European Constitution* (Groningen, Europa Law Publishing, 2007).

[2] N Lupo, 'National Parliaments in the European integration process: re-aligning politics and policies' in M Cartabia, N Lupo and A Simoncini (eds), *Democracy and subsidiarity in the EU. National parliaments, regions and civil society in the decision-making process* (Bologna, Il mulino, 2013) 107–32, spec 130 (arguing that these elements could be deemed as part of the constitutional identity of each Member State).

Therefore, in order to better illustrate and to fully understand the main characteristics of the EWM in Italy, this chapter shall start with a short review of the features of the symmetric Italian bicameralism and will also provide an updated description of the ongoing proposal for its reform, as proposed by the Renzi Government(2014–). An examination of the principle of subsidiarity in the Italian Constitution will follow, noting how this principle appeared, both in its vertical and horizontal versions, in 2001. As we shall see, this helps to understand why, in the Italian Parliament, a rather broad and mainly political concept of subsidiarity has been adopted, at least until now, also concerning the EWM.

In light of the previous considerations, the chapter examines the ways in which the Chamber of Deputies and the Senate of the Republic deal with EU policies and, more specifically, how they implemented the EWM. Neither of the two Houses amended its parliamentary rules of procedures after the Treaty of Lisbon, as the procedures for the EWM have been adopted in a provisional and experimental way. As will be remarked, the procedures for the approval of reasoned opinions, in fact, differ significantly between the two Houses in many aspects: the source of law in which they are contained; the way in which the procedure kicks off; the role assigned to the parliamentary bodies involved in the procedure; and finally, the relationships with the 'Political Dialogue', as well as with the powers of scrutiny and direction of the government in EU affairs.

The second part of the chapter offers some data on the implementation of the EWM and deals with the actual content of a handful of reasoned opinions approved by the Chamber and the Senate: four case studies are analysed more closely, selected from different phases of the implementation of the new procedure, including draft legislative acts that raised the attention of other national parliaments, as well as some of the most controversial cases.

By relying on general documents approved by the Chamber and the Senate, the chapter also reconstructs some tendencies emerging in the five years of implementation of the EWM. It comes out that the bicameral and polycentric nature of the Italian Parliament is also reflected in the content and style of the reasoned opinions approved, which vary considerably, mainly according to the aims pursued in each case by the standing committees involved. In any case, a rather broad and political concept of subsidiarity seems dominant. As for the procedural side, it will be argued, in light of the established institutional practice, that the procedure of the Senate is more efficient and more consistent with the predominantly political nature of the EWM, although at the price of some inefficiencies and inconsistencies. Finally, a normative proposal is advanced, in the direction of a prompt formalisation and homogenisation of the procedures for the issuing of reasoned opinions by the two Houses, which, independently from the approval of the undergoing constitutional reform, would help not only the political actors to interiorise them, but also the European institutions not to get lost in the Italian procedural 'Byzantinism'.

II. The Italian Parliament: A Symmetric Bicameralism, Currently Under Revision

The Italian Constitution, which entered into force on 1 January 1948, establishes a symmetric bicameral system for the Italian Parliament. This means that the two Houses hold exactly the same functions: the Executive needs the confidence of both the Senate of the Republic and the Chamber of Deputies (article 94 Constitution); and the two Houses jointly exercise the legislative function (article 70 Constitution). Therefore, each bill may equally start from the Chamber or from the Senate but, for a bill to become law, both Houses must approve the identical text.

For as long as the two Houses, directly elected at the same time by the citizens, were formed according to a proportional electoral system (as was the case from 1948 to 1992),[3] the symmetric bicameral system did not represent a problem. Neither the distribution of votes—notwithstanding a considerable difference regarding the age limits both to vote and to be elected[4]—nor the allotment of seats was much differentiated between the two Houses. Moreover, strong political parties were in fact able to ensure a consistent behaviour of the Chamber and the Senate: through a strict control of the activity of the legislative committees, this consistency could be ensured both in the confidence relationship with the government and throughout the legislative process.

The exigency to reform the bicameral system, already felt during the '80s, became much stronger after the adoption, in 1993, of a majoritarian electoral system and the outbreak of the crisis of the political parties upon which the Republican Constitution of 1947 had been founded. Both elements, in fact, converged to increase the risks of divergences between the two Houses and deadlock, which actually occurred, rather dramatically, in the aftermath of the February 2013 elections. It is not a coincidence that after these elections the process of constitutional reform, already attempted many times in the last three decades with very limited outcomes, has started again, and seems to be proceeding at a much higher speed.[5]

The bill submitted by the Renzi Government and then approved by the two Houses, but still to be passed through a popular referendum, provides for a rather radical reform of Italian bicameralism, aimed at transforming the current symmetric system into an asymmetric one, with a new Senate indirectly elected (by Regional Councils), deprived of the confidence relationship and normally unable

[3] With the only exception, for the Chamber, of the 1953 elections, with took place according to a majoritarian electoral law (although producing a proportional distribution of seats).

[4] In order to vote for the Chamber or the Senate the age limits are respectively 18 and 25 years; in order to be elected respectively 25 and 40 years.

[5] See S Ceccanti, 'Constitutional change: an explanation' (2015) 20 *Journal of Modern Italian Studies* (special Issue on 'Italy 1990–2014: The Transition That Never Happened') 202–12.

to veto the laws approved by the Chamber. Furthermore, according to this draft reform, the new Senate would be representative of territorial autonomies and would hold, among others, some functions specifically concerning the relationships with the EU: namely, it would exercise a connection function between the state, the territorial autonomies and the European Union, as well as participate 'in the decisions aimed at forming and implementing EU normative acts and policies' and assess the impact of EU policies on territories.[6]

III. The Principle of Subsidiarity in the Italian Constitution

Before examining how the principle of subsidiarity—introduced in the EU legal order by the Treaty of Maastricht and then slightly modified by the Treaty of Lisbon in order to take into account the internal structure of Member States—has been interpreted and implemented by the two Italian Houses in the EWM, it is important to highlight the fact that almost a decade after the signature of the Treaty of Maastricht, the principle of subsidiarity made its own appearance in the Italian Constitution.

More precisely, the expression 'principle of subsidiarity' was introduced by the Constitutional law no 3/2001, which is the main constitutional revision approved to date, extensively revising the Fifth Title of the Constitution (on regional and local authorities). The principle has two clearly different meanings: 'vertical' (ie, among different levels of government: Article 118(1)) and 'horizontal' (ie, between public institutions and civil society: Article 118(4)).

In previous years, this principle, mainly in its first (vertical) meaning, had already appeared in ordinary legislation (namely, Article 4(3)(c), law no 59/1997: the so-called 'Bassanini law') in order to accomplish, together with other general principles (such as differentiation, efficiency, responsibility, cooperation, adequacy), a further step in the devolution of administrative functions to regional and local authorities. More particularly, according to this principle, the exercise of public responsibilities should preferably be given to the authorities that are closest to the citizens.[7]

[6] See Atto Camera, XVII legislatura, no 2613-B (*Disposizioni per il superamento del bicameralismo paritario, la riduzione del numero dei parlamentari, il contenimento dei costi di funzionamento delle istituzioni, la soppressione del CNEL e la revisione del titolo V della parte II della Costituzione*), as approved by the Senate on 8 August 2014, modified by the Chamber on 10 March 2015 and again by the Senate on 13 October 2015. Our translation.

[7] A Maltoni, 'The Principle of Subsidiarity in Italy: its Meaning as a "Horizontal" Principle and its Recent Constitutional Recognition' (2002) 4 *The International Journal of Not-for-Profit Law*, available at: www.icnl.org/research/journal/vol4iss4/art_3.htm.

This means that in some ways the principle of subsidiarity initially entered the Italian constitutional order as a multi-purpose concept,[8] as a justification of some elasticity in the process of determining the functions exercised by each level of government and, more generally, by public institutions. In this context, Italian legal scholars outlined that, conversely to the principle of conferral, subsidiarity is not a technique for the distribution of functions, but—consistently with its own origins—a principle aimed at limiting the exercise of public functions, to be enforced through 'ad hoc' procedures. In other words, it is not a rule that identifies the competent institution on a subject-matter, but a principle to be used in order to evaluate which is best adapted to exercise that function in a concrete context.[9]

This flexible and multi-purpose nature of the principle of subsidiarity is made even clearer by the case law of the Italian Constitutional Court, especially decision no 303/2003. This important decision, qualified by some scholars as a sort of rewriting of the content of Constitutional law no 3/2001,[10] attached the principle of subsidiarity, and the flexibility it entails, not only to the allocation of administrative functions, but also to the concrete distribution of legislative competences. According to the Constitutional Court's interpretation of subsidiarity, the state can move an administrative function upward also bringing with it, thanks to the legality principle, the legislative competence. This requires the measure to be proportionate, not unreasonable, and in some way also supported by the Regions. In this way, the principle of subsidiarity has been interpreted as a flexible instrument, able to act as 'Trojan horse'[11] against the legislative competences of the Regions, which the Constitutional reform of 2001 had significantly enlarged, reverting the distribution criterion between the Regions and the state.

IV. EU Affairs in the Italian Parliament

The current symmetry of Italian bicameralism is also mirrored in the powers regarding EU affairs. There are, in fact, two standing committees on EU Policies: one for each House, both of which are composed proportionally according to parliamentary groups and hold similar functions (with the exception of the EWM, as we will see in the next paragraph).

[8] More generally, in the sense that subsidiarity principle is 'somewhat of a chamaleon' see, for instance, M Evans and A Zimmermans, 'Editors' Conclusions: Future Directions for Subsidiarity' in M Evans and A Zimmermans (eds), *Global Perspectives on Subsidiarity* (Heidelberg, Springer, 2014) 221 ff, spec 223.

[9] A D'Atena, *Diritto regionale*, II edn (Torino, Giappichelli, 2013) 77 f. and 201 f.

[10] See, among many, A Morrone, 'La Corte costituzionale riscrive il titolo V' (2003) XXIII *Quaderni costituzionali* 818–20 and E Arban, 'Re-centralizing subsidiarity: Interpretations by the Italian Constitutional Court' (2015) 25 *Regional and Federal Studies* 129.

[11] G Martinico, 'The impact of "regional blindness" on the Italian Regional State', STALS Research Papers, no 2/2011, available at: stals.sssup.it (ISSN: 1974-5656) 20.

The histories of the two Italian EU Policies Committees, however, differ slightly. The Senate was the first to build, in 1968, an 'ad hoc' body specialised in EU affairs, at the time called '*Giunta per gli affari europei*'. Being a '*Giunta*' instead of a '*Commissione*' meant that it was composed of fewer senators and that, in the beginning, it did not hold any real power in the legislative process, but only advisory powers.[12] In 2003 it was transformed into a standing committee, the 14th and final one of the Senate, with a wider composition similar to the other standing committees and with some (minor) legislative functions. The main difference in comparison with the other Senate standing committees, however, can be seen in the fact that its members are also members of another standing committee (two or three from each of them).[13] There is, therefore, a case of 'dual mandate', which is specifically requested by the rules of procedure (also in order to avoid a further reduction of the average membership of each of the other Senate standing committees) and almost unheard of for the standing committees of the Italian Parliament.[14]

In the Chamber of Deputies an 'ad hoc' committee for EU affairs was established much later, only in 1990.[15] It is not a coincidence that it came into being around the time of the establishment of COSAC[16] and in the aftermath of the entry into force of law no 86/1989, which reformed the instruments for implementing EU directives in Italy, establishing the annual 'Community Law'.[17] Initially called 'special Committee for Community policies', it was transformed in 1996 into the 14th standing committee, and, accordingly, made fully equivalent to the other 13 standing committees. Contrary to the composition of the 14th committee of the *Senate*, however, its members are normally not members of other standing committees.

[12] E Vinci, 'La giunta consultiva del Senato per gli affari comunitari' (1968) 1 *Studi parlamentari e di politica costituzionale* 135–42.

[13] See Art 21.4-*bis* of the Senate rules of procedure, giving to the Speaker of the Senate the power to promote agreements among parliamentary groups in order to follow the proportionality principle and, in the meantime, to ensure that its members consist of 3 from each of the committees on Constitutional Affairs, Foreign Affairs and Budget, while 2 from each of the other 10 standing committees.

[14] See C Fasone, *Sistemi di commissioni parlamentari e forme di governo* (Padova, Cedam, 2012) 219 f.

[15] Previously, the competence on EU affairs was included in that of the standing Committee for Foreign Affairs (which still retains the denomination 'Affari esteri e comunitari'): see M Cartabia and JHH Weiler, *L'Italia in Europa. Profili istituzionali e costituzionali* (Bologna, Il mulino, 2000) 146 f and V Guizzi, *Manuale di diritto e politiche dell'Unione europea*, IV edn (Napoli, Editoriale scientifica, 2015) 598 f.

[16] On the pressure that the setting up of COSAC exerted in favour of the establishment of EU Committees in national parliaments and on their different features, see T Bergman, 'National Parliaments and EU Affairs Committees: Notes on Empirical Variation and Competing Explanations' (1997) 4 *Journal of European Public Policy* 373–87. For an updated picture see C Hefftler, C Neuhold, O Rozenberg, J Smith (eds), *The Palgrave Handbook of National Parliaments and the European Union* (Basingstoke, Palgrave Macmillan, 2015).

[17] The annual 'Community Law', introduced in 1987, serves to implement EU law at domestic level: see F Bindi, *Italy and the European Union* (Washington DC/Rome, Brookings-SSPA, 2011) 101–5, and P Falletta and N Lupo, 'Mechanisms for Implementing EU Law at State Level' in G Di Cosimo (ed), *The implementation of EU Environmental Law in Italy* (The Hague, Eleven International Publishing, 2013) 23–38.

The implementation of the Treaty of Lisbon into the Italian legal system took place with some delays. As its order of execution was timely issued, like all those regarding the founding Treaties and their revisions,[18] by an ordinary law (no 130/2008), no constitutional amendment was deemed necessary. By contrast, the ordinary law necessary for updating all the procedures for participating in and implementing EU law and policies was approved only at the end of 2012 (law no 234/2012), more than three years after the entry into force of the Treaty of Lisbon. Law no 234/2012 includes new provisions on all of the most important EU procedures (among which is the parliamentary scrutiny reserve, introduced in 2005, but substantially devoid of any real application)[19] and it also refers to the EWM and the 'Political Dialogue' (respectively, Articles 8 and 9), including the right to resort to the ECJ in case of violation of the principle of subsidiarity (Article 42). However, as for the parliamentary procedures, it expressly requires (namely, in Articles 7 and 8) that they be completed by 'ad hoc' provisions to be included in the rules of procedure of the Chamber and of the Senate.

This notwithstanding, the updates of the rules of procedure have not yet been approved, although some of them are foreseen in the framework of a more general draft reform of the rules of procedure of the Chamber of Deputies.[20] This inactivity of the two Houses seems to be part of a more general trend, not confined to EU affairs, not to update parliamentary rules of procedure, giving way to non-written norms and to institutional practice: that is, to decisions taken case-by-case or in more general terms, by the Speakers or by the Rules Committee ('*Giunta per il regolamento*'), without formally amending the text of the rules of procedure—thereby, evading the provision of Article 64(1) Constitution, which requires the rules of procedures of each House to be approved with an absolute majority of votes.[21]

Consistently with this trend, as we will see, the main adaptations of the current EU procedures of the Italian Parliament were adopted, in both Houses, through interpretations taken 'on an experimental basis' and without a modification of the text of the rules of procedure, by the Rules Committee of the Chamber and by the Speaker of the Senate. In any case, without the possibility of going into further

[18] See M Cartabia, 'The ratification of the Constitutional Treaty in Italy' in A Albi and J Ziller (eds), *The European Constitution and National Constitutions: Ratification and Beyond* (The Hague, Kluwer, 2007) 39–44, spec 41.

[19] See G Casalena, C Fasone and N Lupo, 'Comment to Protocol No. 1' in HJ Blanke and S Mangiameli (eds), *The Treaty on the European Union. A Commentary* (Berlin/Heidelberg, Springer, 2013) 1531–634, spec 1536 f, and S Cavatorto, 'Italy: Still Looking for a New Era in the Making of EU Policy' in *The Palgrave Handbook of National Parliaments and the European Union*, n 16 above, 209–31, spec 211 ff.

[20] See, commenting the reform proposal, L Bartolucci and C Fasone, 'Le procedure di raccordo con l'Unione europea: un bilancio in attivo, ma con qualche occasione persa', available at: www.osservatoriosullefonti.it, 2014, no 1.

[21] On this trend see the contributions collected in N Lupo (ed), *Il precedente parlamentare tra diritto e politica* (Bologna, Il mulino, 2013).

detail, it seems important to underline that, as a result, some powers provided by the Treaty of Lisbon still need updated parliamentary procedures for their implementation: namely, some special veto powers, which are not the object of any provision of law no 234/2012.[22]

V. The Different Implementation of the EWM in the Two Houses

Notwithstanding the symmetric bicameralism, the Chamber and the Senate adopted very different parliamentary procedures for implementing the EWM. The main differences relate to: a) the source of law in which these procedures are provided; b) the decision to start the subsidiarity check; c) the role assigned to the parliamentary bodies involved in the procedure, namely the distribution of roles between EU Policies Committee and sectoral committee; d) the involvement of the Plenary; e) and the relationships with the other EU procedures concerning the same draft legislative acts; that is the 'Political Dialogue', as well as with the powers of scrutiny and direction of the government in EU affairs. Each of these differences needs to be specifically addressed and, where possible, explained.

A. Sources of Law

While in the Chamber the implementation of the EWM took place through two opinions approved by the Rules Committee, in the Senate the procedure was provided only by a letter of the Speaker of the Assembly. The Rules Committee of the Chamber approved two '*pareri*' (literally, 'opinions', but it is perhaps more appropriate to refer to them as 'interpretative decisions', in view of their binding value, their innovative character and their general effects[23]): one in the wake of the entry into force of the Treaty of Lisbon, on 6 October 2009, and the other, after some months of practical experience, on 14 July 2010, partly specifying and partly reviewing some provisions of the first one (especially on the involvement of the Plenary). In contrast, in the Senate the procedure was determined by a letter signed by the then Speaker, Renato Schifani, sent to all the standing committees' chairpersons, on the very day of the entry into force of the Treaty of Lisbon, 1 December 2009.

[22] See G Piccirilli, '*Il Parlamento italiano: le procedure europee nella legge n. 234 del 2012*' in A Manzella and N Lupo (eds), *Il sistema parlamentare euro-nazionale. Lezioni* (Torino, Giappichelli, 2014) 205–26, spec 221.

[23] On the importance of the 'opinions' of the Rules Committee (*Giunta per il regolamento*) see, in general, A Manzella, *Il parlamento*, III edn (Bologna, Il mulino, 2003), spec 52 ff.

This variation in the sources of law used also implies a different publicity regime for the rules governing the EWM procedures: while the letter of the Speaker of the Senate is not made public in any way (although frequently quoted in parliamentary proceedings, as well as by some scholars),[24] the texts of the two interpretative decisions of the Rules Committee are available on the website of the Chamber.[25]

However, in both Houses the solutions were adopted expressly on an experimental basis (and in the Senate also on a provisional basis)—a feature, indeed, not completely unknown to recent parliamentary practice, as similar expressions have also accompanied other interpretative decisions taken by the two Rules Committees. In our case, as well as in others, the experimental character does not impede the procedures so constructed from being able to stay in place for years, if not for decades. Since 2010, in fact, no change has been made regarding their content, and the (Italian components of) EWM procedures have not been modified further.

Moreover, it can be highlighted that the first interpretative decision approved by the Rules Committee of the Chamber (that of 6 October 2009), which addressed the main procedures linking the Chamber with the EU institutions, expressly contained, precisely with regard to the EWM, an 'evaluation clause'. According to this clause, 'once the Treaty enters into force, the experimental procedure here envisaged will be the object of an evaluation with the particular aim of verifying the possibility, where certain circumstances are met, to involve the Plenary on decisions regarding subsidiarity'.[26] This is exactly what happened with the subsequent 'opinion' approved by the same Rules Committee on 14 July 2010, which is almost completely dedicated to the EWM: it complements the previous interpretative decision, allowing the possibility of an involvement of the Plenary and providing for the relevant norms governing the debate in that case.

B. The Kick-Off of the Procedures

As with regards to the crucial kick-off of the procedure, the two Houses adopted very different solutions. In the Senate, all of the draft legislative acts transmitted according to Protocol no 2—that is on which a subsidiarity scrutiny could be exercised—are automatically assigned to the sectoral committee competent on the subject-matter, as well as to the Committee on EU Policies. The exception to the general rule, which leaves the request for a deferral of an EU draft legislative act to the sectoral committee's discretion (Article 144(1) of the rules of procedure),

[24] See, for instance, DA Capuano, 'Il Senato e l'attuazione del trattato di Lisbona, tra controllo di sussidiarietà e dialogo politico con la Commissione europea', available at: www.amministrazioneincammino.luiss.it/wp-content/uploads/2011/01/Capuano_Senato-e-Trattato-Lisbona.pdf, January 2011, p 7 s.

[25] Respectively, at: www.camera.it/leg17/593?conoscerelacamera=236, and www.camera.it/leg17/593?conoscerelacamera=241.

[26] Our translation.

is the result of a wish to respect, whenever possible, the eight-week deadline.[27] That is why in the assignment decision the Speaker of the Senate automatically indicates a deadline for the expression of the opinion by the sectoral committee, as well as for the other committees consulted on the same issue (including the Committee on EU Policies, which, as we will see in the next paragraph, can also substitute for, in case of inactivity, the sectoral committee).

By contrast, in the Chamber the selection of the draft legislative acts relevant for the EWM procedure is left entirely to the Committee on EU Policies, to whom all these acts are assigned. The Chamber, in fact, decided not to systematically scrutinise all of the EU draft legislative acts transmitted according to Protocol no 2 and, instead, to select only the proposals in which the respect of the principle of subsidiarity could be problematic and therefore be deemed worthwhile for the Committee on EU Policies to begin an examination.[28] This selection is decided by the Bureau, integrated with the group representatives (that is, the chairpersons of every parliamentary group in that committee), of the Committee on EU Policies. This body, which normally meets once a week and whose meetings are devoid of any form of transparency, selects the acts to be examined also on the basis of technical notes prepared by the staff of the Chamber (EU Affairs Department).

As we will see, this difference in the kick-off of the procedures contributes to the explanation as to why, for the most part, there is a much higher number of reasoned opinions approved by the Senate. However, this data can also find further explanations in other divergences that exist between the procedures adopted in the two Houses.

C. EU Policies Committee and Sectoral Committees

The most significant difference between the two Houses relates to the allotment of tasks between the Committee on EU Policies and the other standing committees (hereinafter, called sectoral committees, as they mostly deal with specific policies).

In the Chamber, the 'reasoned opinion', included in a 'document' on the compliance with the principle of subsidiarity, can be issued exclusively by the Committee on EU Policies: to be expressed, in principle, within 40 days and in theory—as this provision has never been implemented—with the participation of the rapporteur in the sectoral committee, who is invited to attend. The sectoral committees, instead, are competent regarding the substance of the draft legislative acts, as well as for the respect of the principle of proportionality. On these aspects, the

[27] DA Capuano, 'Funzioni delle Camere italiane nel procedimento legislativo dell'Unione europea' (2011) 52 *Rassegna parlamentare* 519–50, spec 544.

[28] A Esposito, 'La legge 24 dicembre 2012, n. 234, sulla partecipazione dell'Italia alla formazione e all'attuazione della normativa e delle politiche dell'UE. Parte 1, Prime riflessioni sul ruolo delle Camere' (2013) 9 *Federalismi.it: rivista di diritto pubblico italiano, comunitario e comparato* 41 (available at: www.federalismi.it).

Committee on EU Policies can also, eventually, add something, issuing an opinion addressed (only) to the sectoral committee, which has to decide whether to use this opinion in drafting its own document, to be sent to the government and to the EU institutions.

Meanwhile, in the Senate, the Committee on EU Policies, in its opinion (called 'resolution'), is asked to deal with any aspect of the draft legislative act. In principle, its opinion should be addressed to the sectoral committee also called to scrutinise the draft legislative act in its entirety and to issue a resolution, directed to the Executive and to the EU institutions, relating to all the aspects of the proposal. However, in the case of inactivity of the latter, the resolution approved by the Committee on EU Policies can be transferred directly to the Executive and to the EU institutions. In this way, a sort of substitutive power is given to the Senate Committee on EU Policies, which is founded on a (very) extensive interpretation of Article 144(5) of the rules of procedure: this provision, indeed, does not refer to the EWM and requires a second vote, with a higher attendance quorum,[29] by the Committee on EU Policies on the resolution sent to the Executive (doc XVIII-*bis*).[30]

If one resorted to the classification proposed for the different models of national parliaments' scrutiny of EU draft legislative acts when reviewing subsidiarity,[31] then it ought to be concluded that the Senate adopted a decentralised scrutiny system, while the Chamber opted for a centralised model (or if you wish to rely on a very recent classification, a 'mixed model' with the lead by the Committee on EU Policies).[32]

In some ways, the option preferred by the Chamber presupposes the possibility of a clear-cut distinction between the evaluation of the substance of the draft legislative act, on one hand, and the scrutiny of its compliance with the principle of subsidiarity, on the other hand. Both tasks should be accomplished by the same political institution, the Chamber, although by different internal bodies: the first, probably deemed more important, by the sectoral committee (with the opinion of the Committee on EU Policies); the second exclusively by the Committee on EU Policies, in order to develop a set of well-established criteria by which to assess the compliance with the principle of subsidiarity. As we will see further, it indeed

[29] The attendance quorum for the second vote is higher (50% + 1 of the committee members, instead of one-third), as it is on a document which is going to be sent to another institution and thus does not qualify as an issue which the committee has to refer to the Plenary (or to another committee), according to Article 30 of the rules of procedure.

[30] Normally, the resolutions approved by the Committee on EU Policies are published as Doc XVIII. When transmitted directly to the Executive and to the EU institutions, they are (re-)published as Doc XVIII-*bis*.

[31] See P Kiiver, *The National Parliaments in the European Union. A Critical View on EU Constitution-Building* (The Hague, Kluwer Law, 2006) 47 f.

[32] Cf K Granat, *National Parliaments and the Policing of the Subsidiarity Principle* (PhD Thesis, European University Institute, Florence, December 2014) 134 f (who does not include the Italian parliament in her proposed typology).

seems to be a fascinating attempt—however, unfortunately highly unlikely to succeed in practice, as members of Parliament naturally tend to express a positive evaluation, in respect of the principle of subsidiarity or independently from it, if they agree with the content of the draft legislative act. By contrast, they would assess negatively, according to any possible parameter, a provision whose content they do not deem acceptable from a political point of view.

D. The Involvement of the Plenary

In both Houses, according to experimental rules currently in force, the involvement of the Plenary is possible, but in practice in neither of the two Houses has the Plenary exercised any role in the EWM, at least not to date. However, the mechanisms for involving the Plenary are conceived in a different way in each of the two Houses.

In the Chamber, by analogy with what the Italian Constitution (Article 72(3)) provides in general for the legislative process, the power to move the procedure from the committee to the Plenary is attributed to the Executive, to 1/5 of the committee members, or to 1/10 of the deputies. This option seems consistent with the choice to apply to the examination of EU acts by the Chamber's committees some provisions of the rules of procedure regarding the legislative process in the committee phase '*in sede referente*' (namely, Article 79(4), (5) and (6), to which the interpretative decision of the Rules Committee of 6 November 2009 expressly refers).

The interpretative decision of 14 July 2010 clarifies that this possibility must be exercised within the five days following the approval of the document by the Committee on EU Policies (as already said, to be approved in the first 40 days). If the document is itself a reasoned opinion, no other requirement will be provided. But if the document contains instead a positive evaluation of the draft legislative act, a further document, called '*ordine del giorno*', will also be required, to be proposed in the Plenary (by at least 20 deputies or by a president of a parliamentary group composed of at least 20 deputies). This latter provision was introduced in order to comply with the need to justify, with some arguments, the negative opinion that could possibly be approved by the Plenary, as it would reverse the positive decision previously issued by the Committee on EU Policies.

By contrast, the Senate, consistently with the choice to make use of the resolution as a multi-purpose instrument, opted for the analogy with the procedure constructed for the exercise of political directions ('*indirizzo politico*') to the Executive through resolutions in standing committees (article 50(3), recalled by article 144(6), of the rules of procedure). This means that the power to involve the Plenary is attributed to the Executive or to 1/3 of the Committee members: that is, the same subjects that have the power to move the discussion of a resolution from any standing committee to the Plenary.

E. The Overlapping with the Political Dialogue and the Function of Scrutiny and Direction

Another important difference, strictly connected with those previously noted, is the way in which the procedure for the EWM overlaps—wherever all the three procedures can be used, that is in the case of EU legislative proposals—with the Political Dialogue and with the scrutiny and direction powers that both Houses are entitled to exercise in the framework of their confidence relationship with the government.

This overlapping is tackled differently by the two Houses. However, both Houses agree on the coincidence between the documents through which the Parliament expresses its position in the exercise of the function of scrutiny and direction (toward the government), on the one side, and the contributions issued in the context of the Political Dialogue (towards the European Commission), on the other side. In other words, in both Houses the pre-Lisbon procedures for the scrutiny and direction powers have been used also for the newly established Political Dialogue, from 2006 onwards and, at least in part, for the EWM.[33]

In the Chamber, as has just been shown, the evaluation on the proportionality and on the substance of the proposals is a task for the competent sectoral committee, which may receive an opinion on these elements from the Committee on EU Policies. Similarly, it is up to each sectoral committee to exercise the function of scrutiny and direction of the EU activity of the government: normally, through the approval of a document, after consultation with the Committee on EU Policies (Article 127 of the rules of procedure). As has already been seen, the EWM, instead, pivots around the Committee on EU Policies. The task of issuing opinions on the compliance with the subsidiarity principle is attributed exclusively to this Committee. If negative, it can stand alone as a 'reasoned opinion'; if positive it is not qualified as such, but is in any case transmitted to the EU institutions in the context of the Political Dialogue.

Contrastingly, in the Senate an almost complete overlap between the EWM and the other two procedures, which respectively create a relationship between the Senate and the government and the Senate and the EU institutions, is intentionally pursued both in the Committee on EU Policies and in the sectoral committees.[34] Normally, the first one should express its opinion earlier, so that, in case of inactivity of the sectoral committee in the subsequent 15 days, this opinion can be sent directly to the government and to the EU institutions (embedded in a resolution and after a second vote, as has already been stated). This implies that at least the Senate shares the idea that the EWM is not a separate procedure, but it is strictly

[33] For an interpretation of the EWM as a form of Political Dialogue see Chapter 3 by J Hettne, 'Reconstructing the Early Warning Mechanism?' in this volume.

[34] See DA Capuano, 'Funzioni delle Camere italiane nel procedimento legislativo dell'Unione europea', n 27 above, 520.

intertwined with the Political Dialogue and with its powers of scrutiny and political direction towards the government.[35]

Finally, it can be recalled that a certain degree of overlapping between the EWM and the Political Dialogue, on the one side, and the scrutiny and political direction powers, on the other side, seems to have been codified by Articles 8 (for the EWM) and 9 (for the Political Dialogue) of law no 234/2012. According to these provisions, all reasoned opinions and all contributions expressed in the EWM and in the Political Dialogue are to be sent also to the government. They are embraceable provisions, aimed at avoiding any bypasses of the government in Houses' activity related to the EU. A fear, indeed, which for the moment has to be excluded, as the current parliamentary rules of procedure already contain provisions with the same aim, but such occurrences could not be ruled out in the future. Apart from some criticisms regarding the language they use or the fact that the latter codifies an informal procedure,[36] the two provisions of the law no 234/2012 seem to further underline the necessary connections between all channels, national and European, that each House is able to use in order to represent its own position on an EU draft legislative act. These provisions were promptly implemented in the more recent reasoned opinions, in which a final formula was inserted, clarifying that their content is also guidance for the EU activity of the Italian government.[37]

VI. The Reasoned Opinions Submitted

As already remarked, the examined procedural differences between the two Houses contribute to explain some variations of data. Both the overall number of documents on EU draft legislative acts approved and reasoned opinions submitted are, in fact, much higher in the Senate than in the Chamber.

Up until 3 June 2015, starting from 1 December 2009, the Senate had examined 403 acts, out of which eight reasoned opinions were enacted.

In the Chamber, the most recent data available is from the end of 2013 and offers a very different picture: 90 acts have been examined, of which four qualified as reasoned opinions (although the European Commission recognised just two as such). The correspondent data for the Senate were 204 and seven.[38]

[35] Similarly, see S Cavatorto, 'Italy: Still Looking for a New Era in the Making of EU Policy', n 16 above, 222ff, referring indeed to both Houses and especially to the relationships between EWM and Political Dialogue, seen as 'two sides of the same coin'.

[36] A Esposito, 'La legge 24 dicembre 2012, n 234, sulla partecipazione dell'Italia alla formazione e all'attuazione della normativa e delle politiche dell'UE', n 28 above, 45.

[37] The closing formula runs as follows: '*This document is to be understood as guidance to the Government within the meaning of Article 7 of Law No 234 of 24 December 2012*' (for instance, see the resolution on zootechnics, examined below).

[38] See Osservatorio sulla legislazione, *Rapporto 2014 sulla legislazione tra Stato, Regioni e Unione europea* (Roma, Camera dei deputati, 2015) vol 2, Tomo II, cap V, p 512 (available at: www.camera.it/application/xmanager/projects/leg17/file/documenti/TOMO_II.aggiornato_31_dicembre.pdf).

All the four reasoned opinions of the Chamber were approved by the Committee on EU Policies, whilst in the Senate the eight reasoned opinions were all approved by the sectoral committees. For the rest, around three-quarters of the acts issued by the Senate have been approved by the sectoral committees, normally after an opinion of the Committee of EU Policies. In 111 cases out of 403 the document has been issued instead by the latter, exercising its substitutive power, as already mentioned.

Different explanations could be found for this higher level of EU activity in the Senate. Such explanations could be either down to typical features of the Italian system, or else those common to all the EU second chambers. The first kind of explanation does not seem particularly meaningful, as in Italy the two Houses hold, as has been shown above, the same powers and are both directly elected by citizens. Eventually, we might suppose that the more active role of the Senate can be seen, to a certain extent, as a sort of a preview or a forecast of the future role of the new Senate. In fact, after the constitutional reform currently under discussion, the new Senate could not issue a vote of confidence for or against the government and therefore would not have scrutiny and direction powers in relation to the government. Instead, it should be called to exercise a connective function between the state and the territorial autonomies and between the latter and the EU, as well as to participate in the decisions aimed at forming and implementing EU normative acts and policies.[39] In a way, a similar phenomenon of early implementation of the constitutional reform of the Italian bicameral system seems currently to be taking place, specifically regarding the procedure ensuring some forms of dialogue among the Senate and the Regions.[40] However, for our ends, this does not explain much, as the activism of the Senate dates back to the first years of the EWM application and of the Political Dialogue, which was during a time when the constitutional reform of the Senate, at least in the text that has been described, was quite far from even being conceived.

The second kind of explanation finds its roots in the observation according to which the EWM could represent an opportunity for the 'rise of the Senates'. The observation, in simplified terms, goes as follows: as Senates are generally more independent from the government than lower Houses, because they cannot take a vote of confidence, and as they are less engaged in legislative activity, the EWM could 'offer a greater prospect that their opinion will not merely be a repetition of what the government thinks already'.[41] Although following very different patterns,

[39] See n 7 above, and Chapter 8 by C Fasone, 'Italian Regional Councils and the Positive Externalities of the Early Warning Mechanism on National Constitutional Law' in this volume.

[40] See L Bartolucci, 'In attesa del "nuovo" Senato, un canale di collegamento più fluido con i Consigli regionali negli affari dell'Unione europea' in: www.osservatoriosullefonti.it, no 3, 2014, and C Fasone, 'In attesa della riforma costituzionale, alcune recenti evoluzioni nella 14ª Commissione del Senato sui raccordi tra Stato, Regioni e Unione europea' in: www.forumcostituzionale.it, 13 January 2015.

[41] See P Kiiver, *The Early Warning System for the Principle of Subsidiarity*, n 31 above, 64 ff (also underlying the fact that 'under the EWS Senates enjoy a voice that is completely out of proportion with the voice that they have' regarding domestic legislative competences).

more recent data seem to confirm that 'upper houses—in absolute terms—were much more active than lower houses', when considering both the reasoned opinions and the contributions expressed through the Political Dialogue.[42]

This explanation, which for the Italian case complements the procedural reason already illustrated, also seems consistent with the observed inverse relationship between the institutional strength of a chamber and its European activity towards the EU institution, both in the EWM and in the Political Dialogue. As has been remarked, most of the institutionally strong parliaments 'see no added value in engagement in a dialogue with the European Commission and instead focus on domestic influence on their government', while some 'upper chambers in bicameral systems try to evade the dominance of the lower chamber by getting involved directly at EU level'.[43]

Of course, this is not (yet) the case with the Italian Senate, given its symmetric powers. However, up to a certain extent, the overall trend of a higher level of EU activity by the other European Senates could have exercised some influence in encouraging the Italian Senate to take the new instruments seriously, also involving Regional Councils,[44] and to design procedures that would allow it to keep pace with other Upper Chambers in the EU—even more so nowadays that the symmetry of the Italian bicameral system is probably going to be overcome.

VII. Four Examples of Reasoned Opinions

In order to better understand the features and the main trends in the reasoned opinions issued by the Italian Parliament, four case studies of EU draft legislative acts were selected and will be analysed in more detail. The selection operated according to the year (attempting to consider cases taken from different phases

[42] See the analysis developed by M Romaniello, *Upper Chambers in EU Parliamentary Democracies* (PhD Thesis, IMT Institute for Advanced Studies, Lucca, 2014), 86. From the data reported there (Appendix 1, containing data from 2006 to 2013), the main exceptions are those of Belgium and Slovenia (while in the Netherlands and in Romania the two Houses seem more or less at the same level of activity in EU affairs). Considering that in Spain the two Houses need to act together, in the other eight Member States upper Houses are more active: clearly in Germany, Austria and France (see the chapters on these countries in this volume). More specifically, four main groups have been observed: 'First, there are very active upper chambers, participating both in the political dialogue and in the EWS (Germany, Austria and France). Second, there are upper chambers mostly on equal footing in terms of subsidiarity concerns with the lower ones, but strongly involved in the "political dialogue" (Czech Republic, Italian Senate; House of Lords). Third, there are upper chambers participating on the same grounds with the lower ones (Spain; Ireland; Netherlands; Poland; Romania). Finally, there are upper chambers characterised by a low degree of involvement in EU affairs (Belgium; Slovenia)'.

[43] In these terms, K Auel, O Rozenberg and A Tacea, 'Fighting Back? And, If So, How? Measuring Parliamentary Strength and Activity in EU Affairs' in *The Palgrave Handbook of National Parliaments and the European Union*, n 16 above, 60–93, spec 86 ff.

[44] See Chapter 8 by C Fasone, 'Italian Regional Councils and the Positive Externalities of the Early Warning Mechanism on National Constitutional Law' in this volume.

of the implementation of the new procedure, both before and after the entry into force of law no 234/2012), the interest of the draft legislative act (also selecting some cases that have raised the attention of other national parliaments) and the kind of assessment made by the sectoral and/or EU Policies Committees of the Chamber and/or the Senate (trying to include some of the more controversial cases).[45]

A. Fishery Products: A Reasoned Opinion Founded Only on the Substance of the Proposal

The first case of a reasoned opinion, issued by the Senate, was on a draft Council decision about imports of fishery products into the EU from Greenland (COM(2010) 176).

The reasoned opinion was approved on 8 June 2010 unanimously by the standing Committee on Agriculture, in its fourth sitting, invoking at least formally subsidiarity, proportionality and substance. In all three sections of the reasoned opinion[46] the Committee essentially focused on the 'negative effects on economic and social cohesion in the territories of many EU Member States which could be caused by the import of products not originating from Greenland': this element is noted regarding subsidiarity (it would cause the absence of the evident advantages required by the subsidiarity), proportionality (it would exceed the aims of the Treaties and be unjustified by the declared goals of the proposal) and substance (it would represent a risky precedent for the common agriculture policy).

It could be noted that on the same proposal the EU Policies Committee of the Senate (or better its subcommittee for the so-called ascending phase)[47] had expressed 20 days earlier, on 19 May 2010, a positive opinion favourably assessing the proposal concerning the legal basis, the proportionality and the subsidiarity principles.

As has been remarked,[48] the proposal could be interpreted as referring to a specific field, fisheries, included in the exclusive competence of the EU, and which in any case contains a mere application of an international agreement already in force

[45] A negative criterion was also followed: we opted to exclude cases in which a specific role has been played by Regional Councils, as a specific chapter of this book has been entirely devoted to this topic: C Fasone, 'Italian Regional Councils and the Positive Externalities of the Early Warning Mechanism on National Constitutional Law', Chapter 8 in this volume (where two case studies are examined: the reform of the common agricultural policy and reform of the cohesion policy in 2011–12).

[46] See Atto Senato, XVI legislatura, doc XVIII, no 41.

[47] On this internal articulation of the EU Policies Committee of the Senate and of the Chamber, which varied significantly according to different legislative terms, and parliamentary dynamics, see C Fasone, *Sistemi di commissioni*, n 14 above, 254 ff.

[48] See C Fasone, 'Il Senato approva il primo parere contrario sul rispetto del principio di sussidiarietà' in (2010) XXX *Quaderni costituzionali* 824–27 (available also on: www.forumcostituzionale.it/wordpress/images/stories/pdf/documenti_forum/temi_attualita/parlamento/0012_fasone.pdf).

without altering either the tariffs or the sanitary requirements of the products imported in the EU. This is also confirmed that the Italian Chamber of Deputies decided not to discuss this proposal and that no other reasoned opinion was issued. Other national parliaments expressed support, without any negative remarks on subsidiarity grounds (for example, the German *Bundestag*, the Portuguese Assembly, the UK House of Commons, the Spanish Parliament and the Swedish Parliament).[49]

These counter-arguments were used for the reply signed by the EU Commission Vice-president Šefčovič to the Speaker of the Senate Schifani, on 26 August 2010, which formally referred only to the points referable to the proportionality and subsidiarity principles, ignoring the remark on the substance included in the reasoned opinion.

However, notwithstanding the formal qualification of the remarks, in this case the intent of the Italian senators is rather evident—and especially of the chairman of the standing committee, who also appointed himself as rapporteur on this proposal—to use this opportunity in order to highlight that 'the fishing industry in Italy and other Mediterranean countries is currently facing very serious difficulties', as was recalled in one the premises of the reasoned opinion. It is, therefore, clearly a reasoned opinion based on political reason, almost devoid of any legal argument to support it.[50]

B. European Patent: A Support to the Italian Government on its Action for Annulment before the Court of Justice

The second case briefly analysed here refers to two draft Regulations implementing enhanced cooperation in the area of the creation of unitary patent protection, also with regard to the applicable translation (COM(2011) 215/216). On these two parallel proposals a reasoned opinion was issued, this time only by the Chamber (the first, in this House), by its EU Policies Committee, exactly one year after the first one issued by the Senate, on 8 June 2011.

The reasoned opinion was approved by the Committee on EU Policies, after an examination that lasted only one sitting.[51] First it invokes the choice of a wrong legal basis. As article 118 TFEU confers exclusive competence on the EU in the area of the creation of unitary patent protection, the decision of the Council authorising enhanced cooperation and its implementation in this field would not comply with article 20, paragraph 1, TEU, according to which enhanced cooperation could

[49] C Fasone, 'Il Senato approva il primo parere contrario sul rispetto del principio di sussidiarietà', and for further info: www.ipex.eu/IPEXL-WEB/scrutiny/CNS20100097/itsen.do.

[50] See B Guastaferro, 'Reframing subsidiarity inquiry from an "EU value-added" to an "EU non encroachment" test?' in *Democracy and subsidiarity in the EU*, n 2 above, 133–56, spec 150.

[51] During this exam, however, the chairman of the EU Policies Committee and the rapporteur recall the previous acts approved by the Chamber in support of the position of the Italian government on the European patent.

be established only regarding Union's non-exclusive competences. Secondly, it signals an alleged violation of article 326, paragraph 2, TFEU, according to which any enhanced cooperation 'shall not undermine the internal market or economic, social and territorial cohesion', 'shall not constitute a barrier to or discrimination in trade between Member States, nor shall it distort competition between them'.

Moreover, an inconsistency with the principle of proportionality is foreseen, concerning the excessive sacrifice it would impose on competitors, as the proposals do not offer a detailed motivation about the choice of the solution in favour of English, French and German, instead of the solution of 'English only' as proposed by the Italian government. In the reasoned opinion, however, there is no mention at all of any subsidiarity check: as stated in its premises, 'before the national Parliaments perform their subsidiarity checks … it is necessary, firstly, to appraise the soundness of the legal basis'.

It is quite clear that in these two draft Regulations the Chamber sees an opportunity to support the Italian government in its struggle against the prevalent solution at the EU level, with the option in favour of the three languages (English, French and German). It is because of the opposition of the Italian and the Spanish governments that the Council, on 10 March 2011, decided to trigger an enhanced cooperation, involving all of the other EU Member States.[52] Thus, the reasoned opinion here examined, as well as the one approved by the Joint Committee on EU Policies of the Spanish Parliament on 16 June 2011,[53] can be seen as just two further steps of this struggle, in which both the Italian and the Spanish parliaments clearly move in tune with their respective Executives,[54] possibly in defence of an aim, the protection of their languages, that could even be deemed to be part of their national identities.[55]

[52] For an analysis of the main steps of this saga see S Peers, 'The Constitutional Implications of the EU Patent' (2011) 7 *European Constitutional Law Review* 229–66.

[53] It is symptomatic that on these two draft regulations only the Italian Chamber and the Spanish Parliaments issued reasoned opinions. The one approved by the Spanish Joint Committee, also referring jointly to the two draft Regulations, is focused on the violation of the legal basis (mainly of article 12 of the first regulation, which should be found in article 118, para 2, instead of article 118, para 1, TFEU), which would originate also a lack of compliance with the subsidiarity principle. It could be remarked that the Spanish reasoned opinion was issued also after a report transmitted by the Spanish government, upon request of the Joint Committee, and after a report sent by the Basque Parliament and that, in contrast to what happened to the Italian reasoned opinion, Spain received a reply from the European Commission, in which, although formally insisting on the correctness of the legal basis, recognised the problem and insisted on the connection between the two draft regulations (one founded on article 118, para 1, and the other on article 118, para 2, TFEU).

[54] See C Fasone, 'Il "parere motivato" sul rispetto del principio di sussidiarietà deve riguardare esclusivamente l'osservanza di quest'ultimo?' in *Amministrazione in cammino*, 15 maggio 2011, available at: www.amministrazioneincammino.luiss.it/?p=16248 and Fasone, 'La cooperazione rafforzata in materia di brevetto europeo: un difficile test per il coinvolgimento dei Parlamenti nel processo decisionale europeo' in *Osservatorio sulle fonti online* 3/2011, November 2011, available at: www.osservatoriosullefonti.it/component/docman/cat_view/199-note-e-commenti/200-note-e-commenti-n-32011.

[55] Advancing the hypothesis that in this way the Italian and Spanish Parliaments aimed substantially at protecting their national constitutional identity see P Faraguna, 'A Living Constititutional Identity: The Contribution of Non-Judicial Actors', NYU Jean Monnet Working Paper 10/2015 (available at: jeanmonnetprogram.org/wp-content/uploads/JMWP-10-Faraguna.pdf) p 62 f. On the connection

It should also be noted that just two days after the approval of the reasoned opinion, the Italian government presented, on similar legal grounds, an action for annulment of the Council decision of 10 March 2011 authorising the enhanced cooperation, to the Court of Justice of the EU, expressly mentioning the reasoned opinion of the Chamber. The action was rejected by the Court of Justice of the EU (*Spain and Italy v Council*, 16 April 2013, Cases C-274/11 and C-295/11), in a decision which dismissed the actions, specifically holding unfounded all the arguments used by the Italian and the Spanish government, including those which referred to the legal basis.[56] Along with another couple of parallel decisions, both released on 5 May 2015, the European Court of Justice has dismissed both the actions that the Spanish government brought—alone, as the Italian government had in the meantime changed its position[57]—against the two Regulations, once they had entered into force (*Spain v Parliament and Council*, C-146/13; *Spain v Council*, C-147/13), declaring again that the alleged violations of the legal bases were unfounded.[58]

Therefore, this case seems, for the moment, one of the occasions in which national parliaments went closer to the application of the procedure foreseen in Article 8 of Protocol no 2, through which they are allowed to promote, through their governments, actions for infringement of the principle of subsidiarity by a legislative act, and that has never been experienced to date.[59]

C. Tobacco Products: The Only Proposal on which Both Houses Expressed their (Different) Opinions

While in both of the previous cases one of the two Houses of the Italian Parliament was alone in issuing a reasoned opinion (with the only exception of the Spanish Parliament on the European patent), the example of the draft Directive on Tobacco products (COM(2012) 788) concerns a proposal which also received

between the reasoned opinions issued within the EWM and the protection of constitutional identities see B Guastaferro, 'Reframing subsidiarity inquiry from an "EU value-added" to an "EU non encroachment" test?', ibid, p 150 ff. and M Goldoni, 'The Early Warning System and the Monti II Regulation: The Case for a Political Interpretation' (2014) 10 *European Constitutional Law Review* 90–108, spec 101 ff.

[56] On this decision see A Plomer, '*Spain v Parliament & Council* (C-146/13)—a giant step towards (dis)integration of the European patent system', 11 May 2015, available at: eutopialaw.com/2015/05/11/spain-v-parliament-council-c-14613-a-giant-step-towards-disintegration-of-the-european-patent-system/,.

[57] See, eg, the resolutions approved by the joint Committees on Industry and on EU Policies of the Chamber on the 23 June 2015 in which they asked to the Italian government to take part in the enhanced cooperation.

[58] The first of the two decisions (C-146/13) recalls the previous one (C-274/11 and C-295/11) in interpreting the expression 'throughout the Union' used in Article 118(1) TFEU, in the sense that, 'since the power conferred by that article is exercised within the ambit of enhanced cooperation, the European intellectual property right so created and the uniform protection given by it must be in force, not in the Union in its entirety, but only in the territory of the participating Member States'.

[59] See C Fasone, 'La cooperazione rafforzata in materia di brevetto europeo', n 54 above.

reasoned opinions on the part of other national parliaments (six in this case, for a total of 11 votes).[60] Most importantly, it saw the involvement of both the Senate and the Chamber.[61]

Actually, according to the European Commission,[62] only the Senate is deemed to have issued a 'real' reasoned opinion on this draft directive: the one approved by the Health Committee on 30 January 2013, after opinions were issued by the EU Policies Committee (in fact, on the same day, also expressing doubts on the compliance with the principle of subsidiarity) and the Industry and Trade Committee (on 16 January 2013, expressing a positive opinion on the proposal). In an attempt to summarise a rather long, articulated and partially contradictory document (deriving from the juxtaposition of texts issued by three different Committees, one favourable and two rather more critical),[63] the Senate invoked, generally speaking, several violations of the principle of subsidiarity. More specifically, it referred both to the choice of the legal basis—a point on which the part of the opinion approved by the EU Policies committee published immediately after, affirmed, on the contrary, the correctness—and to the conferral of a too wide provision for delegated acts on the Commission. Furthermore, another three points were raised, two of them presented as violations of the principle of subsidiarity, although they seem to be related instead to the substance of the draft Directive (the new generation tobacco products; the standardisation of packages; and the advertising on electronic cigarettes).

As for the Chamber, in fact, there were both a reasoned opinion, approved by the EU Policies Committee on 19 February 2013, and a document, on the substance of the proposal (although quoting the reasoned opinions expressed by the Chamber and by the Senate), issued by the Health Committee on the subsequent day. Actually, the latter expressed, although with some observations, support for the proposal (consistently with what the Health Committee of the Senate had already done).

[60] Reasoned opinions were issued by Denmark, Greece, Portugal and Sweden and by the Chamber of deputies of the Czech Republic and Romania: see European Commission, *Annual Report 2013 on Subsidiarity and Proportionality*, Brussels, 5.8.2014 COM(2014) 506 final, p 11 ff. From IPEX the numbers look different: 8 national parliaments and 14 votes, but the difference can be rather easily explained considering that, as the *Annual Report 2013* states, Two chambers (the Bulgarian one and the Italian Chamber of Deputies) 'sent opinions arguing that the proposal was not in line with the subsidiarity principle, but these were submitted after the deadline and therefore could not be included when calculating whether the threshold had been met', although qualified anyway for the Political Dialogue. For a synthesis of different reasoned opinions see S Petitjean, 'Tobacco directive passes subsidiarity test', 19 March 2013, available at: tobacco.cleartheair.org.hk/?p=7112.

[61] This being the unique case, according to M Romaniello, 'Assessing Upper Chambers' Role in the EU Decision-Making Process', *Luiss School of Government Working Paper*, 26/2015, available at: sog.luiss.it/sites/sog.luiss.it/files/SOG%20Working%20Papers%20WP26-2015%20Romaniello.pdf, p 14.

[62] See European Commission, *Annual Report 2013 on Subsidiarity and Proportionality*, n 60 above, 11.

[63] Atto Senato, XVI legislatura, doc XVIII, no 183. The document, 14 pages long, has been only partially translated into English in the IPEX website (that is, only the opinion issued by the EU Policies Committee).

The content of the opinion of the EU Policies Committee of the Chamber is also quite broad in its assessment of the draft Directive, disputing the legal basis of the proposal, which it deemed not to be in line with the CJEU's decisions on the issue,[64] arguing that the harmonisation of market conditions within the Community is merely a secondary consequence of the proposal. Furthermore, the Chamber argued that the proposal would have a negative impact on the very objective it was aiming to achieve, as 'by encouraging Member states to act independently in certain areas … [it would] bring about a situation of significant divergences among Member States with the consequent effect of restricting the free movement of goods'.[65]

The delay with which the reasoned opinion issued by the Chamber was sent to the European Commission is not easy to explain. It could in part be attributed to the already remarked informal character of the procedures currently in force: a feature that helps neither their efficiency nor their understandability from the perspective of the EU institutions. Due to this delay, as already recalled, the reasoned opinion issued by the Chamber was only considered through the Political Dialogue.

What can be noted is that the opinions of national parliaments seem to have had some sort of follow-up. Not only because the European Commission replied to the rather contradictory reasoned opinion of the Senate,[66] but because the final text of the Directive 2014/40/EU cites a wider legal basis (not only article 114 TFEU, but also articles 53(1) and 62 TFEU) and contains a provision on electronic cigarettes.[67]

It is difficult to say to what extent these amendments directly derive from the activity of national parliaments. What seems certain is that the tobacco producers also decided to make use of them, and more specifically of the yellow card procedure, in order to try to obtain something that they did not manage to get from the Commission in the draft Directive.[68] And that, specifically in the case of the Italian Parliament, this triggered at least three out of five standing committees to express their critical positions on that proposal.

[64] Case C 491/01 *The Queen v Secretary State for Health, ex parte British American Tobacco (Investments) and Imperial Tobacco*, Judgment of 10 December 2002, paragraph 60; and Joined Cases C-154/04 and C-155/04, *The Queen (on the application of Alliance for Natural Health and Nutri-Link Ltd) v Secretary of State for Health* and *The Queen (on the application of National Association of Health Stores and Health Food Manufacturers Ltd) v Secretary of State for Health and National Assembly for Wales (Nutritional Supplements)*, judgment of 12 July 2005, paragraph 28.

[65] See M Romaniello, *Upper Chambers in EU Parliamentary Democracies*, n 42 above.

[66] See the 3-page letter of Vicepresident Sevkovic to President Grasso on 25 June 2013.

[67] On the points in which the Directive differed from the Commission's initial proposal regarding issues raised by national parliaments, see European Commission, *Annual Report 2014 on relations between the European Commission and National Parliaments*, COM(2015) 316 final, 2 July 2015, p 6ff.

[68] S Peeters, H Costa, D Stuckler, M McKee and AB Gilmore, 'The revision of the 2014 European tobacco products directive: an analysis of the tobacco industry's attempts to "break the health silo"', Research paper, 24 February 2015, available at: tobaccocontrol.bmj.com/content/early/2015/02/06/tobaccocontrol-2014-051919.full#ref-136.

D. Zootechnics: A More Stabilised Assessment, Founded also on a (Non-Published) Government Report

Finally, specific attention can be drawn on a reasoned opinion issued, after three meetings, by the Agriculture Committee of the Senate on 26 March 2014—along with the opinion approved by the EU Policies Committee on 19 March 2014—regarding a draft Regulation and a draft Directive, both on Zootechnics (COM(2014) 4–5).

In this case, consistently with the opinion expressed by the EU Policies Committee, the Agriculture Committee maintained the existence of alleged infringement of both subsidiarity and proportionality principles,

> due to the absence of any detailed reason regarding compliance with the principle of subsidiarity, the excessive use of delegated powers, the adoption of a regulation rather than a directive as an instrument, and the impact on the principles underlying Italy's zootechnical legislation.[69]

Other than the content, which confirms the rather broad and political assessment made by the Italian Parliament, some formal aspects can be underlined as they show a progressive consolidation of the instrument of the reasoned opinion. In this case, in fact, the assessment was grounded on: 1) an overview of the situation through the IPEX website, relating to the other national parliaments' activity, contained in the opinion of the EU Policies Committee, according to which none of the eight Chambers that started examining the proposal expressed 'any reservations or concerns regarding compliance with the principle of subsidiarity'; 2) the referral to the 'highly critical observations submitted by the main relevant professional associations'; 3) most of all, the quotation of the report by the government, highly critical of the draft Regulation, according to which it would have a particularly severe impact on the organisation of Italian zootechnical improvement measures.

The latter element seems particularly relevant, as it makes reference to one of the first reports tabled by the government to the Parliament, in compliance with Article 6, paragraph 4, law no 234/2012. According to this provision, in fact, the competent administration should produce, on every EU legislative draft act of a particular importance, a report on the following elements: a) the respect of the principle of conferral, verifying the legal basis and the compliance with the principles of subsidiarity and proportionality; b) an overall assessment of the draft and its perspectives in the EU negotiations; c) the impact of the draft, financially, legally, as well as on regional and local authorities on public administration and on citizens and undertakings activities. According to the following paragraph 5 of Article 6, this report has to be timely transmitted to the Department of EU Policies

[69] Atto Senato, XVII legislatura, doc XVIII, n 63 above. This time the English translation available on IPEX is complete.

and then to the two Houses, together with a table showing the provisions of the draft legislative act and the corresponding Italian legal provisions.[70]

However, it must be noted that these reports, already used and even quoted in the reasoned opinions expressed within the EWM, quite oddly are not always published in parliamentary proceedings. In fact, this is indeed the case of the report that was expressly quoted by the reasoned opinion on zootechnics. We do not know if this choice in favour of a regime of secrecy is due, in this case—given that some of these reports were instead published on the Parliament's website—to the fact that such reports could contain sensitive elements, especially with regard to the ongoing negotiations at EU level.[71] However, partial publication could have been considered obviously omitting the negotiation strategy but allowing for the impact assessment absolutely essential for a better understanding of the origins and the justifications of reasoned opinions and contributions issued by parliamentary committees.

VIII. Some Trends from the Italian Experience

A series of further important elements concerning the way in which the Italian Parliament conceives and uses the EWM can be derived from some more general documents approved by the Committees on EU Policies of the two Houses. Here, we consider the two documents by which the EU Policies Committee of the Chamber approved, on 16 December 2014, the two Reports of the European Commission issued in 2014;[72] and the joint resolution issued on 6 November 2014 by the EU Policies Committee of the Senate on the same two Reports, with the opinion of the Foreign Policies Committee.[73] In these documents, in fact, the Italian Parliament expresses its own position on some debated features

[70] This provision regarding the concordance table, modelled on the UK experience and already present since law no 11/2005, has received no implementation: see A Esposito, *La legge 24 dicembre 2012, n. 234, sulla partecipazione dell'Italia alla formazione e all'attuazione della normativa e delle politiche dell'UE*, n 28 above, 32. Only recently has a decree of the President of the Council of Ministers been enacted, containing a (very essential, indeed) blank example of the concordance table: see DPCM 17 March 2015, in *Gazzetta Ufficiale*, 2 April 2015 (available at: www.politicheeuropee.it/comunicazione/19278/atti-legislativi-dellue-modalita-di-redazione-della-tabella-di-corrispondenza).

[71] See C Fasone and D Fromage, 'National parliaments and the EU Commission's agenda: limits and recent developments of a difficult partnership' in C Fasone, D Fromage and Z Lefkofridi (eds), *Parliaments, public opinion and parliamentary elections in Europe*, European University Institute Max Weber Working Paper Series, MWP 2015/18.

[72] See, respectively, Atto Camera, XVII legislatura, doc XVIII, n° 18 and n° 19 (available at: www.camera.it/_dati/leg17/lavori/documentiparlamentari/IndiceETesti/018/018/INTERO.pdf and www.camera.it/_dati/leg17/lavori/documentiparlamentari/IndiceETesti/018/019/INTERO.pdf).

[73] See Atto Senato, XVII legislatura, doc XVIII, n° 79 (available at: https://www.senato.it/service/PDF/PDFServer/BGT/813584.pdf). For a synthesis of all these documents see E Albanesi, 'Le Camere si esprimono sulle Relazioni 2013 della Commissione europea sui principi di sussidiarietà e di proporzionalità e sui rapporti con i Parlamenti nazionali (mentre prosegue il cammino verso il "nuovo" Senato', available at: www.osservatoriosullefonti.it/rubriche/raccordi-parlamentari-italia-ue-nei-procedimenti-normativi, March 2015.

of the EWM, the Political Dialogue and, more generally, on the role of national parliaments in the EU.

In particular, the Chamber of Deputies is very clear in qualifying the EWM as a primarily political instrument 'rather than legal-formal in nature'. More precisely, it is seen as a 'complementary instrument to support the national interest'. Both the subsidiarity and the proportionality principles are interpreted in a dynamic sense: that is, not merely as a way of avoiding the increase of EU jurisdiction, but as a means to allow for the enlargement of its policy areas only where required by the circumstances.[74]

Furthermore, the individualistic approach to both EWM and Political Dialogue seems absolutely dominant:[75] inter-parliamentary cooperation mechanisms are recalled, but no collective subsidiarity check is envisaged and bilateral dialogue is encouraged above all other means. Under this point of view, the higher number of contributions compared to the reasoned opinions and the fact that only two yellow cards had been issued do not represent an inefficient use of the mechanism.[76] As it known a third yellow card was issued in May 2016. I do not think it is considered in this volume. And in any case, the passage refers to documents approved in 2014, when the yellow cards were just two. On the contrary, as was stated by the Senate, these data confirm that parliaments have heterogeneous political interests, follow different priorities in choosing the proposals to be examined in the EWM, and also apply distinct criteria in order to verify the compliance with the subsidiarity principle.[77]

Of course, there are some differences between the Chamber and the Senate. While the latter underlines its higher position in the ranking of the most active parliaments in the EWM and in the Political Dialogue, and repeatedly recalls the observation expressed by the Conference of the Presidents of the Regional Assemblies,[78] the former insists on the correctness of some of its procedural choices, in particular, on the selection of the draft legislative acts to be examined; on the extension of the EWM for the assessment of the legal basis, consistently with the approach followed by most national parliaments; and on the distinction between subsidiarity and proportionality, which seems to imply, mainly for the Italian legal order, different methodologies.[79] Both Houses, however, agree on asking the European Commission for more accurate impact analysis and subsidiarity review due to the adoption of programming documents and with quantitative and qualitative indicators, as well as for more timely replies and more accurate

[74] Atto Camera, XVII legislatura, doc XVIII, n° 18, 2 ff.

[75] On the general trend towards individual use of the EWM see N Lupo, 'National parliaments in the European integration process', n 2 above, 124 ff. In the opposite sense, I Cooper, 'A "virtual third chamber" for the European Union? National parliaments after the Treaty of Lisbon' (2012) 35 *West European Politics* 441–65.

[76] Atto Camera, XVII legislatura, doc XVIII, n° 18, 3.

[77] Atto Senato, XVII legislatura, doc XVIII, n° 79, 3.

[78] Atto Senato, XVII legislatura, doc XVIII, n° 79, 4 and, more specifically, the chapter by C Fasone, 'Italian Regional Councils and the Positive Externalities of the Early Warning Mechanism on National Constitutional Law', Chapter 8 in this volume.

[79] Atto Camera, XVII legislatura, doc XVIII, n° 18, p 3.

reconstructions of the follow-up of the contributions and reasoned opinions issued by national parliaments.

The appraisal of these more general documents helps to draw some indications from the Italian experience regarding the implementation of the EWM and the Political Dialogue, underlining the wide, dynamic and political conception of subsidiarity (including legal basis and sometimes proportionality), which emerged rather evidently from the examination of the case studies taken more specifically into consideration. Some further elements can be noted here.

It is interesting that, although provided for—as seen, according to different requirements—by experimental procedures, there has been no involvement of the Plenary, until now, on subsidiarity grounds, even when different committees expressed positions that were not perfectly consistent. The rather strict time-frame, that both the MPs and the bureaucratic structure of the Parliament and Government struggle to follow, is probably one of the reasons for the missed involvement of the Plenary, together with the reduced level of political debate usually linked to most of the topics address by EU draft legislative acts.

The difficulties met in respecting the time-frame can also contribute to explaining why, in most of the cases, there has been almost no form of coordination between the two Houses. However, this lack of coordination—particularly striking in some cases—could simply be deemed a permanent feature of the Italian symmetric bicameral system, especially after the disappearance of the big political parties that, until the beginning of the '90s, were able to ensure coherent legislative behaviour between the Chamber and the Senate.

Finally, it may be remarked that parliamentary committees usually approve acts which substantially coincide with the position of the Executive,[80] although normally the members of the Executive do not play an active role in the debates that take place within the committees and on these votes most of the times the cleavage between majority and opposition is not particularly significant. However, after the entry into force of law no 234/2012 the Executive looks better equipped, at least in theory, to follow more actively the parliamentary processes. Some signals of this new position have appeared, for instance through the quotation of the reports on the impact of some draft legislative acts. It is still too early to assess whether this trend will be encouraged and whether it will determine a transformation of the procedures here examined.

[80] For an exception, see—in the first years of application of the EWM and in a very special period of the Italian form of government, between the end of the Berlusconi government (2008–11) and the start of the Monti government (2011–13)—the reasoned opinion expressed by the Committee on EU Policies on 14 December 2011 on a draft Regulation 'laying down common provisions on the structural funds' (COM(2011) 615 final).

IX. Conclusion: Towards a more Formalised and Homogeneous Procedure?

Drawing some conclusions from a procedural viewpoint, it seems that the procedure adopted by the Senate, which does not isolate the principle of subsidiarity from the substance of the proposal, looks more effective and more suitable for the kind of involvement of national parliaments encouraged by the Commission (through the Political Dialogue) and concretely followed by the Italian Parliament. The procedure imagined by the Chamber, although with the aim of ensuring a higher level of consistency in the subsidiarity scrutiny conferred exclusively on the EU Policies Committee, seems too ponderous and too subtle to be fully understood and clearly implemented. MPs are inevitably inclined to (also) express a political assessment of each proposal, which tends to overlap and often to prevail over a legal assessment, although often using legal arguments.

However, the procedure followed in the Senate can also be criticised. In fact, it gives, at least potentially, in case of inactivity of sectoral committees, an overly significant role to the EU Policies Committee and, at the same time, it lets the other standing committees make an instrumental (and occasional, during the first years of application) use of the principle of subsidiarity. It also enhances—especially if the Plenary continues to be uninvolved—the risk of including contradictory positions in the text of the single document that is sent 'to Brussels', clearly written by many different hands.

The bicameral and highly polycentric nature of the Italian Parliament—and also of the Italian government—is reflected in the content and style of the approved 'reasoned opinions', which vary considerably, mainly according to the concept of subsidiarity adopted in each assessment and to the political aim pursued through it.

More generally, the high level of informality, due to the fact that the procedures for the EWM and the Political Dialogue are still not provided for in the rules of procedures of the two Houses, increases neither transparency nor clarity. Some positive, although partial, effects seem to have been produced after the entry into force of law no 234/2012, but it remains insufficient to ensure effective forms of coordination, regarding procedure as well as substance, between the Chamber and the Senate.

When called to apply clearer and more stringent procedures, possibly coherent and coordinated between the two Houses, MPs would probably be able to elaborate and define, thanks in part to the constant interface with the EU institutions and the use of numerous instruments of inter-parliamentary cooperation, a more consistent, but not legalistic, concept of subsidiarity.

When and if this will happen is not easy to foresee. A window of opportunity might open in parallel with the Constitutional reform of the Senate, which would call upon this branch of the Parliament to develop its European powers, especially working on the coordination among different levels of government. However, this could also happen earlier, and independently from the constitutional reform, in order to improve the efficiency and the effectiveness of the positions expressed by the Italian Parliament in the EU decision-making process.

12

Speaking with One Voice? The French Parliament's Use of the EWM

ANGELA TACEA

I. The French Parliament and The Early Warning Mechanism: A Politicised Use of A Legal Instrument

In March 2013, the French Minister for Justice, Christiane Taubira, together with her German counterpart, Heiko Maas, signed a common declaration through which they asserted their common will for the creation of a European Public Prosecutor. Christiane Taubira's[1] support for this project was further reiterated on different occasions (eg during the Justice and Home Affairs Council in Luxembourg on 7 October 2013). But, although in its resolution of 15 January 2013, the Senate supported the European Public Prosecutor's project, on 28 October, the senators adopted a reasoned opinion on the European Commission's Proposal for a Council Regulation on the establishment of the European Public Prosecutor's Office (EPPO).[2] The French senators considered that the proposal breaches the subsidiarity principle. On the contrary, the Assemblée Nationale issued not only a resolution supporting the Commission's proposal but, on 6 November 2013, in a public communication to Viviane Reding, several members of the Law Committee, together with the chair of the European Affairs Committee affirmed their support for the proposal.

This example shows that five years after its introduction, the Early Warning Mechanism (EWM) is far from building consensus at the national level. Moreover, bicameral parliaments might not speak with one national voice in their relations with the European institutions.

[1] Ministère de la Justice France, *Communiqué de presse de Christiane Taubira, Garde des sceaux, ministre de la Justice: Conseil JAI—Protection des données—Parquet européen* (Ministère de la Justice, 2013).

[2] Council Regulation on the establishment of the European Public Prosecutor's Office, COM/2013/0534 final—2013/0255 (APP).

Scholars have presented the EWM as the major innovation of the Treaty of Lisbon and as a step forward,[3] mostly because it empowers national parliaments to play a direct role in the EU decision-making process, which could reduce the European democratic deficit.[4] National parliaments would no longer be the 'sleeping beauties' of the European decision-making process, but would become a group of 'warriors' that have the capability to oppose European legislation and to constitute themselves in a cooperative manner in what Ian Cooper calls 'the virtual third chamber'.[5] National parliaments are no longer dependent on their governments, either in terms of information (because they receive directly from the European institutions all European documents), or in terms of action (because they can directly communicate with the European institutions and veto legislation). However, while some scholars consider that the introduction of the EWM will have a positive, although moderate, impact on the legitimacy of the EU,[6] others did not find any good argument for parliaments to bypass their governments in EU decision-making.[7] The EWM would blur existing channels of delegation and accountability in the EU and it would support neither the control functions of the parliaments nor those of representation.[8] Scholars have used a broad spectrum of measures to assess the positive or negative impact of the EWM. They range from the impact on the European legislative process[9] to the improvement of EU's democratic deficit[10] and the extent to which the EU offers better justification for its legislation.[11] However, with a few exceptions,[12] current studies focus more on the impact of the EWM on the role of national parliaments in the EU and on the

[3] I Cooper, 'The Watchdogs of Subsidiarity: National Parliaments and the Logic of Arguing in the EU' (2006) 44 *Journal of Common Market Studies* 281.

[4] A Follesdal and S Hix, 'Why There is a Democratic Deficit in the EU: A Response to Majone and Moravcsik' (2006) 44 *Journal of Common Market Studies* 533.

[5] I Cooper, *A 'Virtual Third Chamber' for the European Union? National parliaments after the Treaty of Lisbon* Working Paper 7/2011 (Oslo, Arena Centre for European Studies, June 2011).

[6] G Barrett, 'Introduction' in G Barrett (ed), *National Parliaments and the European Union: The Constitutional Challenge for the Oireachtas and Other Member State Legislatures* (Dublin, Clarus Press 2008), M Dougan, 'The Treaty of Lisbon 2007: Winning Minds, Not Hearts' (2008) 45 *Common Market Law Review* 617.

[7] A Fraga, 'After the Convention: The Future Role of National Parliaments in the European Union (and the Day After … Nothing Will Happen)' (2005) 11 *Journal of Legislative Studies* 49, P Kiiver, *The National Parliaments in the European Union: A Critical View on the EU Constitution-Building* (The Hague, Kluwer Law International, 2006).

[8] Pi De Wilde, 'Why the Early Warning Mechanism Does not Alleviate the Democratic Deficit', *OPAL Online Paper* 6/2012.

[9] P Kiiver, 'The Treaty of Lisbon, the National Parliaments and the Principle of Subsidiarity' (2008) 15 *Maastricht Journal of European and Comparative Law* 77.

[10] Barrett, 'Introduction' (n 6 above), Fraga, (n 7 above), J O'Brennan and T Raunio, *National Parliaments within the Enlarged European Union: From 'victims' of integration to competitive actors?* (London, Routledge, 2007).

[11] Cooper (n 3 above).

[12] R Matarazzo and J Leone, 'Sleeping Beauty Awakens: The Italian Parliament and the EU after the Lisbon Treaty' (2011) 46 *The International Spectator* 129.

European decision-making process itself, rather than explaining the actual use of reasoned opinions in the national legislatures and the impact of the EWM on the national balance of powers.

Through the study of the constitutional provisions and of the actual use of reasoned opinions in the Assemblée Nationale and in the Senate, this chapter aims at understanding the perspective of the French parliament on the EWM and the impact of the former on the French institutional balance. It shows that the EWM reverses the logic of parliamentary regime, as it expects the parliamentary majority to break its solidarity with the government and to act autonomously. Without being detrimental to the national balance of powers, the EWM and the scrutiny of European affairs, more broadly, generated a redefinition of roles of the two chambers in the French parliamentary system. While the introduction of the EWM has been beneficial to the upper house of the French parliament, it did not bring any substantial change for the lower house. In this sense, the minimal use of reasoned opinions under EWM by the Assemblée Nationale could be explained by the close proximity of the parliamentary majority and the government. The Senate have seen the EWM as the opportunity to enhance its own role in French 'asymmetrical bicameralism' and to overcome the traditional executive dominance.

To do so, this chapter will first argue that although the constitutional revision of 2008 and the Treaty of Lisbon granted similar capacities to both houses for controlling the respect of the subsidiarity and proportionality principles, the specificities of the French institutional setting generated a differentiated use of the EWM. The French parliamentary involvement in EU affairs is defined by the cooperative relationship between a rather cohesive parliamentary majority and the government. Moreover, members of the government majority see their main task as 'alerting' the government to potentially politically sensitive issues[13] and not controlling the actions of the government in EU affairs. The subsidiarity principle is often understood in political rather than legal terms,[14] which creates fewer incentives for parliamentary majorities to bypass or to go against their governments. The parliamentary majority would rarely want to go against the government in the parliamentary arena,[15] because this could be considered as a failure to reach a compromise between ministers and government backbenchers.[16] Parliamentary majorities would prefer to support the government rather than to challenge its

[13] A Thomas and A Tacea, 'The French parliament and the EU "Shadow control" through the government majority' in C Hefftler et al (eds), *Palgrave Handbook on National Parliaments and the European Union* (New York, Palgrave Macmillan, 2015).

[14] Cooper (n 5 above).

[15] RB Andeweg and L Nijzink, 'Beyond the Two-Body Image: Relations Between Ministers and MPs' in Herbert Döring (ed), *Parliaments and Majority Rule in Western Democracies* (Frankfurt am Main, Campus, 1995).

[16] K Auel, 'Democratic Accountability and National Parliaments: Redefining the Impact of Parliamentary Scrutiny in EU Affairs' (2007) 9 *European Law Journal* 73.

views on European issues. In this sense, *the parliamentary majority of the Assemblée Nationale uses the EWM when their reasoned opinion goes in the same direction as the government's position.*

Secondly, French bicameralism is unequal and asymmetrical. Lower and upper houses are elected according to different electoral systems and at different times and they have different powers. The Assemblée Nationale represents the citizens and is elected by direct suffrage in a two-round majoritarian system, while the Senate represents the territorial entities and is indirectly elected by local representatives and members of the Assemblée Nationale. As in most of the bicameral systems,[17] the upper house is less powerful than the lower chamber. The government is responsible only to the lower house, and in case of a failure of the conciliatory procedure on a draft legislative act the government can decide to give the final reading—under certain conditions (article 45 of the Constitution)—to the lower house. Moreover, the timing of elections—deputies in the Assemblée Nationale are elected only one month after the presidential election, while the senators are elected two years after the lower chamber—creates a higher dependence of the lower house on the government compared to the upper one and opens the possibility of different partisan compositions of the two houses. Considering the greater independence of the Senate in relation to the government, *the Senate might challenge the government on EU issues using the EWM.*

Thirdly, in addition to the different use and understandings of the subsidiarity principle, the two houses express relatively different views regarding the European integration. The Senate has traditionally been more Eurosceptic than the Assemblée Nationale, in part due to the rather stable right-of-centre senatorial majorities, compared to fluctuating majorities in the Assemblée Nationale,[18] but also due to the stronger attachment of senators to the national territorial entities. Thus, *in the absence of a common coordination parliamentary body in EU affairs, the French parliament would hardly formulate a cohesive opinion on subsidiarity.*

The chapter will be structured as follows: section I describes the procedural aspects and the institutional framework of the subsidiarity check within the French constitutional system and the use of the EWM by the two houses of the French parliament both in qualitative in quantitative terms; section II accounts for the possible explanations of the differentiated use of the EWM and for its impact on the national balance of powers, section III looks at the cooperation with other national parliaments and section IV concludes.

[17] With the exception of the Italian parliament. For more information see Chapter 11 by Nicola Lupo in this volume.

[18] O Rozenberg and A Szukala, 'The French Parliament and the EU: Progressive Assertion and Strategic Investment' in A Maurer and Wolfgang Wessels (eds), *National Parliaments on their Ways to Europe: Losers or Latecomers?* (Baden-Baden, Nomos, 2001) 232.

II. The Control of Subsidiarity within The National Constitutional System: Similar Formal Competences, Differentiated Use Between The Two Houses

A. Constitutional Procedural Aspects

In contrast to most of the European Member States,[19] the new prerogatives concerning the subsidiarity principle laid out in the Lisbon Treaty were introduced in France at two normative levels. First, following the French Constitutional Council ruling of December 2007, the Constitution was revised in order to meet the philosophy of the European legislator and reinforce the role of the French parliament in the European decision-making process (Constitutional Law No 2008-103 of 14 February 2008). Secondly, at a less formal level, the new prerogatives were implemented through the standing orders of the two houses.

Articles 88-4, 88-5 and 88-6 transpose into the French Constitution the prerogatives outlined by Protocol No 1 of the Lisbon Treaty concerning the role of national parliaments. While article 88-4, introduced in 1992 as part of the constitutional revision after the Maastricht Treaty and updated by the 2008 constitutional revision, sets up the so-called 'European resolutions' (*resolutions europénnes*)—the instrument through which the houses communicate their opinion on European documents to the government—article 88-6 organises the control of the subsidiarity principle in the French parliament. In addition to the right to issue European resolutions or reasoned opinions if the chambers consider that a draft legislative act breaches the subsidiarity principle, article 88-6 reinforces also the role of the parliament in relation to the government. Paragraph 2 of the article mentioned above states that the houses have the right to appeal to the Court of Justice of the European Union against a draft legislative act, independently of the government. In other words, the constitutional revision reinforced the role of the parliament in EU affairs, while empowering it in relation to the executive. At the constitutional level, the French parliament becomes autonomous in EU affairs, while the government is reduced to a rather passive role: it only communicates the appeal by the parliament to the CJEU without any right of interfering in or countering the houses' projects.

As a consequence of the constitutional revision, the standing orders of the two houses have been modified. The Assemblée Nationale transposed articles 88-4 to 88-6 of the Constitution into its Standing orders, section III 'Parliamentary control', chapter IX 'European affaires', articles 151-1 to 151-12. For visibility and

[19] Germany was the only other European Member State to operate a constitutional revision.

clarity concerns, the procedures regarding the adoption of reasoned opinions were aligned to the same model of 'European resolutions'. A single parliamentarian, a group of MPs or any committee can propose a resolution or a reasoned opinion. This procedure reveals the centrality of the European Affairs Committee (EAC), which plays the role of a filter, as it is always consulted even though it is not the initiator of the procedure. The EAC can even stop the procedure if it considers the reasoned opinion to be unjustifiable. In the case of a reasoned opinion being adopted by the EAC, it is afterwards sent to one or more standing committees according to its salience for the particular committee. If the committees do not take a decision within a period of one month, the EAC's position stands as the final reasoned opinion of the chamber.

Moreover, a cooperative relationship exists between the EAC and the standing committees. This cooperation is reinforced by the dual membership of MPs: the members of the EAC are also members of a standing committee.[20] In practice, the standing committees are rarely involved and until 2014 none of the standing committees adopted a reasoned opinion. The Law Committee of the Assemblée Nationale adopted for the first time a resolution on a European document on the proposal aiming to create the European Public Prosecutor and the Finance Committee of the Senate decided for the first time upon a subsidiarity issue in 2011 on the 'Two pack' regulations.[21] At the request of the government, of the leader of one of the party groups, or of the chair of a Committee, a draft reasoned opinion could be debated by the plenary. However, in practice the latter is rarely involved. The only reasoned opinion debated by the plenary of the Assemblée Nationale concerned the proposal to reform the Schengen governance in 2011, an issue of high political salience. Once adopted, the Speaker of the house sends the reasoned opinion to the presidents of the European Parliament, the European Commission and the Council. The government is also informed. The MPs and the parliamentary staff have almost absolute independence from the executive when it comes to the EWM. However, the Assemblée Nationale's Standing orders give a small opportunity to the executive to ask for a second re-examination by the Conference of the Committees' Chairs, which can refuse.

The Standing orders, chapter XI *bis* of the Senate establish a similar procedure as that of the Assemblée Nationale regarding the adoption of European resolutions (article 73 *quinquies*) and of reasoned opinions (73 *octies*).

[20] Interview with a clerk from the French Senate, 02/05/2012, Paris.

[21] Proposal for a Regulation of the European Parliament and the Council on common provisions for monitoring and assessing draft budgetary plans and ensuring the correction of excessive deficit of the Member States in the euro area (COM/2011/0821 final—2011/0386 COD) and Proposal for a Regulation of the European Parliament and the Council on the strengthening of economic and budgetary surveillance of Member States experiencing or threatened with serious difficulties with respect to their financial stability in the euro area (COM/2011/0819 final—2011/385 COD), Europa, 23 November 2011.

B. Subsidiarity Check in Practice

While, as we have seen in the previous section, the two houses of the French parliament were granted similar rights concerning the control of the subsidiarity principle, in practice until 2014 the Assemblée Nationale and the Senate made different use of the EWM, which reveals a different understanding of the instruments, as well as a different practice.

As Figure 1 shows, from 2009 to 2014 there is a considerable difference in the use of the Early Warning Mechanism between the Assemblée Nationale and the Senate. While the Senate regularly uses the tool, by 2014 the Assemblée had done so only four times since its introduction: for the reform of the Schengen governance, for energy and electricity taxation, for the EU framework on market access to port services and for novel foods.

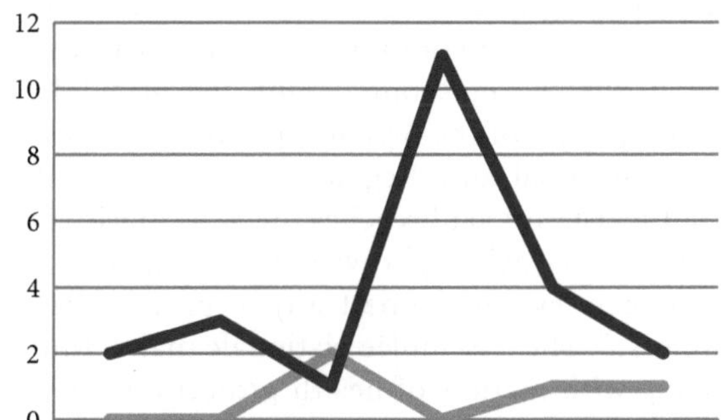

	2009	2010	2011	2012	2013	2014
Assemblée Nationale	0	0	2	0	1	1
Sénat	2	3	1	11	4	2

Figure 1: Overview reasoned opinions (2009–14)

Source: Author's compilation based on the Assemblée Nationale and Senate's web sites.

From a qualitative point of view, the French houses make heterogeneous use of reasoned opinions and their style differs considerably. While the Senate understands the subsidiarity control as a legal examination, the Assemblée Nationale makes a more political use of the EWM. The creation of a working group on subsidiarity in the Senate is a case in point. Simon Sutur, the former left-of-centre chairman of the Senate, put in place in autumn 2011 a working group on subsidiarity; the Assemblée Nationale has not seen any procedural adaptations of this kind. Presented as the political will of the chairman, who wanted to highlight how he differed from his predecessor,[22] the working group

[22] Interview with a clerk from the French Senate, 04/05/2012, Paris.

on subsidiarity is composed of one representative per party group. They meet before the EAC meetings and select the acts that require further scrutiny, without, however, taking any decision. If the group considers that there is a problem of subsidiarity, they nominate a rapporteur, who then presents a draft reasoned opinion to the whole EAC.

A simple content analysis of the reasoned opinions of the two houses helps us understand those difference interpretations the houses give to the same instrument. For example, the last reasoned opinion sent by the Senate in 2014 concerns the proposal for a Regulation on structural measures improving the resilience of EU credit institutions.[23] Senators justify their reasoned opinion based on the Commission's impact assessment, which according to them lacks a real analysis and 'does not allow them to assess whether the European Commission has correctly defined the appropriate level of action in accordance with the principles of subsidiarity and proportionality'. Moreover 'the quantitative abuse of delegated acts exceeds the provisions of Article 290 of the Treaty on the Functioning of the European Union and therefore they [the delegated acts] do not comply with the principle of subsidiarity'[24] The last reasoned opinion of the Assemblée Nationale issued on 14 January 2014 concerns the proposal for a Regulation on novel foods.[25] The MPs consider that the draft legislative act breaches the subsidiarity principle because 'under the law in force the [existing] division of competences between the national and the European level is the best way to protect the health and interests of EU consumers'.[26] The Assemblée Nationale makes thus reference to 'the best way' of dealing with matters of health protection, which is more a matter of proportionality than of subsidiarity. This shows that MPs do not make a clear distinction between the two concepts. Moreover, while in the Senate there is no control of proportionality, MPs in the Assemblée Nationale prefer to focus more on proportionality aspects and even on political recommendations, than on subsidiarity itself, which explains why the Assemblée Nationale is more active in the 'political dialogue' with the European Commission, as per the Figure 2.

[23] Proposal for a Regulation of the European Parliament and of the Council on structural measures improving the resilience of EU credit institutions, COM/2014/043 final—2014/0020 (COD) /

[24] France Sénat, *Résolution européenne portant avis motivésur la conformité au principe de subsidiarité de la proposition de règlement du Parlement européen et du Conseil relatif à des mesures structurelles améliorant la résilience des établissements de crédit de l'Union européenne* [COM(2014) 43] (Sénat, 2014).

[25] Proposal for a Regulation of the European Parliament and of the Council on novel foods COM/2013/0894 final—2013/0435 (COD).

[26] France Assemblée Nationale, *Résolution européenne portant avis motivéur la conformité au principe de subsidiarité sur la proposition de règlement du Parlement européen et du Conseil relatif aux nouveaux aliments* (Assemblée Nationale, 2014).

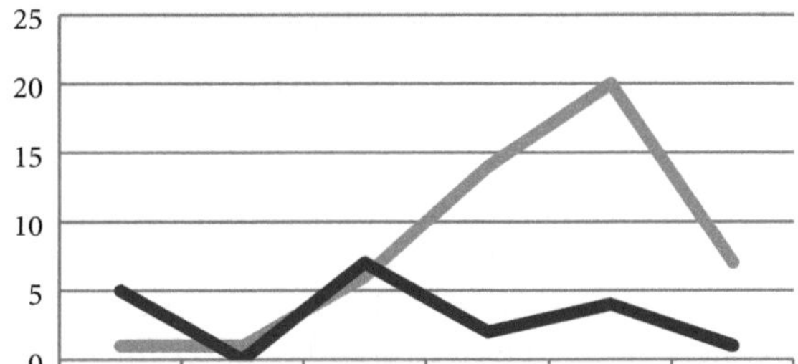

	2009	2010	2011	2012	2013	2014
Assemblée Nationale	1	1	6	14	20	7
Sénat	5	0	7	2	4	1

Figure 2: Overview opinions sent in the framework of the Political Dialogue (2009–14)
Source: Author's compilation based on the 'Political Dialogue' web sites.[27]

The working group on subsidiarity in the Senate has set itself the objective to comment only on matters relating to subsidiarity and not on the content of draft proposals.[28] However, although the senators have become accustomed to making this clear distinction and (as an experienced clerk says) 'You can now observe Senators contradict their colleagues if they consider that a judgement was made on the grounds of the content and not only on the grounds of subsidiarity',[29] this evolution has been a rather slow one, which is mainly due to the political nature of their mandate. Looking only at the legal aspects of a draft legislative act requires not only legal but also a technical expertise on the policy issue.[30] Moreover, inspecting whether a European proposal respects the subsidiarity principle without any reflection on the content of the proposal and without any political exploitation does not make the EWM a very interesting instrument for parliamentarians, who might find this procedure difficult to understand and to put into practice, but most of all difficult to discern any political advantages from using it. MPs are first and foremost politicians and not legal experts and with the exception of this working group most of the use of subsidiarity control is done in political rather than legal terms.

[27] ec.europa.eu/dgs/secretariat_general/relations/relations_other/npo/index_en.htm, retrieved on 30 January 2015.

[28] Thomas and Tacea (n 13 above).

[29] Interview with a clerk from the French Senate, 04/05/2012, Paris, quoted also in Thomas and Tacea (n 13 above).

[30] T Raunio, 'Les parlements nationaux sont-ils mal conseillés ? Examen critique du Mécanisme d'alerte précoce' (2013) 20 *Revue internationale de politique comparée* 73, 83.

III. The EWM: An Instrument Reversing the Fusion of Powers in Parliamentary Systems?

Although parliaments fulfil a multitude of functions, both classic (Walter Bagehot)[31] and modern analyses agree that control, along with legislation and representation, is one of the main functions of parliaments. Control takes mainly the form of the control of the government. Consequently, control over other levels of authority, like the European ones, is 'control via the government', because control is exercised indirectly by controlling the government.[32] In this sense, the EWM, by granting national parliaments an autonomous role in the European decision-making process breaks the fusion of powers, which is the main feature of parliamentary democracies wherein the executive and legislative branches are intermingled.[33] In this context the question arises whether parliaments and parliamentarians are willing to bypass their governments by sending reasoned opinions that go against the executive's position? The answer is not so straightforward as some scholars have presented it[34] and the French case offers a more balanced perspective. While indeed the lower house and more traditional committees in the Senate see the EWM as a strategic tool to support the government in its negotiations in Brussels and they even ask the government's position before issuing a reasoned opinion on a European proposal, the upper house and particularly the EAC might challenge the government on subsidiarity grounds. This different usage of reasoned opinions is a reflection of the role of the French parliament in the national political system and of the rather limited role of the Senate, as well as of the European feelings of its members. Moreover, the different political composition of the Senate (left-wing) and of the Assemblée Nationale (right-wing), from September 2011 to June 2012 and from September 2014 to now, allows us to verify the hypothesis of political exploitation of the subsidiarity check.

A. The EWM: An Instrument of Political Solidarity between the Executive and the Legislative Branches

The Assemblée Nationale makes a parsimonious usage of the EWM, as MPs do not have sufficient incentives to bypass the government in EU affairs. MPs tend to use subsidiarity scrutiny rather in a cooperative manner and to legitimise the

[31] W Bagehot, *The English Constitution*, 2nd edn (London, Fontana/Collins, 1883).

[32] C Gusy, 'Parliaments and the Executive: Old Control and New Control Contexts in Germany' in KS Ziegler, D Baranger and AW Bradley (eds), *Constitutionalism and the Role of Parliaments* (Oxford, Hart Publishing, 2007) 129.

[33] Raunio (n 30 above).

[34] ibid, Kiiver (n 7 above), Wilde (n 8 above).

government's position. They perceive reasoned opinions as an instrument to support the government and not as an instrument to control it. This type of instrumental political usage of the EWM is not surprising if we consider that parliamentary democracies bring together 'governments emanating from a democratically elected parliamentary majority, and unable to work except in accordance with it'[35] and that the very essence of a parliamentary system is that the houses are not in opposition to the government but in support of it. The close cooperation with the government is a common practice in the lower house. Some of the parliamentary actors in the Assemblée Nationale are not accustomed to acting independently of the government: 'There are some clerks in the EAC that cannot imagine drafting an opinion on subsidiarity without asking for the green light of the government'.[36] However, even more traditional committees, like the Finance Committee, in the Senate act in the same way. When the Senate's Finance Committee had to decide upon the respect of subsidiarity of the 'Two pack' proposals,

> the first thing the clerks did was to call the Ministry of Finance. Bercy told them that there was no problem as far as concerning subsidiarity. The EAC found a subsidiarity problem, but the Finance committee did not. What resulted was a reasoned opinion quite ambiguous.[37]

The content of the four reasoned opinions issued by the Assemblée Nationale confirms that MPs do not pursue ministerial accountability through the EWM, unlike other Member States like the United Kingdom. Consequently, one way of explaining the low usage of reasoned opinions under the EWM by the Assemblée Nationale is that the lower chamber will usually send a reasoned opinion only if this supports the position of the government. A good illustration is the reasoned opinion adopted by the Assemblée Nationale regarding the reform of the Schengen governance (COM(2011) 559, 560). The French government considered that border control was the full responsibility of Member states and that communitising the procedures would be against the principle of subsidiarity. Following the same line, the Assemblée Nationale adopted on 12 February 2012 a reasoned opinion stating that the proposal aiming at transferring the reintroduction of internal border controls to the European institutions was not respecting the subsidiarity principle because only Member States were competent in this area.[38] Moreover, the report presented by Didier Quentin, rapporteur

[35] A Le Divellec, 'Cabinets as the Leading Part of Parliament: the Westminster Model in Europe' in KS Ziegler, D Baranger and AW Bradley (eds), *Constitutionalism and the Role of Parliaments* (Oxford, Hart Publishing, 2007) 100.

[36] Interview with a clerk from the Assemblée Nationale, 10/05/2012, Paris.

[37] Interview with a clerk from the French Senate, 04/05/2012, Paris.

[38] France Assemblée Nationale, *Proposition de résolution européenne de MM Jérôme Lambert et Didier Quentin sur la proposition de règlement du Parlement et du Conseil modifiant le règlement (CE) n° 562/2006 afin d'établir des règles communes relatives à la réintroduction temporaire du contrôle aux frontières intérieures dans des circonstances exceptionnelles (E6612)* (Assemblée Nationale, 2012).

for the Schengen reform in the Assemblée Nationale, makes specific reference to the government's position:

> Claude Gueant, Hans-Peter Friedrich and Antonio Camacho consider that the respect of national sovereignty is essential for the Member States. They do not approve of the European Commission's wish to take responsibility for operational measures in the field of security.[39]

In addition, actors consider reasoned opinions less important than European resolutions since they are addressed in the first place to the European institutions and they are sent before the Council's negotiations.[40]

The 'policing' nature of the procedure does not offer a strong incentive for MPs to issue reasoned opinions. The EWM transforms them into 'subsidiarity watchdogs'[41] and they prefer spending time and resources on scrutinising the government on national matters rather than challenging or opposing it on European ones. Moreover, the EWM is structured to allow only a 'negative' intervention by national parliaments, which can only reject the proposal without making constructive suggestions for improving legislative initiatives.[42] A majority of deputies, together with the former chair of the EAC in the Assemblée Nationale, Pierre Lequiller perceive the subsidiarity check as sort of 'integration-brake' or exclusive 'power to say no', not capable of securing the constructive participation of national parliaments in EU decision-making processes.[43] This explains why the Assemblée Nationale is focusing more on the Political Dialogue with the European Commission then on the EWM. According to parliamentary clerks the same was also true until 2011 for the Senate, where Jean Bizet, the former chairman of the EAC, did not see any interest in using the EWM.[44] His lack of interest could explain the low number of reasoned opinions issued by the Senate until 2011.

B. The EWM as an Opportunity to Redefine the French Bicameralism

In spite of some political variations,[45] since de Gaulle's referendum of April 1969 proposing the abolition of the Senate in parallel with further regionalisation, the

[39] D Quentin, *Rapport d'information déposé par la Commission des Affaires Européennes sur la conformité au principe de subsidiarité de la proposition de règlement du Parlement européen et du Conseil modifiant le règlement (CE) no 562/2006 afin d'établir des règles communes relatives à la réintroduction temporaire du contrôle aux frontières intérieures dans des circonstances exceptionnelles* (COM(2011) 560 final/no E 6612) (Assemblée Nationale, 2011) 15. Translation by the author.

[40] Interview with a clerk from the Assemblée Nationale, 10/05/2012, Paris.

[41] Cooper (n 3 above).

[42] Cooper (n 5 above).

[43] Thomas and Tacea (n 13 above).

[44] Interview with a clerk from the French Senate, 04/05/2012, Paris.

[45] Association française des constitutionnalistes, *Le bicamérisme: [actes des] journées d'études du 17 mars 1995* (Economica, Presses universitaires d'Aix-Marseille, 1997).

French Senate has been on a continuous quest to legitimise its existence. This is perfectly illustrated by Jean-Pierre Raffarin's speech in September 2014, right after the right-wing regained the Senate,

> the Senate really needs to be aware that its future is now at stake, that the Senate is endangered if it is not able to demonstrate its efficiency. Victor Hugo, when he was senator, already said: 'Senators, show your utility!'[46]

Moreover, following a public survey published on 22 January 2014 by the newspaper *Le Point* and quoted by several other French newspapers, 81 per cent of the voters affirmed the need to abolish the Senate. Members of the lower house seemed to share the same opinion. An EAC clerk of the Assemblée Nationale ironically stated, 'the Senate always needs something to be present in the debate, otherwise people would forget about them'.[47]

The EWM and European affairs more broadly are considered as the opportunity to make a difference to the lower chamber. Senators, 'insulated from electoral politics',[48] have the shared feeling of going into European affairs beyond the pure control of the government. If the members of the Assemblée Nationale see their main role in EU affairs as 'fire alarms' or support for the government, senators perceive their institution as a 'European debate chamber'.[49] This trend was established by the former left-wing chair of the EAC, Simon Sutour, but following the low number of reasoned opinions issued by the Senate in 2014, does not seem to be followed by his successor (and simultaneously his predecessor), Jean Bizet.[50]

Due to the different timing of elections, the senators are more independent of the five-year mandate of the president and of the political majority in the Assemblée Nationale. This independence enables them to have a long-term policy perspective on European policy issues compared with the lower house. While MPs in the Assemblée Nationale might find themselves trapped in the short national electoral cycle and focus only on highly political salient European issues, senators may be inclined to follow a European policy issue over a longer period of time. Consequently, this independence gives them the possibility to sometimes act as a real countervailing power, independently of the political colour of the house, as was the case for the reasoned opinion on the European Public Prosecutor's Office.

However, the willingness of the Senate to focus on the EWM might have been caused by the different political compositions of the Senate (left-wing) and of the Assemblée Nationale (right-wing), from September 2011 to June 2012 and might reflect the Senate's incentive to oppose the right-wing government in the few months before presidential elections.[51] A case in point is the reform of the

[46] 'Raffarin: le Sénat "menacé de disparition"', *Le Figaro*, 29/09/2014 (Paris).

[47] Interview with a clerk from the Assemblée Nationale, 27/06/2012, Paris.

[48] Cooper (n 5 above).

[49] A Gattolin, *Le bicamérisme français en débat* (Sénat, France 2014).

[50] Jean Bizet was chair of the European Affairs Committee of the Senate from March 2010 to September 2011 and was elected again in this position in September 2014.

[51] Thomas and Tacea (n 13 above).

Schengen governance mentioned above. While, the Assemblée Nationale sent a reasoned opinion supporting the right-wing government's views, the Senate did not follow the same path and issued only a European resolution affirming no breach of the subsidiarity principle. Moreover, Catherine Tasca, the rapporteur on the Schengen reform in the Senate, openly criticised in her report the government's attitude in asking the European Commission for a reform that they then contested afterward. At the same time, she criticised the Commission's weakness for succumbing to national pressures.[52] While it might be too early to say if the newly right-wing majority in the Senate will challenge the left-wing governmental majority, it is certainly true that MPs make political use of a legal instrument and that the Lisbon Treaty might have 'delegalized the principle of subsidiarity' to the benefit of its 'repoliticisation'.[53]

C. National Dissensus and the Lack of Cooperation between the Two Houses

An important objection to the efficiency of the EWM concerns the timing of the procedure. Article 4 of the Protocol No 1 of the TFEU stipulates that, with the exception of 'cases of urgency', national parliaments have an eight-week period to scrutinise a draft legislative act between the time of this act being 'made available to national Parliaments in the official languages of the Union and the date when it is placed on a provisional agenda for the Council for its adoption'.

During this period two scenarios are possible: either the government formulates a position before the parliament starts its scrutiny of the document or on the contrary, the national position is defined after the parliament's reasoned opinion. Irrespective of the scenario, the elaboration of the government's position, from which the parliament is in most of the cases excluded, is coordinated at an interministerial level by the General Secretariat of European Affairs (Le Secrétariat général des affaires européennes—SGAE), an institution subordinated to the Prime minister. Thus, a coherent opinion is formulated at the executive level. No such coordination body exists at the parliamentary level. Each house has its own structures dealing with EU affairs and it's up to the houses whether they want to communicate one with the other or if they want to coordinate in order to express the same national position or not. In practice, no such coordination exists.

An example, which speaks for itself, is the yellow card on the Monti II Regulation,[54] which is presented by the members of the Senate as a 'concerted

[52] C Tasca, *Proposition de résolution de Mme Catherine Tasca concernant les contrôles temporaires aux frontières de l'espace Schengen, 17 novembre 2011* (Sénat, 2011).

[53] C Blumann and L Dubois, *Droit institutionnel de l'Union européenne* (Paris, Lexis Nexis, 2010)

[54] Proposal for a Council regulation on the exercise of the right to take collective action within the context of the freedom of establishment and the freedom to provide services COM/2012/0130 final—2012/0064 (APP).

collective effort'.[55] While the chair of the EAC in the Senate, Simon Soutur, played a very active role and sent letters to his counterparts in the other national parliaments pushing for cooperation in order to reach the threshold, he did not really push his colleagues in the Assemblée Nationale in the same direction. This is explained in part by the Senate's awareness of the hostility of the Assemblée Nationale towards this instrument.[56] Parliamentary actors explain this hostility by the pro-European attitude of the Assemblée Nationale and, most all, of the former chairman of the EAC, Pierre Lequiller, 'a convinced European, who thinks subsidiarity checks are dispensable'.[57] The subsidiarity check is perceived rather as an instrument for those who are against Europe than for pro-European MPs.

Thus, the different understandings which the two houses of the French parliament have regarding the EWM have an influence not only on their actual activity, but also on the cooperation between the two of them. The two houses remain insular, but this does not exclude the possibility of a common position in the case of a collective feeling of solidarity in opposition to the government.[58]

IV. Cooperation with other National Legislatures In Subsidiarity Review: More Consideration Than Cooperation

The EWM reinforces the role of national parliaments on a collective level, through the yellow or the orange card. However, some scholars have argued that cooperation is difficult to achieve, most of all because national parliaments are embedded in their domestic political systems.[59]

One should distinguish two levels of cooperation: an institutionalised physical one and a 'virtual' one—in Ian Cooper's perspective—of a community, 'whose members meet online'.[60] However, if we adopt those two meanings to describe the relationship between national parliaments within the EWM framework we could conclude that the French parliament has developed a very limited cooperation with their colleagues in other Member States.

Very little institutional cooperation exists and its efficiency is limited. While, the French parliament participates regularly at the Conference of Parliamentary Committees for Union Affairs of Parliaments of the European Union (COSAC)

55 Interview with a clerk from the French Senate, 25/05/2012, Paris.

56 Interview with a clerk from the French Senate, 25/05/2012, Paris.

57 Interview with a clerk from the French Senate, 04/05/2012, Paris.

58 Kiiver, *The National Parliaments in the European Union: A Critical View on the EU Constitution-Building* quoted in I Cooper (n 5 above) 456.

59 Kiiver, *The National Parliaments in the European Union: A Critical View on the EU Constitution-Building* (ibid).

60 Cooper (n 5 above).

and Conference of Speakers of EU Parliaments meetings, most of the MPs are disappointed and they have the impression 'they leave those COSAC meetings always with empty hands'.[61] This supports scholars' findings about the inefficiency of formal institutionalised cooperation.[62] Several other inter-parliamentary meetings may be organised: for example the parliament of the Member State that holds the EU Presidency may organise conferences every six months with the chairmen of certain specialised committees. However, French MPs share a feeling of lack of responsiveness from their colleagues when they try to push for a certain issue, as Jean Jacques Urvoas reports during an interview:

> We went to Cyprus[63] and it was the discovery, not of the draft directive, which I knew of course, but of the huge indifference of my colleagues regarding the issue of data protection. This is why, here, in the Law Committee we strengthen our actions. There was indeed a real risk for the directive not to be modified, and it would have been a tragedy for us, because we consider some clauses simply not acceptable.[64]

In practice, consensus is very difficult to reach. On 17 September 2014, the EAC of the Assemblée Nationale held an interparliamentry meeting on the European Public Prosecutor's Office and on the issue of data protection, where 16 out of 28 parliamentary delegations were present. The objective of this meeting was to elaborate a common declaration in support to the creation of a European Public Prosecutor's Office. Three delegations refused: the Netherlands, the United Kingdom and Sweden.[65] So, out of 28 Member states not even half of them agreed in spite of the efforts of the French MPs.

Moreover, the lack of cooperation between the two houses of the French parliament generated bilateral cooperation with their European counterparts at the chamber level and not at a joint parliamentary level. For example, the Assemblée Nationale has regular exchanges with the Bundestag. At the same time, the French Senate has regular exchanges with the Italian Senate. Even in the framework of the 'Weimar Triangle'[66] exchanges take place rather at chamber level, and not jointly. A single joint-cooperation of the two houses has been established with the British parliament on security and defence issues. The four parliamentary defence committees of the United Kingdom and France have set up an informal parliamentary

[61] Interview with a clerk from the Assemblée Nationale, 27/06/2012, Paris.

[62] I Cooper, 'A yellow card for the striker: national parliaments and the defeat of EU legislation on the right to strike' (2015) 22 *Journal of European Public Policy* 1406, 1409.

[63] The Cyprus Presidency held in October 2012, in Nicosia, an inter-parliamentary meeting of Justice and Home Affairs Committees around the issue of data protection.

[64] Interview with the Chairman of the Law Committee in the Assemblée Nationale, Jean Jacques Urvoas, 25/10/2013, Paris.

[65] France Assemblée Nationale, '*Communiqué: Commission des affaires européennes: les parlements nationaux mobilisés pour deux enjeux européens majeurs, le parquet européen et la protection des données personnelles—mercredi 17 septembre 2014*' (Assemblée Nationale, 2014), accessed 29/01/2015.

[66] 'Weimar Triangle' is a trilateral relationship between France, Poland and Germany initiated in 1991. Cooperation takes place at both governmental and parliamentary levels: www.assemblee-nationale.fr/europe/triangle-de-weimar.asp.

working group on bilateral defence cooperation. Those examples show that inter-parliamentary cooperation is more efficient at the individual rather than at the collective level.

At the same time, the 'virtual cooperation' is not confirmed either. Cooperation implies according to the Oxford Dictionary 'an action or a process of working together to the same end'. I would thus qualify the relationship between national parliaments rather as consideration and evaluation of the activity of others, than as cooperation with them. Indeed, the French parliament is interested if other national parliaments issue reasoned opinions on European draft legislative acts, but in a rather indirect way by looking at their activities in IPEX and by asking the Parliamentary Representative in Brussels. On certain important issues, like the EPPO, they might even try to take the role of the 'initiator',[67] but this phenomenon is rather marginal.

The difficulties of finding a convergent position of at least 10 parliamentary chambers seems to confirm the idea that the EWM did not generate a reinforcement of inter-parliamentary cooperation[68] and that five years after its implementation it is still difficult to reach the threshold for the yellow card.

V. Conclusions

At a symbolic level, the official recognition of an autonomous role of the national parliaments by the Lisbon Treaty has been important for the French parliamentarians interested in European Affairs. However, the different understandings of the subsidiarity principle by the two houses, as well as the different objectives the houses are pursuing when issuing a reasoned opinion gives the impression of a split parliament unable to speak with one national voice. Explanations are both institutional and sociological.

The Senate seems to exercise a more systematic and depoliticised control of subsidiarity. This conclusion is supported by the higher number of reasoned opinions sent to the European Commission, but also by the creation of the working group on subsidiarity. The EWM has appeared to the Senate as an opportunity to act as a European player, without being trapped in the traditional legislative-executive relationship. By contrast, the use the Assemblée Nationale makes of the EWM is less regular, because it does not understand subsidiarity in pure legal terms. In a parliamentary democracy like France, where the parliamentary majority perceives its role more in a cooperative light than as a watchdog of the executive, subsidiarity has become a political instrument to support the government. Moreover, MPs in the Assemblée Nationale are not accustomed to acting in perfect

[67] Cooper (n 62 above).
[68] Raunio (n 30 above).

independence from their government and they feel like the animal escaped from the zoo that does not know what to do with its liberty. At the same time, the EWM is considered to be costly both in terms of time and resources that could be otherwise devoted either to the scrutiny of the government in EU affairs or accounting to citizens for European legislation.[69] Those tendencies are reinforced by the attitude of each house and of the chairmen of the different committees towards European integration.

Although it might have enhanced the political division between the Assemblée Nationale and the Senate, the EWM has been beneficial to both houses in that for the lower house it created better cooperation with the government in EU affairs, while for the upper house it offered a new role to take on.

[69] De Wilde (n 8 above).

13

Parliamentary Scrutiny of EU Affairs by the UK Parliament: The Primacy of Ministerial Accountability

ADAM CYGAN

I. Introduction

In 1973, following detailed inquiries into the precise structure and remit of their respective Committees, both Houses of the UK Parliament developed individual scrutiny procedures by which they would scrutinise EU legislative proposals.[1] In both Houses, the formal scrutiny of legislative proposals primarily fulfils a formal constitutional function, namely to ensure executive accountability to Parliament. Within both Houses of the UK Parliament, the core aspect of scrutiny is the process whereby both Houses review legislative proposals, within specific terms of reference, and consider the consequences that a legislative proposal will have for the UK. This will include reviewing a legislative proposal to determine the precise financial, administrative and legislative consequences. The purpose is to influence the ministerprior to final adoption in the Council and express the view of Parliament with respect to a legislative proposal. Such scrutiny comes within the broader range of executive scrutiny which both Houses of Parliament conduct in relation to domestic legislation.

Both Houses also seek to engage and influence the European Commission and other EU Institutions and will do so by engaging in free-standing broader policy-based inquiries. This form of scrutiny task, by contrast to the executive scrutiny, is less precise in terms of impact and this can be seen in circumstances when both Houses have issued Reasoned Opinions by which they indicate that a legislative

[1] The Commons established a Committee under the chairmanship of Sir John Foster (more commonly referred to as the Foster Committee) to evaluate options for the scrutiny of European legislative proposals. See HC 143 and HC 463 (1972–73). In the House of Lords the corresponding Committee was chaired by Lord Maybray-King. See HL 194 (1972–73).

proposal has failed to comply with the principle of subsidiarity in Article 5 TEU. Thus for both houses scrutiny of EU legislative proposals provides two potential opportunities to influence the EU legislative process; first to directly influence the Minister through pre-legislative scrutiny; and secondly, through a Reasoned Opinion, expressed directly to the Commission, on whether it is appropriate for the EU to legislate. However, there is no clear consensus between both Houses with respect to Reasoned Opinions, with the Commons issuing 15 to date and the Lords only 7. In both cases Reasoned Opinions take the form of letters from the Committee Chair to the Commission with an explanation of why the Committee considers that the proposal breaches the principles within Article 5 TEU.

To this day, it has remained an enduring feature of the parliamentary scrutiny arrangements that the House of Commons and the House of Lords have sat independently of each other, and rarely follow the same work agenda.[2] Since the establishment of the Select Committees, the main distinction has been rooted in the terms of reference which permitted the House of Lords Select Committee on the European Union to consider the merits of legislative proposals and other non-legislative documents, thereby affording opportunity for inquiries to move more 'upstream' in the decision-making process. The process is document based and the Committee can recommend further scrutiny within one of the specialised sub-committees, which will review not only the legal basis and the policy objectives of the legislative proposal, but also whether it complies with the principle of subsidiarity. In the case of submitting a Reasoned Opinion to the Commission concerning compliance of a legislative proposal with Article 5 TEU, the Committee will do so through formal correspondence with the Commission, which is submitted in the name of the House of Lords.

The terms of reference in the Commons are, by contrast, narrower and require the European Scrutiny Committee to consider whether a legislative proposal has 'raised questions of legal or political importance'.[3] Consequently in the intervening 40 years, the Commons Committee[4] has often been referred to as being reactive, whereas the Lords Committee could be considered proactive in its review of European affairs.[5] As with the Lords, the process is document based and the Committee will carefully select documents which are considered to be both legally and politically important. Significantly, this will include documents which the Committee considers may not comply with Article 5 TEU but this more recent requirement of

[2] See TStJN Bates, 'The Scrutiny of European Secondary Legislation at Westminster' (1975) 1 *EL Rev* 22.

[3] Standing Order No 119 of the House of Commons, which provides the Terms of Reference of the Committee, requires it to consider the 'legal and political importance' of each document which is deposited in the House of Commons.

[4] Between 1974 and 1999 the Committee was known as the Select Committee on European Legislation. This was amended in 1999 to the European Scrutiny Committee in recognition of the fact that the Committee's task was no longer concerned exclusively with the review of legislative proposals.

[5] See A Cygan, *The United Kingdom Parliament and European Union Legislation* (The Hague, Kluwer Law International, 1998).

subsidiarity monitoring has enhanced the process of ministerial accountability by requiring ministers to justify to the committee why they consider that a legislative proposal does or does not comply with Article 5 TEU.

The historic reason for this initial difference in the terms of reference may be attributed to the constitutional position of the Commons. Within the UK Parliament the Commons is the pre-eminent legislative chamber, and by addressing the immediate political and legal questions which arise out of European legislative proposals, the Commons undertakes a vital constitutional function of considering the legislative, financial and administrative implications of an EU proposal. The Commons has traditionally perceived its role of scrutiny as fulfilling the primary objective of executive accountability within the EU legislative process and the criteria of political and legal importance have proved particularly well suited to this function. Moreover, this corresponds to the exacting scrutiny and accountability procedures that exist in the Commons (for domestic measures) through the work of the Departmental Select Committees.

The House of Commons has therefore positioned itself to ensure that the executive remains accountable to the Chamber for decisions which are taken in the Council, but this has proved challenging, primarily as result of the normative development of the use of qualified majority voting within the ordinary legislative procedure. In response to this, the European Scrutiny Committee has sought to extend its influence and extend its scrutiny activities, and in order to continue to ensure the executive remains accountable it has more recently adopted what may be defined as a hybrid modus operandi, which overlaps with the policy-focused scrutiny that is undertaken by the House of Lords Committee. In doing so it combines pre-legislative scrutiny with stand-alone inquiries into the EU policy agenda. This move upstream in the EU legislative process is recognition that, in the context of EU integration post-Lisbon, the maintenance of effective accountability of ministers requires the Committee to look beyond legislative proposals. In particular, as the EU utilises diverse modes of governance, not all of which necessarily lead to hard legislation, it has been recognised by both parliamentary committees that they need to be more flexible in their working methods to mitigate against the use of non-legislative acts to achieve EU policy objectives.

The purpose of this chapter is to evaluate how, in over 40 years of UK membership of the EU, Parliament has sought to retain both influence and control over the executive in the EU decision-making process and whether the scrutiny activities have any real influence beyond the UK Parliament. In particular, this chapter examines how, more recently, the UK Parliament has sought to balance the pursuit of ministerial accountability with the requirement of subsidiarity monitoring and the production of Reasoned Opinions under Protocol no 2 on the application of the principles of subsidiarity and proportionality which prima facie presume some horizontal coordination between national parliaments. The chapter will consider the terms of reference of the EU affairs Committees and how these enable the Committees to fulfil their obligations to Parliament as well as the procedures under Protocol no 2. Finally, the chapter will consider the importance of the Scrutiny Reserve as a parliamentary mechanism through which to control the Minister and how this could be developed to address concerns that ministerial accountability is undermined when a legislative proposal changes during the course of the legislative process.

II. The Political, Legal and Constitutional Context of Scrutiny

Both the Houses of the UK Parliament use similar parliamentary methods by which they undertake the scrutiny of EU legislation and affairs. The principal methods are questioning government ministers, debating, and the investigative work of committees. Questions to government ministers may be answered orally or in writing. Both houses have permanent and temporary committees, and parliamentarians in the Commons and Lords also work together in Joint Select Committees. The government issues responses to most committee reports. However, it would be incorrect to conclude that scrutiny of EU legislative proposals is complete and that it raises no particular accountability or procedural questions beyond those which would be relevant in the context of wholly domestic legislation. EU law, though part of the UK legal order, is not made by the UK Parliament, but rather by a political and legislative process over which the UK Parliament has no direct control. Parliament has no direct role in the EU legislative process and its participation arises from the scrutiny and review procedures of the select committees.[6] Yet, despite this remoteness from the formal decision-making procedures, the UK Parliament is bound to accept the outcome from the legislative process and it is arguably this remoteness from the legislative process which continues to create the scrutiny challenge for the Committees. In short, how can they exercise any influence over a process in which they are not an institutional actor and which they cannot amend?[7]

The general authority for EU legislation to apply in the UK comes from section 2(1) of the European Communities Act 1972, but most EU legislation requires specific implementation by UK law to be passed by the Parliament. Regulations from the EU are directly applicable, but may need to be supplemented by national legislation for their full implementation, for example to give effect to specific administrative obligations which may arise from the Regulation. Directives

[6] See M Wyrzykowski, et al, 'General Report: The Role of National Parliaments in the European Union' in GCR Iglesias and LO Blanco (eds), *The Role of National Parliaments in the European Union: Proceedings of the FIDE XXIV Congress*, Madrid 2010, (2011) vol 1, p 26.

[7] T Raunio, *Destined for Irrelevance? Subsidiarity Control by National Parliaments, Elcano Royal Institute Working Paper* 36/2010 (Madrid, 19 November 2010), argues that scrutiny remains a major challenge for national parliaments notwithstanding the improved arrangements under Protocol no 2. Available at: www.realinstitutoelcano.org/wps/portal/rielcano_eng. (accessed 24 January 2015).

generally require national legislation to implement them and thus enable Parliament to have a greater involvement in the transposition process, which may suggest that there is increased opportunity for Parliament to be involved. However, the role of Parliament in the implementation of Directives does not enable Parliament to reject or amend the legislation once agreed, and even in the course of the scrutiny process the role of the EU Committees is to act as guardians and raise the alarm bell if there are specific legal, political, financial or administrative questions for the UK. According to Rodgers and Walters the scrutiny process may

> identify an EU proposal that might damage UK interests; and a burglar alarm can tell you that someone is attempting to get into your house through the kitchen window. But just as a bit more action is required to apprehend the burglar, so the scrutiny system depends on MPs (and anyone else affected by an EU proposal or policy) making effective use of the product.[8]

Yet despite the debate in the UK about the future relationship with the EU, EU affairs within the UK Parliament do not attract significant interest. The former Leader of the House, Peter Hain MP, wrote:

> [T]he sad fact is that European Scrutiny is something of a minority interest: the great majority of Members take little interest in the reports of the European Scrutiny Committee or in the debates which it recommends. Meetings of the European Standing Committees to which it refers some documents are badly attended and seen to be irrelevant. European issues are seen as something separate and avoidable, while they should be in the mainstream of our political life.

With the Commission retaining primary responsibility for the initiation of European legislative proposals, the position of the UK Parliament is undoubtedly weaker than when it scrutinises wholly domestic legislation. This may account for the observations of the former Minister for Europe, Peter Hain, and indicate that many MPs and Peers continue to believe that their work will make limited or no difference to the EU policy agenda and the EU legislation is somehow 'set apart' from the work of Parliament. However, it is important to consider whether in the light of the introduction of Protocol no 2 in the Treaty of Lisbon this position has altered? Until the adoption of Protocol no 2 within the Treaty of Lisbon, Committees of the UK Parliament, and any other national parliament, had no formal role assigned to them within the Community method of decision-making. Moreover, since UK Accession in 1973, the Committees have not developed any formal relationship with the Commission, primarily because the objective of scrutiny is to influence the executive.[9] Even the Reasoned Opinion process, through which the Committee communicates directly with the Commission, is merely a procedural mechanism. For similar reasons, the Committees have not established any formal

[8] R Rogers and R Walters, *How Parliament Works*, 5th edn (London, Longman, 2004) 361.

[9] Though regularly invited to attend the debate in the European Standing Committees, the Commissioners rarely attend.

working relationship with the European Parliament or other EU institutions.[10] The question which is considered below is whether the prerogatives under Protocol no 2 offer the UK Parliament *real and genuine* opportunities to promote the accountability agenda which has been central to UK parliamentary activities since Accession in 1973.

Since UK Accession in 1973, the overriding purpose of scrutiny has been, and remains to this day, to *influence* the Minister prior to casting his/her vote in Council. Consequently, the Commons, in particular, has not always appreciated that with the introduction of the co-decision procedure, the lack of a formal working relationship with the European Parliament may, on occasion, have hampered its scrutiny activities. The European Scrutiny Committee[11] and the European Parliament[12] have previously acknowledged this weakness, but the working relationship between the European Parliament and national parliaments has never been institutionalised, beyond the existing arrangements for COSAC.[13]

A prevailing view within the European Scrutiny Committee, particularly with the extension of the ordinary legislative procedure, has been that the European Parliament may be considered as a competitor institution, executing its own definitive role within the legislative process.[14] In this regard, the UK Committees have tended to view the European Parliament as part of the accountability problem within the EU, and not necessarily part of the solution. The European Parliament competes with the Council and seeks to pursue its own agenda within the legislative process through proposing amendments. From a UK parliamentary perspective, the European Parliament is considered as part of the problem because the ordinary legislative procedure enables it to amend the Council's common position, which forms the starting point for the legislative scrutiny work of the two Committees. Post-Lisbon, the problem is undoubtedly exacerbated as a result in the increase of first reading agreements between the Council and European Parliament within the Trilogues.[15] Increasingly, the Committees will have conducted their scrutiny on the basis of a Council common position that may be significantly amended even before the Committees have concluded their review.

[10] The House of Commons established a National Parliament office in Brussels in 1999, which acts as the eyes and ears of the Committee in Brussels. However, this office has only two members of staff.

[11] HC 152-xxx (2001–02) at para 107 where the Committee proposed a regular six-monthly meeting with all UK MEPs to discuss the Commission's Annual Work Programme and Presidency priorities. Other national parliamentary committees have their own individual relationships with MEPs, for example German MEPs have a right to attend all meetings of the Bundestag's EU Affairs Committee. See Bundestag Rules of Procedure, Section 93a, para 6.

[12] European Parliament resolution of 7 February 2002 on relations with national parliaments (P5-TA (2002) 0058) and the *Napolitano Report* of January 2002 which considered how a closer working relationship may be developed with domestic legislatures (A5-0023/2002).

[13] See A Cygan, 'COSAC: Birth, Evolution, Failures and Perspectives' in N Lupo and C Fasone (eds), *Inter-parliamentary Cooperation in the Composite European Constitution* (Oxford, Hart Publishing, 2015).

[14] HC 109-I *Reforming the Scrutiny System in the House of Commons* (2013–14) at para 75.

[15] Ibid at paras 75–77.

Since they were established, both Committees within the UK Parliament have tried to compensate for the limited influence which they may exert over the EU Institutions through seeking to maximise the effectiveness of their own internal procedures. This focus reflects the enduring political and constitutional culture within the United Kingdom that Parliament remains supreme and that ministers remain accountable. This may be defined as 'the individual scrutiny function' and is distinct from the 'collective scrutiny' that Protocol no 2 necessitates in order to secure the thresholds for the yellow card.[16] More generally, Protocol no 2 is an example of the organic nature of EU integration and that with each Treaty reform there are new prerogatives, competences and procedures that are introduced and which will impact upon national parliaments. Parliaments such as that of the UK have sought to adapt to this deeper integration and since 1973 there have been a number of procedural and substantive changes made to scrutiny procedures in both Houses which were introduced in response to Treaty changes and the transfer of further competences. Both the Foster and Maybray-King Committees,[17] which were established in 1972 in the Commons and Lords respectively to consider arrangements for the scrutiny of EU legislative proposals, acknowledged that internal procedures would need to evolve in parallel with the development of European integration.[18] This was essential if the Committees were to maintain influence over the executive. However, neither Committee anticipated the existence of Protocol no 2, which requires the Committees to look beyond the domestic parliamentary agenda and, if possible coordinate scrutiny with other parliaments. Thus in the context of fulfilling the obligations within Protocol no 2, to what extent are the UK Committees able to ensure that ministers remain fully accountable?

Perhaps the most significant development, which seeks to ensure the effective accountability of ministers, has been the introduction of the Scrutiny Reserve Resolution, which applies to both Chambers, and which was first introduced in 1990. The Reserve was modified in 1998[19] in order to respond to the changes introduced by the Treaty of Amsterdam (1997) and the significant extension of qualified majority voting. The Reserve, though significant in domestic parliamentary terms through control over ministerial action, cannot place a complete brake on the overall legislative process. In particular, the demise of the veto and the norm of qualified majority voting have altered significantly both the relationship between

[16] P Kiiver, *The National Parliaments in the European Union: A Critical View on EU Constitution Building* (The Hague, Kluwer Law International, 2006) 134. By contrast, elsewhere in this volume, Cooper considers that the yellow card can operate as a dynamic mechanism through which national parliaments can engage and are able to put pressure upon the Commission to withdraw legislation. See also F Fabbrini and K Grannat, '"Yellow Card but no Foul": The role of national parliaments under the subsidiarity protocol and the Commission proposal for an EU Regulation on the right to strike' (2013) 50 *Common Market Law Review* 115–43.

[17] See HC 143 and HC 463 (1972–73) and HL 194 (1972–73).

[18] HC 143 and HC 463 (1972–73) at p 25 and HL 194 (1972–73) at p 41.

[19] HC Debs 17 November 1998 Col 779.

Parliament, and the executive and the centre of gravity of EU decision-making, which create problems for both Committees that were not necessarily anticipated in 1973. It may be argued that the Scrutiny Reserve is the parliamentary response to the demise of the veto and seeks to exert some control over the Minister in order that Parliament's views are formally considered as part of the EU legislative process. However, the Scrutiny Reserve is the best example of the exercise of the individual scrutiny function which has only limited impact outside of the UK Parliament. Even if the Reserve is exercised, no other Member State has any constitutional obligation to accept the UK's negotiating position.

It would therefore be accurate to conclude that, since 1973, the substance of the problems facing both Committees has not changed; rather those problems have become more acute. The Committees are continually aware of their scrutiny function, but practical arrangements have not always secured this objective.[20] Exerting influence over the Minister and how to engage with an ever-increasing volume of documentation in good time in order to complete the requisite scrutiny remain significant challenges for the Committees. Since the Treaty of Maastricht 1993, the work of the Committees has been dominated by one additional question, namely what are the most appropriate mechanisms and criteria by which to monitor the application of the subsidiarity principle? The growth of EU competence that has occurred through successive Treaty amendments, has challenged the constitutional omnipotence of all domestic legislatures and raised uncertainty with respect to how and by whom subsidiarity should be policed.[21]

Post-Lisbon, the answers come in the form of Article 12 TEU and Protocol no 2 which allocate this task to national parliaments. Yet the effectiveness of subsidiarity monitoring in its present form is open to question, especially as Protocol no 2 requires some form of collaboration between national parliaments and leads to a *collective* decision that a legislative proposal infringes the principle of subsidiarity.[22] This criticism, based upon the experience to date to secure the necessary thresholds under Protocol no 2, challenges not only the viability of such collective scrutiny but also the assertion that, post-Lisbon, national parliaments may in exercising their prerogatives under Protocol no 2 constitute a form of virtual third chamber in the EU which, inter alia, improves the democratic accountability and legitimacy of EU legislation.[23]

[20] For example the number of European Standing Committees has not remained constant and fluctuated between five and two since introduced in 1991. The current number stands at three.

[21] S Weatherill, 'Better Competence Monitoring' (2005) 30 *European Law Review* 23.

[22] G Barrett, '"The King is Dead, Long Live the King": The Recasting by the Treaty of Lisbon of the Provisions of the Constitutional Treaty Concerning National Parliaments' (2008) 33 *European Law Review* 66.

[23] See See D Jančić, 'A New Organ of the European Union: "National Parliaments Jointly"' (February 2008) Federal Trust Policy Commentary. Available at: www.fedtrust.co.uk/uploads/Parliaments_Jointly.pdf, and P Kiiver, 'The Early Warning System for the Principle of Subsidiarity—The National Parliament as a Conseil d'etat for Europe' (2011) 36 *European Law Review* 98. See also I Cooper, Chapter 2 in this volume and Fabbrini and Granat (n 16 above) 127–29.

Following the introduction of Protocol no 2 both parliamentary scrutiny Committees have issued Reasoned Opinions with respect to a number of legislative proposals and in which the Committees have contended that a legislative proposal infringes the subsidiarity principle. However, both Committees remain unconvinced that Protocol no 2 will deliver any long-term transformative impact upon accountability within the legislative procedure.[24] Central to this conclusion is the acknowledgment that overcoming difficulties with respect to regularly reaching a consensus amongst national parliaments in order to satisfy the thresholds in Protocol no 2 remains a challenge. It may be argued that it was the prospect of this failure to secure Reasoned Opinions which led to both Committees re-evaluating their role in the scrutiny process in the aftermath of the Treaty of Lisbon and how they may best maximise their efforts. While neither Committee is wholly dismissive of the value of Protocol no 2, both recognise that maintaining a focus on ministerial accountability remains the paramount objective.[25]

III. The Work of The EU Scrutiny Committee

The House of Commons' scrutiny system may be defined as a document-based process. It covers all European Union documents, as defined in the House's Standing Order No 143.[26] It is worth noting that the terms used in the Standing Order No 143 are outdated because they do not reflect the changes introduced by the Treaty of Lisbon, especially with respect to the use of policy coordination and soft law in circumstances where, previously, hard law might have been used. However, notwithstanding the focus of the Committee on the ordinary legislative procedure, the Standing Orders do appear to have proved to be broad and flexible enough to offer sufficient discretion that the Committee has not been hampered in its tasks, and, as noted earlier, the Committee has, in recent years, developed its modus operandi to undertake more policy-based reviews.

Today, under the terms of Standing Order No 143 the Committee conducts scrutiny at different stages of the policy and legislative cycle. This includes the review of Green Papers and Commission Communications, as well as scrutiny of formal legislative proposals in the form of Regulations, Directives and Council Decisions. Over 1,000 documents a year fall within these categories, necessitating that the Committee carefully selects those documents which do raise matters of legal and political importance and which require further debate. In the case of legislative proposals, legal and political importance encompasses application of the procedures within Protocol no 2 and includes a review of whether a legislative proposal complies with the principle of subsidiarity.

[24] See HC 109-I (2013–14) and HL 151 (2013–14).
[25] ibid.
[26] Standing Order No 143 (European Scrutiny Committee), 17 March 2008.

A key challenge for the European Scrutiny Committee, and indeed all parliamentary committees across the EU, is that the EU legislative timetable proceeds without reference to the work of national parliaments. The eight-week time period contained within Protocol no 2 and by which time scrutiny is to be competed, is challenging within the overall context of parliamentary activity.[27] For the European Scrutiny Committee the challenge arises within the framework of scrutiny of legislative proposals because it will, under its Standing Orders, consider the domestic implications of a legislative proposal, seek to establish a formal position that will be communicated to the Minister, and, consider the question of subsidiarity.

Clearly, the Committee must be selective and thus the Standing Orders require the Committee to consider each document and formally determine its legal or political importance. Only those documents which are considered to raise such issues will be subjected to further scrutiny. To this extent the Committee's activities are objective and have the purpose of fulfilling the Standing Orders and thus do not formally distinguish between scrutiny for the purposes of Protocol no 2 and scrutiny falling within the scope of political dialogue with the Commission. Once a document is deemed cleared the scrutiny process is complete, or it will be followed up through a further inquiry which may or may not lead to the issuing of a Reasoned Opinion or correspondence to the Commission. Scrutiny is therefore a value-based process utilising information provided from several sources, including Commission Green and White Papers, the legislative proposal and the Government's Explanatory Memorandum, the latter of which concerns the precise scope and impact of a legislative proposal. For this Committee, and indeed its Lords counterpart, a crucial part of the equation which enables it to determine the legal and political importance will be the formal position of the UK Government.

However, the scrutiny process in this form, though procedurally efficient, may be subjected to criticism. Parliamentary scrutiny of EU legislation suffers from a lack of transparency. Even if a member of the public (or indeed many MPs) had the inclination, they would find it hard to track the process of inspecting individual proposals.[28] The agendas for the meetings of the European Scrutiny Committee are only published the day before the Committee sits and do not give a clear indication as to on what day an item will be discussed (though a rolling agenda shows which documents are awaiting scrutiny). However, it should be said that the tight schedule is not necessarily the Committee's fault, as it can only consider documents after an Explanatory Memorandum is received, which is the responsibility of the Government. The Scrutiny Reserve may offer some assistance to the Committee in such circumstances and it can request that the Government does not agree to a proposal in the Council of Ministers until such time as the scrutiny

[27] HC 109-I *Reforming the Scrutiny System in the House of Commons* (2013–14) at para 66.

[28] R Rogers and R Walters, *How Parliament Works*, 5th edn (London, Longman, 2004) 320.

process is completed. In the context of benchmarking a legislative proposal against the principle of subsidiarity, the Scrutiny Reserve would enable the Committee to complete its scrutiny and if necessary issue a Reasoned Opinion.

All EU documents arrive at the Foreign and Commonwealth Office and within 10 working days of the deposit of a document, the lead Government department should submit an Explanatory Memorandum. The requirements of an Explanatory Memorandum are two-fold and intended to simplify the task for the Committee. First, an Explanatory Memorandum needs to provide the Committee with an explanation of the objective of the proposal. Secondly, it must state clearly the Government's view with respect to the proposal, which will be expressed at the Council. As part of determining whether a proposal is legally or politically important the Explanatory Memorandum must address key questions concerning the appropriate exercise of EU competence including the legal base that is being used, the timetable for implementation and any financial implications. In addition, the Explanatory Memorandum needs to identify the subsidiarity implications for the UK and the Government's position with respect to this question. Once the Committee has reported its conclusions on the document, and unless it recommends a document for debate, the proposal will have cleared the scrutiny hurdle, which in practical terms lifts the Scrutiny Reserve and permits the Minister to vote in Council.

The Explanatory Memorandum is the central element of the scrutiny process because it constitutes the Minister's evidence to Parliament and it is a public document which confines the actions of the Government to the principles set out in the Explanatory Memorandum.[29] In doing so, the Explanatory Memorandum may be considered as the embodiment of ministerial accountability and the individual scrutiny function. It provides a formal benchmark of the UK Government's negotiating position within the legislative process and enables the Committee to pursue the Minister for explanations and justifications in the event of the Council arriving at a different conclusion to the UK's negotiating position, or if the Minister departs from the negotiating position in the course of Council deliberations.

This form of scrutiny of the executive, which is both ex ante and ex post, provides a degree of oversight that is unmatched within many parliaments, perhaps with the exception of those Nordic parliaments such as Denmark's that employ a scrutiny system which mandates the minister in advance of the Council taking a final decision.[30] By contrast, the document-based system, though less rigid, is arguably no less effective and the defining feature of this scrutiny is that it is a formal parliamentary process the purpose of which is to pursue ministerial accountability to Parliament. Yet, the system remains questionable with respect to the

[29] HC 109-I *Reforming the Scrutiny System in the House of Commons* (2013–14) at paras 52–56.

[30] See further S Møller, 'Learning in Denmark? The Case of Danish Parliamentary Control over European Union Policy' (2008) 31 *Scandinavian Political Studies* 441.

precise extent to which the Commons has been able to mitigate against the loss of legislative sovereignty through its scrutiny activities, and the question of whether this form of scrutiny constitutes only a form of substitute sovereignty is explored later in this chapter.

IV. The House of Lords EU Select Committee

The constitutional position of the House of Lords is one of an unelected revising Chamber whose members undertake no constituency duties. Consequently, by comparison to MPs, peers have, historically, had significantly greater time available to dedicate to the process of in-depth scrutiny and review of EU affairs as part of the overall process of securing ministerial accountability to Parliament. Such scrutiny is particularly suited to a Chamber which is composed of a cross-section of peers, who bring to the task of EU scrutiny their vast experience and knowledge.[31] The in-depth specialist inquiries conducted by the Lords which, when considered alongside the more mechanical scrutiny work of the Commons, may be highlighted as the key contributing features to why the UK Parliament is consistently described as a strong parliament within academic literature.[32] The complementary package of scrutiny in both Houses seeks to maximise executive accountability through different procedures.

The House of Lords appoints the European Union Committee 'to consider European Union documents deposited in the House by a minister, and other matters relating to the European Union'. It is clear, from these terms of reference, that, by contrast with the Commons, the ability of the Lord's Committee to consider 'other matters relating to the European Union' has been both a procedural and substantive advantage.[33] From a constitutional perspective, EU documents must clear the scrutiny process in *both* Houses before the minister can give agreement to them in Council and to this extent the Scrutiny Reserve Resolution applies equally within the Lords. On this basis there is no need for either House (Commons or Lords) to have the last word with respect to a document, notwithstanding that, as noted above, the Common's primary focus on scrutiny of a legislative proposal and influencing the minister prior to the Council has historically been viewed as reflecting the constitutional pre-eminence of the Commons and replicates the scrutiny which domestic legislation is subjected to.

The scrutiny processes differ between the two Houses in certain respects, but the overall objectives remain similar; namely that of securing ministerial

[31] HL 101 (Session 2004–05) *Strengthening national parliamentary scrutiny of the EU—The Constitution's early warning mechanism.*

[32] See P Kiiver, *The National Parliaments in the European Union: A Critical View on EU Constitution Building* (The Hague, Kluwer Law International, 2006).

[33] HL 151 (Session 2013–14) *The Role of National Parliaments in the European Union*, para 21–22.

accountability. Simply stated, the Lords Select Committee has a wider mandate to scrutinise the merits—rather than only the legal or political importance—of emerging EU policy that it has singled out through a weekly sift of the EU documents it receives. This difference in modus operandi is significant because it has enabled the Committee to conduct stand-alone policy based inquiries where the target audience is not just the UK Government, but also the EU Institutions. Perhaps, most significantly, it has enabled the Committee to move upstream in the legislative process and focus on the Commission's Annual Work Programme and anticipate the potential impact upon of future policy on the UK, in some instances even before the Government has formally established a negotiating position. From the perspective of securing accountability of the executive this is a real advantage as the Lords Committee may be in a position to set the scrutiny agenda once the formal proposal is deposited within Parliament with an accompanying Explanatory Memorandum.

The House of Lords Select Committee carries out most of its investigations through its six sub-committees which have responsibility for:

- Economic and Financial Affairs
- Internal Market
- EU External Affairs
- Energy and Environment
- EU Justice
- EU Home Affairs

The sub-committees conduct inquiries based either on the scrutiny of EU documents or on wider subject areas chosen by the sub-committees from within their fields of activity. The sub-committees look at the policy implications of EU proposals, including whether they are matters which the EU (not the UK) should be legislating for, by reviewing the compatibility of the proposal with the principle of subsidiarity in Article 5 TEU.[34] In arriving at this conclusion the Committee will consider whether the proposal has been subject to a proper cost analysis through a regulatory impact assessment and whether it inappropriately delegates power to EU official committees to exercise decision-making powers under the so-called comitology procedure.

As the discussion above thus far illustrates, both Houses of the UK Parliament have rigorous scrutiny procedures and take their responsibility very seriously.[35] To that extent, the UK Committees generally fulfil the provisions of Article 12 TEU which states that 'national parliaments contribute actively to the good functioning of the Union'. However, it would be optimistic to conclude that these procedures,

[34] In evidence to the House of Lords Select Committee on the European Union Sir David Edward stated that if national parliaments did not raise Subsidiarity objections at the yellow card stage then it may be harder for any party to run Subsidiarity arguments later. See HL 62-1 (2007–08) *The Treaty of Lisbon: an Impact Assessment* at para 11.40.

[35] See HL 151 at 33 above at para 31.

and indeed more generally the work of EU committees across the EU, are sufficient to address the concerns of legitimacy, accountability and democracy that the EU legislative process still raises.[36] This brings to light the question of what is the value of the individual scrutiny function and whether in the context of subsidiarity monitoring under Protocol no 2, national parliaments should consider shifting their focus to developing more coordinated scrutiny and activities that would create a form of 'virtual third chamber'.

V. UK Parliamentary Scrutiny as a Form of Substitute Sovereignty?

The discussion of the scrutiny arrangements in the Commons and Lords underscores the importance which is attached to Parliament securing executive accountability. However, though the scrutiny procedures are effective, this impact is primarily internal and confined to the UK Parliament. It should not be forgotten that the UK Parliament is unable to exert decisive influence over what the Council decides, nor can it control the activities of other parliaments. The primary effect of EU integration for national parliaments is that they no longer legislate in areas where the EU has exclusive competence. Even where competence is shared, the Commission's interpretation of the justification for EU legislation and why, for example, the principle of subsidiarity should not be applied, has led to the EU legislating in the overwhelming majority, if not all cases, when competence is shared.[37] Moreover, this choice of EU legislative action has been consistently upheld by the European Court of Justice which has accepted the Commission's dual Internal market justifications of 'necessity' and 'effectiveness'.[38]

The constitutional change which the reduction of legislative competences has had in some so-called stronger national parliaments, such as the UK, is that they have continually sought to enhance their own individual scrutiny mechanisms accordingly in response to these developments. On this analysis, the process of detailed and vigorous national parliamentary scrutiny of EU affairs may be considered as a cathartic exercise for national parliaments and gives an impression of control. Yet, given the challenge of limited political control and influence over the

[36] S Weatherill, 'Better Competence Monitoring' (2005) 30 *European Law Review* 23; J Van Dijk, 'National Parliaments and Political Accountability in Europe' in L Vehey, P Kiiver and S Loeffen (eds), *Political Accountability and European Integration* (Groningen, Europa Law Publishing, 2009) 85.

[37] See further Wetter, Chapter 4 in this volume.

[38] See for example Case C-58/8 *Vodafone Ltd, Telefonica O2 Europe plc, T-Mobile International AG, Orange Personal Communication Services Ltd v Secretary of State for Business, Enterprise and Regulatory Reform* [2010] ECR I-4999 and Case C-49/01 *R v Secretary of State for Health ex parte British American Tobacco and Imperial Tobacco* [2002] ECR I-11453 in particular paras 177 and 185.

EU legislative process, then, individual national parliamentary scrutiny processes may be assessed as constituting merely some form of substitute sovereignty.[39] That is to say, from the UK parliamentary perspective the more scrutiny that occurs then the more this is deemed to make up for the loss of legislative competence and the less politically impotent parliament feels. In many strong national parliaments, the rigorous scrutiny process corresponds in large part to the exacting scrutiny that occurs of the domestic policy and legislative process and may be viewed as the parliamentary chamber merely discharging its duty of pursuing executive accountability. For this reason it may be inaccurate to suggest that the prerogatives of Protocol no 2 offer significantly improved avenues through which to secure improved legitimacy or that it will encourage systematic collective participation in EU affairs. Though pan-EU collaboration should not be dismissed and both the Commons and Lords have recognised in their recent reports that it has a place in the overall scrutiny process,[40] the focus of these Committees will continue to remain on influencing the Minister.

Despite the criticism that this form of enhanced ministerial scrutiny may be considered as substitute sovereignty, the requirement of executive scrutiny should not be understated. It is a crucial task, and remains the only method of direct control over the executive throughout the entire EU legislative procedure. To this end, while the prerogatives of Protocol no 2 may be viewed as offering more attractive opportunities for involvement in the legislative process and create an impression of pan-EU accountability the UK objective that individual ministers to be directly answerable to parliament at all times remains both constitutionally significant and readily attainable Ultimately, for the Committees it remains essential that they exert their influence in a manner in which *they* consider it to be most effective and Protocol no 2 has not yet provided sufficient opportunity to exert consistent and effective influence in the legislative process.

Irrespective of the scrutiny, whether of the Minister or in the guise of subsidiarity monitoring this can only be effective if it is pre-legislative and based upon the *timely* provision of all available documentation. Pre-Lisbon national parliaments were largely reliant upon their governments to provide EU documentation that formed the basis of their scrutiny activities. To this end many parliaments have adopted Scrutiny Reserves similar to those of the UK Parliament in order to restrain ministers from voting on a legislative measure in Council, prior to completion of the scrutiny process. The objective of the Scrutiny Reserve now recognised in Protocol no 1 of the Treaty of Lisbon and the precise scope and operation of which varies in the national parliamentary chambers, has been to provide a minimum guarantee that some form of inquiry can take place prior to

[39] See the example of the United Kingdom Parliament by A Cygan, 'EU Affairs before the United Kingdom Parliament: A Case of Scrutiny as Substitute Sovereignty?' in O Tans, C Zoethout and J Peters (eds), *National parliaments and European Democracy* (Groningen, Europa Law Publishing, 2007) 75.

[40] See HL 151 (2013–14) at para 205.

the final vote. Though the Treaty of Lisbon provides for more direct transmission of documents to national parliaments directly from the Commission, the challenges of timely scrutiny remain.

VI. The Provision of Information and Scrutiny Reserves

The two key issues for the UK Parliament since EU Accession in 1973, and which have consistently inhibited the conduct of scrutiny activities, are the need for adequate time and the prompt provision of the necessary information which forms the basis of scrutiny.[41] Given that the overriding objective of the scrutiny process is to influence the minister *prior* to the Council adopting its definitive common position it is essential that documentation is available sufficiently in advance. Moreover, it is difficult to see how national parliaments can fulfil the objectives of Article 12 TEU without this documentation. The dependency of all national parliaments on their government for the provision of information had been consistently highlighted as a significant weakness of the scrutiny arrangements that were put in place by the Treaty of Amsterdam.[42] Kiiver[43] and Tans[44] identified that executive dominance and control of information was the norm in the majority of Member States and consequently impaired the process of securing executive accountability. Within the Constitutional Convention, the single most highlighted restriction to effective parliamentary review that was universally identified was the late provision of the relevant documentation that forms the basis of scrutiny.[45] More broadly, within the context of the prerogatives under Protocol no 2 what may be described as a continuing information deficit, notwithstanding the provisions of Protocol no 1, raises question marks over the extent to which co-ordinated horizontal subsidiarity monitoring by national parliaments is achievable. The information deficit continues to remain as a historical hangover of the scrutiny process from the pre-Lisbon era, albeit in an environment in which the worst excesses of this information deficit have been mitigated against.

Recognising the improved provision of information to all national parliaments as a pre-requisite for effective scrutiny has been a constant. However, Treaty recognition of the challenges faced by national parliaments which are the consequence of an information deficit has failed to address the substance of the problem. For example, Declaration 13 annexed to the Treaty on European Union and Protocol

[41] HC 152-xxxiii-I (Session 2001–02) at 26 above at 24, para 33.

[42] HC 563 (Session 2007–08) *Subsidiarity, National Parliaments and the Lisbon* Treaty at p 4.

[43] Kiiver, *The National Parliaments in the European Union* (n 32 above) at 58.

[44] O Tans, 'Conclusion: National Parliaments and the European Union; Coping with the Limits of Democracy' in O Tans, C Zoethout and J Peters (eds), *National Parliaments and European Democracy: A Bottom-UP Approach to European Constitutionalism* (Groningen, Europa Law Publishing, 2007) 229.

[45] CONV 353/02 at 9–15.

no 13 annexed to the Treaty of Amsterdam both purported to involve national parliaments to a greater extent in EU matters. Declaration 23 annexed to the Treaty of Nice invited national parliaments to participate in the debate on the future of the Union, and the Laeken Declaration proposed specific questions about the role of national parliaments that the Convention should tackle. In practice these made no substantive difference to the daily scrutiny activities of national parliaments.[46]

Working Group IV on the role of national parliaments identified some basic factors influencing the effectiveness of scrutiny and especially the provision of information, but also acknowledged that not all national parliaments would always make use of the powers they had to scrutinise their governments.[47] In addition to recommendations on the provision of documents directly to national parliaments, which Protocol no 1 of the Treaty of Lisbon incorporates, Working Group IV also highlighted the need for improved coordination between the European Parliament and national parliaments as a means for improving both accountability and participation in EU affairs.

Scrutiny Reserves, such as that which operates within the UK Parliament were formally recognised by the Amsterdam Protocol[48] and this development, though important, cannot be considered as a constitutional counterbalance to the gradual de-parliamentarisation that has accompanied integration. Moreover, the recognition of Scrutiny Reserves arguably serves the individual scrutiny activities of national parliaments. Scrutiny Reserves are individual to each parliament, reflect national priorities, exist without any reference to other parliaments and cannot be said to create a framework for horizontal cooperation. Thus, within the UK Parliament, the Scrutiny Reserve operates both as a procedural step within the scrutiny process and encapsulates the constitutional requirement that the executive remains accountable to Parliament. To that extent, the Scrutiny Reserve may be considered as the formal procedural mechanism by which substitute sovereignty is exercised within the EU scrutiny process.

While Scrutiny Reserves such as that within the UK Parliament may prove to be effective within a wholly domestic context, their ability to secure some form of pan-EU coordinated scrutiny, of the kind discussed within Working Group IV, remains open to question. This is because scrutiny conducted by the UK Parliament, which seeks to influence the Minister prior to the final adoption of the

46 In the Convention and the subsequent debates many have voiced concerns about national parliaments becoming only involved in the initial stages of the legislative process, as the amendments by Council and the European Parliament may significantly alter the contents of the proposal, and hence also at least theoretically make it problematic in terms of subsidiarity even if the original draft act did not violate the subsidiarity principle. See further A Maurer, 'National Parliaments in the Architecture of Europe after the Constitutional Treaty' in G Barrett (ed), *National Parliaments and the European Union: The Constitutional Challenge for the Oireachtas and Other Member State Legislatures*, (Dublin, Clarus Press, 2008) 47 at 58.

47 CONV 353/02 at para 9.

48 For a comprehensive overview of the functioning of Scrutiny Reserves in the Member States see generally Tans (n 44 above).

measure by the Council, has minimal impact outside of the UK Parliament and essentially focuses upon the domestic impact of the proposed legislation. Furthermore, this form of scrutiny has not been without difficulty, not least because of the weaknesses with, for example, the Amsterdam Protocol for National Parliaments in relation to the transmission of documentation to national parliaments. Under the Amsterdam Protocol parliaments were wholly dependent upon their governments for the provision of information[49] and the systematic late provision of a limited number of documents impaired executive accountability.[50] In relation to legislative proposals the Amsterdam Protocol was weak because it required the Commission to make these available in good time for governments to distribute them to parliaments as appropriate. This inconsistent access to documents across the Member States reinforced the disparity between what were considered weak and strong parliaments and helped to create an information deficit within many legislatures.

Yet despite this continuing information deficit national parliaments have not been wholly hampered to the point of impotence in their individual oversight of EU activities. By contrast, rather than remaining passive and isolated institutions, many national parliaments have, at least in the context of information transmission, taken the initiative and improved their internal parliamentary procedures by which they have secured ministerial accountability. Since 2006, the so-called Barosso Initiative has also assisted national parliaments who have received a diverse range of documents directly from the Commission as well as paving the way for a dialogue between national parliaments and the Commission.

However, in the UK it remains the case that Parliament has recognised its constitutional position, and notwithstanding developments such as the Barosso Initiative, Parliament recognises that only through exercising its powers can it effectively control the minister. In particular this has arisen through obtaining guarantees from the executive in relation to parliamentary scrutiny of EU affairs. The most common way that this was achieved was through the introduction of Scrutiny Reserves, the existence of which can be considered as the cornerstone of the scrutiny process within the UK.[51] This is primarily because the Scrutiny Reserves includes binding guarantees from the executive and recognised within the Treaty, that no agreement will be given to a legislative proposal in Council until the domestic scrutiny process is complete, save in cases of 'urgency'.

[49] See HC 563 (Session 2007–08) *Subsidiarity, National Parliaments and the Lisbon Treaty*, at p 4.

[50] See CONV 353/02 at paras 21–36. See also Tans (n 44 above).

[51] See A Cygan, National Parliaments in an Integrated Europe: An Anglo-German Perspective (The Hague, Kluwer, 2001) at 63. See generally on the importance of Scrutiny Reserves in the Member States A Maurer, 'National Parliaments in the European Union Architecture; From Latecomers Adaptation Towards Permanent Institutional Change' in A Maurer and W Wessels (eds), *National Parliaments on their Ways to Europe: Losers or Latecomers*? (Baden-Baden, Nomos, 2001) 432.

VII. Concluding Remarks—The Impact of EU Scrutiny within The UK Parliament

It is difficult to assess precisely what effect parliamentary scrutiny in general has in practice and perhaps only ministers and civil servants can give a meaningful answer to the question. However, several observations may be offered regarding the work of both Select Committees within the UK Parliament. First, it remains correct to continue to view the UK Parliament as a strong actor in EU affairs. Secondly, the discipline of ministers having to submit Explanatory Memoranda and to respond, in writing and sometimes in person, to questions raised by the Scrutiny Committees should not be dismissed. This is a more subtle form of ministerial accountability. There can be little doubt that it is an important and efficient means of keeping the Government of the day accountable to Parliament. Though there have been a substantial number of occasions when the Scrutiny Reserve has been over-ridden by the Government, it remains a real and effective check on ministers. In particular the requirement that they must explain their actions in public ensures that any decision to bypass Parliament is not taken lightly. In this context ministers cannot rely on the support of their own party members who are appointed to the Committees. Finally, EU scrutiny continues to be considered as part of the constitutional obligations of Parliament to ensure that the executive remains accountable at all times.

In the Commons, though the composition of the Committee is in proportion to the number of MPs elected and thus favours the party in government, the Committee tends to act with a high degree of collegiality and consensus, and this is also the case in the House of Lords. This behaviour reinforces the constitutional convention of ministerial accountability which in such circumstances the Committee secures on behalf of Parliament. Such a consensus is an undoubted strength, and one which is generally lacking within the Chamber of the House of Commons where adversarial politics are the norm.

Going forward, the challenge remains how to maintain relevance of the scrutiny work of the Committees within an EU where competence has increased and decision-making in the form of policy coordination and new modes of governance is difficult to review.[52] These governance processes though not leading to hard law are highly likely to have financial, administrative and legislative implications for the UK and the Committees need to review their procedures in order to ensure that this form of decision-making does not slip through the scrutiny net. If the role of the Committees is to sound the burglar alarm when there are implications for UK law and policy then under existing procedures this will not always be the case.

[52] See HL 151 (Session 2013–14) *The Role of National Parliaments in the European Union* at para 55 where the House of Lords put forward the idea of a 'green card' which would enable a 'group' of national parliaments working together to make a constructive suggestion for a legislative initiative.

Effective scrutiny by national parliaments of the activities of their own governments in the European Union is essential. It is fundamental to ensuring that there is accountability, and legitimacy, for the actions of the Union. It should be recognised as core business for every parliament. There is no doubt that, as far as the UK Parliament is concerned, securing effective ministerial accountability is seen as, first and foremost, the gateway to ensuring that EU legislation is subjected to rigorous review.

In 2014, the Commission received only 21 Reasoned Opinions from national parliaments, a decrease by 19 per cent by comparison with the 2013 statistics, and this is the first significant decrease since the first year of functioning of the early warning mechanism. During 2014, the threshold for the yellow card was not reached and this overall decrease in the use of Reasoned Opinions is strongly indicative of the premise that national parliaments, including the United Kingdom Parliament, do not consider Protocol no 2 as being sufficiently effective. Moreover, these 21 Reasoned Opinions represent less than five per cent of the total number of 506 opinions received by the Commission in 2014 as part of its broader political dialogue with national Parliaments.[53] This would indicate that all legislatures, including the United Kingdom Parliament are searching for alternative methods of participation within the decision-making process and, in addition to expanding the political dialogue with the Commission, they continue to see value in exerting influence over their ministers.

[53] COM(2012) 373 final, Report from the Commission on Subsidiarity and Proportionality (19th Report on Better Law-Making covering the year 2011).

14

Able and Willing? Early Warning System and Political Dialogue in the Bundestag and the Nationalrat

KATRIN AUEL

When the Treaty of Lisbon finally came into force in December 2009, it was hailed as the 'Treaty of Parliaments'. Indeed, it strengthened the position of national parliaments within the domestic arena, primarily by giving them direct access to European documents, and for the first time, provided them with direct input in the legislative process at the European level. Not only does the Treaty grant national parliaments a role in the Treaty amendment process through the Convention on the Future of Europe, but it also explicitly mentions national parliaments and areas of their involvement for the first time (Article 12 TEU).[1] This role is then further outlined in two protocols annexed to the Treaty. According to the first, the 'Protocol on the Role of National Parliaments in the European Union', national parliaments are to receive all draft European legislative acts directly (rather than via their governments); in addition, they receive a broader range of non-legislative documents, such as the annual reports of the Court of Auditors and the Commission's annual legislative programme. The second, the 'Protocol on the Application of the Principles of Subsidiarity', outlines the provisions for the control of the subsidiarity principle by national parliaments: the so-called Early Warning System (EWS).[2]

Both the Austrian Nationalrat and the German Bundestag were among the first national parliaments to use the EWS by submitting reasoned opinions that identified a breach of the principle of subsidiarity regarding the Directives on Seasonal Workers (COM/2010/379) and on Deposit Guarantee Schemes (COM/2010/0368), respectively. At the time, the German opinion, especially,

[1] The Treaty also empowers national parliaments in other ways. For an exhaustive list, see P Kiiver, *The Early Warning System for the Principle of Subsidiarity. Constitutional Theory and Empirical Reality* (London, Routledge, 2012).

[2] For details on the EWS see the Introduction to this volume (Chapter 1).

made newspaper headlines[3] that saluted it as a strong signal to Brussels or 'the Bundestag's "sharpest weapon"'[4] and speculated about the first defeat of a Commission proposal by national parliaments. As we know now, nothing much has come out of these reasoned opinions—both attempts failed, as the necessary quorum was missed by a wide margin—or out of the Early Warning System altogether. Thus far (July 2016), the quorum for a 'yellow card' has been reached three times,[5] and all have—ultimately—been unsuccessful (see also below).

The Early Warning System is, however, not the only instrument national parliaments have at their disposal to try and influence at the European level. Since 2006, as part of the 'Political Dialogue', the Commission also sends all legislative proposals and consultation documents directly to national parliaments, inviting them to express their opinions on these documents without any restriction to issues of subsidiarity. In turn, the Commission promised not only to reply to all opinions, but also to take them into due consideration.[6]

Since the introduction of the Political Dialogue, the Bundestag has submitted 20 opinions, the Austrian Nationalrat twice as many, with 41 opinions (until December 2014). Of these, only three each were reasoned opinions submitted within the EWS since 2010.[7] Compared to the other national parliaments, both are among the least active chambers when it comes to submitting reasoned opinions (Figure 1). For the Bundestag, this is also true for the Political Dialogue, while the number in Austria is only a little lower than the average across all chambers (Figure 2).

Against this background, the aim of this chapter is to explain the engagement of both chambers in the EWS and the Political Dialogue. The chapter is structured as follows. The next section will discuss some of the challenges parliaments were expected to face when participating in in the EWS or the Political Dialogue. As will be shown, problems such as the lack of a clear definition of subsidiarity, time pressure or weak (administrative) capacities cannot adequately explain either similarities or differences between the two parliaments.

[3] See, for example: *Süddeutsche Zeitung*, 'Neues Frühwarnsystem', 6.10.2010; *Süddeutsche Zeitung*, 'Widerstand gegen Einlagensicherung', 7.10. 2010; *Süddeutsche Zeitung*, 'Stoppzeichen nach Brüssel' 8.10.2010; *Der Standard*, 'Widerstand gegen EU-Sparerschutzpläne', 6.10.2010; *EurActiv*, 'Machtvolles Signal an die EU-Kommission', 5.10.2010; *EurActiv*, 'Deutschland scheitert mit EU-Rüge', 22.10.2010.

[4] *Frankfurter Allgemeine Zeitung*, 'Prallschutz für Bankkunden', 16.12.2010.

[5] 12 parliaments with 19 votes overall submitted a reasoned opinion on the 'Proposal for a Council Regulation on the exercise of the right to take collective action within the context of the freedom of establishment and the freedom to provide services' (Monti II) (COM/2012/130). On the proposal for the European Public Prosecutor's Office (COM/2013/534), the Commission received reasoned opinions from 11 parliaments representing 19 votes, and 22 from 11 parliaments on the proposal for the 'Posting of Workers Directive' (COM/1991/230).

[6] C Preising, 'Der Umgang nationaler Parlamente mit den neuen Rechten des Vertrags von Lissabon—die Perspektive der Europäischen Kommission' in G Abels and A Eppler (eds), *Auf dem Weg zum Mehrebenenparlamentarismus? Funktionen von Parlamenten im politischen System der EU* (Baden-Baden, Nomos, 2011) 152.

[7] The data is based on the information provided by the Interparliamentary Exchange platform IPEX.eu as well as the European Commission's Website for the relations with national parliaments (ec.europa.eu/dgs/secretariat_general/relations/relations_other/npo/index_en.htm).

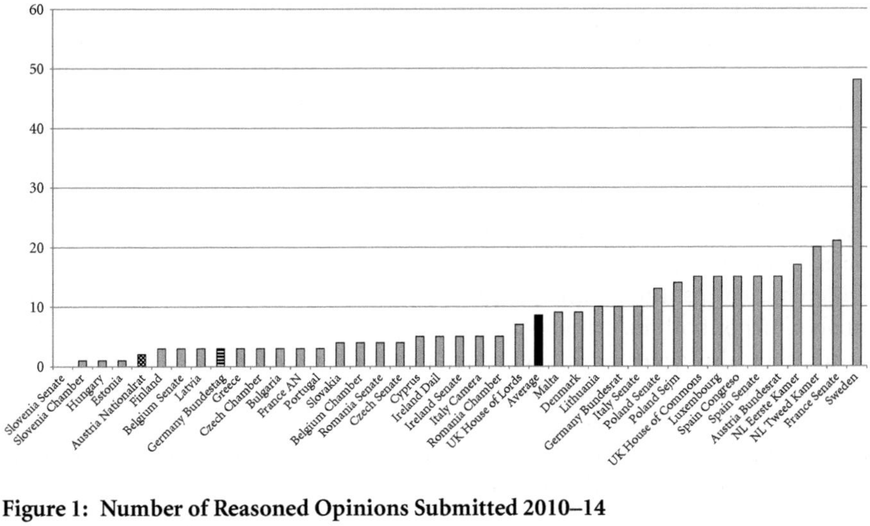

Figure 1: Number of Reasoned Opinions Submitted 2010–14

Source: OPAL data set[8] and own calculations.

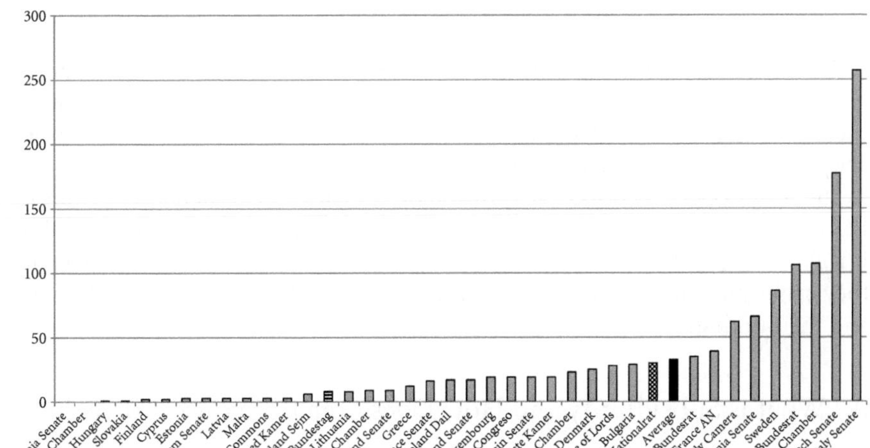

Figure 2: Number of Political Dialogue Opinions Submitted 2010–14

Source: OPAL data set and own calculations.

[8] K Auel, O Rozenberg and A Tacea, 'Fighting Back? And if Yes, How? Measuring Parliamentary Strength and Activity in EU Affairs' in C Hefftler et al (eds), *Palgrave Handbook of National Parliaments and the European Union* (Basingstoke, Palgrave Macmillan, 2015).

This suggests that explanations have to take the political *willingness* to become engaged in the EWS or the Political Dialogue into account. One of the main insights of neo-institutionalism is that institutions do not determine, but rather interact with, and are subject to, the behaviour of individuals working with and through them. As Fenno has argued, 'representatives are context interpreters. And they will make choices and take actions not in the abstract, but accordingly to what they believe to be rational and/or appropriate in the circumstances or context in which they find themselves'.[9] From a neo-institutionalist perspective, behaviour can thus be explained by both institutional context and actors' preferences or motivations. Different neo-institutionalist approaches, however, are based on distinct conceptualisations of both institutions and the origin or formation of preferences. As a result, they also generate different hypotheses on the way actors interpret their institutional context and develop different explanations for the motivations and incentives driving behaviour. Sections III and IV therefore present an analysis of parliamentary motivation drawing on rational choice and sociological institutional approaches, respectively. Section V discusses the findings and concludes.

I. The Challenges: Getting It Right In Time

Within the early literature, national parliaments were expected to face a number of challenges related mainly to the EWS, but also the Political Dialogue.[10] Among the most frequently discussed were the lack of any stringent definition of subsidiarity, the limited time available for the adoption of the reasoned opinions, as well as the resources needed to deal with the onslaught of documents sent from the EU institutions. In short, scholars doubted that national parliaments would get it right in time. The following will take up these arguments and analyse whether they can explain the use of the EWS and the Political Dialogue in the Nationalrat and the Bundestag.

A. What is Subsidiarity and How Does One Recognise a Breach?

One of the fundamental problems related to the new provisions in the Treaty is the lack of a precise definition of subsidiarity. Article 5 of the Treaty only provides a rather broad and vague definition, and the 'Protocol on the Application

[9] RF Fenno, 'House Members in Their Constituencies: An Exploration' (1977) 71 *American Political Science Review* 883.

[10] For the following see V Knutelská, 'National Parliaments as New Actors in the Decision-making Process at the European Level' (2011) 7 *Journal of Contemporary European Research* 327; V Paskalev, 'Lisbon Treaty and the Possibility of a European Network *Demoi*-cracy', *European University Institute Working Paper* 2009/20 (Florence); T Raunio, 'Destined for Irrelevance? Subsidiarity Control by National Parliaments', *Real Instituto Elcano Working Paper* 36/2010 (Madrid).

of the Principles of Subsidiarity and Proportionality' is not very helpful in this regard either, as it mainly contains procedural provisions, but shies away from spelling out what exactly is being applied. So far, even the EU Court of Justice has found the assessment of subsidiarity issues difficult, although it did eventually declare the principle justiciable in its '*American Tobacco*'[11] decision. While actions on subsidiarity grounds have been brought before the Court on a number of occasions, it has never annulled an act on the basis of a breach of the principle or developed a detailed procedure specifying the examination of its observance. As a result, national parliaments have little guidance when it comes to the scrutiny of EU documents in terms of the subsidiarity principle, and tend to define the principle differently according to domestic traditions and interests, which makes it difficult for them to identify similar problems and to reach the necessary quorum for a subsidiarity complaint through the EWS (see also below). While the Austrian parliament does not see this as a problem, stating that there was 'no need for further clarification',[12] the Bundestag indicated that it should be clarified.[13] Yet while both the Nationalrat and the Bundestag would be in favour of greater cooperation on a common definition or understanding of the principle of subsidiarity, neither parliament would agree to formal guidelines, let alone binding rules.[14]

B. Dealing with Information Overload

The new provisions of the 'Protocol on the Role of National Parliaments in the European Union' provide for the direct transmission of a broad range of EU documents to national parliaments. This can indeed be helpful, in particular for parliaments that have so far not been fully informed by their own governments. However, the sheer quantity of European documents coupled with the complex decision-making procedures means that national parliaments are far more often faced with an enormous problem of information overload. Thus, to be able to deal with European affairs, national parliaments have to develop effective systems to filter important European developments out of the mass of documents they receive, and they need to be able to process all that information.

Both parliaments have set up administrative prioritising processes to deal with EU documents: In the Bundestag, the prioritising process is part of the responsibilities of the European Affairs Directorate. Established in 2013,[15] it is the largest

[11] Case C-491/01, *The Queen v Secretary of State for Health, ex parte British American Tobacco (Investments) Ltd and Imperial Tobacco Ltd*, EU:C:2002:741.

[12] COSAC, 'Annex Eighteenth Bi-annual Report, Responses Austrian Nationalrat' (2012) online at: www.cosac.eu/documents/bi-annual-reports-of-cosac.

[13] COSAC, 'Annex Eighteenth Bi-annual Report, Responses German Bundestag' (2012), online at: www.cosac.eu/documents/bi-annual-reports-of-cosac.

[14] COSAC, 'Annex Eighteenth Bi-annual Report, Responses Austrian National'; COSAC, 'Annex Eighteenth Bi-annual Report, Responses German Bundestag'.

[15] The Directorate brings together the Secretariat of the Committee on the Affairs of the European Union; two analytical divisions supporting all of the *Bundestag*'s committees; the European Affairs

administrative EU unit among EU national parliaments with 59 members of staff. The European Affairs Directorate drafts a first proposal on what documents to refer (prioritisation) and to which committees (lead committee and other committees in advisory capacity). It also provides a first assessment of the proposal's conformity with the principle of subsidiarity. The suggestion is then forwarded to the Chairman of the EAC, who drafts a formal proposal on the selection of documents for scrutiny and the responsible committees in agreement with the other committee chairs. The final decision is taken by the President of the Bundestag in agreement with the parliamentary secretaries (*parlamentarische Geschäftsführer*) of the parliamentary party groups. Further guidance is provided by the government, which—according to §4 of the Act on Cooperation between the Federal Government and the German Bundestag in Matters concerning the European Union (*Gesetz über die Zusammenarbeit von Bundesregierung und Deutschem Bundestag in Angelegenheiten der Europäischen Union*, EUZBBG) and §13 of the Responsibility for Integration Act (*Integrationsverantwortungsgesetz*, IntVG)—has the obligation to provide the Bundestag with an assessment regarding the competence of the European Union to adopt a proposed legislative act and its compatibility with the principles of subsidiarity and proportionality 'within two weeks following their referral to the Bundestag committees but no later than the start of their discussion by the Council bodies' (§13.6 IntVG).

The process in the Nationalrat is somewhat similar. Within the 'EU and International Services' of the Parliamentary Directorate (*Parlamentsdirektion*), two units are responsible for EU affairs, the 'EU Coordination and Information' division and the 'European Relations' division. Although both are involved,[16] the latter is the main unit responsible for dealing with incoming documents. It submits all incoming legislative proposals to a first, purely legal, subsidiarity check and informs EAC members by email.[17] The *political* relevance of these documents is then assessed by the so-called 'group advisors' of the parliamentary party groups, who also take the final decision on the documents to be put on the EAC's agenda in a weekly meeting with the EU affairs staff.[18] Since 2003, the government also provides explanatory memoranda, including an assessment of the compatibility of a proposal with the principles of subsidiarity and proportionality for those issues that have been put on the agenda of the EAC. In addition, all ministries provide parliament with an overview of the issues on the Council's agenda over the coming year.[19]

Office, which is the central unit that receives all of the documents sent to the *Bundestag*; the German *Bundestag*'s Liaison Office in Brussels; and the European Affairs Research Section (b).

[16] E Mastenbroek, P Zwaan, A Groen, W van Meurs, H Reiding, N Dörrenbächer and C Neuhold, *Engaging with Europe—Evaluating national parliamentary control of EU decision making after the Lisbon Treaty* (Nijmegen, Radboud University, 2014) 72.

[17] E Miklin, 'The Austrian Parliament and EU Affairs: Gradually living up to its legal potential' in C Hefftler, C Neuhold, O Rozenberg and J Smith (eds), *Palgrave Handbook of National Parliaments and the European Union* (Basingstoke, Palgrave Macmillan, 2015) 396.

[18] E Miklin, 'The Austrian Parliament' (n 16 above).

[19] J Pollak and P Slominski, 'Zwischen De- und Reparlamentarisierung—Der österreichische Nationalrat und seine Mitwirkungsrechte in EU-Angelegenheiten' (2009) 38 *Österreichische Zeitschrift für Politikwissenschaft* 193, 205.

While existing differences in the pre-screening process in both parliaments may not explain the differences in the overall number of opinions sent, they do provide some indication regarding the type of documents both chambers submit opinions on. For the Nationalrat, legislative proposals have been the main focus, while the opinions of the Bundestag are more evenly spread across different types of documents (Figure 3).

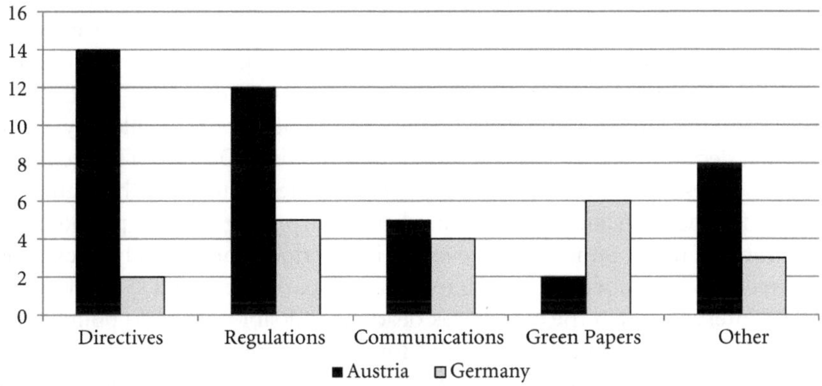

Figure 3: Number of opinions by type of document (2006–14)

Source: OPAL data set and own calculations.

Note: 'Other' includes documents such as white papers, reports from the Commission to the EU institutions, Commission working documents or proposals for decisions.

One explanation Miklin[20] puts forward for the Nationalrat's focus on legislative proposals is that the EWS is the only field where a comprehensive pre-screening of documents by the administration takes place. Suggestions for scrutiny are usually taken up by the Subcommittee on EU affairs, but often result in a Political Dialogue opinion rather than a reasoned opinion 'simply because it is the political content that parliamentarians are interested in or concerned with'.[21] In the Bundestag, in contrast, the pre-screening process is not limited to legal subsidiarity issues under the EWS and thus to legislative proposals. As a result, the administration also flags up other types of documents for parliamentary scrutiny.

C. Getting it Done in Eight Weeks

One of the main challenges related to parliamentary scrutiny in general, and the EWS in particular, is time issues, as parliaments have to complete the subsidiarity check within eight weeks following the proposal's publication. For the German Bundestag, time issues, and the eight-week period for the EWS in particular, are

[20] Miklin (n 16 above).
[21] Miklin (n 16 above) 397.

indeed challenging due to the lengthy process of selecting and transferring EU documents to the relevant committees. While the EAC is the committee responsible for all fundamental matters of European integration, the specialised committees deal with EU policies within their policy areas and are also responsible for the drafting of opinions. Thus, the Bundestag first needs to decide not only which EU documents to select for further scrutiny, but also which committee(s) will be responsible. Although the process is mainly paper-based and, as outlined above, prepared by the Bundestag's administration, it still takes about four weeks.[22] The selected documents then need to be put on the agenda of the responsible committees. Once the lead committee has debated the document, made a proposal for an opinion and has given the other committees involved (especially the EAC) the opportunity to comment, the draft opinion has to be put on the plenary agenda for a final decision (see §§ 93a–93c Bundestag Standing Orders). These cumbersome processes make it more difficult for the Bundestag to meet the eight-week deadline for the EWS, and it is therefore hardly surprising that the period is seen as insufficient. In the Bundestag's view, the time period should ideally be extended to 12 weeks.[23] A number of German members of parliament (MPs) did, however, agree in interviews 'that the eight-week deadline is doable if there is political will, and that no reasoned opinion ever failed for lack of time'.[24]

In the Nationalrat, in contrast, the procedures for the scrutiny check are much leaner.[25] Although the Grand Committee of the Nationalrat is officially the main parliamentary body dealing with EU affairs, most of the actual EU business has been delegated to the Subcommittee on EU affairs, which also deals with subsidiarity checks and submits most opinions both within the EWS and the Political Dialogue.[26] Thus, once the prioritising and selection process is done, no further cooperation with other committees or involvement of the plenary are necessary. The Subcommittee has also increased its meeting frequency. It now meets about once a month, twice as often as compared to before Lisbon.[27] Overall, interviewees 'perceive the procedure in the Nationalrat to be fast and simple, because it does not involve many layers and actors'[28] and, accordingly, the eight weeks are considered sufficient.[29]

[22] J Koch and M Kullas, *Subsidiarität nach Lissabon—Scharfes Schwert oder stumpfe Klinge?* (Freiburg im Breisgau, CEP, 2010) 11, see also the timeline in COSAC, 'Thirteenth Bi-annual Report: Developments in European Union Procedures and Practices Relevant to Parliamentary Scrutiny' (2010), online at: www.cosac.eu/documents/bi-annual-reports-of-cosac, p 74.

[23] COSAC, 'Annex Nineteenth Bi-annual Report, Responses German Bundestag' (2013), online at: www.cosac.eu/documents/bi-annual-reports-of-cosac.

[24] Mastenbroek et al, *Engaging with Europe* (n 15 above) 91f.

[25] For the following, see also Mastenbroek et al (n 15 above) 73f.

[26] Miklin (n 16 above).

[27] E Miklin, 'From vote-seeking towards policy-seeking: The Austrian parliament's engagement in EU affairs after Lisbon', paper presented at EUSA 13th Biennial International Conference, May 2013, Baltimore MA, online at: euce.org/eusa/2013/papers/4i_miklin.pdf, 12.

[28] Mastenbroek et al (n 15 above) 45.

[29] COSAC, 'Annex Nineteenth Bi-annual Report, Responses Austrian Nationalrat' (2013), online at: www.cosac.eu/documents/bi-annual-reports-of-cosac.

To sum up, while the above-mentioned problems of interpretation, information overload, time pressure etc certainly present challenges for both parliaments, they can hardly explain the reluctant use of the new instruments. The scrutiny process in Germany is cumbersome and time consuming, but no other national parliament in the EU has an administrative workforce similar to that of the Bundestag. In addition, the decentralised scrutiny process allows the Bundestag to deal with several EU proposals or documents simultaneously in different specialised committees. The Austrian Nationalrat, in contrast, has to make do with much less administrative support, but makes up for that with leaner—and thus faster—scrutiny procedures; the eight-week period is not seen as a major problem. Indeed, the Nationalrat submitted, as mentioned, as many reasoned opinions and twice as many Political Dialogue opinions as the Bundestag. Thus, the problem seems less the capacity to draft opinions, but rather the *willingness* to do so. The following will therefore analyse several factors that might explain the (lack of) political will to get involved in the EWS or the Political Dialogue.

II. Is it all Worth the Effort? MPs as Rational Actors[30]

Rational Choice approaches view actors as rational utility maximisers who have fixed, exogenous preferences and make decisions based on an analysis of costs and benefits. Here, institutions 'merely' act as constraints on or provide opportunities for specific behaviour and strategies to pursue the realisation of these preferences. As regards the preferences of parliamentarians, much of the rational choice literature on legislative behaviour focuses on career goals, conceptualising legislators as 'single minded reelection seekers'.[31] While there is a general consensus on the importance of the re-election preference, other scholars have criticised this approach as too parsimonious and 'not totally persuasive … It makes little sense to assume that parties value votes for their own sake … votes can only plausibly be instrumental goals'[32] to achieve policy influence and/or the spoils of office. Budge and Laver,[33] for example, argue that policy goals play an important role for legislators as well, either because they sincerely care about the policies in question, or because they regard them as a means for some other goal, for example

[30] The following draws on K Auel and T Christiansen, 'After Lisbon: National Parliaments in the European Union' (2015) 38 *West European Politics* 261.

[31] D Mayhew, *Congress: The Electoral Connection* (New Haven CT, Yale University Press, 1974) 5; see also GC Cox and MD McCubbins, *Legislative* Leviathan*: Party Government in the House* (Berkeley CA, University of California Press, 1993) 100.

[32] K Strøm and WC Müller, 'Political Parties and Hard Choices' in WC Müller and K Strøm (eds), *Policy, Office or Votes? How Political Parties in Western Democracies Make Hard Decisions* (Cambridge, Cambridge University Press, 1999) 9.

[33] I Budge and M Laver, 'Office Seeking and Policy Pursuit in Coalition Theory' (1986) 11 *Legislative Studies Quarterly* 485.

electoral support. For De Swann, 'considerations of policy are [even] foremost in the mind of actors … the parliamentary game is, in fact, about the determination of major government policy'.[34]

On the basis of these considerations, we can assume that legislators will make use of institutional opportunities, ie get engaged in the Early Warning System or the Political Dialogue if they expect such activities to result in either electoral benefits or in actually having a policy impact.[35]

Regarding the latter, a policy impact through the EWS or the Political Dialogue is rather difficult to achieve. First of all, the subsidiarity check is merely a 'negative' right with a rather narrow remit. Thus, it does not give national parliaments the right to reject a proposal for reasons related to the policy content, nor does it provide them with the opportunity for more constructive input. Secondly, the right can only be used collectively; individual reasoned opinions have no formal impact. Thirdly, the EWS does not provide national parliaments with an absolute veto. Rather, the final decision, at least in the case of the 'yellow card', remains with the European Commission. Here, the Political Dialogue is overall a more flexible instrument, as opinions do not have to be limited to issues of subsidiarity and can include more constructive suggestions for improvement. The effectiveness of the Political Dialogue, however, also depends on the ability to convince the European Commission.

Whether, in turn, the engagement in the EWS or the Political Dialogue can provide electoral benefits depends mainly on public opinion on EU integration. A general argument here is that in Member States where EU issues are more salient and public opinion is more critical of EU integration, MPs have greater incentives to become active in EU affairs to signal to their voters that they safeguard national interests. Where, in contrast, European affairs play no role in voting decisions or where the permissive consensus prevails, there are no electoral benefits to be gained from investing in scrutiny. In addition, Saalfeld[36] has argued that the motivation to engage in scrutiny activities may also vary according to the policy area and specific policy issue: Given the general preference structure of MPs, they can be expected to engage more actively in the scrutiny of highly salient EU issues, ie issues that affect clearly defined (large) groups at the domestic level and which the domestic public is highly aware of.

The following will in turn discuss both sets of incentives for the German Bundestag and the Austrian Nationalrat.

[34] A De Swann, *Coalition Theories and Cabinet Government. A Study of Formal Theories of Coalition Formation Applied to Nine European Parliaments After 1918* (Amsterdam, Elsevier, 1973) 88.

[35] T Saalfeld, 'The *Bundestag*: Institutional Incrementalism and Behavioural Reticence' in K Dyson and K Goetz (eds), *Germany, Europe and the Politics of Constraint* (Oxford, Oxford University Press, 2003), see also T Saalfeld, 'Delegation or Abdication? Government Backbenchers, Ministers and European Integration' (2005) 11 *Journal of Legislative Studies* 343; T Winzen, 'European integration and national parliamentary oversight institutions' (2013) 14 *European Union Politics* 297.

[36] T Saalfeld, 'Delegation or Abdication?' n 34 above.

A. Making a Difference: Does it Actually Have any Impact?

In the early literature, institutionally strong parliaments were expected to use the new opportunities more frequently to extend their influence beyond the domestic level to the EU level.[37] However, with regard to the Nationalrat and the Bundestag, the opposite seems to apply: both parliaments already have strong scrutiny powers vis-à-vis their governments. Any additional instrument thus needs to have some added value in terms of influence. Yet both parliaments consider not only the EWS, but also the Political Dialogue, rather ineffective and without much impact. One reason is certainly that in all instances where the quorum for a so-called 'yellow card' has been reached, the reaction of the European Commission was what national parliaments were hoping for. In the case of the Monti II regulation, the Commission subsequently withdrew the proposal, but stated that this was not due to parliamentary concerns, since a breach of the subsidiarity principle was not evident in the opinions. Rather, the Commission explained, the proposal was withdrawn because it was 'unlikely to gather the necessary political support within the European Parliament and the Council'.[38] With regard to the proposals concerning the European Public Prosecutor's Office and the 'Posting of Workers Directive', the Commission simply decided to maintain the proposals despite the yellow card.[39] Although neither the Bundestag nor the Nationalrat submitted a reasoned opinion on either of these two proposals, the outcome cannot have been encouraging. The same holds true for the Political Dialogue, which also does not seem to have had any discernible impact. Not even the Commission points to a single concrete instance in its annual reports[40] in which it actually took parliamentary concerns into account and amended a proposal accordingly.

However, the success of the EWS—and certainly of the Political Dialogue—can and should not only be measured in successful yellow or orange cards. Just

[37] C Neuhold and A Strelkov, 'New opportunity structures for the "unusual suspects"? Implications of the Early Warning System for the role of national parliaments within the EU system of governance', *OPAL Online Paper Series* 4/2012, p 11.

[38] European Commission, *Commission decision to withdraw the Proposal for a Council Regulation on the exercise of the right to take collective action within the context of the freedom of establishment and the freedom to provide services* – COM(2012) 130, online at: ec.europa.eu/dgs/secretariat_general/relations/relations_other/npo/letter_to_nal_parl_en.htm. For a more positive interpretation of the Monti II yellow card see I Cooper, 'A yellow card for the striker: national parliaments and the defeat of EU legislation on the right to strike' (2015) 22 *Journal of European Public Policy* 1406.

[39] European Commission, 'Communication from the Commission on the review of the proposal for a Council Regulation on the establishment of the European Public Prosecutor's Office', online at: ec.europa.eu/commission_2010-2014/sefcovic/documents/2013_11_27_ com851_public_prosecutor_en.pdf. European Commission, 'Communication on the proposal for a Directive amending the Posting of workers Directive', online at: europa.eu/rapid/pressrelease_IP-16-2546_en.htm.

[40] See the European Commission's annual reports on 'Subsidiarity and Proportionality—Better Lawmaking' online at: ec.europa.eu/dgs/secretariat_general/relations/relations_other/npo/subsidiarity_reports_en.htm, and on 'Relations Between the European Commission and National Parliaments', online at: ec.europa.eu/dgs/secretariat_general/relations/relations_other/npo/political_dialogue_en.htm#annualreports.

as important is the establishment of a constructive and meaningful exchange of arguments between national parliaments and the Commission with the aim of making viewpoints at both levels clear and accessible to each other. However, so far the EWS and the document-based part of the Dialogue do not seem to live up to the Bundestag's or the Nationalrat's expectations: both parliaments have repeatedly criticised especially the fairly late, vague and too general replies by the European Commission to reasoned opinions.[41] As the Nationalrat criticised, 'Until now, only in a few cases the doubts expressed in a reasoned opinion were treated in substance within the answers received'.[42] Accordingly, 'the European Institutions should inform the National Parliaments in a more precise way on the effect of the opinions received by the National Parliaments'.[43] Similarly, the Bundestag complained about the 'often general'[44] responses of the Commission and demanded that 'The Commission should give answers to the specific concerns of every [reasoned opinion], not only general remarks why in its opinion the proposal complies with the principle of subsidiarity'.[45] As a result,

> the low number of reasoned opinions and even lower number of contributions under the political dialogue from the *Bundestag* on the one hand, and the non-committal reactions by the Commission (compared to the clout of the federal government) on the other hand, seem to have produced a downward spiral of decreasing interests in these instruments and decreasing expectations about the reactions of the Commission.[46]

As Figures 4 and 5 demonstrate, the same may be true for the Austrian Nationalrat.

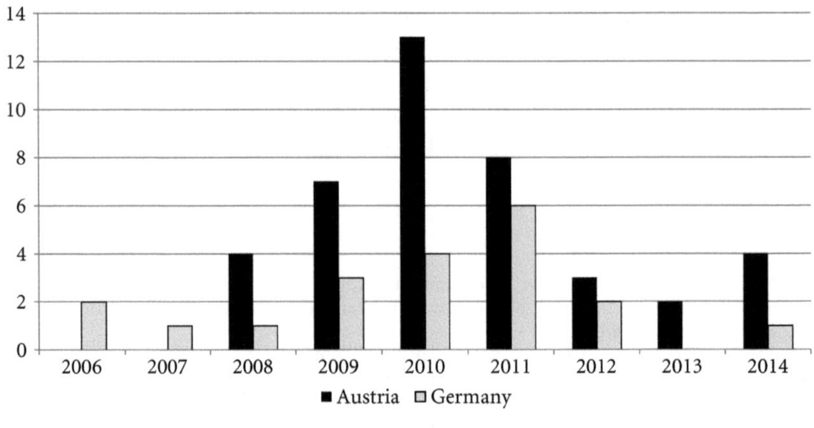

Figure 4: Number of all opinions by year (2006–14)

Source: OPAL data set and own calculations.

[41] See also Mastenbroek et al (n 15 above) section X, and the contribution by Anna Wetter, Chapter 4 in this volume.

[42] COSAC, 'Annex Nineteenth Bi-annual Report, Responses Austrian Nationalrat' (n 28 above).

[43] COSAC (n 11 above).

[44] COSAC, (n 12 above).

[45] COSAC (n 28 above).

[46] Mastenbroek et al (n 15 above) 87.

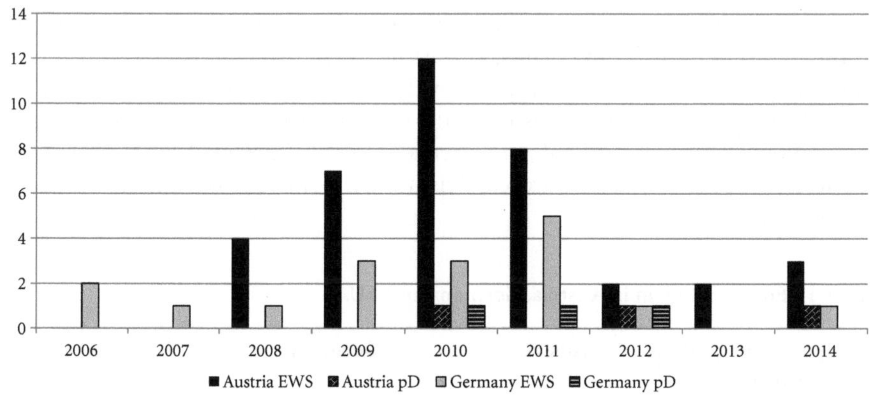

Figure 5: Number of opinions by type and year (2006–14)
Source: OPAL data set and own calculations.

The Nationalrat also sees the need to improve the Political Dialogue more generally. While both parliaments regard visits between the European Commission and national Parliaments to discuss Commission proposals as an effectively used tool within the Political Dialogue, the Nationalrat would clearly like to see them strengthened through more direct contacts with the Commission, both through presentations of Commission proposals in parliament and discussions with Commissioners in COSAC meetings.[47] In addition, both parliaments would be in favour of a closer cooperation with the Commission to discuss proposals that are of particular concern to national parliaments and for which a large number of reasoned opinions were sent, even though the threshold set out under the Lisbon Treaty was not met. The Nationalrat, for example, proposes that such concerns should be brought to the attention of the College of Commissioners, and be dealt with through the informal Dialogue with national parliaments' representatives in Brussels,[48] while the Bundestag suggests the strengthening of the informal Dialogue at staff level.[49]

B. Electoral Benefits: Public Euroscepticism and Salience

Despite a surge in EU criticism due to the eurozone crisis, which also led to the emergence of a new party critical of the common currency and the EU's eurozone crisis management ('*Alternative for Germany*', AfD), the German public is usually considered as less Eurosceptic than the EU average, and certainly less so than the rather Eurosceptic Austrian public.[50] As Table 1 indeed shows, generally (but not

[47] COSAC (n 11 above), no reply from Bundestag.
[48] COSAC (n 11 above).
[49] COSAC (n 12 above).
[50] Miklin (n 16 above).

always), fewer Germans have a negative image of the EU or consider membership in the EU to be 'a bad thing'. Thus, at least for these two countries, the assumption that greater Euroscepticism will provide MPs with incentives to intervene at the EU level is supported for Austria in the case of the Political Dialogue. Analysing opinions across all national parliaments in the EU, Auel et al,[51] however, have found no impact of public Euroscepticism on the number of opinions sent by national parliaments.

Table 1: Euroscepticism in Austria, Germany and EU.

'Negative image of the EU' in %	Austria	Germany	EU average
2010	37.5	24.5	19.5
2011	36.5	23.5	23
2012	35	24.5	28.5
2013	34	24.5	28.5
2014	35	20	23.5
'EU membership is a bad thing' in %	**Austria**	**Germany**	**EU average**
2010	23	20	18
2011	25	16	18
2012	29	8	16
2013	21	7	17
2014	–	–	–

Note: Entries for 'negative image of the EU' provide the averages across both bi-annual Eurobarometer waves for each year. Entries for 'bad thing membership' draw on the Standard Eurobarometer surveys EB 73 (Spring 2010) and 75 (Spring 2011) as well as on the European Parliament Eurobarometer (EB/EP 79.5) for the 2012 and 2013 data. Please note that the two sets of surveys are not strictly comparable. Data for 2014 is not available for this item.

One of the reasons is that opinions are majority instruments. As a result, Eurosceptic parties that would have the greatest incentive to make use of these instruments are usually unable to do so on their own and especially against the will of the governing parties. More importantly,

> parties that are eager to enhance their public profile in European affairs (and tap into the limited popular resentments against a European leviathan) will not opt for the highly arcane and ineffective Lisbon instruments. Instead, they will embrace any issue of public

[51] K Auel, O Rozenberg and A Tacea, 'To Scrutinise or Not to Scrutinise? Explaining Variation in EU-Related Activities in National Parliaments' (2015) 38 *West European Politics* 282.

enragement against Brussels—typically a specific issue that voters can personally relate [to] and that has a direct impact on their lives.[52]

For mainstream parties (and especially governing parties), in contrast, EU issues are often more a liability than an electoral asset.[53] Reasons for this are internal dissent over EU integration,[54] or the fact that they are generally more Europhile than their voters.[55]

Public attitudes towards the EU as such, however, tell us little about the salience of EU issues. In particular, it should not be assumed that a more sceptical attitude toward the EU necessarily means a greater salience. Unfortunately, the general salience of EU integration in public opinion is very difficult to measure due to the lack of data. When it comes to specific issues that the public considered most important at the EU level, the eurozone crisis played a big role: the state of Member States' public finances, unemployment and the economic situation top the lists in both countries.[56] Yet crisis issues played only a fairly small role in both countries regarding the EWS or the Political Dialogue. The Nationalrat submitted four opinions on documents related to anti-crisis measures, and the Bundestag, three, one of which was a reasoned opinion on the deposit guarantee scheme. As Auel and Höing[57] have found, this is also true for national parliaments in general: about 11 per cent of all submitted opinions from 2010 to 2012 were crisis related.

Yet Figure 6 does give an indication that issue salience may have had an impact on the Political Dialogue opinions submitted.[58] While the reasoned opinions were sent on proposals from different policy fields (Austria: employment, health and service companies; Germany: banking, internal market, social policy), there is a much clearer pattern to the salience of specific policy areas for Political Dialogue opinions sent in the period 2006 to 2014. In both parliaments, opinions on issues relating to the Area of Justice, Security and Freedom clearly dominated (Austria 15 out of 38; Germany 6 out of 17). Within this area, we mainly find opinions on issues related to immigration and asylum policy, on issues related to family matters such as matrimonial property regimes, child support and divorce laws as well as on issues related to crime (human trafficking and child pornography)—and thus on issues that can be expected to resonate with the public. All other

52 Mastenbroek et al (n 15 above) 87f.

53 CE De Vries, 'EU Issue Voting: Asset or Liability? How European Integration Affects Parties' Electoral Fortunes' (2010) 11 *European Union Politics* 89.

54 EE Edwards, 'Products of Their Past? Cleavages and Intra-Party Dissent over European Integration' *IHS Political Science Series*, Paper no 118 (February 2009).

55 M Mattila and T Raunio, 'Drifting Further Apart: National Parties and their Electorates in the EU Dimension' (2012) 35 *West European Politics* 589.

56 See, for example, Standard Eurobarometer 80, Autumn 2013, 'Public Opinion in the European Union—First Results', online at: ec.europa.eu/public_opinion/archives/eb/eb80/eb80_en.htm, 15ff and Standard Eurobarometer 82, Autumn 2014, 'Public Opinion in the European Union—First Results', online at: ec.europa.eu/public_opinion/archives/eb/eb82/eb82_en.htm, 15ff.

57 K Auel and O Höing, 'National Parliaments and the Eurozone Crisis: Taking Ownership in Difficult Times?' (2015) 38 *West European Politics* 375, 385.

58 See also D Finke and T Dannwolf, 'Domestic scrutiny of European Union politics: Between whistle blowing and opposition control' (2013) 52 *European Journal of Political Research* 715.

opinions are fairly evenly spread out over the policy fields in Austria, while the German Parliament focused on a smaller number of policy areas due to the overall smaller number of opinions.

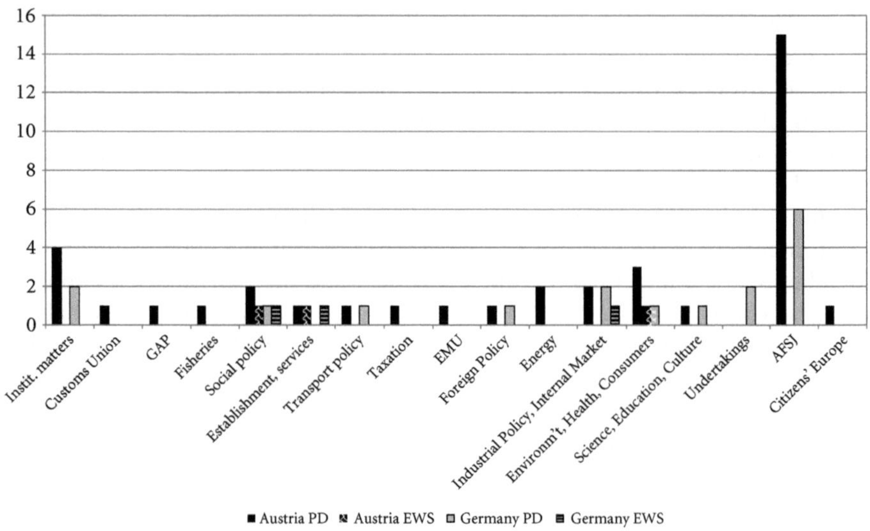

Figure 6: Number of opinions by type and Eurlex Category (2006–14)
Source: OPAL data set and own calculations.

Finally, based on the assumption that the salience will be higher for acts proposing *new* legislation as opposed to those that amend or repeal existing legislation,[59] Gattermann and Hefftler[60] have also found that salience thus defined did indeed have a positive impact on the probability of parliaments sending a reasoned opinion. Whether this is also true for the Bundestag and the Nationalrat is difficult to say given the very low number of reasoned opinions. The six reasoned opinions submitted were indeed all on new legislation, but only on a very small proportion of all new legislation proposed.

C. Reaching the Audience?

As the above suggests, public Euroscepticism as well as the salience of legislative proposals (both in terms of new legislation and in terms of the policy area covered),

[59] See R De Ruiter, 'Under the radar? National parliaments and the ordinary legislative procedure in the European Union' (2013) 10 *Journal of European Public Policy* 1196, 4; D Finke and T Dannwolf 'Domestic scrutiny', (n 57 above) 17.

[60] K Gattermann and C Hefftler, 'Beyond Institutional Capacity: Political Motivation and Parliamentary Behaviour in the Early Warning System' (2015) 38 *West European Politics* 305.

may have an impact on the willingness of MPs to use the new instruments. At the same time, we can observe a clear disillusionment in both parliaments with the effectiveness of the instruments—regarding both the direct impact on EU legislation and the establishment of a meaningful dialogue with the Commission. Yet as argued above, the new instruments can also be used to mobilise the public—or at least to signal parliamentary engagement.

> The EWS gives the national parliament a voice, however minimal, in European legislative politics; and while its main interlocutor is in theory the Commission, in practice the intended audience of its intervention is likely to be its own national government as well as the press and the public. The EWS allows the national parliament to intervene early and vocally in the European legislative process, with the potential to mobilize domestic public opinion.[61]

Whether these aims are met, however, depends crucially on whether the intended audience actually can and does take note of the opinions sent. Both parliaments provide a short description of the EWS and their related scrutiny procedures on their websites (but not for the Political Dialogue) as well as a direct link to IPEX. But neither parliament provides direct access to a list of submitted opinions. The opinions are published on the websites, but can only be accessed through a search of the general parliamentary database. Yet as welcome as the provision of information via parliamentary websites is, most citizens experience politics through the media. As mentioned above, the first reasoned opinions sent by the Bundestag and Nationalrat did receive some press coverage. In addition, newspapers in both countries published a few articles outlining the rights of both parliaments under the Lisbon Treaty more generally.[62] Since then, the novelty, and thus the news value, of reasoned opinions seem to have worn off. Reasoned opinions, let alone opinions submitted for the Political Dialogue, hardly receive any coverage in the three main newspapers in each country beyond mere mentions in passing.[63] The fact that reasoned opinions have to be decided by a plenary vote in the Bundestag seems to make little difference, as does the fact that both parliaments send out press releases at least on reasoned opinions. If at all, reasoned opinions are taken up by EU online press publications such as *EurActiv*, which reported on the reasoned opinions by the Bundestag regarding the legislative proposals on the deposit

[61] I Cooper, 'The Watchdogs of Subsidiarity: National Parliaments and the Logic of Arguing in the EU' (2006) 44 *Journal of Common Market Studies* 281, 292; for a similar argument Paskalev, 'Lisbon Treaty' (n 9 above).

[62] See, for example, *Die Presse*, 'Parlament: Neue Mitwirkungsrechte in der EU', 12.7.2010, *Die Presse*, 'Neue Außenpolitik abseits der Ministerien: nationale Parlamente müssen kooperieren', 28.1.2011.

[63] Based on data collected in the context of the PACE project (see: www.ihs.ac.at/pace/). See, for example, *Frankfurter Allgemeine Zeitung*, 'Gegen Kaufrecht auf EU-Ebene', 3.12.2011; *Frankfurter Allgemeine Zeitung*, 'Leutheusser gegen EU-Kaufrecht', 25.5.2012; *Frankfurter Allgemeine Zeitung*; 'EU will eigenes Kaufrecht durchsetzen', 25.5.2012; *Frankfurter Allgemeine Zeitung*, 'Konkurrenz fuärs BGB', 4.6.2012 on the Bundestag's reasoned opinion on the EU sales law regulation.

guarantee scheme[64] and the Common European Sales Law,[65] but also on the three yellow cards that have been issued so far.[66]

To sum up, the lack of effectiveness seems to be a clear disincentive in both parliaments to become involved in the EWS or the Political Dialogue. Public opinion and especially the salience of some policy issues seem to provide a greater incentive, but even here the ability of both parliaments to signal parliamentary engagement in EU affairs through these instruments to their citizens is hampered by the general lack of interest by the media. Thus, from a rational choice perspective, MPs in both parliaments have little incentive to make frequent use of the new instruments, and it is not very surprising that the number of opinions sent has decreased rather dramatically in both parliaments over the last three years.

III. The Role of Norms and Values[67]

In contrast to rational choice approaches, sociological neo-institutionalist approaches see preferences as neither stable, nor exogenous.[68] Moreover, institutions 'do not just constrain options; they establish the very criteria by which people discover their preferences'[69] and thus 'mould their own participants, and supply systems of meaning for their participants in politics'.[70] Thus, behaviour is the result of conscious choices, but these choices are not purely guided by the expected rational pay-off; they are influenced by institutional values and norms.[71]

One expression of institutional norms and values is parliamentary culture. Elkins and Simeon describe political culture as 'a short-hand expression for a "mind set" which has the effect of limiting attention to less than the full range of alternative behaviours, problems, and solutions which are logically possible'.[72] Thus, from a sociological institutionalist point of view, legislative behaviour in EU affairs will depend on and be influenced by general parliamentary traditions and political culture. In a system characterised by a culture of party discipline and

64 *EurActiv*, 'Machtvolles Signal an die EU-Kommission', 5.10. 2010; *EurActiv*, 'Deutschland scheitert mit EU-Rüge', 22.10.2010.

65 *EurActiv*, 'Deutsche Vorbehalte gegen Europäisches Kaufrecht', 3.12. 2011.

66 *EurActiv*, 'Brussels drops plans for EU law limiting right to strike', 14.9.2012; *EurActiv*, 'Commission to press ahead with European Prosecutor's Office, without France and Britain', 30.10.2013. *Euractiv. National parliaments invoke 'yellow card' in response to revised Posted Workers Directive, 10.05.2016.*

67 The following draws on K Auel and T Christiansen, 'After Lisbon' (n 29 above).

68 JG March and JP Olsen, *Rediscovering Institutions: The Organizational Basis of Politics* (New York, Free Press, 1989) 163.

69 PJ DiMaggio and WW Powell, 'Introduction' in PJ DiMaggio and W Powell (eds), *The New Institutionalism in Organizational Analysis* (Chicago IL/London, University of Cambridge Press, 1991) 11.

70 BG Peters, *Institutional Theory in Political Science: The 'New Institutionalism'* (London, Continuum, 1999) 26.

71 Peters, *Institutional Theory in Political Science*, n 69 above, p 29.

72 DJ Elkins and REB Simeon, 'A Cause in Search of Its Effect, or What Does Political Culture Explain?' (1979) 11 *Comparative Politics* 127, 128.

executive dominance, submitting an opinion on a legislative proposal against the wishes of the government 'could be potentially damaging for the government that has been consulted in drafting the initiative (and has probably already discussed this initiative in the Council)',[73] something that governing parties will generally try to avoid.[74] In addition, the findings of a study by Weßels[75] suggest that different parliamentary norms and role perceptions will have an impact not only on the general motivation of MPs to engage in scrutiny, but also, for example, on the extent to which they consider it appropriate and feel the need to become directly involved in the policy process at the EU level through such instruments such as the EWS or the Political Dialogue. Similarly, Sprungk[76] argues that the general attitude of MPs towards European integration may impact on their motivation to engage in scrutiny activity. A party in favour of European integration may view parliamentary scrutiny as a factor impeding smooth European policy-making and thus as inappropriate.

In both parliaments, we can find a culture of rather strict party discipline and executive dominance, and as a result opinions formulated against the position of the government are rare: In Germany, 'risking a governmental crisis triggered by a cross-party ad hoc vote against a governmental initiative or European legislation is next to unthinkable'.[77] Rather, both EWS and Political Dialogue opinions are usually coordinated with the government. Similarly, in Austria,

> the two largest political parties (Austrian Social-Democrats and the Austrian People's Party) that form the government coalition are seen to coordinate and thus 'pre-cook' their opinions with the respective ministry and each other, so as to find a consensual position.[78]

While Pollak and Slominski[79] argued 10 years ago that strong party discipline coupled with grand coalition governments severely hampered parliamentary scrutiny in EU affairs in the Nationalrat, the Nationalrat has since become somewhat more active in EU affairs,[80] especially since the Lisbon Treaty,[81] which also led to

[73] T Raunio, 'National legislatures and the Constitutional Treaty' in J O'Brennan and T Raunio (eds), *National Parliaments within the Enlarged European Union: From 'victims' of integration to competitive actors?* (Abingdon, Routledge, 2007) 86; see also A Vergés Bausili, 'Rethinking the methods of Dividing and Excercising Powers in EU: Reforming Subsidiarity and National Parliaments' *Jean Monnet Working Paper* 9/2002 (New York, 2002).

[74] K Auel, 'Democratic Accountability and National Parliaments—Re-Defining the Impact of Parliamentary Scrutiny in EU Affairs' (2007) 13 *European Law Journal* 487.

[75] B Weßels, 'Roles and Orientations of Members of Parliament in the EU Context: Congruence or Difference? Europeanisation or Not?' (2005) 11 *Journal of Legislative Studies* 446.

[76] C Sprungk, 'National Parliamentary Scrutiny in The European Union: The German Bundestag and the French Assemblée Nationale—Key Players or Side-Shows?' Paper presented at the EUSA Conference, Nashville TN, 27–30 March 2003.

[77] Mastenbroek et al (n 15 above) 86.

[78] Mastenbroek et al (n 15 above) 72f.

[79] J Pollak and P Slominski, 'Influencing EU Politics? The Case of the Austrian Parliament' (2003) 41 *Journal of Common Market Studies* 707.

[80] J Pollak and P Slominski, 'Zwischen De- und Reparlamentarisierung' (n 18 above).

[81] Miklin (n 16 above); Miklin (n 26 above).

a greater engagement in the Political Dialogue in 2010–11. Reasons for this are MPs' increased awareness of EU decision-making as well as improvements regarding the information provided to the Nationalrat and regarding administrative support. Whether this is a long-term development seems questionable, however, given that the number of submitted opinions has decreased dramatically since.

A second question is whether parliaments actually considerate it appropriate to intervene in the legislative process at the EU level. Here, differences between the two parliaments are rather strong, which may explain why the Bundestag is less engaged in the Political Dialogue than the Nationalrat: While the Nationalrat unequivocally considers accountability to include European institutions,[82] the Bundestag does not consider them to be accountable to national parliaments.[83] What is more, Bundestag MPs feel that parliamentary scrutiny of EU affairs should not impede either the government's negotiations in Brussels or EU policy-making more generally. Such views were readily visible in the plenary debates over the implementation of parliamentary participation rights in the Bundestag following the German Federal Constitutional Court's decision on the Lisbon Treaty.[84] Similarly, Mastenbroek et al[85] report that in interviews German MPs voiced 'the concern that the EWS turns into a weapon in the hands of radical Eurosceptic parties throughout Europe'.

IV. Conclusion

The chapter started with the observation that—despite a somewhat more enthusiastic start—both the Austrian Nationalrat and the German Bundestag are not very engaged in either the Early Warning System or the Political Dialogue. Although the Nationalrat has overall been more active regarding the Political Dialogue, the number of opinions sent by both parliaments remains below the EU average and has decreased substantially over the last few years. As the analysis demonstrated, this reluctance to make use of the new instruments is not primarily a result of a lack of capacity to deal with the scrutiny of EU documents in time. Both parliaments have implemented scrutiny provisions that are efficient, albeit in different ways. The Bundestag can rely on strong administrative support, an encompassing pre-screening process and detailed information by the government, which counterbalances the fact that the decentralised scrutiny process and the responsibil-

[82] COSAC, 'Annex Twentieth Bi-annual Report, Responses Austrian Nationalrat', online at: www.cosac.eu/documents/bi-annual-reports-of-cosac.

[83] COSAC, 'Annex Twentieth Bi-annual Report, Responses German Bundestag', online at: www.cosac.eu/documents/bi-annual-reports-of-cosac.

[84] T Auberger and W Lamping, 'Die richtige Auffuährung auf der falschen Buähne? Das Bundesverfassungsgericht und die Politisierung der europäischen Integration', (2009) 2 *dms—der moderne staat—Zeitschrift für Public Policy, Recht und Management* 271.

[85] Mastenbroek et al (n 15 above) 91.

ity of the plenary make the process more time-consuming. The Nationalrat, in contrast, makes up for its more limited administrative support with the advantage of lean and therefore fast scrutiny processes. Even though the more limited pre-screening seems to focus MPs' attention mainly on legislative proposals and less on other documents, the Nationalrat still submitted more opinions under the Political Dialogue than the Bundestag.

These findings emphasise that it is not so much the capacity of parliaments to deal with the new instruments, but rather their willingness to do so, which plays a role. And indeed, MPs in both parliaments seem to have few incentives to use the new instruments. EWS and Political Dialogue are neither seen as effective regarding parliamentary influence at the EU level—concerning both the actual impact on EU legislation as well as the development of a meaningful dialogue with the European Commission—nor do they prove successful in signalling parliamentary engagement in EU politics to the national public, and thus as a means to reap potential electoral benefits. The ability of parliaments to reach their audience depends to a large extent on the coverage of their activities by the media, but in both countries reasoned opinions seem to be of limited news value for the press. While they were hardly covered in Austria at all, they were mentioned slightly more often in the German Press, but usually only in passing and within a broader context. It is therefore hardly surprising that MPs in both parliaments seem to feel an increasing frustration with the new Lisbon instruments and prefer to focus their scrutiny efforts towards their own governments where attempts at exerting influence may be more successful. This reluctance also relates to the fact that the new instruments' rationale of giving national parliaments a voice at the EU level independently of (or even against) their governments is not easily compatible with a parliamentary culture characterised by party discipline and executive dominance, where a parliamentary opinion contradicting the view of the government is usually not considered appropriate.

To conclude, the Lisbon Treaty may indeed deserve to be hailed as the 'Treaty of Parliaments', given the many provisions that strengthened both national parliaments and the European Parliament. In addition, the introduction of the Early Warning System has certainly led to an overhaul of parliamentary scrutiny provisions and the establishment of greater parliamentary administrative capacities in EU affairs—not only in the Bundestag and the Nationalrat, but also in many other national (and indeed regional) parliaments. Yet although they are certainly *able* to deal with the EWS or the Political Dialogue, both the German Bundestag and the Austrian Nationalrat, never all that enthusiastic to begin with, seem less and less *willing* to do so. There are also indications that this may be the case for other, previously more active, parliaments as well.[86] Of the most active chambers in the EWS, the French Senate has sent only two reasoned opinions since January 2014 (see also the contribution by Tacea (Chapter 12) in this volume), the Dutch Upper

[86] For the following, see: ec.europa.eu/dgs/secretariat_general/relations/relations_other/npo/index_en.htm.

and Lower Chambers one and two reasoned opinions, respectively, and the House of Commons three, to name just a few. Even the Swedish Riksdag, the most active parliament when it comes to sending reasoned opinions, seems to have grown tired of the instrument. Having submitted 11, 20 and 9 reasoned opinions in 2011, 2010 and 2013, respectively, the Riksdag has not sent a single one since then (May 2015). In a recent interview,[87] Frans Timmermans, European Commission Vice President responsible—inter alia—for promoting a new relationship with national parliaments, promised that the new Commission will take parliaments' concerns more seriously.[88] It remains to be seen whether this promise will lead to greater changes than merely the recent re-design of the Commission's 'National Parliament opinions' website.

[87] See *Financial Times Brussels Blog*, 19.5.2015: blogs.ft.com/brusselsblog/2015/05/19/timmermans-interview-the-annotated-transcript/.

[88] See also the contribution by Jörgen Hettne, Chapter 3 in this volume for a discussion of various proposals for the development of the EWS.

15

Like Two Peas in a Pod? The Functioning of the Early Warning Mechanism in the Czech Republic and Poland

KATARZYNA GRANAT

I. Introduction

This chapter deals with the functioning of the Early Warning System in two EU Member States belonging to the Visegrád Group: Poland and the Czech Republic. These Member States are similar along many relevant dimensions but exhibit significant differences in their activities within the EWM. Following the model of studying 'most similar cases' a detailed comparison thus offers insights into what the causes behind these differences in their activity may be.[1] The similarities are extensive. Both Member States acceded to the EU in 2004 and their parliamentary systems follow the same model of asymmetric bicameralism. Moreover, both apply to a large extent centralised scrutiny for the EWM, with some role for standing committees. However, in terms of outcomes the differences are stark. The Polish parliament belongs to the most active group of parliaments under the EWM and is much less involved in the Barroso initiative, whilst the Czech parliament has barely taken part in the EWM, but its Senát is one of the most active parliaments in the political dialogue process. The aim of this chapter is to analyse possible reasons for their different approaches to the subsidiarity scrutiny through careful study of the details of debates and votes on reasoned opinions and the text of those reasoned opinions themselves.

The chapter first describes the general position of the Polish and the Czech parliaments within their constitutional systems (section II). The next section presents procedures implemented in Poland and the Czech Republic to accommodate the EWM (section III). Next, the chapter explores the reasoned

[1] R Hirschl, 'The question of case selection in Comparative Constitutional Law' (2005) 53 *American Journal of Comparative Law* 125, 134.

opinions and discusses the issues that the chambers criticise: subsidiarity, legal basis, proportionality, delegations to the Commission to adopt non-legislative acts, fundamental rights protection and contents of the proposals (section IV). Moreover, the chapter analyses the debates and votes taken under the EWM (section V). The aim is to establish whether the parliamentary chambers gained some independence from their national government under the EWM and whether reasoned opinions integrate the whole political spectrum at the national level. The chapter concludes with an exploration to explain the differences in the functioning of the EWM in each of the Member States under analysis (sections VI and VII).

II. Position of Parliament In The Constitutional System of Poland and The Czech Republic

The Polish Constitution vests legislative power in two chambers of the parliament: the Sejm and the Senat, both elected for a four-year term of office.[2] The Sejm is composed of 460 deputies who are elected in universal, equal, direct and proportional elections by secret ballot.[3] The Senat, re-established after the fall of communism in 1989, consists of 100 Senators who are chosen in universal and direct elections by secret ballot.[4] After a 2011 reform, Senators are chosen in majority elections, held in single-member constituencies.[5] Only the lower chamber, the Sejm, exercises control over the Council of Ministers, has the power to overturn by an absolute majority the Senat's rejection of a bill or amendments proposed to it, and adopts the state's budget.[6] Moreover, the Sejm may overturn a presidential veto.[7] The Sejm and the Senat, however, share some functions such as initiating the legislative process and the constitutional amendment process.[8] The Polish bicameralism is hence described as unequal or incomplete, the Senat being regarded as a chamber of reflection.[9]

Since 2007, in the period relevant for the EWM analysis, the governing coalition in Poland consisted of the liberal-conservative Civic Platform (PO) and the centrist Polish People's Party (PSL), a force reflected in the composition of the Sejm and Senat. The opposition included the conservative Law and Justice (PiS), liberal Palikot's Movement (RP), social-democratic Democratic Left Alliance (SLD) and right-wing United Poland (SP).[10]

[2] Art 95(1) of the Polish Constitution.

[3] Art 96 of the Polish Constitution.

[4] Art 97 of the Polish Constitution.

[5] Art 260 §1 Ustawa z 5 stycznia 2011 r—Kodeks wyborczy, DzU 2011 nr 21 poz 112 (Election Code).

[6] Arts 95(2), 121(3) and 219(1) of the Polish Constitution.

[7] Art 122(5) of the Polish Constitution.

[8] Arts 119(1) and 235(1) of the Polish Constitution.

[9] L Garlicki, *Polskie Prawo Konstytucyjne: Zarys Wykadu* (Warsaw, Liber, 2006) at 199.

[10] Ruch Palikota and SLD have no representatives in the Senat, similar to in the period of 2007–11.

Similarly to Poland, the Czech bicameral system consists of the Poslanecká sněmovna and the Senát, which were established in 1992 after the dissolution of Czechoslovakia.[11] The Poslanecká sněmovna consists of 200 deputies chosen for a four-year term in universal, equal, proportional and direct elections by secret ballot.[12] In the Senát 81 Senators are elected for a term of six years, with one-third of the Senators renewed every two years in universal, equal and direct elections by secret ballot and under the principles of the majority system.[13] The Czech bicameralism is also an asymmetrical one: while both chambers may put forward legislative proposals,[14] the government is accountable only to the Poslanecká sněmovna, which also has a final say (by absolute majority) within the legislative procedure and with regard to the presidential veto of bills, and it approves the state's budget.[15]

Although the Social Democrats (ČSSD) gained the largest number of seats in the 2010 elections to the Poslanecká sněmovna, between July 2010 October 2013 the conservative Civic Democratic Party (ODS), TOP 09 and populist Public Affairs (VV) formed the government. Since the October 2013 elections the Social Democrats are in the centre-left governing coalition together with populist ANO 2011 and centrist Christian and Democratic Union (KDU–ČSL). In October 2010 the Social Democrats gained a majority in the Senát, traditionally dominated by the Civic Democrats. Subsequent elections in October 2012 and 2014 further enhanced the majority of the Social Democrats in the Senát.

III. EWM Procedures

In this section, I explore the institutional design concerning subsidiarity scrutiny in Poland and the Czech Republic. The Lisbon Treaty, by granting new competences to national parliaments, has in fact equalised the unequal bicameralism in both Member States, since both Senates gained equal rights under the EWM and this was also translated to national provisions.[16]

A. Poland

Before the Lisbon Treaty, it was argued that despite its relatively strong position vis-à-vis the government in the constitutional system, in EU affairs the parliament

[11] Art 15(2) of the Czech Constitution.

[12] Arts 16(1) and 18(1) of the Czech Constitution.

[13] Arts 16(2) and 18(2) of the Czech Constitution.

[14] Art 41(2) of the Czech Constitution.

[15] Arts 68(1), 47(1), 50(2) and 42(1) of the Czech Constitution.

[16] On this conclusion for the Polish parliament see Z Witkowski, M Serowaniec, 'Przesłanki naruszenia zasady pomocniczości przez akty ustawodawcze Unii Europejskiej w świetle uzasadnionych opiniii przyjętych przez Sejm i Senat RP' (2014) 31 *Gdańskie Studia Prawnicze* 997, 1001.

was 'more an accidental hero than an effective actor'.[17] The early involvement of the parliament in EU affairs related to the approximation of national law to EU law prior to Poland's accession to the EU.[18] After EU accession, the parliament adopted the Act on Cooperation between the Council of Ministers and Parliament in EU Affairs, granting the parliament powers with regard to aspects such as cooperation in the EU legislative process, adoption of laws implementing EU law and appointments to EU institutions.[19] Also in 2005, whilst controlling the compatibility with the Constitution of the Act on Cooperation, the Constitutional Court underlined the necessity to ensure that both the Sejm and the Senat participate in the process of EU law-drafting.[20]

The new powers of the parliament in EU affairs significantly strengthened its impact on the government's policy-making.[21] Other activities of the Polish parliament in that period included debates of EU-related issues and resolutions in this respect, as well as engagement in inter-parliamentary cooperation.[22] However, observers criticised the early years of the Polish parliament in the EU for the quite limited expertise and understanding of EU law by its deputies and the political reality of parliamentary work.[23] The position of the parliament in EU affairs was described as 'modest' as understood in the categories developed by Maurer and Wessels, and a 'cooperative model' in which the parliament's position cannot be forced on the government.[24]

In the judgment assessing the Lisbon Treaty the Polish Constitutional Court stressed the significance of national parliaments in issuing reasoned opinions on Commission proposals allowing the Polish parliament to shape the content of EU law 'to the extent … that it is possible to narrow down the scope

[17] A Łazowski, 'The Polish Parliament and EU affairs. An effective actor or an accidental hero?' in J O'Brennan and T Raunio (eds), *National Parliaments within the enlarged European Union. From 'victims' of Integration to Competitive Actors* (London, Routledge, 2007) at 203.

[18] ibid at 204ff.

[19] Ustawa z dnia 11 marca 2004 r. o współpracy Rady Ministrów z Sejmem i Senatem w sprawach związanych z członkostwem Rzeczypospolitej Polskiej w Unii Europejskiej, Dz.U. Nr 52, poz. 515 oraz z 2005 r. Nr 11, poz. 89 i Nr 160, poz. 1342.

[20] Trybunał Konstytucyjny, K 24/04 judgment of 12 January 2005, inequality in competences of Sejm and Senat committees in respect of European Union legislative proposal. The Court stated that influencing the position of the government is in fact a legislative function. As long as the bicameral parliament is to be maintained, both chambers should be guaranteed equal participation in activities concerning the shaping position of Poland in the field of adopting EU law. See A Łazowski, 'The Polish parliament and EU affairs: an effective actor or an accidental hero?' in J O'Brennan and T Raunio (eds), *National parliaments within the enlarged European Union: from 'victims' of integration to competitive actors?* (London, Routledge, 2007) at 212–14.

[21] J Barcz and A Pudło, 'The Polish Parliament and EU Affairs' in C Hefftler, Ch Neuhold, O Rozenberg and J Smith (eds), *The Palgrave Handbook of National Parliaments and the European Union* (Basingstoke/New York, Palgrave Macmillan, 2015) at 605.

[22] Łazowski (n 17 above) at 211.

[23] ibid at 215.

[24] Barcz and Pudło (n 21 above) at 608.

of its "external character" in relation to the Polish state'.[25] In this respect, the Constitutional Court left it to the legislature to take the legal measures to accommodate the EWM and shape the cooperation of the government with the Sejm and the Senat in EU affairs.[26] With the entry into force of the Lisbon Treaty, the Polish parliament gained a number of new powers which are reflected in the Rules of Procedure of the Sejm[27] and the Senat[28] and in the new Cooperation Act (2010), however its role in EU affairs has not radically changed from the national perspective.[29]

The question of subsidiarity scrutiny of Commission proposals was not completely new for the Polish parliament because it assessed subsidiarity while opining on Commission proposals for the Polish government.[30] Since the Lisbon Treaty, of course, the chambers may send a reasoned opinion to the Commission. In this regard, the lower chamber applies the centralised model in which the European Affairs Committee (EAC) remains the main actor,[31] whereas the upper chamber uses a mixed one, whereby the EAC and standing committees cooperate on expressing a reasoned opinion. This section hence presents the centralised subsidiarity scrutiny of the EAC of the Sejm and mixed system of the Senat.[32] The Cooperation Act and the Rules of Procedure of each of the chambers regulate subsidiarity reviews in the Polish parliament.

In the Sejm, the Marshall forwards EU draft legislative acts to the EAC of the Sejm.[33] Usually once per week, the Presidium of the EAC, on the basis of the Sejm's Bureau of Research analysis, choses proposals for further consideration and assigns rapporteurs to them.[34] Next, the EAC itself or a group of 15 MPs can take

[25] Trybunał Konstytucyjny, K 32/09 judgment of 24 November 2010, p 31. The Court, following the Polish doctrine, sees EU law as an order that is 'partially external' to Polish law, meaning that although EU legal acts have a legal force in Poland it is not the Polish legislator who creates EU law.

[26] ibid.

[27] Uchwała Sejmu Rzeczypospolitej Polskiej z dnia 30 lipca 1992 r., Regulamin Sejmu Rzeczypospolitej Polskiej, M.P. 1992 nr 26 poz. 185. (Sejm Rules of Procedure).

[28] Uchwała Senatu z dnia 23 listopada 1990 r., Regulamin Senatu, M.P. 1991 nr 2 poz. 11. For the description of new powers see also Barcz and Pudło (n 21 above).

[29] Barcz and Pudło (n 21 above) at 608.

[30] A Fuksiewicz, 'Sejm i Senat rok po wejściu w życie Traktatu Lizbońskiego-dostosowanie do reformy instytucjonalnej': www.isp.org.pl/uploads/pdf/1827766553.pdf, at p 11.

[31] However, see the written evidence from the EU Affairs Committee of the Polish Sejm to the House of Lords, which pointed out that the Sejm's standing committees are now more involved in scrutiny work and that joint meetings between the EU affairs committee and standing committees are sometimes held. House of Lords, European Affairs Committee, 9th Report of Session 2013–14, The Role of National Parliaments in the European Union, published 24 March 2014: www.publications.parliament.uk/pa/ld201314/ldselect/ldeucom/151/151.pdf, at 13.

[32] The Senat's system represents a mixed system of the participation of the dominating EAC with a prior facultative consultation of the standing committees. For the possible constellations of the mixed systems see K Granat, *National Parliaments and the Policing of the Subsidiarity Principle* (European University Institute PhD Thesis, 2014).

[33] Art 148b(1)4) Sejm Standing Orders.

[34] See: oide.sejm.gov.pl/oide/en/images/files/badanie_pomocniczosci/subsidiarity_sejm_table_pl.pdf.

a resolution, with a reasoned opinion attached to a motion stating the grounds.[35] The first reading of this resolution takes place in the EAC while the second one occurs at a plenary session of the Sejm.[36] If the Sejm adopts the reasoned opinion, the Marshall of the Sejm forwards the resolution to the Commission.[37]

In the Senat, the Marshall forwards all EU documents to the EAC and to the standing committees, if requested so by the chairman of the EAC.[38] In the EAC the chairman and the two Deputy Chairs sift the EU draft legislative acts prior to the committee sitting, and assign rapporteurs for documents selected for debate in the committee.[39] If the EAC or any standing committee adopts an opinion that the EU draft legislative act violates the subsidiarity principle, it next puts a motion to the Marshall of the Senat for a resolution of the Senat together with the draft opinion.[40] This draft opinion is forwarded to all relevant committees, including the EAC.[41] They should prepare a joint report that is later voted on in the plenary sitting of the Senat.[42]

The Cooperation Act of 2010 compels the government to cooperate with the Sejm and the Senat in 'affairs connected to the membership in the EU'.[43] Specifically, the Council of Ministers must forward an opinion on EU draft legislative acts within 14 days after receipt thereof.[44] This opinion should include an assessment whether the EU proposal is compatible with the subsidiarity principle.[45]

B. The Czech Republic

Before the Czech Republic's accession to the EU, in 2001, the Czech Constitution was amended to incorporate provisions on the relationship between government and parliament in EU affairs, including the duty to inform parliament and the possibility for parliament to express its views.[46] The amendment, together with new provisions in the Rules of Procedure of each of the chambers, reflected the political willingness for more involvement of the Czech parliament in EU affairs after the Czech EU accession.[47] The position of the Poslanecká sněmovna at that

[35] Art 148cc(1) and (2) Sejm Rules of Procedure.

[36] Art 148cc(3) Sejm Rules of Procedure.

[37] Art 148cc(5) Sejm Rules of Procedure.

[38] Art 75a Senat Rules of Procedure.

[39] See: www.ipex.eu/IPEXL-WEB/parliaments/institution/plsen.do.

[40] Art 75d(1) Senat Rules of Procedure.

[41] Art 75d(2) Senat Rules of Procedure.

[42] See: www.ipex.eu/IPEXL-WEB/parliaments/institution/plsen.do.

[43] Ustawa z dnia 8 października 2010 r. o współpracy Rady Ministrów z Sejmem i Senatem w sprawach związanych z członkostwem Rzeczypospolitej Polskiej w Unii Europejskiej, Dz. U. Nr 213 Poz. 1395 (Cooperation Act). See Arts 1 and 2 Cooperation Act.

[44] Art 7(1) Cooperation Act.

[45] Art 7(3)(3) Cooperation Act.

[46] Art 10b of the Czech Constitution.

[47] L Pitrová and M Coxová, 'Parliamentary Control of EU Decision-making in the Czech Republic' in O Tans, C Zoethout and J Peters (eds), *National Parliaments and European Democracy. A Bottom-up Approach to European Constitutionalism* (Groningen, Europa Law Publishing, 2007) at 207.

time was assessed as being of medium strength vis-à-vis the government, while the Senát was more modest, since the government was not bound by the Senát's opinions during the negotiations at EU level.[48]

The following changes in the Rules of Procedure of the Czech chambers were connected to the entry into force of the Lisbon Treaty.[49] They included the introduction of the EWM procedures and the 'mandating' rights of the parliament with regard to the flexibility clause, passerelle clauses and the simplified revision procedure.[50] The Czech Constitutional Court highlighted these changes in its Lisbon Treaty judgment and underlined that 'national parliaments of Member States can play an important role in protecting the limits of competences which the Member States conferred on the Union' since they were granted a role in this process in accordance with Protocols No 1 and No 2.[51]

The Rules of Procedure describe the practices applicable to subsidiarity review which are rather centralised systems of scrutiny in the EAC, with some characteristics of a mixed scrutiny since also the standing committees are consulted.[52] In the Poslanecká sněmovna, the Parliamentary Institute proposes documents for scrutiny and the chairman of the EAC does the final selection.[53] For the selected document, the government submits its opinion to the EAC which is then a basis for deliberation in the committee.[54] The EAC can also forward the draft EU act to a standing committee.[55] An expert of the EU Unit prepares for the rapporteur an analysis of the scrutinised proposal.[56] The rapporteur, together with the expert, drafts a resolution on the proposal, which includes a reasoned opinion.[57] On the basis of the obtained information, the EAC can take a resolution on issuing a reasoned opinion that counts as an opinion of the whole chamber if not sent for the approval to the plenary.[58] The reasoned opinion is then sent by the president of the chamber to the government, the Senát and to EU institutions.[59]

[48] ibid at 215.

[49] So-called 'Lisbon Amendment' to the Act on the Rules of Procedure of the Chamber of Deputies and Standing Rules of the Senát of the Czech Republic (Act No 162/2009 Col).

[50] See M Hrabálek and A Strelkov, 'The Czech Parliament and European Integration' in C Hefftler, Ch Neuhold, O Rozenberg and J Smith (eds), *The Palgrave Handbook of National Parliaments and the European Union* (Basingstoke, Palgrave, 2015) at 501.

[51] Czech Constitutional Court, Pl ÚS 19/08: Treaty of Lisbon I, 26 November 2008, para 140.

[52] See, however, that other authors identify the Czech system as centralised: www.houseofrepresentatives.nl/sites/www.houseofrepresentatives.nl/files/news_items/engaging_with_europe_management_report_2nd_edition.pdf. The Czech scrutiny system is similar to that of the Polish Senat; although it is dominated by the EAC, the standing committees might also be consulted. See also Granat (n 32 above).

[53] Hrabálek and Strelkov (n 50 above) at 496.

[54] §109a(1) and (2) Rules of Procedure of the Chamber of Deputies.

[55] §109a(2) Rules of Procedure of the Chamber of Deputies. However, the opinion of the standing committee is not binding for the EAC. See Hrabálek and Strelkov (n 50 above) at 497.

[56] Scrutiny of documents coming from the European Union and monitoring compliance with the principle of subsidiarity at: www.ipex.eu/IPEXL-WEB/parliaments/institution/czpos.do.

[57] ibid.

[58] §109a(4) Rules of Procedure of the Chamber of Deputies.

[59] §109a(6) Rules of Procedure of the Chamber of Deputies.

In the Senát, the EAC chairman together with the Head of the EU Unit and the committee's advisor select EU documents for scrutiny from the weekly overview prepared by that Unit, and appoints a rapporteur for the chosen piece of legislation.[60] The EAC may request information on the proposal at stake from the government within 14 days.[61] In addition the EAC may ask a standing committee to submit its opinion on the proposal under consideration within an agreed time-limit.[62] The member of the EU Unit prepares an analysis for the EAC.[63] The Committee rapporteur, assisted by the advisor to the Committee and expert from EU Unit, drafts a resolution on the proposal incorporating a subsidiarity assessment; if a breach is confirmed a reasoned opinion is prepared.[64] Having obtained the draft resolution, the EAC decides either only to take note of the proposal or to refer it to the plenary not later than three days before the elapse of the eight-week deadline set by Protocol No 2.[65] If it is approved, the President of the Senát forwards the reasoned opinion directly to the EU institutions.[66]

C. Assessment of the Functioning of the EWM by the Parliaments

Since the entry into force of the Lisbon Treaty until the end of 2014, the parliaments under analysis have participated in the EWM and the 'Barroso initiative' to different extents as presented in the table below. In addition, the Polish Sejm participated in the first 'yellow card' on the Monti II proposal,[67] while the Czech Senát contributed to the second one, on the EPPO proposal.[68]

	Polish Sejm	Polish Senat	Czech Poslanecká sněmovna	Czech Senát
Reasoned opinion	12	11	3	4
Opinion under Barroso Initiative	10	23	28	219

Source: Own compilation on the basis of 2010–14 Commission Annual Reports on Relations between the European Commission and National Parliaments.

[60] §119d(1) Standing Rules of the Senát. See also information on the website of the Senát: www.senat.cz/senat/evropa/vybory_a_plenum/index-eng.php?ke_dni=8.5.2015&O=10. This procedure is not exclusively for subsidiarity issues. See 'Scrutiny of documents coming from the European Union and monitoring compliance with the subsidiarity principle' at: www.ipex.eu/IPEXL-WEB/parliaments/institution/czsen.do.

[61] §119d(3) Standing Rules of the Senát.

[62] §119d(4) Standing Rules of the Senát. The involvement of standing committees is higher in the Senát than in the chamber. See Hrabálek and Strelkov (n 50 above) at 497.

[63] See 'Scrutiny of documents coming from the European Union and monitoring compliance with the subsidiarity principle' at: www.ipex.eu/IPEXL-WEB/parliaments/institution/czsen.do.

[64] ibid.

[65] §119f(2) and (3) Standing Rules of the Senát.

[66] §119i(1) Standing Rules of the Senát.

[67] Polish Sejm, Reasoned Opinion of 11.5.2012 on COM(2012) 130.

[68] Czech Senát, Reasoned Opinion of 9.10.2013 on COM(2013) 534.

Despite the fact that the parliamentary chambers under analysis have been active in the EWM to different extents, they share a rather negative assessment of the functioning of the EWM.[69] The chairman of the Senat's EAC, in his evidence to the UK House of Lords, noted a set of problems.[70] First, he raised the question of common definition of subsidiarity and its political character, which leads to an overly narrow scope of reasoned opinions. Secondly, the chairman underlined that the eight-week deadline to submit a reasoned opinion does not take relevant parliamentary breaks such as end of term into account. Thirdly, the lack of common interests of parliaments on EU policies was raised as a weakness of the EWM.

Moreover, the parliaments under comparison negatively assess the Commission's replies to reasoned options. In the view of the Polish Senat's EAC chairman, the Commission answers with a delay and neglects the views of national parliaments.[71] The views expressed by the Sejm's representative seem compatible with that of the Senat with regard to the impact of the reasoned opinions.[72] In the same vein, the Czech Senát suggests that the Commission should monitor and disclose the impact of the EWM on the legislative procedure.[73]

With a view to improving the functioning of the EWM, in May 2015, preceding the COSAC meeting, the Polish Sejm organised a working group meeting with an aim to improve the 'yellow card' procedure.[74] The discussion focused on the involvement and cooperation by national parliaments with regard to the Commission Work Programme; inclusion of the proportionality principle under the EWM; timing and quality of the Commission's replies and the extension of the submissions deadline from eight to 12 weeks.

Finally, the Czech Poslanecká sněmovna and the Senát, as well as the Polish Sejm, support the introduction of a new 'green card', which would build on the existing 'Barroso initiative', allowing parliaments to make constructive suggestions regarding policy or legislative proposals to the Commission without amending the Treaty.[75] In fact, the Czech Senát supported the first 'green card' on the reduction

[69] See, however, that the Czech Poslanecká sněmovna labels the EWM a 'great tool' for national parliaments. Czech Poslanecká sněmovna in Annex to the 23rd Bi-annual Report of COSAC at 115.

[70] Mr Edmund Wittbrodt, Chairman of the European Affairs Committee, Senat, Poland in House of Lords European Union Committee Report HL 151 of Session 2013–14, The Role of National Parliaments in the European Union, Written evidence at pp 312ff.

[71] ibid.

[72] Mr Andrzej Gałażewski, Vice Chairman of European Union Affairs Committee, Sejm, Poland in House of Lords European Union Committee Report HL 151 of Session 2013–14, The Role of National Parliaments in the European Union, Written evidence at p 310.

[73] Mr Miroslav Krejča, Chairman of the Committee on European Affairs, The Senát, Parliament of Czech Republic in House of Lords European Union Committee Report HL 151 of Session 2013–14, The Role of National Parliaments in the European Union, Written evidence at p 105.

[74] See: oide.sejm.gov.pl/oide/en/index.php?option=com_content&view=article&id=14900&Itemid=946.

[75] Annex to the 23rd Bi-annual Report of COSAC at 115, 128, 451 (no reply from the Polish Senat). See also chapter by Hettne in this volume.

of food waste within the EU, put forward by 16 other chairpersons of committees of national parliaments.[76]

IV. Reasoned Opinions

This section deals with the content of the reasoned opinions of Czech and Polish parliaments with the aim to highlight the questions raised under the EWM. First, the chambers conduct subsidiarity scrutiny, which consists of two aspects: the material and the procedural dimensions of the principle of subsidiarity.[77] In accordance with Article 5(3) TEU the material dimension of subsidiarity might be reviewed in the *national insufficiency test* and the *comparative efficiency test* as proposed by Schütze. Under the first test the Union shall act 'only if and in so far as the objectives of the proposed action cannot be sufficiently achieved by the Member States', which means that a Member State has 'inadequate means at its disposal for achieving the objectives of the proposed action'.[78] The second test permits the Union to act when the objectives of the proposed action can rather 'by reason of the scale or effects of the proposed action, be better achieved at Union level'. To put it differently, the EU should not act 'unless it could *better* achieve the objectives of the proposed action'.[79]

In response to a Commission proposal regarding the management of copyrights in musical works, the Polish Sejm in its material subsidiarity control put forward that the Member States themselves might achieve the objective of transparent management within the EU internal market, as it was already happening in Poland and the Commission had not proved that EU action in this respect would be more effective.[80] Subsidiarity is similarly understood in the lower Czech chamber, which argued with regard to the Commission proposal for the third-country seasonal workers directive that seasonal work can be dealt with by existing legislation and an EU action has no added value.[81] In the understanding of the Polish Senat the subsidiarity principle can be breached when a proposal does

[76] 220th Resolution of the Czech Senát of 12.8.2015, on the joint letter of members of parliaments of EU Member States to the European Commission (so-called 'green card') on food waste. For the proposal see the joint letter of 22.07.2015 from the members of parliamentary committees to the President of the Commission available at: www.parliament.uk/documents/lords-committees/eu-select/green-card/green-card-on-food-waste.pdf.

[77] A Estella De Noriega, *The EU principle of subsidiarity and its critique* (Oxford, Oxford University Press, 2002) at 105.

[78] K Lenaerts, 'Subsidiarity and Community competence in the field of education' (1994) 1 *Columbia Journal of European Law* 22.

[79] R Schütze, *From dual to cooperative federalism: the changing structure of European law* (Oxford, Oxford University Press, 2009) at 250.

[80] Polish Sejm, Reasoned Opinion of 12.10.2012 on COM(2012) 372.

[81] Czech Poslanecká sněmovna, Reasoned Opinion of 7.10.2010 on COM(2010) 379. For the Czech Senát see Reasoned Opinion of 9.10.2013 on COM(2013) 534.

not contain a supranational element and there is no need for harmonisation.[82] In some cases, the chambers assess only the fulfilment of the national insufficiency test. For example, the Czech Senát indicated with regard to the Commission proposal initiating the Eurojust reforms that the current systems of Member States could be improved leading to a better functioning of the regulation already in place.[83]

In addition, the substantive assessment of the subsidiarity principle was followed by the procedural scrutiny connected with the 'onus to justify' legislative proposals which rests on EU institutions.[84] Specifically, national legislatures check whether the Commission has justified the compatibility of proposed legislation with the subsidiarity principle.[85] The Czech Senát and to a large extent the Polish chambers found this type of subsidiarity breach in a number of proposals.[86] For example the Czech Senát opined that the Commission did not substantiate the proposed Eurojust reforms from the perspective of their compliance with the subsidiarity principle.[87]

The reasoned opinions of the Polish and Czech chambers focus on a number of relevant issues in the Commission proposals, going beyond the assessment of the subsidiarity principle. While the question on whether national parliaments should apply a broad scrutiny of Commission proposals that steps beyond their competence to monitor subsidiarity compliance indicated in Protocol No 2 is currently under discussion in national parliaments and EU legal scholarship alike, for descriptive purposes the issues raised by the Czech and Polish parliaments in their reasoned opinions are discussed below.[88] These include the evaluation by the chambers under analysis of the legal basis and proportionality of Commission proposals as well as criticism of delegations of executive powers to

[82] See Polish Senat, Reasoned Opinion of 21.10.2010 on COM(2010) 379.

[83] Czech Senát, Reasoned Opinion of 9.10.2013 on COM(2013) 535.

[84] G De Búrca, 'Re-appraising subsidiarity's significance after Amsterdam', *Harvard Jean Monnet Working Paper Series* No 7/99: jeanmonnetprogram.org/archive/papers/99/990701.html, 8.

[85] See X Groussot and S Bogojević, 'Subsidiarity as a Procedural Safeguard of Federalism' in L Azoulai (ed), *The question of competence in the European Union* (Oxford, Oxford University Press, 2014) at 235.

[86] See Sejm Reasoned Opinion of 12.10.2012 on COM(2012) 372 and Sejm Reasoned Opinion of 13.1.2012 on COM(2011) 560. See also in Sejm Reasoned Opinion of 25.11.2010 on COM(2010) 537 and also in Sejm Reasoned Opinion of 25.11.2010 on COM(2010) 539, Sejm Reasoned Opinion of 4.3.2011 on COM(2010) 799; Sejm Reasoned Opinion of 3.2.2011 on COM(2010) 728, Polish Senat Reasoned Opinion of 9.1.2013 on COM(2013) 614.

[87] Czech Senát, Reasoned Opinion of 9.10.2013 on COM(2013) 535.

[88] See Twenty-third Bi-annual Report: Developments in European Union Procedures and Practices Relevant to Parliamentary Scrutiny (6.5.2015) at 29 ff; Folketing, European Affairs Committee, 23 Recommendations to strengthen national parliaments in the changing European governance (January 2015); F Fabbrini and K Granat, 'Yellow Card, but No Foul': The Role of the National Parliaments under the Subsidiarity Protocol and the Commission Proposal for an EU Regulation on the Right to Strike' (2013) 50 *Common Market Law Review* 115; M Goldoni, 'The Early Warning System and the Monti II Regulation: The Case for a Political Interpretation' (2014) 9 *European Constitutional Law Review* 98; M Bartl, 'The Way We Do Europe: Subsidiarity and the Substantive Democratic Deficit' (2015) 21 *European Law Journal* 23.

the Commission, and the standards of protection of fundamental rights included in the Commission proposals (Czech chambers exclusively).[89]

The assessment of the legal basis of Commission proposals is connected with the close links between the principle of conferral and the principle of subsidiarity, both anchored in Article 5 TEU.[90] It is argued that 'if the Union already fails the competence test, a subsidiarity test even if conducted cannot possibly be positive'.[91] Within the Czech and Polish legislatures under analysis, the reasoned opinions of the Polish Sejm exemplify such scrutiny. For example, its reasoned opinion on the Common Consolidated Corporate Tax Base stated that the EU lacks competence of direct taxation and that the proposal was wrongly based on Article 115 TFEU.[92] Hence, in the view of the Sejm, 'exceeding competences conferred on the Union must be considered an infringement of the principle of subsidiarity'.[93] The chamber drew a similar conclusion in the case of the Commission proposal establishing an EU legal framework for determining jurisdiction and the law applicable to the property consequences of registered partnerships, stating that the issue at stake belongs to the area of substantive family law and would, as a result, introduce partnerships to the Polish legal order that currently does not provide for this type of institution.[94]

Thirdly, the compatibility of the Commission proposals with the proportionality principle was a crucial issue in some of the reasoned opinions.[95] Such an assessment requires an evaluation of the necessity of a measure, of its adequacy to achieve a desired goal and its conciliation with competing interests.[96] Both Polish chambers included an assessment of the proportionality principle in their reasoned opinions. Accordingly, the Polish Sejm assessed the Commission 'Women on boards' proposal as being in breach of the proportionality principle, since 'it

[89] For a detailed analysis of the content of the reasoned opinions of the Polish parliament see also C Mik, K Kuszel and M Zreda, 'Parlamenty narodowe wobec zasady pomocniczości w świetle prawa i praktyki Unii Europejskiej', BAS, Prace Studialne, nr 18/12/2014 at 95 available at: orka.sejm.gov.pl/WydBAS.nsf/0/DA2934F5B0C605DBC1257DB200459923/$file/Parlamenty_wobec_pomocniczosci.pdf.

[90] P Craig, *EU Administrative Law* (Oxford, Oxford University Press, 2010) at 40.

[91] Ph Kiiver, *The early warning system for the principle of subsidiarity: Constitutional theory and empirical reality* (Abingdon, Routledge, 2012) at 99. In contrast Judge Thomas Von Danwitz concludes that subsidiarity cannot settle the question of competence, even though that question might be related to the more general idea of subsidiarity. See T von Danwitz, 'Subsidiaritätskontrolle in der Europäischen Union' in K Hansmann K-P Dolde, S Paetow and E Schmidt-Assmann (ed), *Verfassung-Umwelt-Wirtschaft Festschrift für Dieter Sellner zum 75 Geburtstag* (Munich, CH Beck, 2010) at 40.

[92] Polish Sejm, Reasoned Opinion of 13.5.2011 on COM(2011) 121.

[93] ibid.

[94] Polish Sejm, Reasoned Opinion of 27.5.2011 on COM(2011) 127. See also Polish Sejm, Reasoned Opinion of 4.1.2013 on COM(2012) 614 and Reasoned Opinion of 10.10.2012 on COM(2012) 369 where it indicates the 'faulty legal basis' of the Commission proposal, but outside of the subsidiarity violation.

[95] For relationship between subsidiarity and proportionality principles see AG Toth, 'The principle of subsidiarity in the Maastricht Treaty' (1992) 29 *Common Market Law Review* 1079, 1083.

[96] A Stone Sweet and J Mathews, 'Proportionality balancing and global constitutionalism' (2008) 47 *Columbia Journal of Trans national Law* 72.

would suffice to adopt EU-wide measures aimed at standardizing the criteria of appointing members of company boards, without the need to establish binding parities'.[97] Similarly, the Czech Poslanecká sněmovna opined that binding quotas for women on boards are a 'measure of last resort'.[98] Moreover, the Polish Senat indicated that the benefits of maritime spatial planning and integrated coastal management that one of the Commission proposals obliged Member States to conduct were 'disproportionately low' as compared to their costs from a viewpoint of promoting maritime and coastal activities.[99] In the same vein, the Czech Senát argued that fulfilling the objective of increased recycling rates intended by the Commission proposal on waste management was not attainable taking into account its time and costs.[100]

Next, EU draft legislative acts conferring upon the Commission powers to adopt delegated or implementing acts in accordance with Articles 290 and 291 TFEU were the subject of scrutiny in reasoned opinions.[101] Both the Polish chambers and the Czech Poslanecká sněmovna often disapprove of such delegations of power to the Commission provided for in the draft legislative acts assessed under the EWM.[102] For example, the Czech Poslanecká sněmovna argued against the scale of delegations in the proposed tobacco products directive.[103] Similarly, the Polish Sejm and Senat, in a series of reasoned opinions, highlighted problems with the delegations of the basic draft legislative act. Specifically, they criticised the wide scope of powers delegated to the Commission;[104] the unclear choice between delegations by means of delegated or implementing acts;[105] the lack of an indication of the objectives, content, scope and duration of delegated power;[106] delegation of regulatory powers with regard to essential elements of the proposal by means of delegated acts;[107] and the subject-matters that the Commission aims at tackling by means of delegated acts.[108]

Although fundamental rights have found a prominent position in Article 6 TEU in the EU, national parliaments negatively assess their safeguards.[109] This

[97] Polish Sejm, Reasoned Opinion of 4.1.2013 on COM(2012) 614.

[98] Czech Poslanecká sněmovna, Reasoned Opinion of 6.12.2912, COM(2012) 614.

[99] Polish Senat, Reasoned Opinion of 23.04.2013 on COM(2013) 133.

[100] Czech Senát, Reasoned Opinion of 1.10.2014 on COM(2014) 397.

[101] R Schütze, '"Delegated" Legislation in the (new) European Union: A Constitutional Analysis' (2011) 74 *Modern Law Review* 661.

[102] Such an assessment under the EWS is widespread under the EWM. See C Moury, A Heritier and K Granat, 'The Contest for Power in Delegated Rule-Making' in C Bergström and D Ritleng (eds), *Rule-Making by the EU Commission: The New System for Delegation of Powers* (Oxford, OUP, 2016).

[103] Czech Poslanecká sněmovna, Reasoned Opinion of 24.1.2013 on COM(2012) 788, point 2.

[104] Polish Sejm, Reasoned Opinion of 25.11.2010 on COM(2010) 537 and of 4.3.2011 on COM(2010) 799.

[105] Polish Sejm, Reasoned Opinion of 25.11.2010 on COM(2010) 539.

[106] Polish Sejm, Reasoned Opinion of 4.2.2011 on COM(2010) 738.

[107] Polish Senat, Reasoned Opinion of 4.2.2011 on COM(2010) 738 and on COM(2010) 799.

[108] Polish Sejm, Reasoned Opinion of 25.11.2010 on COM(2010) 539; Polish Senat, Reasoned Opinion of 25.11.2010 on COM(2010) 537 and of 25.11.2010 on COM(2010) 539.

[109] R Schütze, 'Three 'Bills of Rights' for the European Union' (2011) 30 *Yearbook of European Law* 131.

is especially visible in the reasoned opinions of the Czech chambers which raised the question of fundamental rights protection offered by Commission proposals. The Czech Senát underlined in its reasoned opinion that the European Public Prosecutor's Office (EPPO) regulation violates fundamental rights guaranteed by the Czech constitutional system and by the ECHR (and in the view of the chamber, in consequence, violates also the Charter of Fundamental Rights). Especially problematic were the right to a lawful judge, due to the EPPO's choice of the competent court, and the right to fair trial, due to single-instance procedures and lack of appeal procedures against the EPPO decisions.[110] In turn the Czech Poslanecká sněmovna argued that the EU might also propose standards that are too high. Specifically, the chamber opined that the Commission proposal on third-country seasonal workers would raise the standard of social rights of the workers from third countries beyond that offered to EU citizens in cases where transitional periods apply.[111]

Finally, in their content the reasoned opinions of the Czech Poslanecká sněmovna are rather succinct as compared to the upper chamber's opinions that contain many more comments on the substance of the proposals. The Polish Sejm also offers some general comments on the proposals, as for example with regard to the proposal 'on clinical trials on medicinal products for human use' where the chamber indicated its reservations about the 'general concept' of the proposal, since it concerns 'matters of strictly national character and of the ethical aspects of the clinical trial'.[112]

V. Debates and Votes under The EWM

This section studies the debates in the parliamentary committees or plenary sessions and the voting patterns for all the reasoned opinions issued by the Polish and the Czech parliaments. The aim is to uncover whether the respective parliamentary chambers gained some independence from their governments under the EWM and whether there is a party division on issuing a reasoned opinion.

A. Parliament's Independence from Government's Views under the EWM

The first issue to consider is the extent to which under the EWM the Czech and Polish parliamentary chambers act independently from their respective

[110] Czech Senát, Reasoned Opinion of 9.10.2013 on COM(2013) 534.

[111] Czech Poslanecká sněmovna, Reasoned Opinion of 22.9.2010 on COM(2010) 379. See in the same vein the Polish Senat, Reasoned Opinion of 21.10.2010 on COM(2010) 379.

[112] Polish Sejm, Reasoned Opinion of 10.10.2012 on COM(2012) 369.

governments. This challenge is based on the assumption that it is rather improbable that a national parliament's majority would take a different position from that of the government on the issue of subsidiarity.[113] The analysis of the debates in the EACs and the plenary debates in Poland and in the Czech Republic shows a different state of affairs in each of the Member States under analysis despite the fact that both depict a consensus model with executive power-sharing in broad coalition cabinets as opposed to the Westminster model characterised by concentration of executive power in one-party and the government dominant vis-à-vis the parliament.[114]

In the Czech Poslanecká sněmovna and the Senát, the position of the government and of the parliament with regard to subsidiarity tends to be the same.[115] However in Poland, the chambers disagreed with the government on a number of occasions. Specifically, this was the case in the Sejm with regard to the Commission proposal on a Common Consolidated Corporate Tax Base;[116] on clinical trials on medicinal products for human use,[117] on the management of copyrights in musical works.[118] Both the Sejm's and the Senat's position differed from that of the government regarding the issuing of the reasoned opinion on the 'Women on Boards' proposal.[119] In addition, for a number of early Commission proposals the government did not deliver any opinion on subsidiarity either in the proceedings

[113] FC Mayer, 'Competences-Reloaded-The Vertical Division of Powers in the EU and the New European Constitution' (2005) 3 *International Journal of Constitutional Law* 493, 502. In addition, de Wilde argues that '[g]overnment frequently cajole their backbenchers into supporting them using the possible loss of a parliamentary majority as a threat. Given such a situation, it seems unlikely that parliament will send a reasoned opinion to the Commission without the consent of its government'. See P de Wilde, 'Why the Early Warning Mechanism does not Alleviate the Democratic Deficit' *OPAL Online Paper* No 6/2012: www.opal-europe.org/index.php?option=com_content&view=article&id=76&Itemid=108, at p 9.

[114] A Lijphart, *Patterns of Democracy, Government Forms in Thirty-Six Countries* (New Haven CT, Yale University Press, 2012). See also Chapter 13 by Cygan in this volume who points out the relatively more important ministerial accountability in comparison to the EWM.

[115] For Poslanecká sněmovna: Minister of Labour and Social Affairs, EAC meeting of 6.12.2012; Minister of Agriculture Czech, EAC meeting of 24.1.2013; For Senát: See Minister of Interior, Stenographic record of 23rd Senát meeting Parliament of the Czech Republic (The first day of the meeting—22.9.2010) and in the reasoned opinion itself on COM(2010) 379; Minister of Justice Czech Parliament, the Senát 9th term Stenographic record of the 14th meeting of the Senát on COM(2013) 534 and 535; Minister of Industry and Trade Czech Parliament, the Senát 9th term Stenographic record of the 25th meeting of the Senát (the first day of the meeting—1.10.2014).

[116] COM(2011) 121. According to the government the directive will resolve transparency issues. See Pełny zapis przebiegu posiedzenia Komisji do Spraw Unii Europejskiej, 26.9.2012, p 5.

[117] COM(2012) 369. Sprawozdanie Stenograficzne z 23. Posiedzenia Sejmu Rzeczypospolitej Polskiej, 10.10.2012, p 8.

[118] COM(2012) 372. Sejm, Sprawozdanie Stenograficzne z 23. Posiedzenia Sejmu Rzeczypospolitej Polskiej, 11.10.2012, p 243.

[119] COM(2012) 614. Sejm, Sprawozdanie Stenograficzne z 31. Posiedzenia Sejmu Rzeczypospolitej Polskiej, 3.1.2013, p 86. The government's representative stated that the position of the government is favourable to the aim of the directive, but the way to achieve this aim should be more flexible. No stance on subsidiarity. See Sprawozdanie Stenograficzne z 25. Posiedzenia Senatu, 9.1.2013, p 151.

before the Sejm or the Senat.[120] The Polish government itself gave a plausible explanation of the different views on subsidiarity. Specifically, during the Sejm debate on the Commission regulation on clinical trials on medicinal products for human use, the representative of the government justified the support for the draft proposal by stating that '[the government] does not want to be seen as blocking all the [EU] initiatives'.[121] This explanation might apply also to the other cases of disagreement between the government and parliament on issuing a reasoned opinion.[122] Nonetheless, it also underlines that the Polish parliament, and especially the Sejm, has gained some independence under the EWM.

In contrast to that, in the Czech Republic, the views of the government and the chambers overlapped in all cases where the reasoned opinion was issued.[123] Interestingly, this was the case also with regard to the EPPO and Eurojust reform proposals, when the Social Democrats had the majority in the Senát while the government was conservative.[124]

B. Unanimity on Issuing the Reasoned Opinions

Secondly, this chapter studies whether the decision to conduct a subsidiarity review through the EWM echoes divisions between the parliamentary majority (coalition) and the minority (opposition) or whether issuing a reasoned opinion is a unanimous decision.

During the votes on the reasoned opinions in the EAC of the Czech Poslanecká sněmovna, the deputies took the resolution to issue a reasoned opinion on the third-country seasonal workers proposal and on the tobacco products directive unanimously (with some of the members abstaining),[125] while there was more

[120] COM(2010) 799: The government does not assess subsidiarity, but expressed criticism with regard to merits similarly to the parliament. See Sejm Biuletyn z posiedzenia Komisji do Spraw Unii Europejskiej, 18.2.2011; COM(2010) 537 and COM(2010) 539: The government did not take a specific stance on subsidiarity, yet criticised the lack of precision of delegation. Sejm, EAC, 5.11.2010, Biuletyn Nr 4349/VI; COM(2010) 728: No position of the government on subsidiarity, but it seconds the EU Affairs Committee in the criticism of extensive implementation powers to the Commission. Sejm, EAC, 21.1.2011, p 7; COM(2010) 745: Not specified. Senat, Zapis Stenograficzny, Wspólne posiedzenie Komisji Rolnictwa i Rozwoju Wsi oraz Komisji Spraw Unii Europejskiej, 3.2.2011.

[121] In response, one of the MPs proposed that a reasoned opinion should change the future position of the government. See Pełny zapis przebiegu posiedzenia Komisji do Spraw Unii Europejskiej, 29.8.2012, p 12.

[122] See opinions mentioned nn 114–117 above.

[123] COM(2010) 379: Minister of Interior, Stenographic record of 23rd Senate meeting Parliament of the Czech Republic (The first day of the meeting—22.9.2010); COM(2012) 614: Minister of Labour and Social Affairs, Czech Chamber of Deputies EAC meeting of 6.12.2012; COM(2012) 788: See the Reasoned Opinion of 24.1.2013 of the Czech Poslanecká sněmovna; COM(2014) 397: Minister of Industry and Trade, Czech Parliament, Stenographic Record 25th meeting of the Senate (1st day meeting—1.10.2014).

[124] Minister of Justice Czech Parliament, the Senát 9th term Stenographic record of the 14th meeting of the Senát (the first day of the meeting—9.10.2013).

[125] On COM(2010) 379: Poslanecká sněmovna EAC, meeting of 7.10.2010, Votes 6-0-0. On COM(2012) 788: Poslanecká sněmovna, EAC meeting of 24.1.2013, Vote 7-0-1.

contestation on 'Women on Boards'.[126] The analysis of voting procedures on the reasoned opinions in the Czech Senát indicates that there was rather a consensus among the senators that the reasoned opinion should be put forward to the Commission. More specifically, the parties on both sides of the political spectrum broadly accepted the reasoned opinions.[127] One explanation of this situation could be that EU issues are no longer as divisive as before accession and are nowadays more technical than strategic.[128]

In the same vein, a noticeable convergence between the coalition and opposition can be found in both the Sejm and the Senat.[129] In principle, when the governing coalition proposes a reasoned opinion, it passes through the chambers. In contrast, it is harder for the parliamentary opposition to succeed in the subsidiarity review. For example, the reasoned opinion sponsored by one of the opposition parties (PiS) regarding the Commission proposal for the programme FISCUS, supporting cooperation between tax and customs authorities of the Member States, failed to get sufficient support.[130]

Although there seems to be a major convergence of views between the political parties with regard to subsidiarity violations regardless of the fragmentation of the domestic party system, visibly some cases display the right-left political cleavage.[131] The party positions on specific policy issues tend to play a role in the question whether to issue a reasoned opinion in the lower chambers of the Member States under analysis.[132] In consequence, the parliamentarians follow their general party programme, rather than the specific party stance on EU affairs.

[126] Poslanecká sněmovna, EAC meeting of 6.12.2012, Vote 7-2-3 (2 disagreed, 3 abstained).

[127] On COM(2010) 379: 23rd meeting, resolution of Senát of 22.9.2010, vote no 562, 44 of ODS, ClubTop9 and some of ČSSD were in favour of the reasoned opinion and 10 abstained (ČSSD and one independent—main argument was protection of third country nationals). On COM(2013) 534 and COM(2013) 535, 14th meeting of the Senát of 9.10.2013, 50 in favour and 4 abstained (mostly ODS) and 48 in favour, 5 abstain (mostly ODS); On COM(2014) 397, 25th meeting, 1.10.2014, 52 in favour and 3 abstain (mostly ODS).

[128] Hrabálek and Strelkov (n 50 above) at 496. Hrabálek and Strelkov put this forward as an argument why it is almost always the EAC taking binding resolutions for the Chamber in EU affairs. This is in contrast to the Senát where the state plenary acts as a 'gatekeeper' especially when the chairmanship in the EAC was of a different political colour than the majority in the Senát.

[129] For the purposes of the study on the Polish parliament, I disregarded single votes of MPs or Senators that were not in favour of issuing a reasoned opinion.

[130] Proposal for a Regulation of the European Parliament and of the Council establishing an action programme for customs and taxation in the European Union for the period 2014–20 (FISCUS) and repealing Decisions N° 1482/2007/EC and N° 624/2007/EC, COM(2011) 607. See Sejm, Sprawozdanie Stenograficzne z 5. Posiedzenia Sejmu, 13.1.2012, p 237 ff.

[131] In addition, the socio-economic cleavage is visible in other Member States. See Granat (n 32 above).

[132] This outcome contrasts with the findings of the study by Gattermann and Hefftler, who argue that 'the traditional conflict along the left-right lines 'hardly matters for the subsidiarity review.' See K Gattermann and C Hefftler, 'Political Motivation and Institutional Capacity: Assessing National Parliaments' Incentives to Participate in the Early Warning System' *OPAL Online Paper* No 15/2013 at p 17. Although the reasoned opinions described in this chapter have been issued and hence the cleavage did not impact on the number of issued reasoned opinions, the analysis of the parliamentary debates shows that arguments along the right-left division are in fact present in the debates of EU legislative proposals.

In the first example, in the Sejm, the Democratic Left Alliance, a party in favour of the introduction of partnerships into the Polish legal order, did not support the reasoned opinion on the Commission proposal on the property consequences of registered partnerships with an objective to enable management and division of property of such couples. The party argued that 'it is in line with the plans or program of the SLD that supports the legalisation of partnerships in Poland'.[133] The second instance of a right-left division took place in the Sejm and in the Czech Poslanecká sněmovna. On the Polish side, the majority of the governing coalition and the conservative MPs of the parliamentary opposition (PiS, SP) supported the reasoned opinion against the Commission's proposal introducing gender quotas on non-executive boards of companies. In contrast, the liberal opposition (SLD, Ruch Palikota) resisted the issuing of a reasoned opinion in this case, highlighting the need for gender equality on boards and the absence of national measures in this respect.[134] Interestingly, the case of the 'Women on boards' proposal was also the only case showing a lack of unanimity in the Czech parliament, beyond the cases where some MPs and senators abstained.[135] The Social Democrats (CSSD) and the communist party (KCSM) MPs who welcomed the Commission proposal underlined the existing inequalities between men and women in labour relations and remuneration in the Czech Republic.[136]

Finally, it has to be emphasised that the divisions are less visible in the Senates of the parliaments under analysis. This might be connected to the higher levels of politicisation of the lower chambers relative to the upper chambers.

VI. Assessment

In summary, the comparison between the Polish and Czech parliaments along the lines of the 'most similar cases' model suggests several plausible explanations (both structural and procedural) for the different approaches they adopt in their scrutiny of the subsidiarity principle, without identifying a strong single causal mechanism.

First, a structural argument has been made that the particular activity of the Czech Senát, the extensive participation in the 'Barroso initiative,' and more recently the participation in the first 'green card', is due to the relative weakness

[133] Own translation. Sejm, Sprawozdanie Stenograficzne z 93. Posiedzenia Sejmu Rzeczypospolitej Polskiej, 25.5.2011, p 92.

[134] Sejm, Sprawozdanie Stenograficzne z 31. Posiedzenia Sejmu Rzeczypospolitej Polskiej, 3.1.2013, p 83. Vote: Sejm, Sprawozdanie Stenograficzne z 31. Posiedzenia Sejmu Rzeczypospolitej Polskiej, 4.1.2013, p 133. See that a number of the governing majority MPs abstained, probably from the more liberal wing; still enough MPs supported the reasoned opinion.

[135] The MPs that voiced their support for the proposal came from KCSM (Communist Party of Bohemia and Moravia) and CSSD (Czech Social Democratic Party).

[136] Poslanecká sněmovna, EAC meeting of 6.12.2012, Vote 7-2-3 (2 disagreed, 3 abstained).

of that chamber in the parliamentary system, which the Senát aims to counter by establishing a strong profile on EU affairs.[137] In the same vein, the upper chambers in other examples of asymmetric bicameralism discussed in this volume, such as the French Sénat, see the EWM as an avenue to enhance their role in the national system.[138] In addition, even in the symmetric Italian bicameralism, the Senato takes a more active role both under the EWM and in the 'Barroso initiative' in the face of possible constitutional reforms diminishing its role and a more general trend of strengthening of the upper chambers by the Lisbon Treaty reforms.[139] Whilst all these explanations are plausible, it is worth noting that the Polish Senat is subject to a similar asymmetry as the Czech and French upper chambers and nonetheless chooses to pursue a different, more balanced route. Thus, the Czech and other examples do not alone warrant inference of causality.

A second group of arguments focuses on the political stance of parties in power towards European integration, pointing out that a particularly Europhile party may prefer to pursue dialogue through the 'Barroso initiative' over a possible confrontation with the Commission through formally issued reasoned opinions. In particular, Hrabálek and Strelkov argue that the Czech Social Democratic party may want to protect its credibility at EU level.[140] Visibly, in the Czech lower chamber, all the reasoned opinions to date have been issued by the governing conservative coalition. In addition, the perception of the EWM as a Eurosceptic tool is evident also in France (low number of reasoned opinions and high number of 'Barroso initiative' opinions in the pro-European French Assemblée nationale in contrast to the traditionally more Eurosceptic Sénat).[141] A similar analysis of pro-European behaviour can be conducted for the parties in power in Poland but, however, offer different results. Since 2007 the Civic Platform, which is seen as a Europe-friendly party, has controlled both houses of parliament, but this situation did not prevent it from actively making its case through issuing reasoned options. The approach taken by the EU-friendly parliamentary majority hence might not be decisive for the participation in the EWM.

Thirdly, procedural aspects of the EWM may play a crucial role in different levels of participation of parliaments: the national scrutiny procedures for the EWM and the eight-week time constraint for submission of the reasoned opinions. Since the EWM procedures at the national level are similar in the Czech and the Polish chambers (centralised and mixed) this aspect seems not to play a role for their activity.[142] Due to the cycles of parliamentary work and not very frequent EACs'

[137] Hrabálek and Strelkov (n 50 above) at 503. For possible explanations of the activity of upper chambers, including the Czech Sénat under the EWM, see M Romaniello, 'Assessing Upper Chambers' Role in the EU Decision-Making Process', *Luiss Guido Carli School of Government Working Paper Series* 26/2015 at 15.

[138] See Chapter 12 by Tacea on the French Parliament in this volume.

[139] See Chapter 11 by Lupo on the Italian Parliament in this volume.

[140] Hrabálek and Strelkov (n 50 above) at 504.

[141] See Chapter 12 by Tacea on the French Parliament in this volume.

[142] In contrast, Lupo shows that the different procedures in the Italian chambers (especially their 'kick off') influence the number of reasoned opinions issued. See Chapter 11 by Lupo in this volume.

meetings the participation in the EWM might be impaired.[143] For example, the Czech Senát adopted a reasoned opinion on the right to strike proposal and on the proposal for recovery and resolution of credit institutions, which however were not submitted within the eight-week period.[144] In contrast the 'Barroso political dialogue' allows for a flexible submission of contributions. The eight-week deadline in the EWM seems less problematic for the Polish parliament. The EAC committees meet regularly; in addition, the reasoned opinions are voted on in the plenary and one evident case where the reasoned opinion was not agreed to was due to the lack of support rather than lack of time. Yet, the wish to increase the time available for drafting the reasoned opinions has also been voiced by the Polish parliament.[145]

VII. Conclusion

This chapter presented the functioning of the EWM in the Czech Republic and in Poland. In these two relatively recent new EU Member States the position of the parliament in the constitutional system is similar, since they represent the unequal bicameralism model. The powers of the legislatures in the Czech Republic and in Poland in EU affairs were also strengthened with the entry into force of the Lisbon Treaty. Accordingly, the Czech and the Polish chambers rely to a large extent on the EACs for the subsidiarity scrutiny. Due to these similarities, the Czech and the Polish parliaments could be perceived as 'two peas in a pod'. Surprisingly, their activity under the EWM is very different. The Polish Sejm and the Senat have issued around a dozen of reasoned opinions each, while their Czech counterparts remained rather quiet in this procedure. Moreover, the Czech Senát relied much more on the 'Barroso initiative', becoming one of the most active parliaments EU-wide in this respect. The aim of this chapter was hence to explore the possible reasons for this discrepancy.

The chapter has first studied the content of the reasoned opinions that the Czech and the Polish parliaments issued under the second Barroso Commission, which covered the period since the entry into force of the Lisbon Treaty until December 2014. The reasoned opinions show that both parliaments apply a rather generous reading of the EWM under Protocol No 2. They assess the material and procedural

[143] Hrabálek and Strelkov (n 50 above) at 502.

[144] Czech Senát, Reasoned Opinion of 14.06.2012 on COM(2012) 130 and Reasoned Opinion of 25.10.2012 on COM(2012) 280. Senator Miroslav Krejča indicated these cases during the sitting of the Senát of 9.10.2013, Stenographic record of the 14th meeting of the Senát (the first day of the meeting—9.10.2013).

[145] See n 70 above.

aspects of the subsidiarity principle, in addition to assessments of the legal basis and proportionality of Commission proposals. Moreover, the Polish parliament's focus is also on the legal basis of proposals and conferrals of the delegated and implementing power on the Commission, while the Czech parliament emphasised the fundamental rights questions raised by the proposed draft acts.

The analysis of the debates and of the voting on the reasoned opinions in the Czech and Polish parliaments has offered some more insights into the application of the EWM in both Member States. In Poland and in the Czech Republic, the political parties usually vote unanimously that a reasoned opinion should be issued. However, some right-left political cleavages are visible in the debates under the EWM. The in-depth study of the EWM in Poland and the Czech Republic shows also that beyond the unequal number of the reasoned opinions issued by the chambers, there is a visible difference in the relationship vis-à-vis the government. Specifically, in a number of cases the Polish Sejm has issued a reasoned opinion although the government did not establish a subsidiarity violation by the Commission proposals at stake. It was hence argued that the chamber became more independent from the government under the EWM than the Polish Senat or the Czech chambers.

Finally, the chapter attempted to give some explanation for the dissimilar application of the subsidiarity scrutiny in the two 'most similar cases'. First, the argument that the Czech Senát has built a strong profile in the 'Barroso initiative' due to its generally rather limited competences in Czech bicameralism was rejected, since the Polish Senat has the same position as its Czech counterpart and did not take a corresponding approach under the EWM. Secondly, the argument that a pro-European stance by political parties bars the parliament from issuing a reasoned opinion does not offer an explanation for the differentiated functioning of the EWM in Poland and the Czech Republic. Visibly, the Polish Euro-friendly coalition parliament, in contrast to the Czech parliament, did not limit its participation under the EWM. Lastly, the concerns of the parliaments with the eight-week limit for submitting the reasoned opinions and its interplay with the agenda of the parliament might offer some—however, probably not the only—explanation for the activity of the EWM in Poland and the Czech Republic.

16

The Trajectory of the Early Warning Mechanism

MARCO GOLDONI AND ANNA JONSSON CORNELL

I. Introduction

Despite the constant growth of scholarship around subsidiarity review, a definitive evaluation of the nature and the performance of the Early Warning Mechanism (EWM) would still remain premature at this stage. One can detect trends and potential changes, but it is still impossible to pass a definitive judgment upon its real impact. As stated in the Introduction to this volume the Lisbon Treaty hoped to achieve two constitutional goods relevant for this study: a democratisation of EU ordinary law-making and a new European activism of the national parliaments through the policing of subsidiarity. Thus, the EWM was introduced in order to strengthen the respect for the principle of subsidiarity, on the one hand, and improve the anaemic role of the national parliaments, on the other hand. This was needed because the political and constitutional contexts would not easily allow it. Several factors still work as variables with a potential impact on the understanding and the functioning of the EWM. For example, as many contributors to this volume have shown, the election of the European Parliament in 2014 and the ensuing political debates have caused the attention of the national parliaments to drift away from subsidiarity review for a conspicuous amount of time. Of course, more compelling and urgent issues were to be discussed by national parliaments at a moment where the stability of the whole Euro area was clearly at stake.[1] National parliaments were also asked to be involved in the new economic governance of the Eurozone. In particular, the European semester and the Fiscal Compact required national parliaments to take up an oversight role in the process, even though it is often claimed that the acceptance of this role is more a sign of marginality rather

[1] On the performance of national parliaments during the crisis see K Auel and O Hönig, 'Parliaments in the Euro Crisis: Can the Losers of Integration Still Fight Back?' (2014) 52 *Journal of Common Market Studies* 1184.

than anything else.[2] Other factors are more of an institutional design and constitutional character, for example whether a centralised or decentralised model for national scrutiny has been adopted, the role of the plenary; the relation between the national parliament and the government; the institutional and administrative capacities of each parliamentary chamber; and the specific sensitivity of each parliamentary chamber toward different subjects of policy-making so that certain issues trigger a heightened level of scrutiny and others a lessened level, etc.

Despite the previous cautionary remarks, certain traits of the EWM have unfolded throughout its practice and the rapidly developing research around it is shedding further light on this institutional tool. Moreover, the political context suggests that there could be further developments in the near future affecting the practice of the EWM. National parliaments (or, at least, some of them) have already taken a reflexive stance upon the EWM and they have formulated possible adjustments to make it more effective. Proposals for reforming this instrument are proliferating and political developments might also trigger further change. For example, the negotiations between the United Kingdom and the EU about Brexit have produced some interesting modifications to subsidiarity review, on which more will be said in the following sections.[3] This chapter will provide a provisional evaluation of the practice of the EWM and of its impact upon national and regional parliaments. It will also focus on the direction that the EWM might take in the near future, with an assessment of the proposals currently on the table.

II. The Nature of the Early Warning Mechanism

It is not by chance that much of the debate on the EWM has focused on its nature. This is due to a number of factors. First of all, the nature of subsidiarity is in itself still a matter of concern. Indeed, how subsidiarity ought to be implemented was one of the concerns behind the introduction of the EWM (the other being the involvement of the national parliaments). It might still be discussed whether subsidiarity is a rule or a principle and, if it is a principle, whether it ought to be applied according to legal or political rationality.[4] Secondly, it is clear that a line ought to be drawn around the political salience of subsidiarity. Given that subsidiarity is involved at the inception of the law-making process and that the

[2] S Puntscher Riekmann and D Wydra, 'Representation in the European State of Emergency: Parliaments against Governments? (2013) 35 *Journal of European Integration* 565.

[3] The conclusions reached at the European Council of 18 and 19 February 2016 on UK membership are a bit vague on the red card (it is stated that 'appropriate arrangements will be made' in order to make sure that the reasoned opinions will be taken into account). The text of the conclusions is available at the following address: www.consilium.europa.eu/en/press/press-releases/2016/02/19-euco-conclusions/ (for subsidiarity review see p 12).

[4] Important reflections on this issue have been provided by A Estella de Noriega, *The EU Principle of Subsidiarity and Its Critique* (Oxford, Oxford University Press, 2002); R Schütze, 'Subsidiarity after Lisbon: Re-inforcing the Safeguards of Federalism?' (2009) 68 *Cambridge Law Journal* 525.

working definition of subsidiarity is predominantly legal as it is the one contained in Article 5.3, there is always a legal dimension pertaining to subsidiarity review. The framing of the process of scrutiny pushes institutional actors to formalise their position by making reference to a legal point. But what is also at stake in this discussion is whether subsidiarity review can and should also accommodate a political dimension in the arguments presented in favour or against the respect of the subsidiarity principle. The answer is dictated not only by the content of the principle of subsidiarity, but actually by the larger context of European integration. More concretely, determining how subsidiarity review ought to be conducted entails a view on the pace and direction of European integration. It also entails an understanding of the role of national and supranational institutions and the respective roles in the European constitutional balance. Thirdly, at a normative level, the nature of subsidiarity review is also critical for the organisation of powers managing it. In other words, the determination of how subsidiarity scrutiny ought to be conducted will have to be reflected in the distribution of competences among institutions.

These are matters of the highest relevance for the practice of the EWM because the latter is dependent upon the understanding of subsidiarity by the national parliaments and the Commission. It is certainly important for a proper reconstruction of the practice of the EWM to bear in mind how national parliaments interpret their contribution to European integration. From the empirical perspective, the chapters of Parts II and III draw a rather clear picture. The vast majority of the parliamentary chambers analysed in this book see in the EWM a 'political process' which might also have a legal dimension. In his chapter (Chapter 2), Ian Cooper reconstructs three different logics of acting in EU law-making and shows how different parliamentary chambers have adopted them. While there are still a number of parliamentary chambers committed to a legalistic understanding of subsidiarity review (for example, the Finnish *Eduskunta* and French *Sénat*), others have by now started using the new instrument in a political way.[5] This is not surprising given that parliamentary chambers, as varied as they can be, are mostly political institutions. Hence, they tend to act under political incentives in ways that have political resonance. Thus, subsidiarity review is generally not understood as limited to a formal process to control the legality of the Commission's legislative proposals. Predictably, the more active chambers are those using the EWM in a wider, political sense, even though, it should be noted, some among them are also using the Political Dialogue rather frequently.[6] Despite palpable

[5] This is the case, for example, of the Dutch *Tweede Kamer*. For the sake of accuracy, it should also be remarked that there are inactive parliamentary chambers, aptly defined by Philip Kiiver as 'absentees': P Kiiver, *The Early Warning System for the Principle of Subsidiarity: Constitutional Theory and Empirical Reality* (Abingdon, Routledge, 2012) 136–39.

[6] The relation between the Political Dialogue and the EWM is not straightforward because some of their features overlap. For a recent and exhaustive analysis see D Jančić, 'The Game of Cards: National Parliaments in the EU and the Future of the Early Warning System' (2015) 52 *Common Market Law Review* 939.

developments toward Europeanisation, the self-perception of their role in European integration still varies, constituting one of the major variables in the explanation of each chamber's policy vis-à-vis subsidiarity review. One cannot judge a national parliament's performance just by sheer numbers (ie, the number of reasoned opinions sent to the Commission, even though this cannot be ignored altogether).[7] The example of the Scandinavian Member States is telling. Hailed as role models for other parliamentary chambers, by a closer look one can detect important differences in their approaches which can be accounted for by bearing in mind the variation in the respective political systems, the peculiarities of the national constitutions and the local political culture. In light of these considerations, it is possible to conclude that national parliaments tend to adopt mostly a political view of subsidiarity review and hence to use the EWM in a political way, which is frequently influenced by the national political and constitutional context. This is manifested in many reasoned opinions sent to the Commission, which are often drafted in a way that goes beyond subsidiarity concerns. We will return to this question in the following section.

Another layer of the debate concerning the EWM takes place at the normative level: how *should* national parliaments understand the EWM and subsidiarity review? Again, the main poles of this debate are between those who advocate a legal conception of subsidiarity and the EWM and those who advocate a political interpretation. In between, it is foreseeable that a third way, trying to make the two sides compatible will grow in the near future. According to the first group, the principle of subsidiarity is legal in nature; hence, it ought to be implemented by legal means and according to legal rationality. National parliaments would be legitimately given this task because they are directly affected by the legal abuse of subsidiarity.[8] A political take on subsidiarity review might subvert the logic of EU law-making and have an impact on the delicate constitutional balance of powers in the EU. A political approach to subsidiarity review might bring about, in the long term, a transformation of functions performed by the EWM. This is the case because arguing or negotiating politically about subsidiarity is a practice that cannot be severed off from other important aspects like proportionality analysis and the respect of certain traits of national identity (Article 4.2 TEU).[9] The second

[7] An attempt at capturing the efficacy of national parliaments' activities not only with the EWM, but in all European affairs, has been made by K Auel, O Rozenberg and A Tacea, 'Fighting Back? And if So, How? Measuring Parliamentary Strength and Activity in EU Affairs' in C Hefftler et al (eds), *The Palgrave Handbook of National Parliaments and the European Union* (Basingstoke, Palgrave Macmillan, 2015) 60–93. See, also, T Winzen, 'National Parliamentary Control of European Union Affairs: A Cross-National and Longitudinal Comparison' (2012) 35 *West European Politics* 657; T Winzen, 'European Integration and National Parliamentary Oversight Institutions' (2013) 14 *European Union Politics* 297.

[8] For a development of this view see F Fabbrini and K Granat, 'Yellow Card, but no Foul: The Role of the National Parliaments under the Subsidiarity Protocol and the Commission Proposal for an EU Regulation on the Right to Strike' (2013) 50 *Common Market Law Review* 115; cf P Kiiver, *The Early Warning System for the Principle of Subsidiarity* (n 5 above) at 138.

[9] It is questionable whether the principle of conferral belongs to the same category of subsidiarity or to a different level: the chapters by Cooper and Hettne (Chapters 2 and 3) put forward alternative views on this matter.

group turns these arguments on their heads: ex ante subsidiarity review makes a difference only by allowing a series of political considerations to come into the picture. Otherwise, subsidiarity review remains without real traction. Either by protecting their national interests or by contributing to a deliberative enhancement of the quality of EU law-making, national parliaments are better predisposed to control the political impact of subsidiarity.[10]

At this stage, a beneficial development would be to find a third way between the political and legal aspects of subsidiarity review. Jörgen Hettne's contribution (Chapter 3) contains such a 'holistic' view of the EWM, which leaves space to legal considerations by involving, in limited circumstances, the CJEU ex ante without sacrificing its political salience.[11] The inspiration comes from the opinion demanded, according to Article 218.11 TFEU, from the CJEU on the compatibility of international agreements with the Treaties. The same, argues Hettne, could be demanded by a certain number of national parliaments if they have serious doubts about the compatibility of a proposal with the constitutional principles of the Union. The main point of Hettne's proposal of what he calls a constitutional dialogue is challenging because it entails an expansion of the scope of the EWM. Anne Wetter's contribution provides a useful addition to this approach by stressing the importance of the procedural aspects of subsidiarity review, again with a view to perfecting the process and to making the eventual contribution of the CJEU more meaningful. These contributions hint beyond ideal types and they try to integrate the multiple aspects concerning subsidiarity review into a coherent and encompassing single process.

III. The Style and Content of Reasoned Opinions

A key indicator of the national parliaments' approach to subsidiarity review is the drafting of reasoned opinions, which represent on this issue the formal means of communication with the Commission. A caveat has to be introduced here: by itself, the style of reasoned opinions does not fully reveal the commitment of the parliamentary chamber to subsidiarity review, nor does the mere fact of the quantity of reasoned opinions sent to the Commission. The first aspect is important

[10] The principle of subsidiarity in the realisation of the Single Market has a de-politicising effect at the national level because it builds in a bias for harmonisation. For a reconstruction of this problem in EU lawmaking cf G Davies, 'Democracy and Legitimacy in the Shadow of Purposive Competences' (2015) 21 *European Law Journal* 2. Another important contribution on the de-politicising effects of subsidiarity is represented by M Bartl, 'The Way We do Europe: Subsidiarity and the Substantive Democratic Deficit' (2015) 21 *European Law Journal* 23.

[11] For an analysis of the Member States' reactions before the possibility was given to national parliaments to resort, through their governments, to the CJEU as introduced by Article 8 of Protocol no 2, see K Granat, 'Institutional Design of Member States for Ex-Post Subsidiarity Scrutiny' in N Lupo, M Cartabia and A Simoncini, *Democracy and Subsidiarity in the EU* (Bologna, Il Mulino, 2013) 421–45.

but it needs to be coupled with the relationship of the parliamentary chamber with its own government in order to have an accurate picture of the legislature's position. By itself, the second aspect may signal a certain disposition toward political activism, but recent quantitative research has proved that the propensity to issue reasoned opinions varies according to the circumstances of the political system and the topicality of the draft legislation under discussion.[12] Despite all of that, an analysis of the content and style of reasoned opinions stands out as the best indicator of a series of important points: how national parliaments conceive the subsidiarity principle; how they have organised the review and drafting process; how they understand their role in EU law-making; and how they frame the communication with the Commission.

In order to appreciate the drafting of reasoned opinions it is essential to make reference to a parliament's understanding of subsidiarity and the organisation of the reviewing process. Unsurprisingly, reasoned opinions drafted by parliamentary chambers committed to a legal approach to subsidiarity review are usually few in number and limited in their scope; two paradigmatic examples are provided by the Finnish *Eduskunta* and the French *Sénat*.[13] The analysis of the reasoned opinions of both chambers made by Anna Jonsson Cornell (Chapter 10) and Angela Tacea (Chapter 12) show that their content is strictly limited to subsidiarity review and the arguments are shaped in a predominantly legalistic form. In the Finnish case, the Grand Committee (the key player in subsidiarity scrutiny) and the plenary have stressed the element of the added value, focusing on the analysis of the Commission's effort to prove it. In the case of the French *Sénat* and its EAC the attention goes to the Commission's justification and in particular to its impact assessment.[14] The advantage of this position is that it is based on a clear working definition of subsidiarity extrapolated from the treaties[15] and, at least in the Finnish case, on a settled and defined strategy, ensuring in this way the stability of roles played by institutions in EU law-making (every institution knows in advance what to expect from the other) and a relatively smooth and limited review of the principle. The French *Sénat* maintains a relatively autonomous position from its government and the other chamber and such autonomy is reflected in the style of reasoned opinions.

Other parliamentary chambers have been either more assertive or less formalistic, and therefore they have drafted reasoned opinions bearing in mind a wider set of arguments. These parliamentary chambers might have a more or less political understanding of subsidiarity but we need to add immediately that the content and number of opinions sent might be explained by a heterogeneous range of

[12] K Gattermann and C Hefftler, 'Beyond Institutional Capacity: Political Motivation and Parliamentary Behaviour in the Early Warning System' (2015) 38 *West European Politics* 305.

[13] Other cases include the Austrian *Nationalrat* and the *Bundesrat*.

[14] Cf D Fromage, *Les Parlements dans L'Union Européenne après le Traité de Lisbonne* (Paris, L'Harmattan, 2015) 257–89.

[15] For an analysis of how subsidiarity ought to be legally reviewed see R Schütze, *From Dual to Cooperative Federalism* (Oxford, Oxford University Press, 2009) 224–35.

factors, ranging from a political use of subsidiarity to a different constitutional organisation of subsidiarity review (eg, the involvement of different parliamentary committees). The adjective 'political', here, has to be taken in a loose sense because it denotes argumentations that are not only legal, but contain different types of considerations. The Swedish *Riksdag* and the Danish *Folketing* are paradigmatic examples of a wide-scope approach to subsidiarity. Their reasoned opinions do not make clear reference to their conception of subsidiarity and they contain references to other principles or simply other remarks. Another example, illustrated by Granat in Chapter 15, concerns the assessment of the legal basis of the Commission's proposals (the principle of conferral) which is integrated into subsidiarity review by the Polish and the Czech chambers according to the idea that the violation of the principle of conferral determines a violation of subsidiarity.

At this point, it should not be surprising that a concern shared by many parliamentary chambers is where to draw the line between the principle of subsidiarity and the principle of proportionality. This preoccupation is confirmed by the recognition by many parliamentary chambers that they have no defined criteria for separating the two principles. To the contrary, certain parliaments state in their reasoned opinions that it is not possible to draw a clear distinction and that in the best case there is always an overlap, as recognised by, among other chambers, the Swedish *Riksdag*[16] and the Polish *Senat*. There are also cases, like the Czech *Senát* on the occasion of the EPPO legislative proposal, where the violation of fundamental rights is mentioned in the reasoned opinions sent to the Commission or, from the other side of the spectrum, the Czech lower chamber, on the Commission proposal on third-country seasonal workers, for raising the standards of social rights too high. Overall, it is extremely difficult to track a common pattern among these active parliamentary chambers for two main reasons: 1) some of them have different conceptions of how competence allocation should work; 2) national political and constitutional peculiarities still play a major role in drafting arguments on subsidiarity and EU law-making.

In light of these considerations, and despite the fact that a degree of homogeneity in the drafting of reasoned opinions would make the whole procedure more intelligible and would make the task of the Commission easier, it remains doubtful whether a standardised form for reasoned opinions would be feasible and even desirable at this stage. As a matter of fact, the recent 24th Bi-Annual COSAC report has documented the lack of consensus on the use of a common template despite the fact that at least 20 parliamentary chambers are using a fixed format for drafting reasoned opinions.[17] Nonetheless, when asked whether they would prefer a common template, national parliaments have voiced their disagreement and expressed a preference for non-binding, informal guidelines and lists of best

[16] On the use of proportionality by the Swedish parliament see A Jonsson Cornell, 'The Swedish Riksdag as Scrutinizer of the Principle of Proportionality' (2016) 12(2) *European Constitutional Law Review* 294–317.

[17] COSAC 24th Bi-Annual Report (2015) 19.

practices.[18] Among these best practices, it is worth mentioning the following ones: stating clearly in the text of the opinion that it is about Protocol no 2 and subsidiarity review; translating the text of the reasoned opinion into English and possibly uploading it onto IPEX as soon as possible, or, at least, providing an abstract of the opinion in English; including a summary of the argumentation. From the last two COSAC reports one can also evince the dissatisfaction of national parliaments concerning the quality of the Commission's replies to reasoned opinions. This specific concern will be taken up in the next section.

IV. The EWM's Internal and External Impact

This section deals with the impact of the EWM on national parliaments both in the relation with their national governments (internal impact) and in the relation with the Commission (external). From a constitutional perspective, both questions are extremely relevant. The former concerns the impact of the EWM on the national balance of powers. It should be noted that one of the arguments against a political use the EWM was indeed its potential for disrupting the separation of powers between national governments and national parliaments. Of course, this objection does not affect the legal dimension of the EWM because in that case national parliaments are basically enforcing the rule of law within EU law-making. But in the (majoritarian) case of a political use of the EWM the relationship between governments and parliaments might suffer because threatened by different institutional interests: parliamentarians being more attentive to the claims coming from their constituencies; national governments being more sensitive to reaching an agreement with their European partners. In theory, national parliamentary chambers might take an initiative against a particular EU legislative draft as a way to attack the national government when it's known that the latter would be in favour of the piece of legislation under discussion. The same argument is usually adopted against the use of the mandate by European Affairs Committees before the Council of ministers. In both cases, the national governments could be put in a difficult position and their efforts to reach an agreement at the European level, or even to remain in a significant bargaining position, might be jeopardised. Predictably, minority governments or coalition governments are those more exposed to these dangers.[19] Such a criticism puts emphasis on government's stability at the expense of a vibrant parliamentary activity.

[18] Even this option was strongly opposed by some parliamentary chambers: The Finnish *Eduskunta*, for example, or the Dutch *Tweede Kamer*, deemed Protocol no 2 of the Lisbon Treaty to be already providing sufficient guidance.

[19] See, for example, the dynamics within the Danish *Folketing* as underlined by Anna Jonsson Cornell in Chapter 10 of this volume.

Are these fears exaggerated? The chapters collected in Parts II and III show that this is the case. The EWM is an expensive and time-consuming procedure concerning issues that rarely are of public interest and visibility. Hence, there are not many incentives for national parliamentary chambers to use the EWM in an instrumental way against their own national governments. Moreover, the sceptics do not take into account that an independent (meaning: independent from the executive) parliamentary scrutiny of EU legislative drafts could represent a healthy practice for parliaments to claim back their political role in EU affairs, and to ensure that the powers referred to the EU by national parliaments are not overstretched.

As it was predicted even before the entry into force of the Lisbon Treaty,[20] a more conspicuous effect can be registered at the level of the relationship between parliamentary chambers in bicameral constitutional systems. The implementation of the EWM has taken different paths in bicameral systems. Given its semi-presidentialist constitutional system, particularly intriguing is the case of France, where, as Angela Tacea highlights in her contribution (Chapter 12), the EWM has had a different impact on its bicameral parliamentary system. In other words, the *Sénat* has taken up a different approach toward subsidiarity review when compared to the *Assemblée Nationale* and it has strengthened the separation between the two levels of parliamentary politics. The former's style is pervaded by technical and systematic scrutiny of the Commission's legislative proposals while the latter is more politicised and clearly more attentive to the government's position. The Polish case is also of great interest because, as Granat shows in Chapter 15, both chambers have sent reasoned opinions against their national government. The *Sénat* has been more active, but also the lower chamber (the *Sejm*) has sent reasoned opinions against the advice of the government. Two factors explain this case: one is that the Polish government has been afraid of appearing at the European level as an aggressive veto-player and the other one is that there have been periods where the parliamentary majority in the *Sénat* differed from the one supporting the government. The same dynamics of differentiation is at play in other parliamentary constitutional systems such as the United Kingdom, Austria, Germany,[21] and even in a state with symmetrical bicameralism like Italy.[22]

The second problematic question previously mentioned concerns the relation between national parliamentary chambers and the Commission. As already noted in the introduction, it is extremely difficult to assess the effective impact of parliaments' opinions upon the legislative draft. In fact, while numbers might help in evaluating how national parliamentary chambers understand their roles in EU

[20] P Kiiver, *National Parliaments in the European Union: A Critical View on the EU Constitution* (Alphen aan den Rijn, Kluwer, 2006) 134.

[21] See the details highlighted in the chapters by Auel, Tacea and Cygan (Chapters 12–14) in this volume. The UK stands out in one particular aspect: the use of the EWM is shaped by the key constitutional principle of political accountability.

[22] See the chapters by Nicola Lupo (Chapter 11) and Cristina Fasone (Chapter 8) in this volume.

affairs and how much they do invest, in terms of resources and political capital, in the functioning of the EWM, the same does not apply to the Commission's reaction to parliaments' opinions and, also, communications within the scheme of the Political Dialogue. The Commission has not recognised a single case where the Political Dialogue made a difference in the drafting of a legislative proposal while the EWM has produced *some* impact (the withdrawal of Monti II) but officially not because of the violation of subsidiarity. This still does not make the EWM utterly ineffective (as already noted, the EWM has brought about further Europeanisation of many parliamentary chambers and in some cases also affected the relation between parliamentary chambers and their national governments), but it highlights the difficulty for a single or a few parliamentary chambers to affect the European law-making process. Interparliamentary cooperation is strategic for reaching concrete outcomes and exercising a visible influence over the Commission. A critical mass (representing, crucially, the parliaments of the biggest Member States) is a necessary pre-condition for influencing EU legislative drafts through the EWM. Whether this ought to be an instrumental cooperation or a deliberative one is probably a matter to be decided according to the context and the circumstances.[23]

The real issue between national parliaments and the Commission concerns the reasoned opinions and in particular the quality of the Commission's reactions to objections concerning subsidiarity and the Political Dialogue. When the Commission took the time to reply to reasoned opinions, as happened with the Monti II, it did not address each and every parliamentary chamber with an ad hoc reply, but circulated a standardised answer to all parliaments. This is the complaint more frequently made by parliamentary chambers, which in the latest COSAC report pinpointed also the timeliness of the answers given by the Commission.[24] The lukewarm attitude of the Commission has a discouraging effect over national parliaments because, in a context of limited time and resources, the latter need to perceive that their efforts will be at least publicly recognised. The Juncker Commission has started by promising a new beginning. An often quoted statement by the vice-president of the Commission, Frans Timmermans,[25] shows that the new Commission is fully aware of the problem and promises to be more sensitive to the dialogue with national parliaments. If anything, this acknowledges the previous neglect by the Commission itself.

[23] A remarkable overview of the practices of interparliamentary cooperation is now available in N Lupo and C Fasone, *Interparliamentary Cooperation in the Composite European Constitution* (Oxford, Hart Publishing, 2016); cf B Crum and J Fossum (eds), *Practices of Interparliamentary Coordination in International Politics* (Colchester, ECPR, 2013).

[24] COSAC 24th Bi-Annual Report (2015) 18.

[25] 'I think that the Commission should be more proactive in coming to national parliaments whenever there is an issue that is of importance related to Europe in national parliaments. If national parliaments take the trouble to scrutinize European proposals, and they then flag a yellow card, the Commission should respond … in a political way'. COSAC meeting (Rome, 1 December 2014).

V. The Role of Regional Parliaments

This volume has shown that the EWM is predominantly but *not only* a two-level game.[26] Regional parliaments with legislative competences[27] or with devolved competences are part of a multi-level parliamentary field or, according to a different perspective, of a Euro-parliamentary system[28] and this position is relevant for subsidiarity review. While regional parliaments cannot participate directly in the EWM (with the exception of Belgium),[29] Article 6 of Protocol no 2 calls on national parliaments to consult with regional parliaments with legislative powers when appropriate to do so. As known, the modalities of the regional parliaments' involvement are left to each Member State, but it is clear that there is legal and political space opening up to these local legislatures.

Yet, obstacles to effective participation by regional parliaments are similar to those faced by national legislatures and they are even more acute. First of all, given the short period of eight weeks for subsidiarity review, time constraints operate in a stricter manner for regional parliaments. By the time they receive the proposal and given that they will have to communicate their views to the national parliament well before the eight-week deadline in order to allow the latter to incorporate them, if possible, in the reasoned opinion, time is short. Secondly, the relations between the regional parliaments and the national government are less strict and this fact limits the flow of information and the possibility of strategic choices. Thirdly, the electoral incentive is less strong for regional parliamentarians, in particular in light of the possibility that their concerns will not even be taken into account by the national parliament.[30] Finally, regional parliaments may voice their concerns about subsidiarity through the Committee of the Regions and its Subsidiarity Monitoring Network. The latter does not participate to the EWM but it has the right to bring ex post action before the CJEU.[31] Allowing

[26] The idea of two-level games has been formalised by R Putnam, 'Diplomacy and Domestic Politics: The Logic of Two Level Games' (1988) 42 *International Organisation* 427; for a recent application of two-level games to national parliaments see R Bellamy and A Weale, 'Political Legitimacy and European Monetary Union: Contract, Constitutionalism and the Normative Logic of Two-Level Games' (2015) 22 *Journal of European Public Policies* 257.

[27] Eight EU Member States have regions with legislative competences: Germany, Austria, Belgium, the United Kingdom, Spain, Italy, Portugal and Finland.

[28] The idea of a multi-level parliamentary field has been introduced by B Crum and J Fossum, 'The Multi-level Parliamentary Field' (2009) 1 *European Political Science Review* 249. For an application to the position of regional parliaments in the EWM procedure see Chapter 7 by Karolina Borońska-Hryniewiecka. Nicola Lupo refers to a Euro-parliamentary system to illuminate the interaction among different types of parliaments (European, national and regional) in A Manzella and N Lupo (eds), *Il sistema parlamentare Euro-nazionale* (Torino, Giappichelli, 2014) 22–24.

[29] See Chapter 9 in this volume, by Popelier and Vandenbruwene.

[30] But see the considerationof the circumstances which led to bestowal of a role upon regional parliaments in N Lupo, 'National and Regional Parliaments in the EU Decision-Making Process, after the Treaty of Lisbon and the Euro-Crisis' (2013) 5 *Perspectives on Federalism* E-1.

[31] E Domorenok, 'The Committee of the Regions: in Search of Identity' (2009) 19 *Regional and Federal Studies* 143, 154.

the Committee of the Regions to participate fully in the EWM would enhance its role in EU affairs. However, the diversity of its members and its proportionally regressive composition make the formation of a common position rather unlikely. As suggested by Fromage, the only concrete possibility would be to bring an action before the CJEU on procedural grounds claiming that the Commission did not take regional parliaments into due account.[32] Another obstacle is represented by the different constitutional positions of each subnational legislature in every Member State. The Treaty refers vaguely to regional parliaments but this notion captures subnational legislatures in both federal and regional states with different scopes of devolved powers. This is another aspect which also makes the horizontal cooperation among regional parliaments more difficult. As Karolina Borońska-Hryniewiecka notes, horizontal regional cooperation is on the rise, as the introduction of REGPEX (a website built after the example of IPEX) and the CALRE network confirm, but remains fragmented and dispersed. Yet, a rationalised horizontal cooperation is an essential precondition for an effective exercise of subsidiarity review by regional parliaments.

In fact, as documented by the chapters collected in Part II, regional parliaments suffer from being subject to two masters (the Commission and the national parliament), with perhaps the notable exception of Belgium. Such diversity of arrangements also shows the absence of a unitary scheme of vertical cooperation between national and regional parliaments. Yet, the recognition of this state of affairs should not lead to a completely negative judgment. By contrasting the relations between subnational and national parliaments in Italy and Spain, Fasone illustrates how, perhaps surprisingly, certain positive externalities can still emerge. While the Spanish case provides a story of disillusionment (after an initial interest, many regional bodies have now fully proceduralised subsidiarity review), the Italian case strikes a different note. Starting from a similar background, ie, non-Europeanised regional legislatures, Italy shows that the awareness of subsidiarity review has mobilised at least some of its regional parliaments, creating a new relation between them and the national parliament. While there is no single scheme encompassing all European experiences of vertical and horizontal cooperation, it can be noted that the successful participation by regional parliaments depends mostly on their own autonomous initiative.[33] Even though there are exceptions, it is fair to conclude that this is actually an unfortunate state of affairs. Regional

[32] The reflections on the use of procedural grounds made in Chapter 4 by Anna Wetter might turn out to be useful also for the case of regional parliaments.

[33] Gracia Vara Arribas and Anna-Lena Högenauer note an outstanding example represented by one Italian region: 'the degree of activity of the Assembly of Emilia-Romagna is notable, in that to achieve maximum visibility it refers its position to a wide range of actors: the Italian Senate and the Chamber of Deputies, the regional government, the Conference of the Presidents of the Legislative Assemblies of the Regions and Autonomous Provinces, the Subsidiarity Monitoring Network of the CoR, European, Italian regional assemblies, Members of the European Parliament and the members of the CoR from Emilia': 'Legislative Regions after Lisbon: A New Role for Regional Assemblies?' in C Hefftler et al (eds), *The Palgrave Handbook of National Parliaments and the European Union* (n 7 above) 143.

parliaments do not have enough resources to invest in trying to catch the attention of their national parliaments. It is worth trying to mobilise this type of institution only in carefully chosen circumstances. Only an attentive selection of the EU draft legislation which might concern subnational legislatures and a strengthening of the coordination and cooperation among these institutional entities might enable a more effective subsidiarity review.

VI. The Future of the EWM

The debate of the reform of the EWM is consubstantial with its history. Concerns on its proper functioning were present from the inception of this new tool. These worries have been constantly growing because of the parsimonious use of the instrument in the first six years of its application. The impression among practitioners and scholars is that the EWM has potential but this has been frustrated up to now. The need for reform is widely acknowledged and it touches upon the nature of the EWM cards and the kind of cooperation necessary to make subsidiarity review effective.

A. Toward a Rainbow of Cards?

The first proposal for a third kind of card, a red one, was already on the table during the working of the Convention for the Constitution in 2004. As is known, the red card was dropped because it was thought to be an unnecessary formal veto given to national parliaments on EU law-making. If such a measure had been introduced, then the Commission's monopoly of legislative initiative would have been possibly damaged. The original logic behind the red card entails that if half of all national parliamentary chambers voted against a Commission's legislative proposal, then the Commission would have a duty to withdraw it. This kind of card would represent an acknowledgement of the role of formal (de jure) veto players for national parliaments. The keenest proponent of the red card is the UK Parliament, which probably sees in its introduction the public acknowledgement that national parliaments' participation in EU law-making stands at least on an equal footing with that of EU institutions. However, it was recognised that there are some disadvantages affecting the red card. Apart from the higher threshold required for issuing a red card, there is the question of the concrete difference between this measure and the orange card. Clearly, the red card would formalise the veto power of national parliaments, but in many quarters it is believed that the orange card would already signal an effective political veto. Moreover, the creation of a formal red card may require Treaty change and possibly the modification of national constitutions. In a nutshell, the creation of a red card option was seen to entail disproportionate costs compared to its advantages.

Despite all these doubts, the recent renegotiation deal between the United Kingdom and the Member States' governments has re-opened the debate with the decisions taken in the meeting of 18 and 19 February 2016. The compromise reached by the Member States looks similar to a red card, but it is not the same as the original proposal.[34] The conclusions, under Section C ('Sovereignty'), illustrate how subsidiarity review might be improved in order to make national parliaments' contribution more effective. Two points stand out in this decision, which, it should be recalled, is legally binding. First, section C.2 stresses the fact that reasoned opinions issued by national parliaments ought to be taken into account by *all* European institutions. Secondly, a new procedure is introduced in Section C.3, which is worth quoting at length:

> Where reasoned opinions on the non-compliance of a draft Union legislative act with the principle of subsidiarity, sent within 12 weeks from the transmission of that draft, represent more than 55 % of the votes allocated to the national Parliaments, the Council Presidency will include the item on the agenda of the Council for a comprehensive discussion on these opinions and on the consequences to be drawn therefrom.

This new provision contains many novelties: it expands the usual eight-week period to 12 (but this seems to be limited to this procedure and not to the yellow and orange card); it sets the threshold at more than 55 per cent of the votes (that is, at least 31 votes), which is slightly more than the orange card;[35] instead of triggering a dialogue between the Commission and the parliaments, the procedure involves the Council immediately, which will have to decide whether to discontinue the legislative proposal or not. In other words, the solution found by the Member States is a compromise which introduces a 'weak' red card. The Council might try to push for amendments in order to accommodate the objections contained in the reasoned opinions, even though, given the high threshold required to trigger such a procedure, it is predictable that it will be extremely difficult to find a compromise which will take into account all these aspects. If the Council then deems the changes either impossible or not sufficient to address national parliaments' concerns, then it can discontinue the draft proposal. It is too early to pass a judgment on how this new procedure will work, so it is impossible to assess whether it will operate de facto as a red card. From the Council's conclusions, it is reasonable to infer that to be effective, such a procedure will still require a dialogue between national parliaments and governments.

The other most recent development in this field concerns the possible introduction of the green card. Interestingly, the idea of a green card, advocated by some parliaments, has received attention in interparliamentary forums in the first place and it has been discussed during the COSAC meeting in Riga which took place

[34] For an insightful commentary on the President of the Council's proposal see K Granat, 'The Draft Renegotiation Deal: A Genuine Red Card?' (2016) *EU Law Analysis Blog* (available at this address: eulawanalysis.blogspot.co.uk/2016/02/the-draft-renegotiation-deal-genuine.html).

[35] Based on past experience, this entails that it will be unlikely that this procedure will be triggered.

at the end of May 2015. A summary of the conclusions reached at that meeting is available in the 24th Bi-Annual COSAC Report.[36]

While the trajectory of the proposal is clear and points toward a more active role for the national parliaments in the EU, there are different available ways of conceiving the green card. This is due, partly, to the causes behind the request for a green card. In a recent intervention, Cristina Fasone and Diane Fromage have offered a plausible list of explanations for the causes behind a request for a green card. They list, as important factors,

> the disappointment expressed by most national parliaments about the replies provided by the Commission to their opinions, the perception of scarce impact on the content of EU legislation, and the understanding of their role as mere negative-veto player in the EU.[37]

Be that as it may, the translation of the proposal into a procedure has been the object of several different 'takes'. The 'Dutch approach' entails the creation of 'a group of parliaments that is gathered around a theme (cluster of interest) [and that] could propose ideas for new European policies to the European Commission, or could propose the amending or revoking of existing legislation'.[38] The 'Danish approach' suggests that the green card ought to operate in a way similar to the EWM and, in contrast to the Dutch proposal, it would intervene only once a legislative proposal had already been made by the EU Commission. A third approach is represented by the House of Lords' take on the green card as an opportunity to make proposals to change already adopted legislation. It also suggests that 'there should be a way for a group of like-minded national parliaments to make constructive suggestions for EU policy initiatives, which may include reviewing existing legislation'.[39] Lord Boswell prepared a discussion paper for an interparliamentary meeting in January 2015, on the basis that 'the green card procedure could build on the existing political dialogue'.[40] According to the latter view, the green card would rather become an 'enhanced' Political Dialogue.

While there seems to be a majoritarian consensus on the introduction of the green card by national parliaments,[41] it has still to be seen which version will prevail in the end. A proof of this uncertainty is given by the 24th COSAC bi-Annual summary, according to which there is no clear consensus over the threshold necessary to trigger the green card or whether it should always be the same for

[36] The report is available at the following address: www.cosac.eu/documents/bi-annual-reports-of-cosac/.

[37] C Fasone and D Fromage, 'National parliaments and the EU Commission's agenda: limits and recent developments of a difficult partnership', *EUI Max Weber Programme Working Paper* 4/2015.

[38] Dutch *Tweede Kamer*, 'Ahead in Europe. On the Role of the Dutch House of Representatives and national parliaments in the European Union', *Final Report on Democratic Legitimacy*, 9 May 2014, p 14.

[39] UK House of Lords European Union Committee, *The Role of National Parliaments in the European Union* (n 50 below) §§ 55–59.

[40] Lord Boswell, *The Green Card discussion paper*, 1.

[41] However, some parliamentary chambers have expressed doubts about the opportunity to introduce a green card. Moreover, the Finnish *Eduskunta* has stated that the green card would require a treaty change.

all issues.[42] Moreover, there is a divide among those parliaments who think that there should not be any Treaty amendment (actually, the majority) and those who think that the green card ought to be recognised through Treaty change. In order to frame how cooperation will have to take place it is necessary to understand the function of the green card, and much depends on its aim. Whether national parliaments ought to act more as a 'virtual third chamber' or, again, just as individual national parliaments trying to find alliances with a view to issuing a green card is relative to the objective of the green card. If the green card is thought to inject democratic legitimacy into the process of EU law-making[43] then one might expect interactions: 1) more attentive to the European dimension of the proposal and 2) more prone to favour a deliberative attitude over a national-interest-based approach. If the green card were used to infuse EU law with the impetus coming from national parliaments, then cooperation ought to be less instrumental in promoting the national interests or preferences of a single chamber or group of chambers. If, on the other hand, a 'reactive' conception of the green card were to prevail (and this would happen if the green card were to be limited to the repeal of a piece of existing EU legislation) then it would be possible to envisage a more individualistic approach toward the required cooperation. Obviously, two distinct attitudes towards the green card might alternate: one more deliberative which would realise the model of the virtual third chamber;[44] the other more instrumental and prone to be receptive of national interests. These notes bring us to the second important point concerning the improvement of the EWM.

B. Interparliamentary Cooperation

Several of the chapters in this volume mention the critical importance of interparliamentary cooperation for strengthening the EWM. This is the case because the required threshold for each card is to be reached in a short amount of time and because of unevenness among parliamentary chambers when it comes to their administrative and political capacities. The importance of cooperation in the framework of the subsidiarity review is further highlighted by the guidelines for interparliamentary cooperation as adopted by the EU Speakers' Conference, gathering together the Speakers of the European and the national parliaments, at the Lisbon meeting in 2008. In the objectives, it is first stated that interparliamentary cooperation is organised in order 'a) To promote the exchange of information and best practices between the national parliaments of the European Parliament with a view to reinforcing parliamentary control, influence and scrutiny at all levels', and after that, it is made clear that the second objective is 'b) To ensure effective

[42] See n 17 above, at p 12.

[43] D Chalmers, *Democratic Self-Government in Europe* (London/New York, Policy Network, 2013).

[44] I Cooper, 'A Virtual Third Chamber for the European Union? National Parliaments after the Lisbon Treaty' (2012) 35 *West European Politics* 447.

exercise of parliamentary competences in EU matters in particular in the area of monitoring the principles of subsidiarity and proportionality'.[45] Bruno Pinheiro's reconstruction (in Chapter 5) of the development of forums for cooperation confirms that national parliaments do have a natural incentive for cooperating with other parliamentary chambers at least under certain circumstances. The proliferation of these forums proves that at least some chambers are very keen on developing cooperation.

The practice has proved that a yellow card can be reached only through some form of networking, communication and cooperation. The two yellow cards triggered until now (Monti II and the European Public Prosecutor's Office, EPPO) are the most evident proof of the importance of cooperation in the context of subsidiarity review.[46] An analysis of the Monti II proposal 'can reveal the extent of interparliamentary coordination'.[47] In this case, cooperation and interaction took place in different places and times. The threshold was reached only thanks to a number of factors: the activism of certain parliaments (in particular the Danish *Folketing*); a timely COSAC meeting; and the informal interaction occurring among the permanent representatives in Brussels. The first lesson to be drawn from this first yellow card is that cooperation *matters*. And its relevance extends beyond the exchanges or networking of parliamentarians. Insightfully, Ian Cooper has noted that

> the National Parliament Representatives in Brussels played an indispensable role by sharing with one another real-time information about the state of play regarding the scrutiny of Monti II in their respective parliaments. Only with this network of representatives in place was it possible to compile an accurate and up-to-date picture of the likelihood of a reasoned opinion from each chamber, and thus a rough 'vote count' as the process unfolded and thus the knowledge that a yellow card was within reach. The representatives shared this information with their home parliaments.[48]

Given that some parliaments had not noticed or even heard of the Monti II proposal, interparliamentary cooperation in formal and informal settings (from COSAC to information exchange on IPEX) was instrumental to the mobilisation of some legislatures. The leading legislatures were able to convince other parliaments of the potential impact of the Monti II proposal upon their constituencies, overcoming in this way the issue of lack of incentive.[49]

[45] *Guidelines for Interparliamentary Cooperation in the European Union*, Lisbon, June 2008, p 3.

[46] For a recent reconstruction of these two cases see A Pintz, 'National Parliaments Overcoming Collective Action Problems Inherent in the Early Warning System: The Cases of Monti II and EPPO', *LUISS School of Government working papers* No 22/2014 (Rome, October 2014).

[47] I Cooper, 'A Yellow Card for the Striker' (2015) 22 *Journal of European Public Policy* 1406.

[48] I Cooper, Oral Evidence to the UK Parliament: available at: www.publications.parliament.uk/pa/ld201314/ldselect/ldeucom/151/15108.htm#n112: (accessed 20 April 2015).

[49] This does not mean that often parliamentarians do not have incentives to participate in subsidiarity review, but it shows that if left to exceptional and rare occasions, MPs can be mobilised. In the case of Monti II, it is not surprising that the Nordic parliaments were easily co-opted when convinced that their peculiar model of industrial relations was at stake.

In the case of EPPO, the context was rather different because, in light of the new institution (already required by the Lisbon Treaty) and the coincidence of the summer break (which does not count for the EWS timetable), parliaments were already aware of the importance of the proposal before the beginning of the eight-week period. A pattern of instrumental cooperation can be detected also in this case. The leading parliamentary chamber was the UK House of Commons, followed by the two Dutch chambers. Very early in the process of review, concerns about the proposal were raised in the Monday morning meetings of the permanent representatives in Brussels and through this channel it became public that some legislatures had already chosen to issue a reasoned opinion. An intensive interaction among permanent representatives and use of the IPEX platform[50] took place, leading to the reaching of the necessary threshold.[51] In this case, the COSAC general meeting did not take place during the eight-week period and could not be used as a forum for information exchange and agenda-setting.

A final important point has to be made. Ian Cooper has proved that informal and administrative settings might be even more effective than formal ones[52] because the latter are often perceived by parliamentary chambers as ineffective. Too many forums might have an opposite effect and they might induce a sense of redundancy. Cooperation too, as it happens for subsidiarity review, ought to be used economically so that it would be made more effective. Even more importantly, the coordination of administrative practices in order to maintain a constant flux of information and contacts is functional to such an economy of cooperation. This function is unjustly underrated, possibly because national parliaments are not regarded as comprising different political and administrative layers, but just as a sum of parliamentarians or, at best, political groups or parties. In fact, the interaction among administrative units of parliaments is often essential for the preparation of interparliamentary meetings.[53] Plenty of contacts take place behind the scenes, usually alongside the COSAC meetings or other types of parliamentary conferences. The setting-up of IPEX under the impulse of the EU Speakers' Conference[54] and the meetings among permanent representatives of national

[50] OJ Gstrein and D Harvey, Written Evidence, in House of Lords/European Select Committee, *The Role of National Parliaments in the European Union*, 9th Report of Session 2013–14, §§ 53–59.

[51] Note that in the process some parliamentary chambers changed their opinion on the EPPO or contradicted the position of their governments.

[52] I Cooper, 'A Yellow Card for the Striker', n 47 above, at 1412.

[53] This point is rightly highlighted by A Esposito, 'La cooperazione interparlamentare: principi, strumenti e prospettive' in Lupo and Manzella (eds), *Il sistema parlamentare Euro-nazionale* (n 28 above) at 181. He explains that the underestimation of informal cooperation by doctrine might be due to the impossibility of measuring this practice.

[54] National parliaments have created various functions and forums to support the functioning of IPEX: the IPEX steering group, the IPEX board and the IPEX correspondents. The first website was created in 2004, fully launched in 2006 and substantially revised in 2011. The *Guidelines for Interparliamentary Cooperation in the European Union* set up by the Conference of the Speakers in July 2004 state the role of IPEX: 'The Objective of IPEX (Interparliamentary EU Information eXchange) is to support

parliaments in Brussels have become permanent features of the current system of cooperation. At this stage of European integration there is constant interaction among the administrative apparatuses of national parliaments and it is not an overstatement to note that this aspect plays a crucial role in the success of parliamentary cooperation. Besides consolidating the links among parliamentary offices, the interaction among parliamentary staff favours the circulation of best practices and procedures.[55]

VII. Conclusions

It is time to take stock of the previous reflections. In light of the chapters of this book and of other recent research, it is possible to pass a cautious first judgment on the impact of the EWM on EU law-making. The usual caveat applies: a quantification of this impact is unrealistic; hence the following points should be taken more as prudential judgments on the practice of the EWM. Any evaluation ought to distinguish between two questions inherent to the introduction of the EWM: Has this new tool been able to strengthen subsidiarity review? Has the EWM enhanced the democratic representativeness of EU law-making?

Despite the initial widespread scepticism around it, the EWM has had some impact on subsidiarity review. The EWM has made parliamentary chambers (and in particular upper chambers) more aware of their European role. In only one case it has been able to produce a concrete impact upon legislation by forcing the Commission to withdraw the Monti II proposal, even though the withdrawal was not based upon the principle of subsidiarity.[56] But further development and reform might increase the chances of impacting directly on future proposed legislation.

As to the second question, the answer ought to be nuanced: at a practical level, it is not the case that the EWM has enhanced the democratic credentials of EU law-making. There is no single case where the influence of inputs coming from

interparliamentary cooperation in the European Union by providing a platform for the electronic exchange of EU-related information between parliaments in the Union including a calendar of meetings and forums for exchange of views on subsidiarity control. Each parliament/chamber has an IPEX correspondent to represent the parliament'. For the use of IPEX in subsidiarity review see V Knutelská, 'Cooperation among National Parliaments: An Effective Contribution to EU Legitimation?' in Crum and Fossum (n 23 above) at 41–45.

[55] For an overall assessment of the role of administrative bureaucracies in interparliamentary cooperation see N Lupo, 'Il ruolo delle burocrazie parlamentari alla luce dei mutamenti dell'assetto istituzionale, nazionale e sopranazionale' (2012) 54 *Rassegna parlamentare* 51, 88. For an evaluation of the rise of administrators in European parliamentary politics see AL Högenauer and C Neuhold, 'National Parliaments after Lisbon: Administrations on the Rise?' (2013) 20 *Journal of European Public Policy* 335. See, also, A Pegan and AL Högenauer, 'The Role of Parliamentary Administrations in Interparliamentary Cooperation' in Lupo and Fasone (eds), *Interparliamentary Cooperation* (n 23 above).

[56] It could be said that national parliaments got what they wanted but for the wrong reasons.

national parliaments has shaped in a significant way the content of EU legislation through subsidiarity review. National parliaments are not well equipped for a positive contribution to EU law-making and their main electoral interests are still circumscribed to their national constituencies. Moreover, the EWM, even when understood in its wider sense and even when enlarged to include the principles of conferral and proportionality, does not lend itself to being an affirmative instrument. In the end, the core question behind subsidiarity review is whether the EU ought to legislate or not on a particular topic. The most that a parliamentary chamber could make out of a reasoned opinion would be to suggest to the Commission how to change the proposal in a way that does not violate the principle of proportionality. Nonetheless, the absence of a positive contribution explains the widespread support for a 'green card' which would enable national parliamentary politics to be infused somehow into EU law-making.

In a negative sense, it is clear that subsidiarity review can contribute to the democratic legitimacy of EU law-making. But this is a minimal contribution: the absence of a clear opposition to EU law-making signals that the legislative proposal might not be stripping national parliaments of their fundamental competence over key national issues. This means that EU law-making is, at a minimum, respectful of national jurisdictions and it does not undermine national democratic processes.[57]

The Euro crisis has changed the European priorities of national parliaments for the time being. The inception of the crisis basically coincided with the entry into force of the Lisbon Treaty and this was, for the EWM, an unfortunate circumstance. First, some of the key provisions enacted by European authorities were actually not European law.[58] Other legislative measures were adopted as EU law, but were supposed to be emergency measures to be quickly approved in order to cope with the Euro crisis (eg the six and the two packs). The haste behind the approval of these measures was certainly detrimental to the quality of parliamentary deliberation but, more importantly for the topic of this book, national parliaments were more concerned with the new measures rather than with their role as subsidiarity watchdogs. It cannot be denied that national parliaments are the losers of the new economic governance adopted after the Euro crisis. But here one should draw a line between parliaments of creditor and debtor Member States. The latter were often reduced to mere rubber-stampers of European proposals. May a revamped subsidiarity review give some leeway to those demeaned national parliaments? Is it reasonable to expect that these same parliaments will go back

[57] B Guastaferro, 'Reframing Subsidiarity Inquiry from an "EU Value-Added" to an "EU Non-Encroachment" test?' in Lupo et al, *Democracy and Subsidiarity in the EU* (n 11 above) at 133.

[58] See, on this point, P Craig, 'Pringle and the Use of EU Institutions Outside the EU Legal Framework' (2013) 9 *European Constitutional Law Review* 243; cf C Kilpatrick, 'Are the bailout measures immune to EU Social challenge because they are not EU Law?' (2014) 10 *European Constitutional Law Review* 393.

to subsidiarity review and use it as leverage for acquiring more influence over the course of European law-making? While it is difficult to give a clear-cut answer, it seems plausible to imply that some of the reforms previously mentioned might actually help. But it will be essential to start looking into the material conditions (of political, economic and cultural nature) under which each parliamentary chamber operates in order to gain a more accurate perspective on the future functioning of the EWM.

INDEX